Shojo Beat

Skip·Beat!

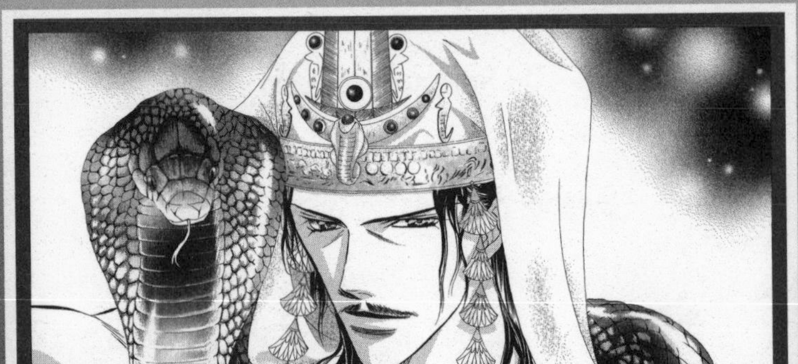

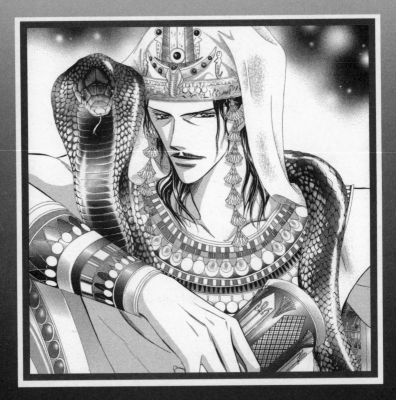

9

Story & Art by Yoshiki Nakamura

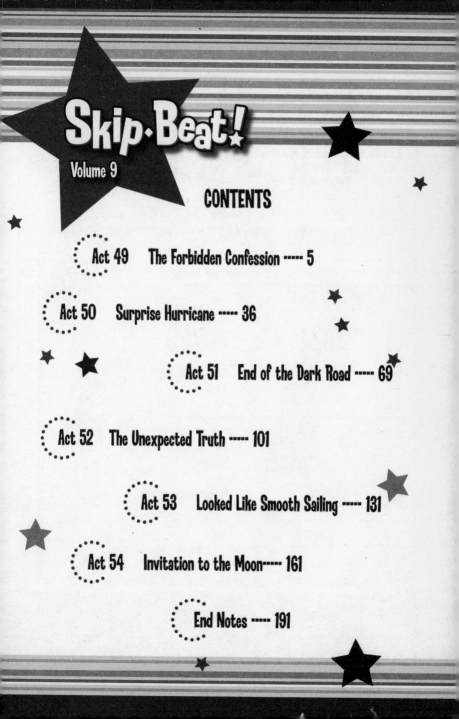

Skip·Beat!

Volume 9

CONTENTS

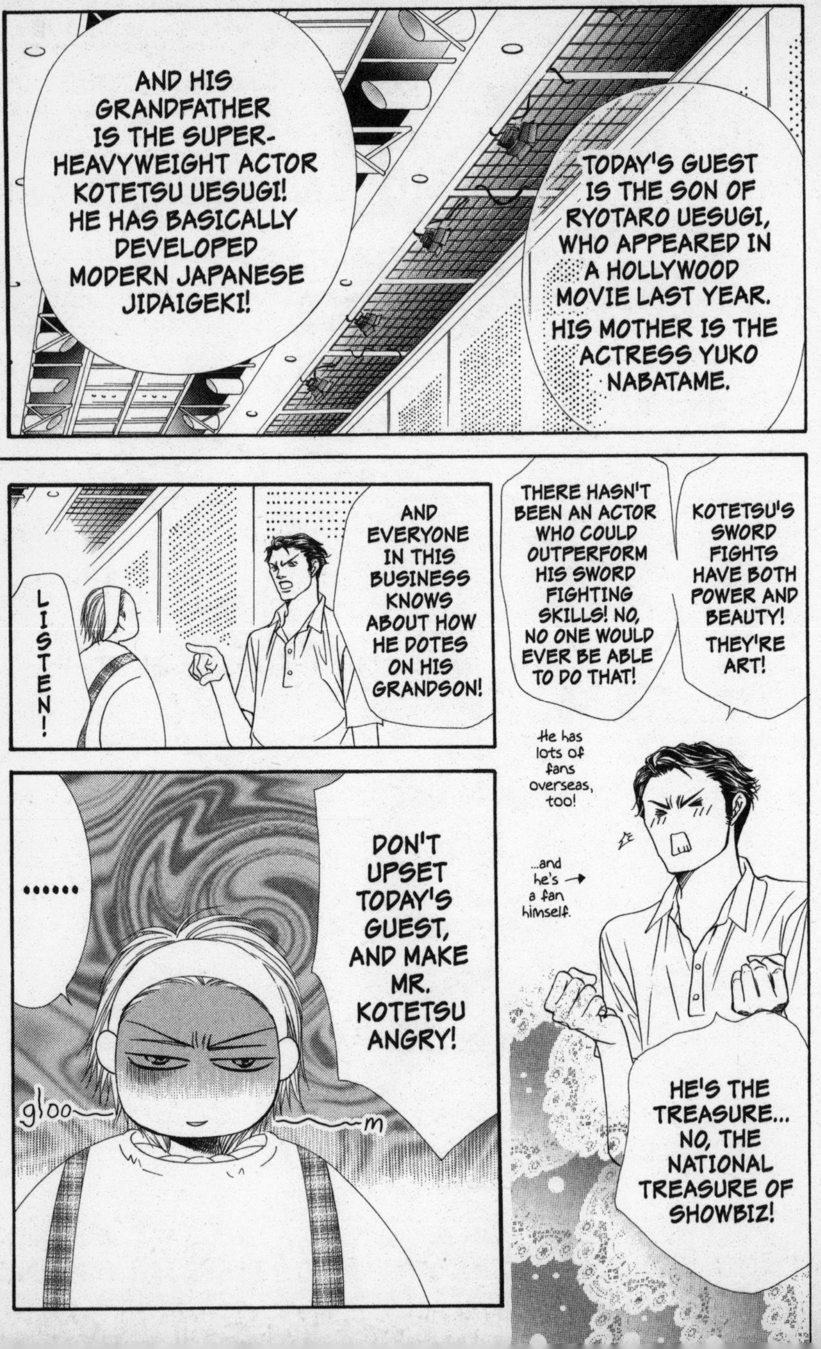
TODAY'S GUEST IS THE SON OF RYOTARO UESUGI, WHO APPEARED IN A HOLLYWOOD MOVIE LAST YEAR.
HIS MOTHER IS THE ACTRESS YUKO NABATAME.
AND HIS GRANDFATHER IS THE SUPER-HEAVYWEIGHT ACTOR KOTETSU UESUGI! HE HAS BASICALLY DEVELOPED MODERN JAPANESE JIDAIGEKI!
KOTETSU'S SWORD FIGHTS HAVE BOTH POWER AND BEAUTY!
THEY'RE ART!
THERE HASN'T BEEN AN ACTOR WHO COULD OUTPERFORM HIS SWORD FIGHTING SKILLS! NO, NO ONE WOULD EVER BE ABLE TO DO THAT!
AND EVERYONE IN THIS BUSINESS KNOWS ABOUT HOW HE DOTES ON HIS GRANDSON!
LISTEN!
He has lots of fans overseas, too!
...and he's a fan himself.
HE'S THE TREASURE... NO, THE NATIONAL TREASURE OF SHOWBIZ!
DON'T UPSET TODAY'S GUEST, AND MAKE MR. KOTETSU ANGRY!
......
gloo~~~~m

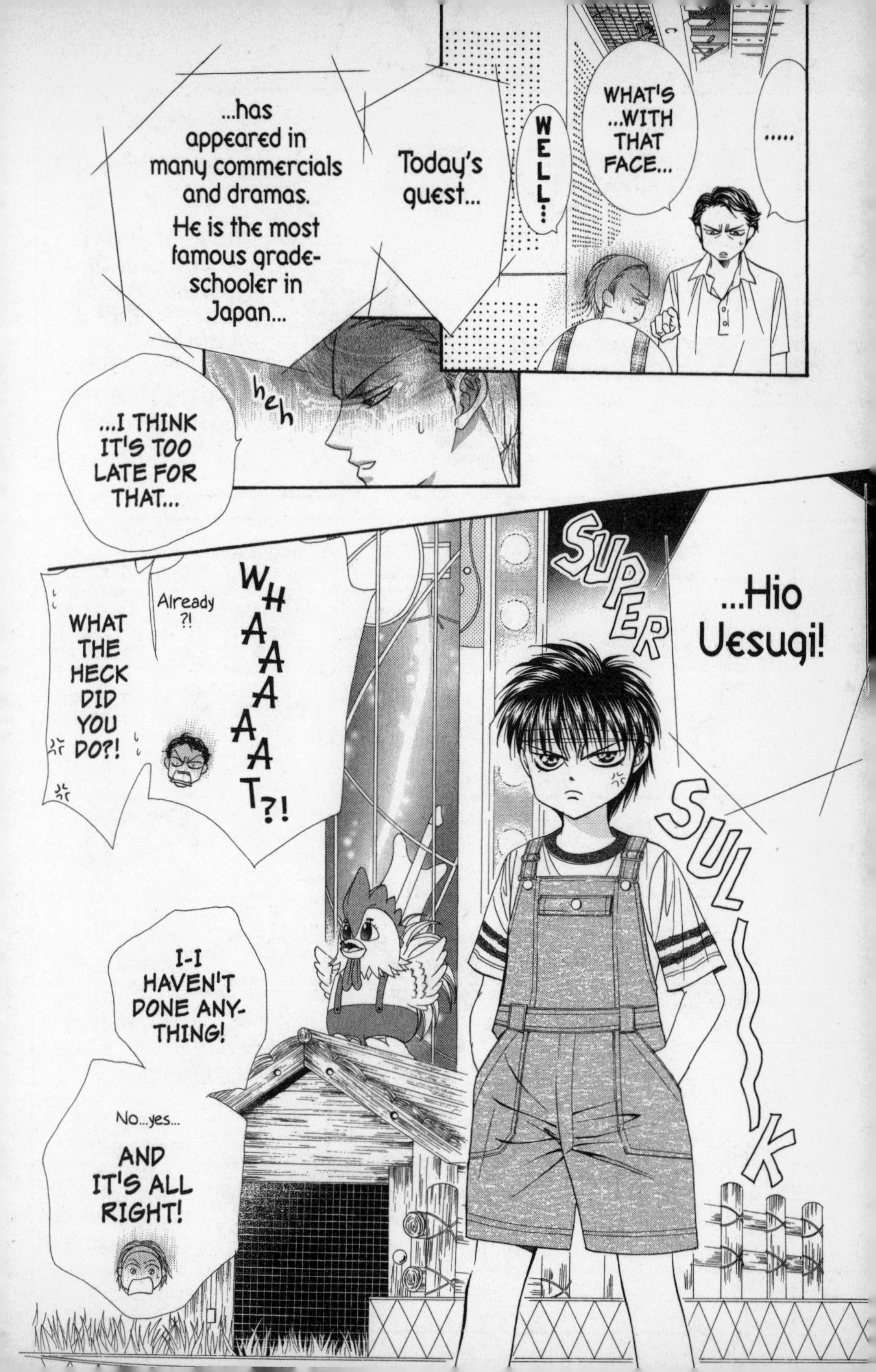
.....
WHAT'S ...WITH THAT FACE...
WELL...
Today's guest...
...has appeared in many commercials and dramas. He is the most famous grade-schooler in Japan...
heh
...I THINK IT'S TOO LATE FOR THAT...
SUPER
...Hio Uesugi!
SULK
WHAAAAAT?!
Already?!
WHAT THE HECK DID YOU DO?!
I-I HAVEN'T DONE ANY-THING!
No...yes...
AND IT'S ALL RIGHT!

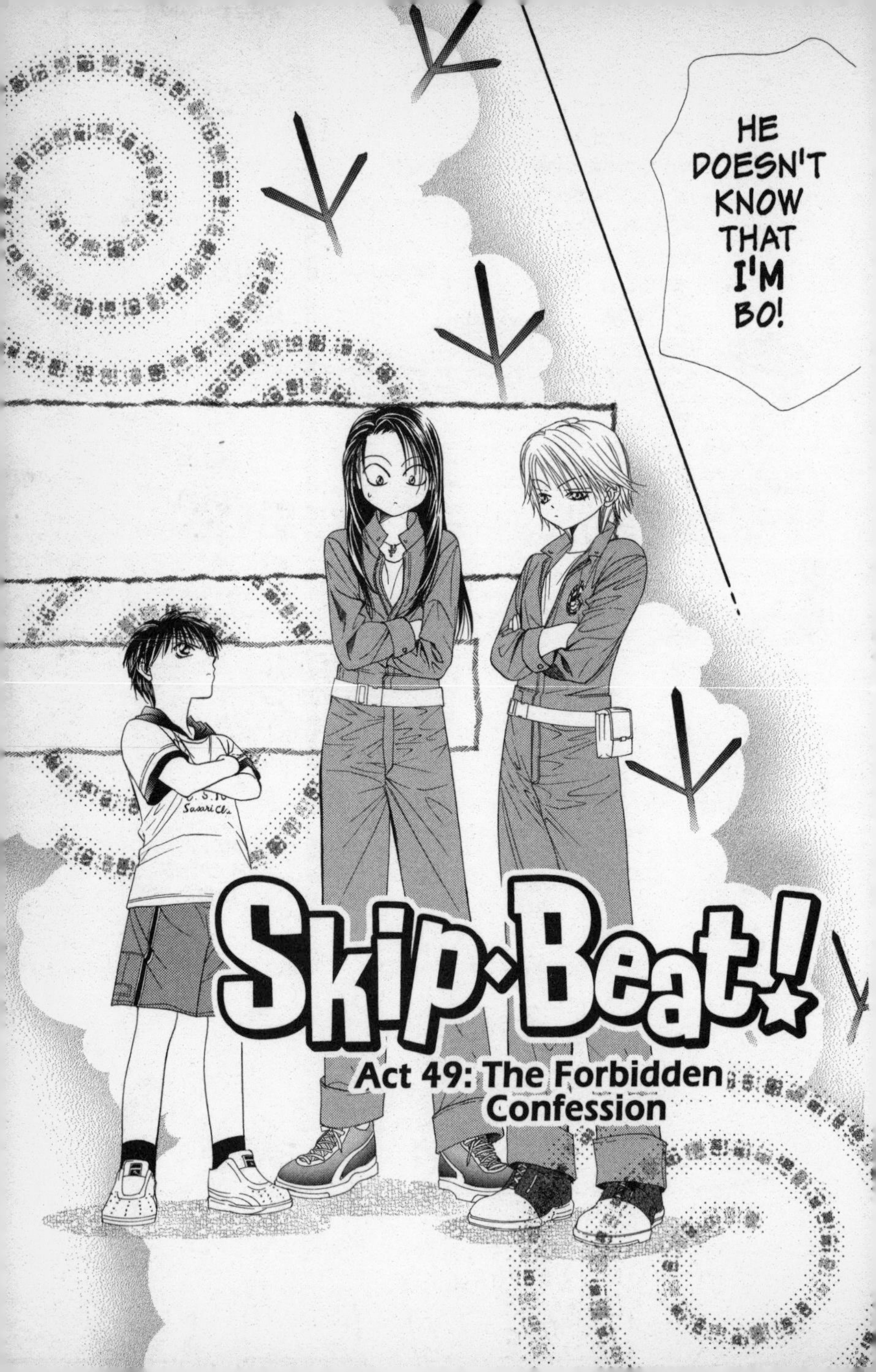
HE DOESN'T KNOW THAT I'M BO!
Skip·Beat!
Act 49: The Forbidden Confession

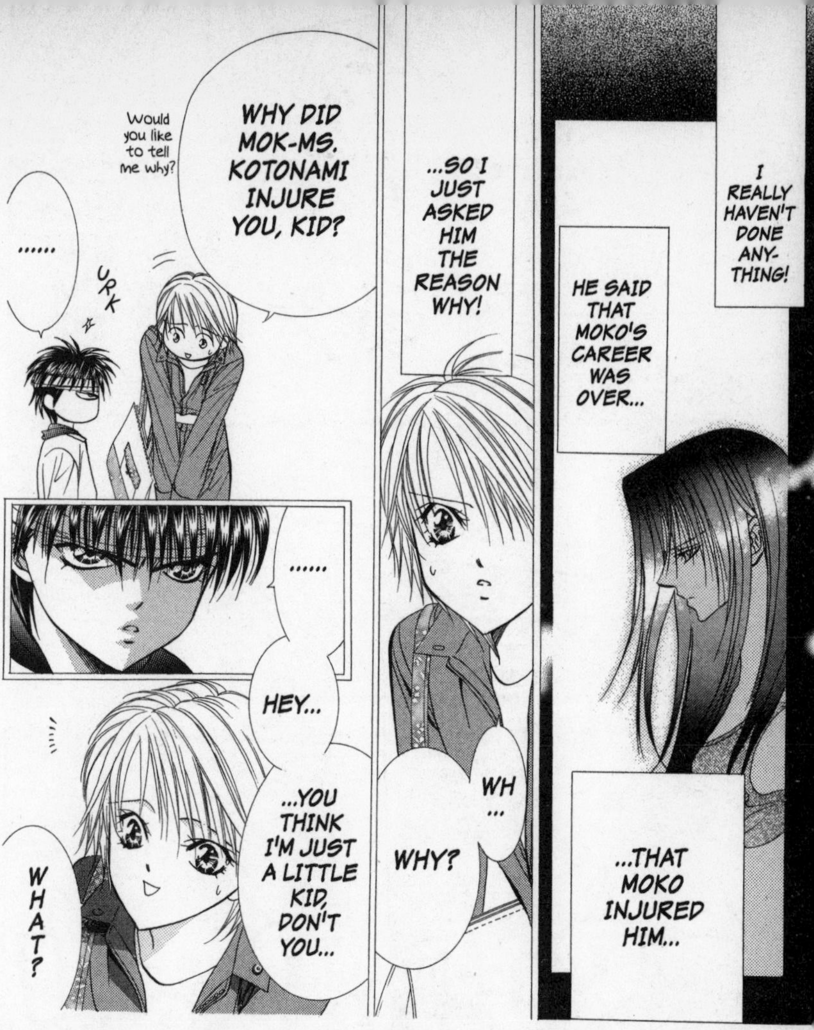
I REALLY HAVEN'T DONE ANYTHING!
HE SAID THAT MOKO'S CAREER WAS OVER...
...THAT MOKO INJURED HIM...
...SO I JUST ASKED HIM THE REASON WHY!
WH...
WHY?
WHY DID MOK-MS. KOTONAMI INJURE YOU, KID?
Would you like to tell me why?
URK
......
......
HEY...
...YOU THINK I'M JUST A LITTLE KID, DON'T YOU...
WHAT?

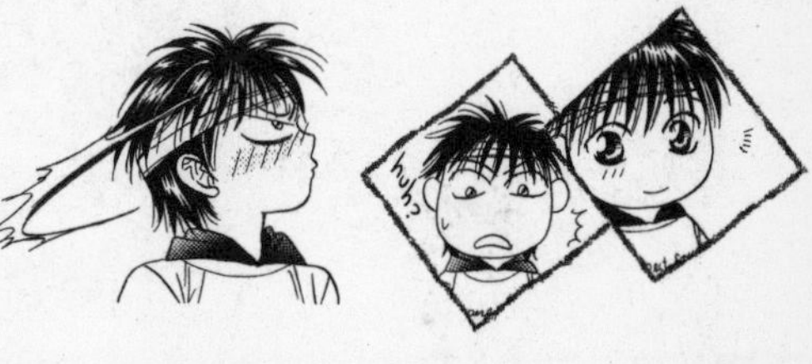
huh?

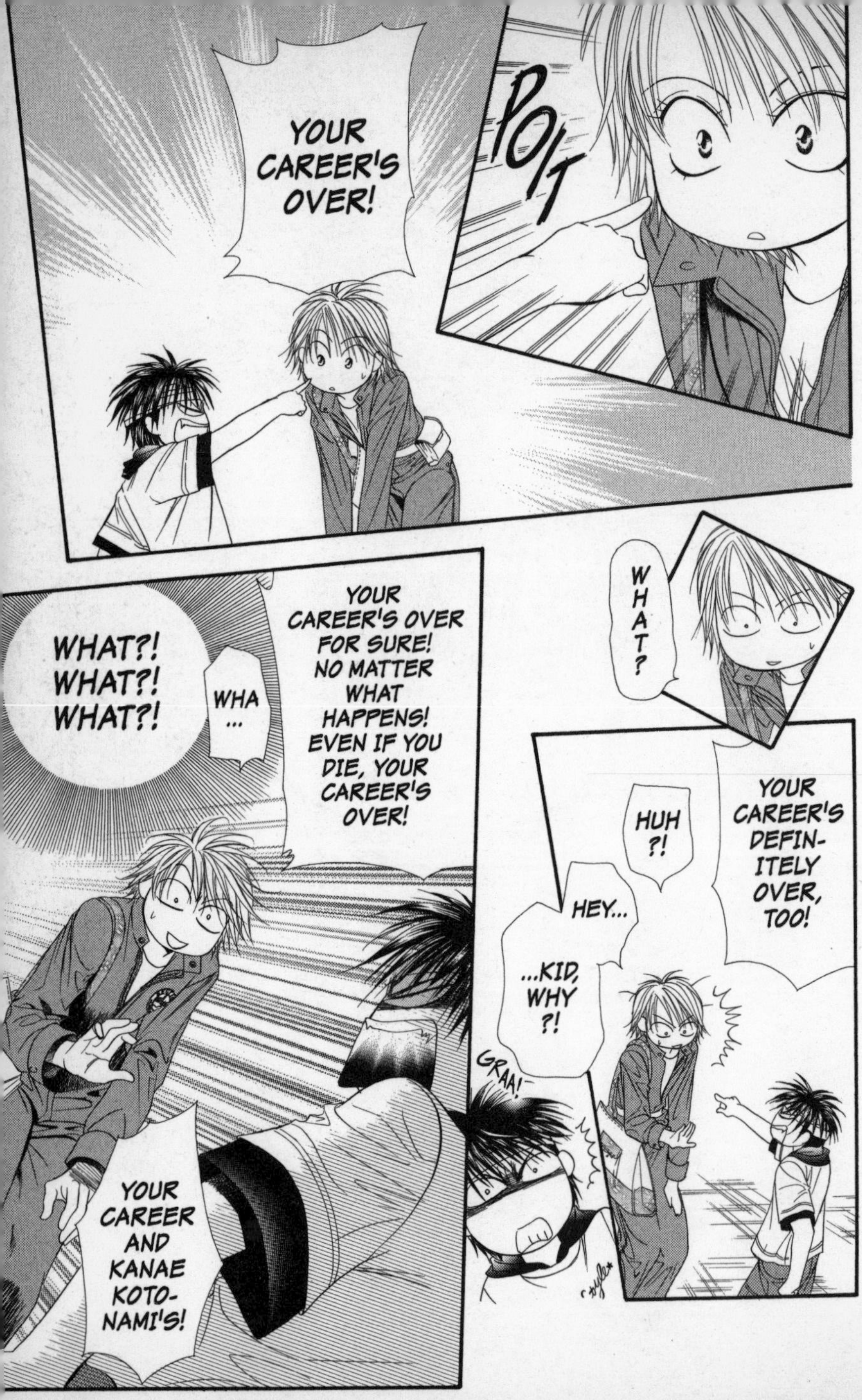
POIT
YOUR CAREER'S OVER!
WHAT?
YOUR CAREER'S DEFINITELY OVER, TOO!
HUH?!
HEY...
...KID, WHY?!
GRAA!
YOUR CAREER'S OVER FOR SURE! NO MATTER WHAT HAPPENS! EVEN IF YOU DIE, YOUR CAREER'S OVER!
WHA...
WHAT?! WHAT?! WHAT?!
YOUR CAREER AND KANAE KOTONAMI'S!

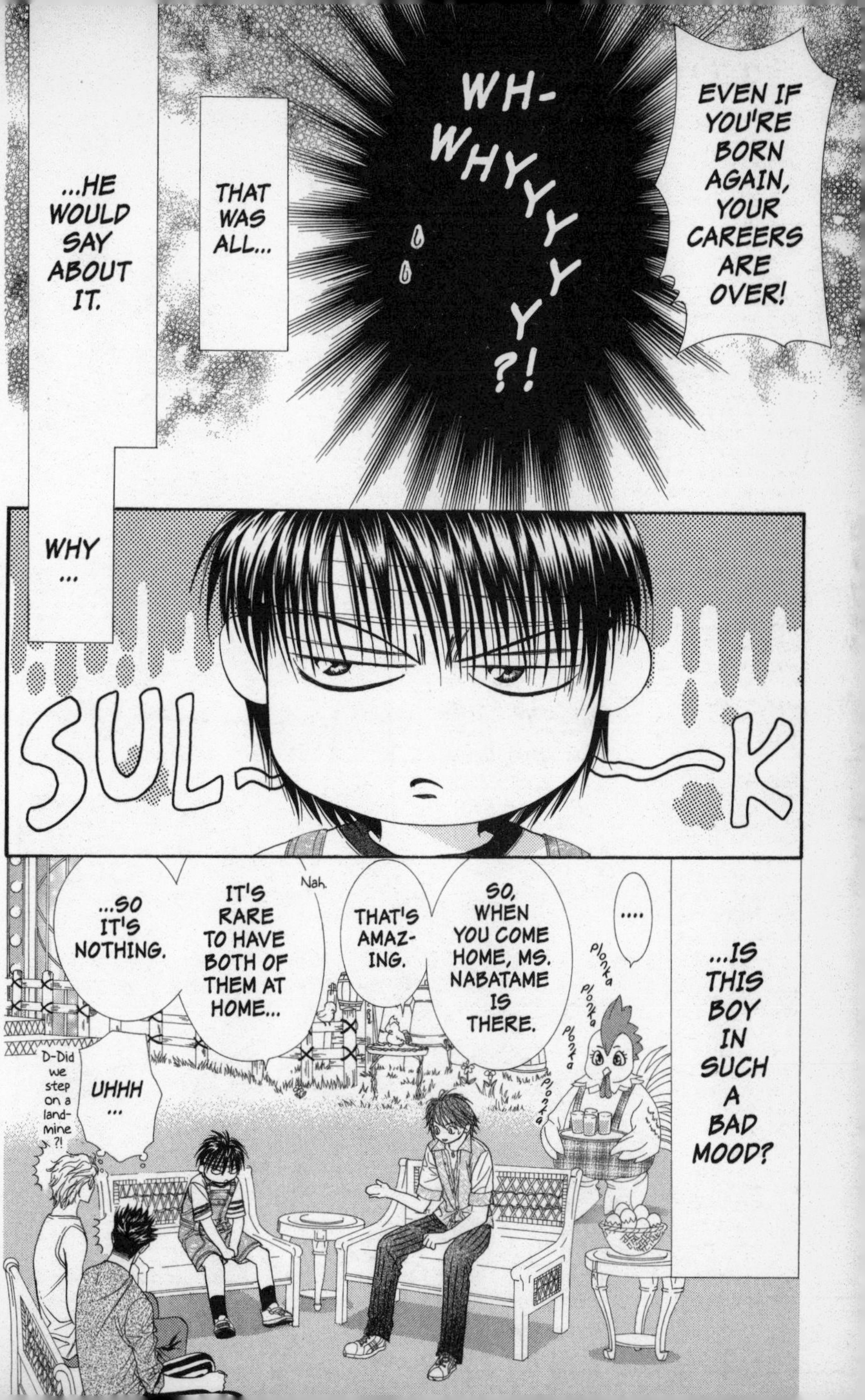
EVEN IF YOU'RE BORN AGAIN, YOUR CAREERS ARE OVER!
WH-WHYYYYY?!
THAT WAS ALL...
...HE WOULD SAY ABOUT IT.
WHY ...
SUL~K
...IS THIS BOY IN SUCH A BAD MOOD?
....
plonka plonka plonka plonka
SO, WHEN YOU COME HOME, MS. NABATAME IS THERE.
THAT'S AMAZ-ING.
Nah.
IT'S RARE TO HAVE BOTH OF THEM AT HOME...
...SO IT'S NOTHING.
UHHH ...
D-Did we step on a land-mine ?!

Greetings

I'll start by apologizing... the blank spaces haven't been filled this time as well... ♁♁ And I think this volume I spent the most time fixing things... ♁

I tend to take time fixing things for the tankobon. This time I did them in bits, because I had three manuscripts to do for the magazine, so the total was about nine days...(that's too long...) Usually, I go over the typesetting, redraw the cuts I don't like, and add effects that I couldn't do when the manuscript was first printed in the magazine. However, this time, the obvious reason is that due to certain circumstances, I re-applied screentones for most of the characters' shadows in this volume. ♁ I really want to say thanks to my assistants. Thank yoooooooou!!

The third round of fixing was for the pages before and after the 2-page Ren cover illustration (the extra episodes), the title page illustration and filling in the blank spaces...I wasn't going to do them because I didn't have the time...but I ended up doing them...without telling my editor... ♁ (Well...since I submit them to the editorial department, they find out anyway... ♁ Wry smile...

So this Vol. 9 really consists of blood, sweat, and tears...I would be very happy if all you readers enjoy it...

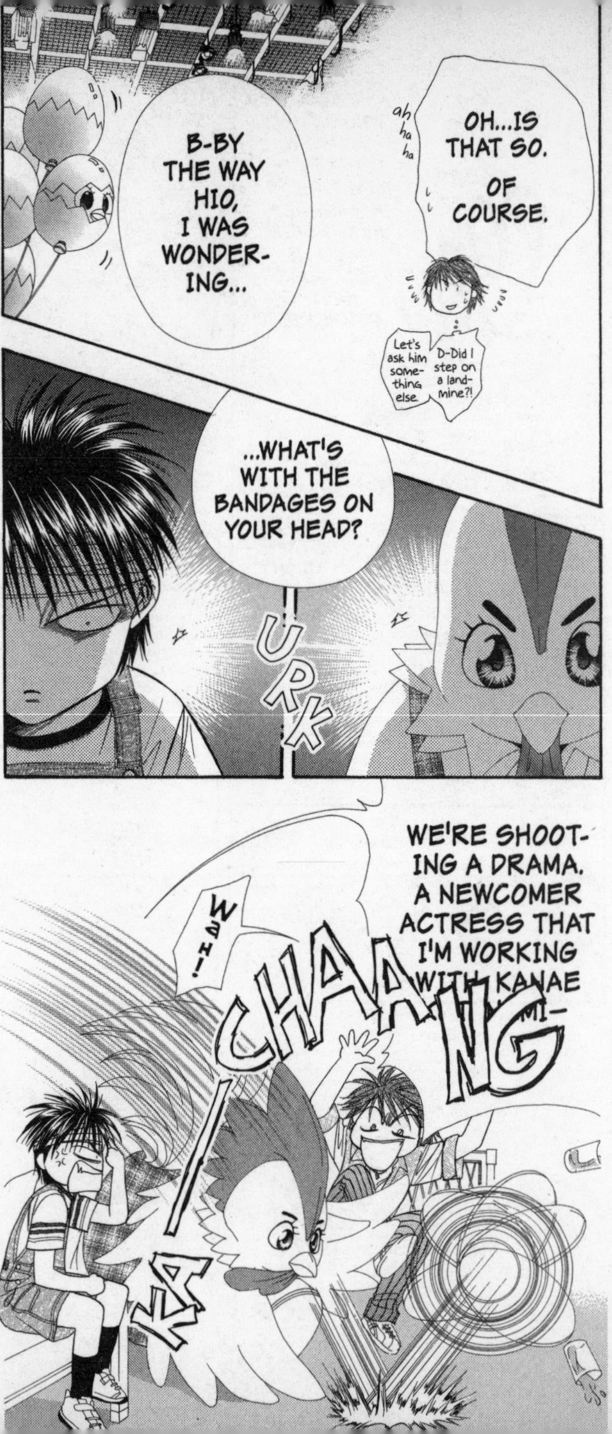

ah ha ha
OH...IS THAT SO. OF COURSE.
B-BY THE WAY HIO, I WAS WONDERING...
D-Did I step on a landmine?!
Let's ask him something else.
...WHAT'S WITH THE BANDAGES ON YOUR HEAD?
URK
WE'RE SHOOTING A DRAMA. A NEWCOMER ACTRESS THAT I'M WORKING WITH KANAE
WAH!
KA-CHAAANG

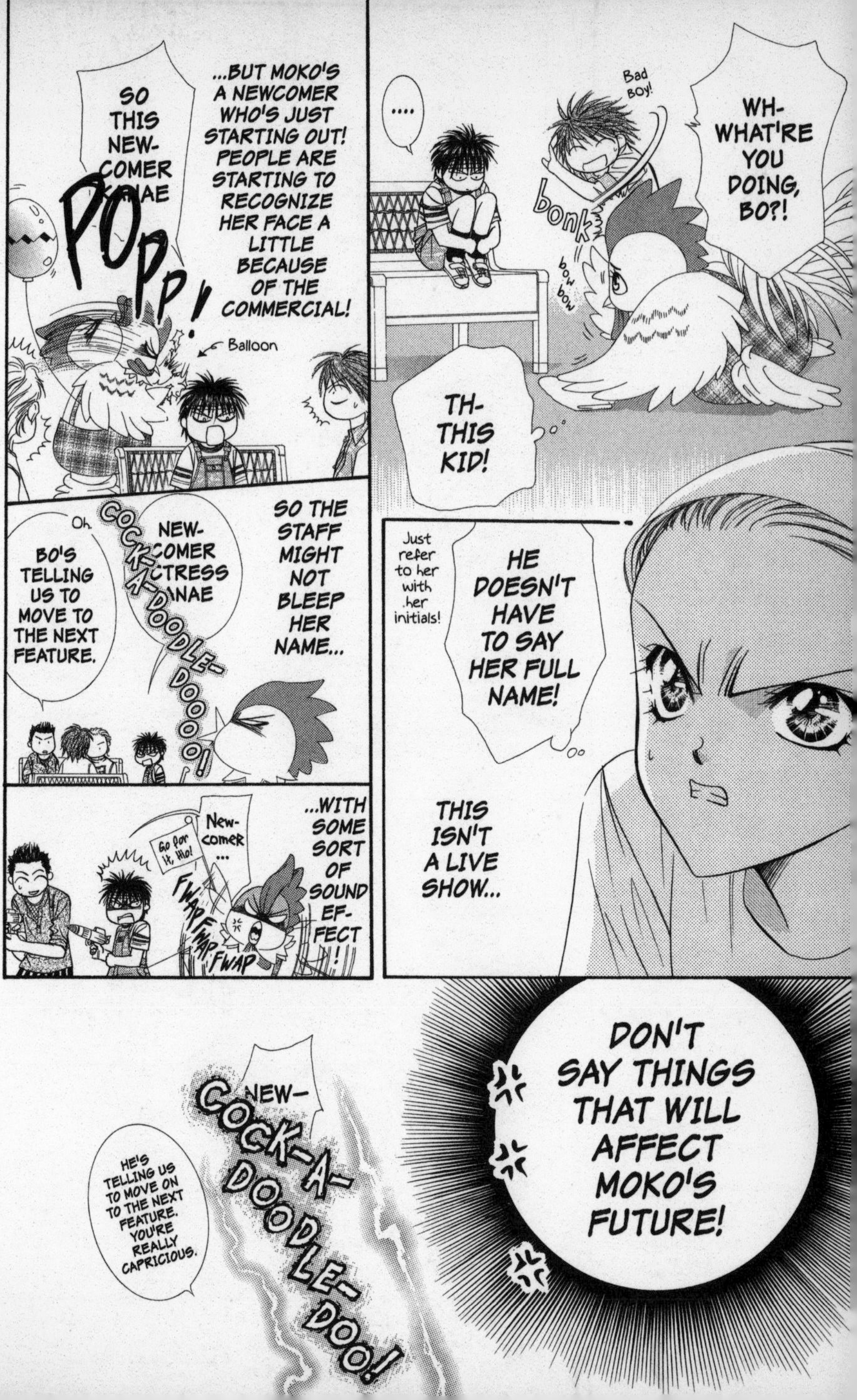
Bad Boy!
WH-WHAT'RE YOU DOING, BO?!
bonk
bow bow
....
TH-THIS KID!
...BUT MOKO'S A NEWCOMER WHO'S JUST STARTING OUT! PEOPLE ARE STARTING TO RECOGNIZE HER FACE A LITTLE BECAUSE OF THE COMMERCIAL!
SO THIS NEW-COMER KANAE
POPP!
Balloon
HE DOESN'T HAVE TO SAY HER FULL NAME!
Just refer to her with her initials!
THIS ISN'T A LIVE SHOW...
SO THE STAFF MIGHT NOT BLEEP HER NAME...
NEW-COMER CTRESS NAE
COCK-A-DOODLE-DOOOOO!
Oh.
BO'S TELLING US TO MOVE TO THE NEXT FEATURE.
...WITH SOME SORT OF SOUND EF-FECT!
New-comer...
Go for it, Hio!
FWAP FWAP FWAP
DON'T SAY THINGS THAT WILL AFFECT MOKO'S FUTURE!
NEW-
COCK-A-DOODLE-DOO!
HE'S TELLING US TO MOVE ON TO THE NEXT FEATURE. YOU'RE REALLY CAPRICIOUS.

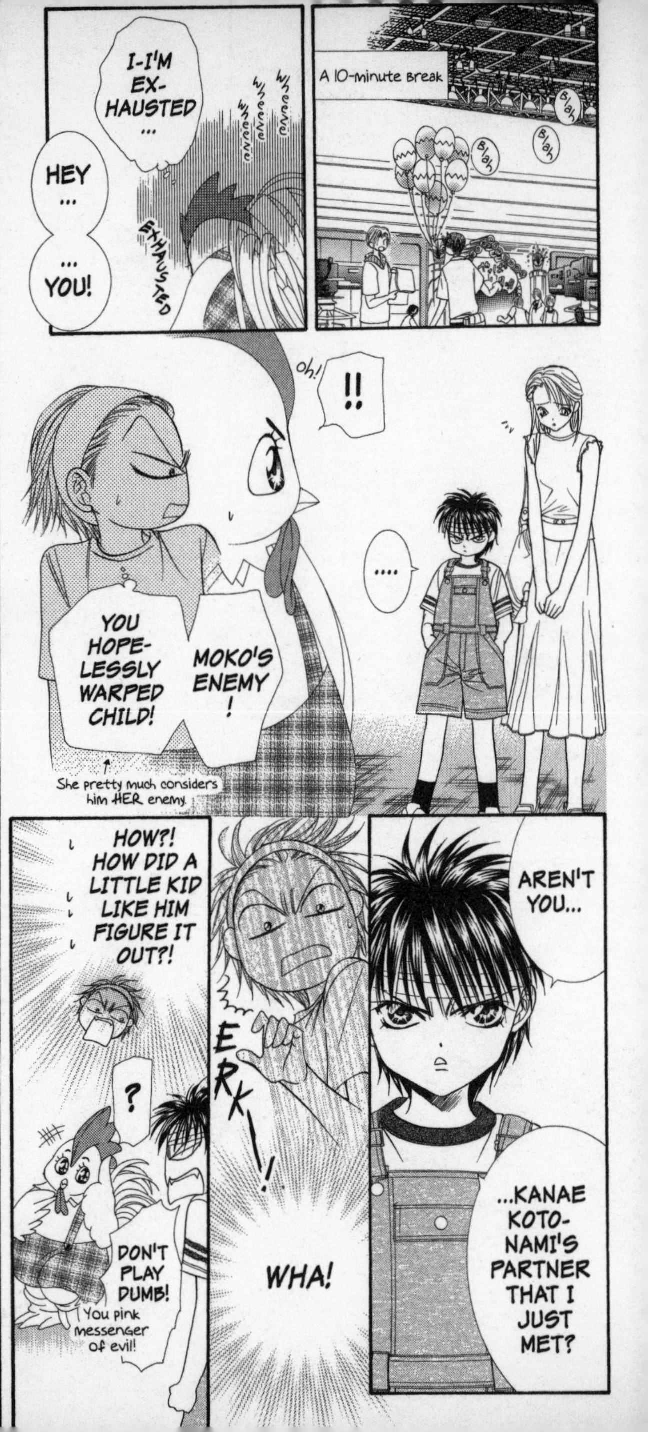
A 10-minute Break
Blah
Blah
Blah
Blah
I-I'M EX-HAUSTED ...
wheeze wheeze wheeze
HEY ...
... YOU!
EXHAUSTED
Oh!
!!
....
MOKO'S ENEMY!
YOU HOPE-LESSLY WARPED CHILD!
She pretty much considers him HER enemy.
AREN'T YOU...
...KANAE KOTO-NAMI'S PARTNER THAT I JUST MET?
ERK!
WHA!
HOW?! HOW DID A LITTLE KID LIKE HIM FIGURE IT OUT?!
?
DON'T PLAY DUMB!
You pink messenger of evil!
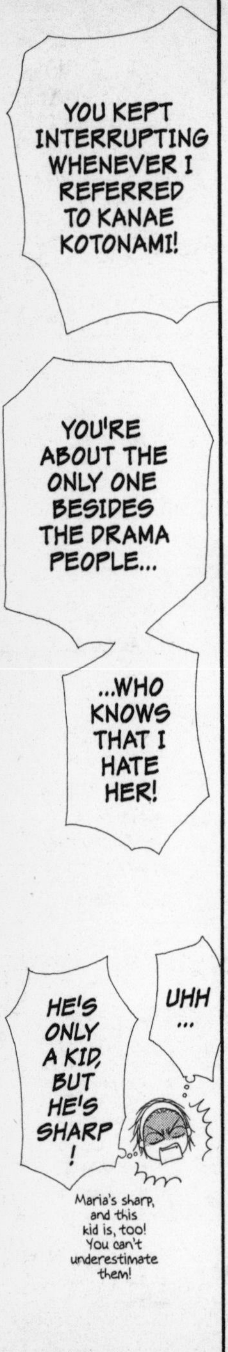
YOU KEPT INTERRUPTING WHENEVER I REFERRED TO KANAE KOTONAMI!
YOU'RE ABOUT THE ONLY ONE BESIDES THE DRAMA PEOPLE...
...WHO KNOWS THAT I HATE HER!
UHH ...
HE'S ONLY A KID, BUT HE'S SHARP!
Maria's sharp, and this kid is, too! You can't underestimate them!

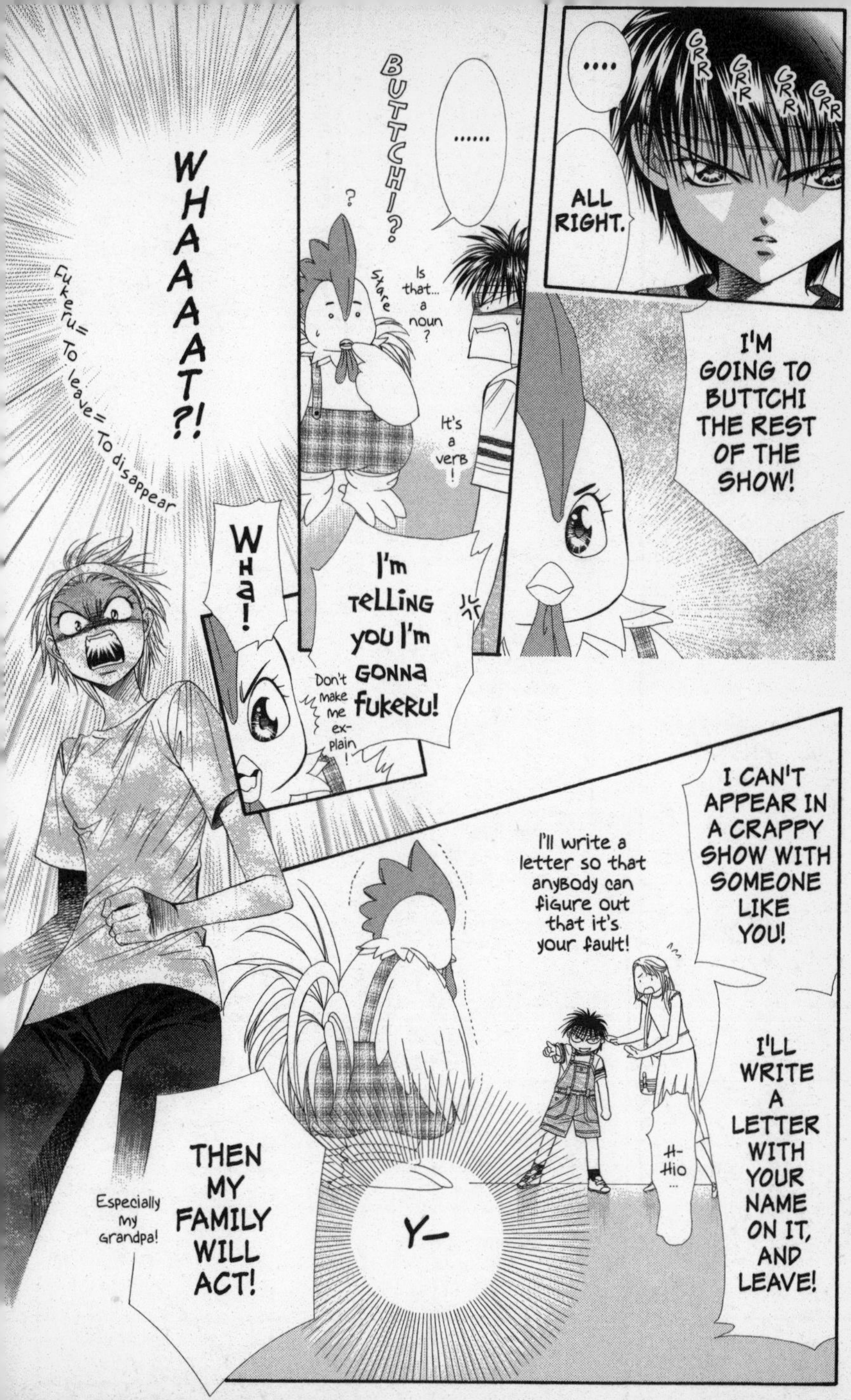
....
GRR GRR GRR GRR
ALL RIGHT.
I'M GOING TO BUTTCHI THE REST OF THE SHOW!
......
BUTTCHI?
?
stare
Is that... a noun?
It's a verb!
I'm telling you I'm gonna fukeru!
Don't make me ex-plain!
WHAAAAAT?!
Fukeru= To leave= To disappear
Wha!
I CAN'T APPEAR IN A CRAPPY SHOW WITH SOMEONE LIKE YOU!
I'll write a letter so that anybody can figure out that it's your fault!
I'LL WRITE A LETTER WITH YOUR NAME ON IT, AND LEAVE!
H-Hio...
Y–
THEN MY FAMILY WILL ACT!
Especially my Grandpa!

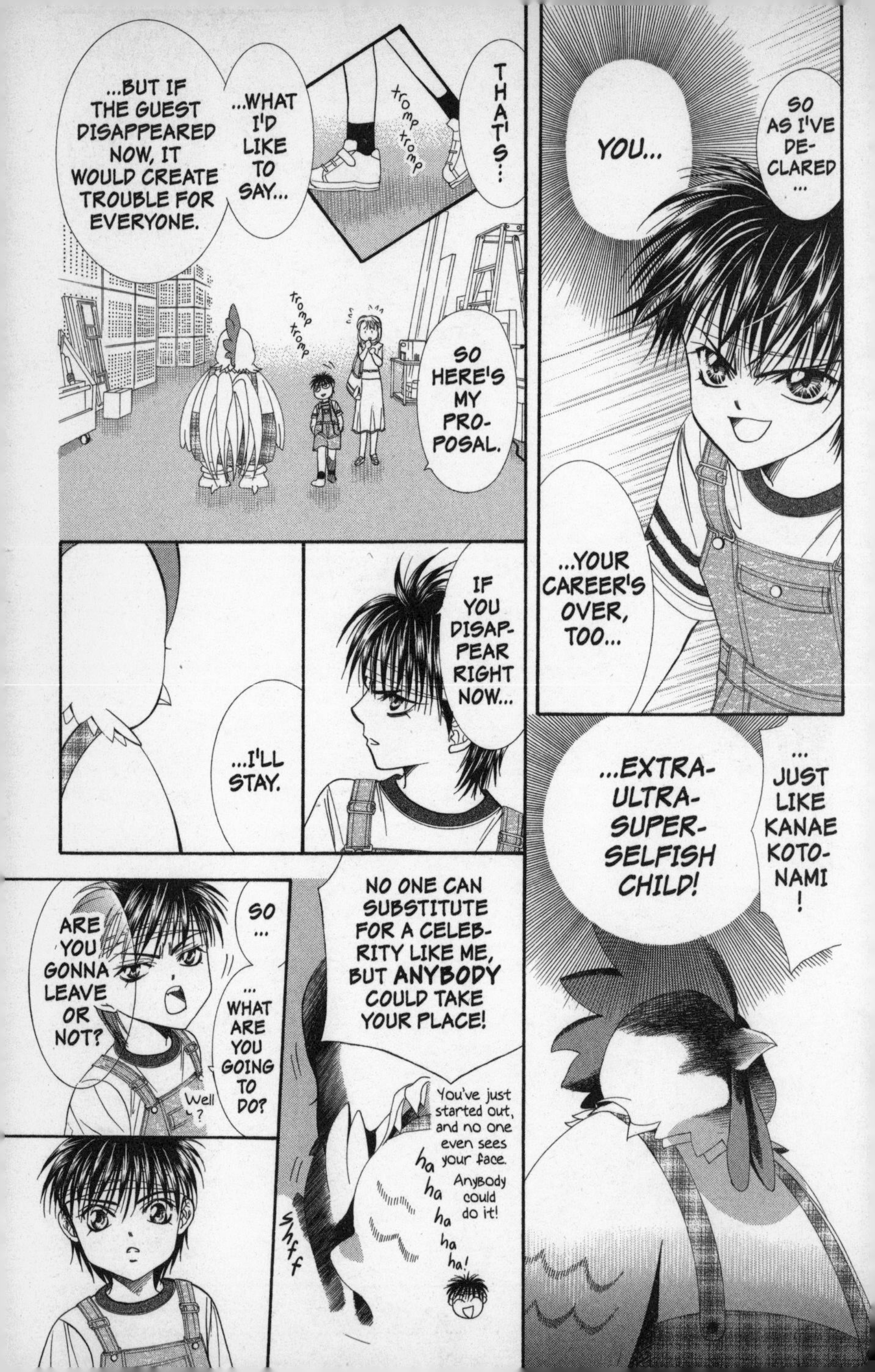
SO AS I'VE DE-CLARED ...
YOU...
...YOUR CAREER'S OVER, TOO...
... JUST LIKE KANAE KOTO-NAMI !
...EXTRA-ULTRA-SUPER-SELFISH CHILD!
THAT'S...
...WHAT I'D LIKE TO SAY...
...BUT IF THE GUEST DISAPPEARED NOW, IT WOULD CREATE TROUBLE FOR EVERYONE.
xromp xromp
xromp xromp
SO HERE'S MY PRO-POSAL.
IF YOU DISAP-PEAR RIGHT NOW...
...I'LL STAY.
NO ONE CAN SUBSTITUTE FOR A CELEB-RITY LIKE ME, BUT ANYBODY COULD TAKE YOUR PLACE!
You've just started out, and no one even sees your face.
Anybody could do it!
ha ha ha ha ha!
shff
SO ...
... WHAT ARE YOU GOING TO DO?
ARE YOU GONNA LEAVE OR NOT?
Well ?

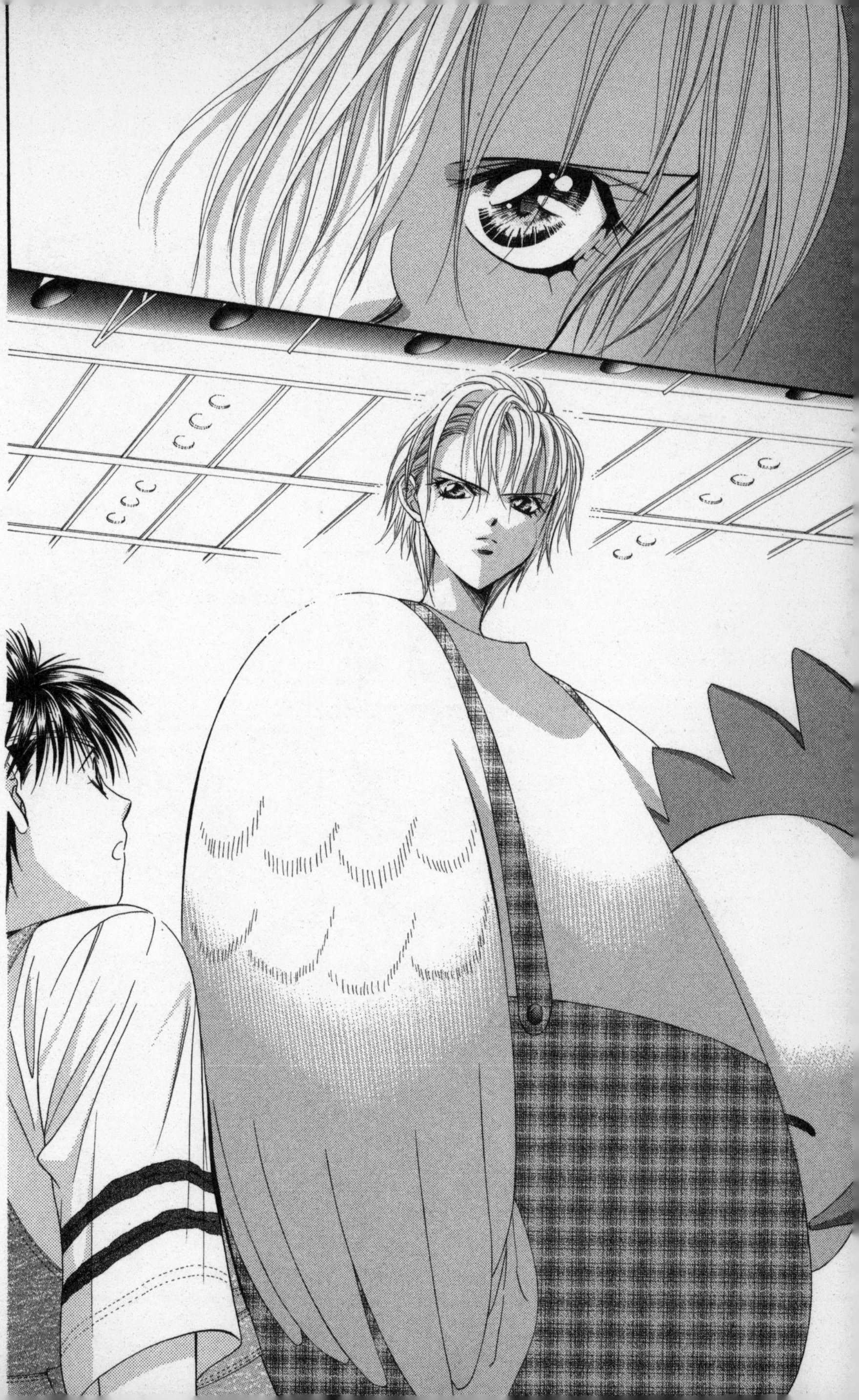

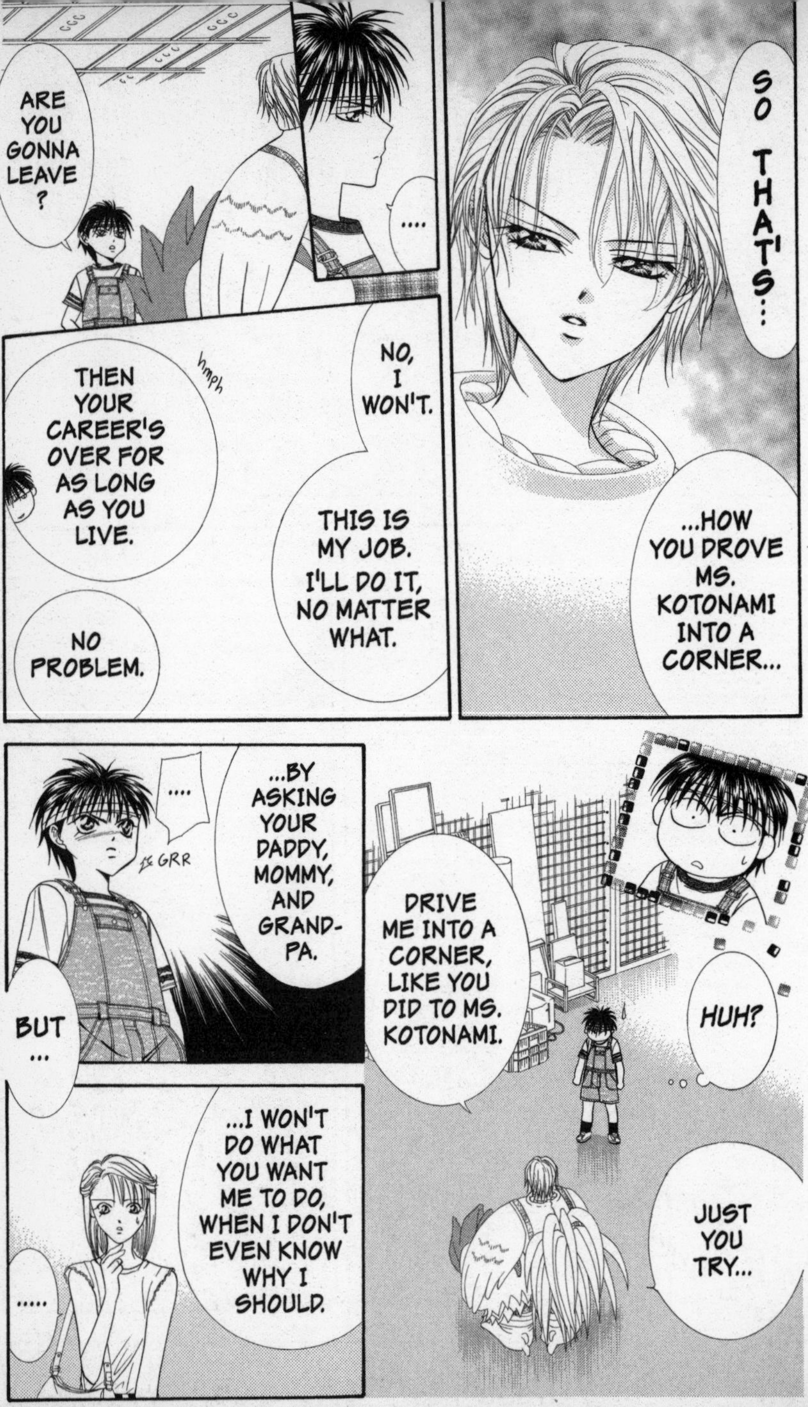
SO THAT'S...
...HOW YOU DROVE MS. KOTONAMI INTO A CORNER...
ARE YOU GONNA LEAVE?
....
NO, I WON'T.
THIS IS MY JOB. I'LL DO IT, NO MATTER WHAT.
hmph
THEN YOUR CAREER'S OVER FOR AS LONG AS YOU LIVE.
NO PROBLEM.
HUH?
JUST YOU TRY...
DRIVE ME INTO A CORNER, LIKE YOU DID TO MS. KOTONAMI.
...BY ASKING YOUR DADDY, MOMMY, AND GRAND-PA.
....
GRR
BUT...
...I WON'T DO WHAT YOU WANT ME TO DO, WHEN I DON'T EVEN KNOW WHY I SHOULD.
.....

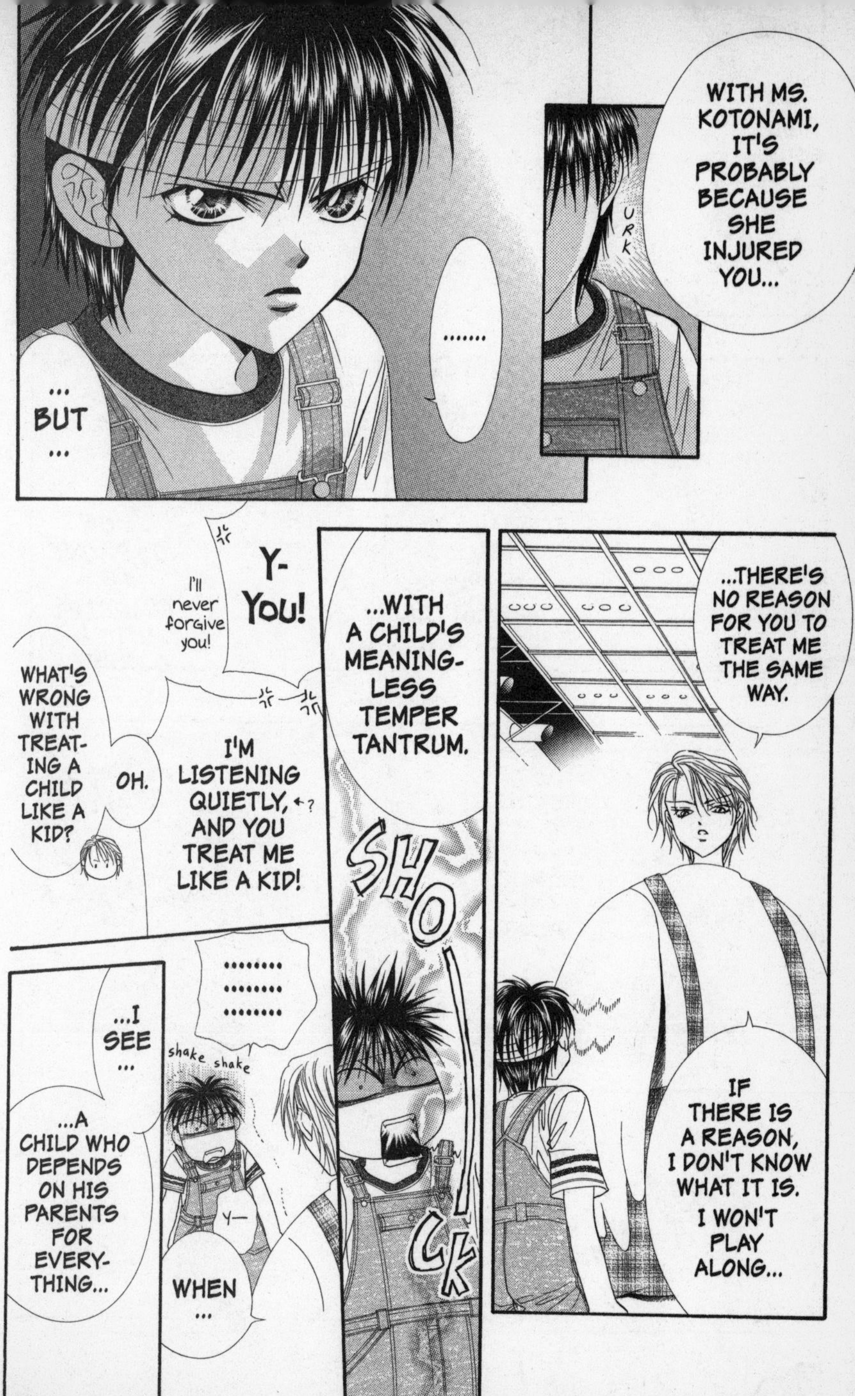
WITH MS. KOTONAMI, IT'S PROBABLY BECAUSE SHE INJURED YOU...
URK
....
...BUT...
...THERE'S NO REASON FOR YOU TO TREAT ME THE SAME WAY.
IF THERE IS A REASON, I DON'T KNOW WHAT IT IS.
I WON'T PLAY ALONG...
...WITH A CHILD'S MEANING-LESS TEMPER TANTRUM.
SHOCK
Y-YOU!
I'll never forgive you!
I'M LISTENING QUIETLY, AND YOU TREAT ME LIKE A KID!
?
OH.
WHAT'S WRONG WITH TREATING A CHILD LIKE A KID?
....
....
....
...I SEE...
shake shake
Y—
...A CHILD WHO DEPENDS ON HIS PARENTS FOR EVERYTHING...
WHEN...

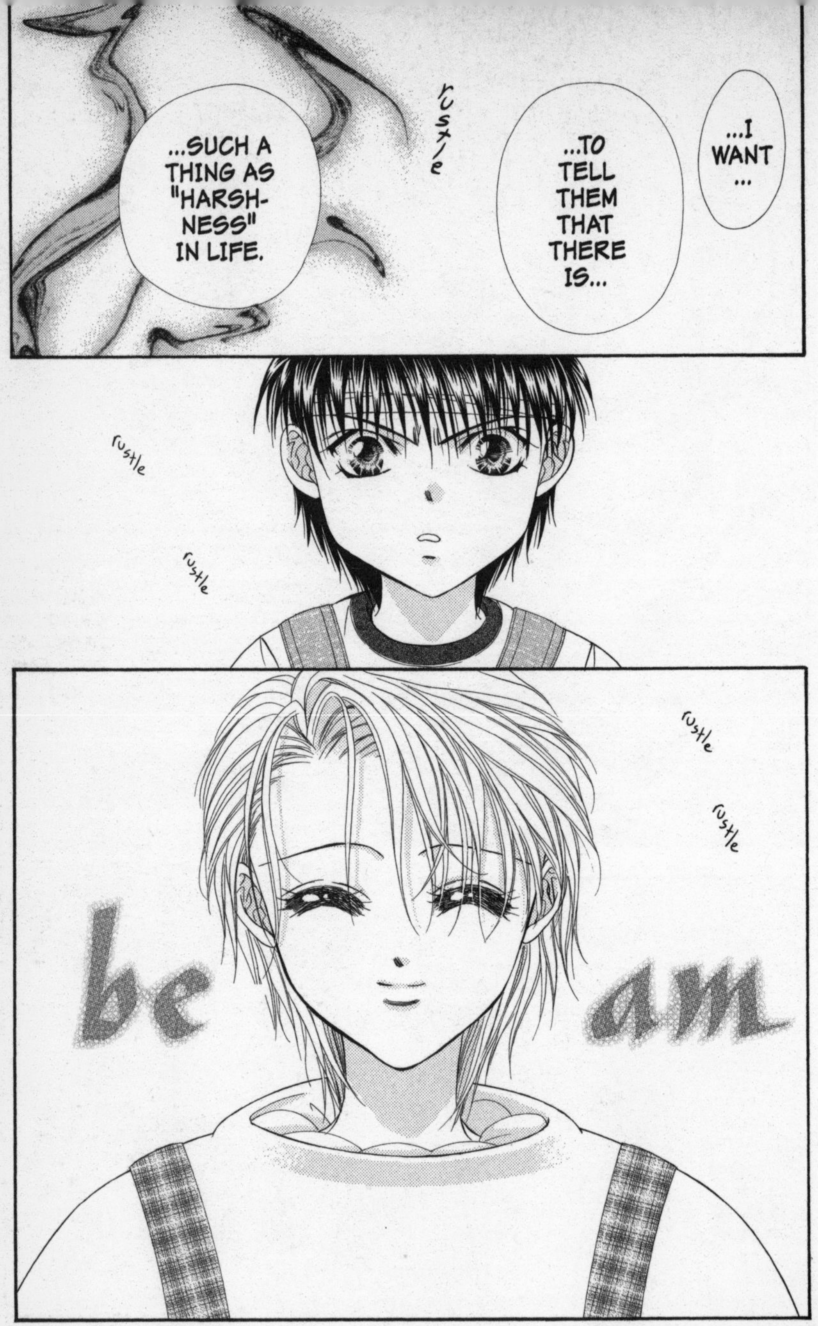

...I WANT...
...TO TELL THEM THAT THERE IS...
rustle
...SUCH A THING AS "HARSHNESS" IN LIFE.
rustle
rustle
rustle
rustle
be am

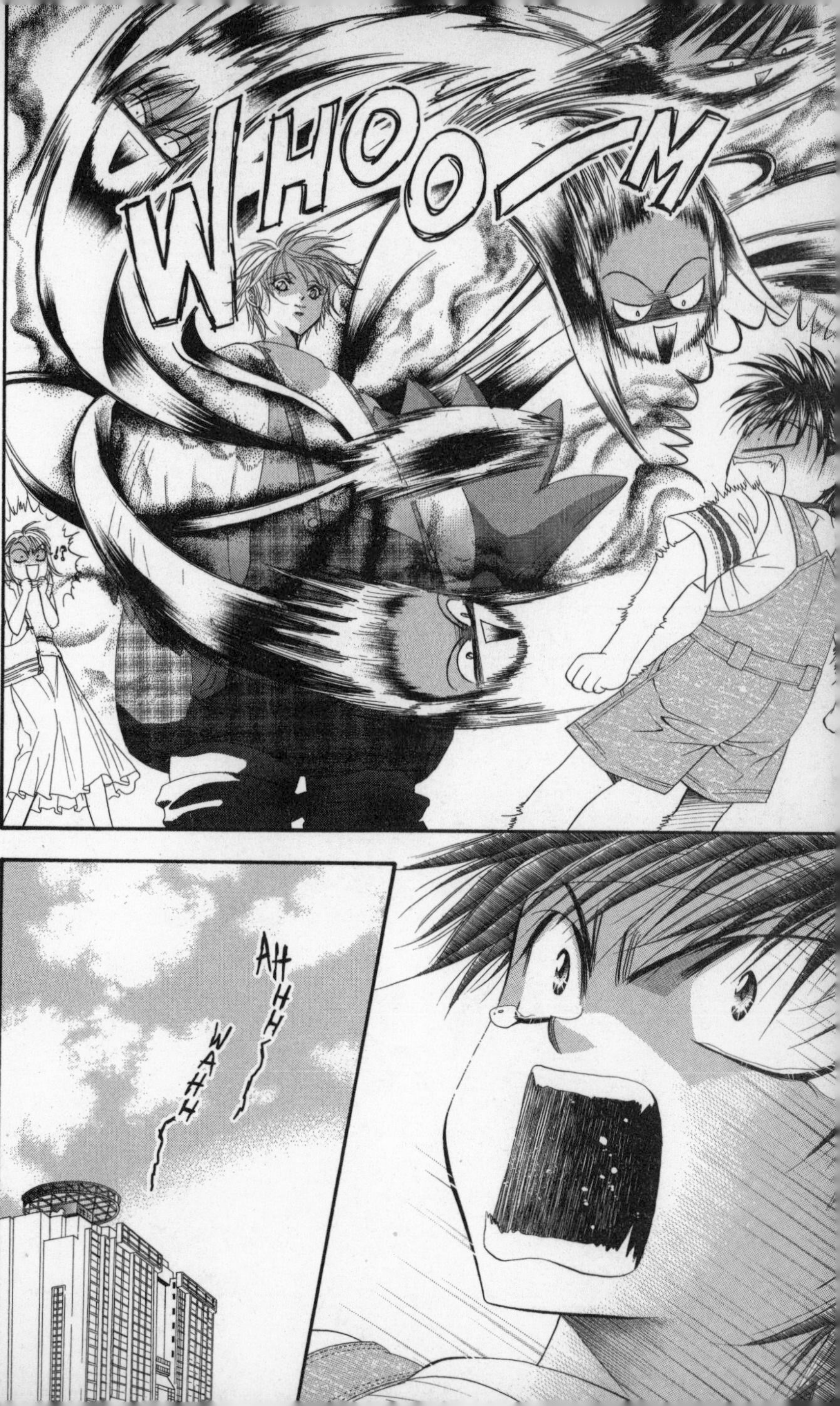
W-HOO—M
!?
AHHH
WAHHH

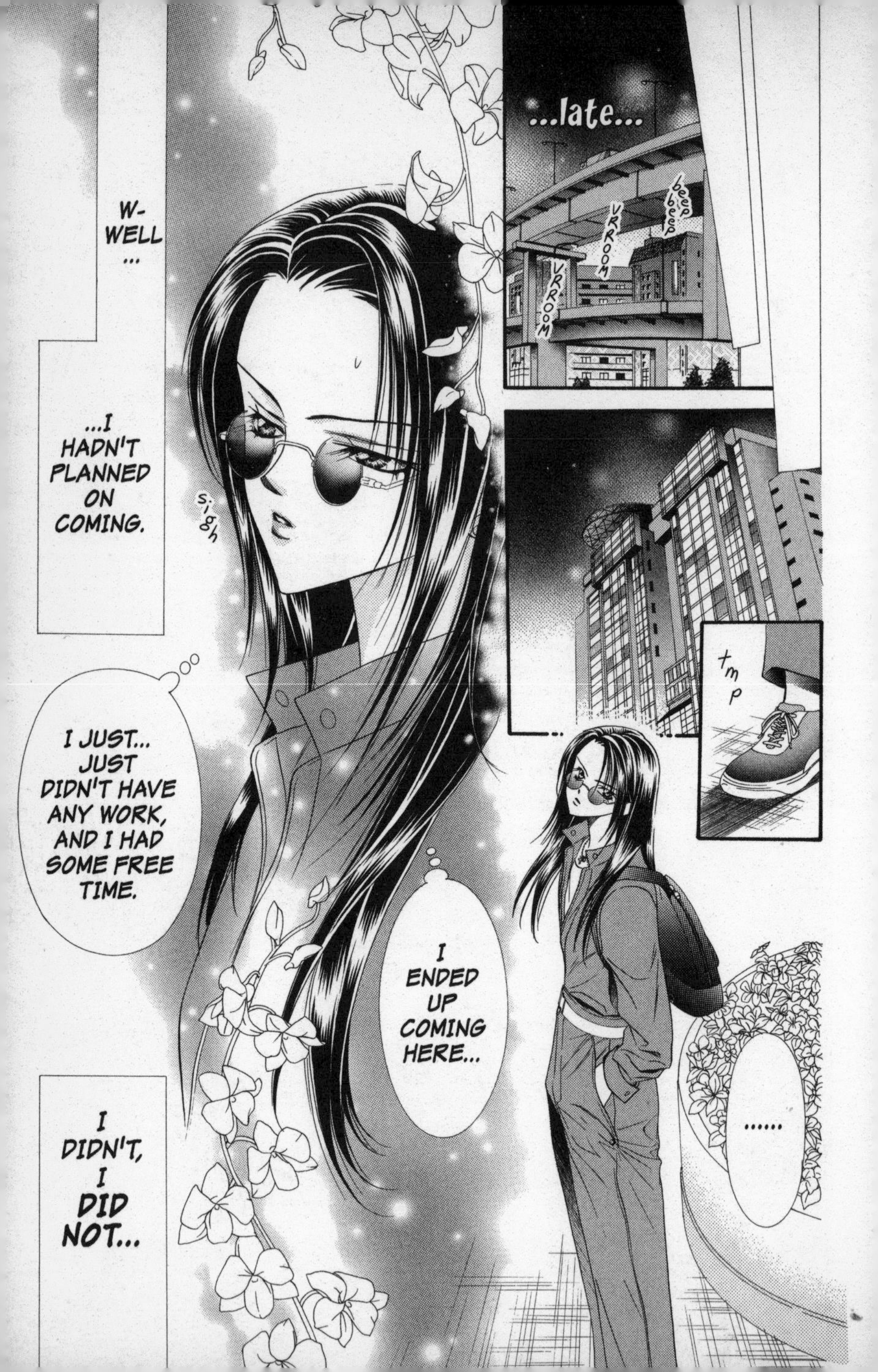
...late...
beep beep
VRROOM
VRROOM
tmp
I ENDED UP COMING HERE...
......
W-WELL...
...I HADN'T PLANNED ON COMING.
sigh
I JUST... JUST DIDN'T HAVE ANY WORK, AND I HAD SOME FREE TIME.
I DIDN'T, I DID NOT...

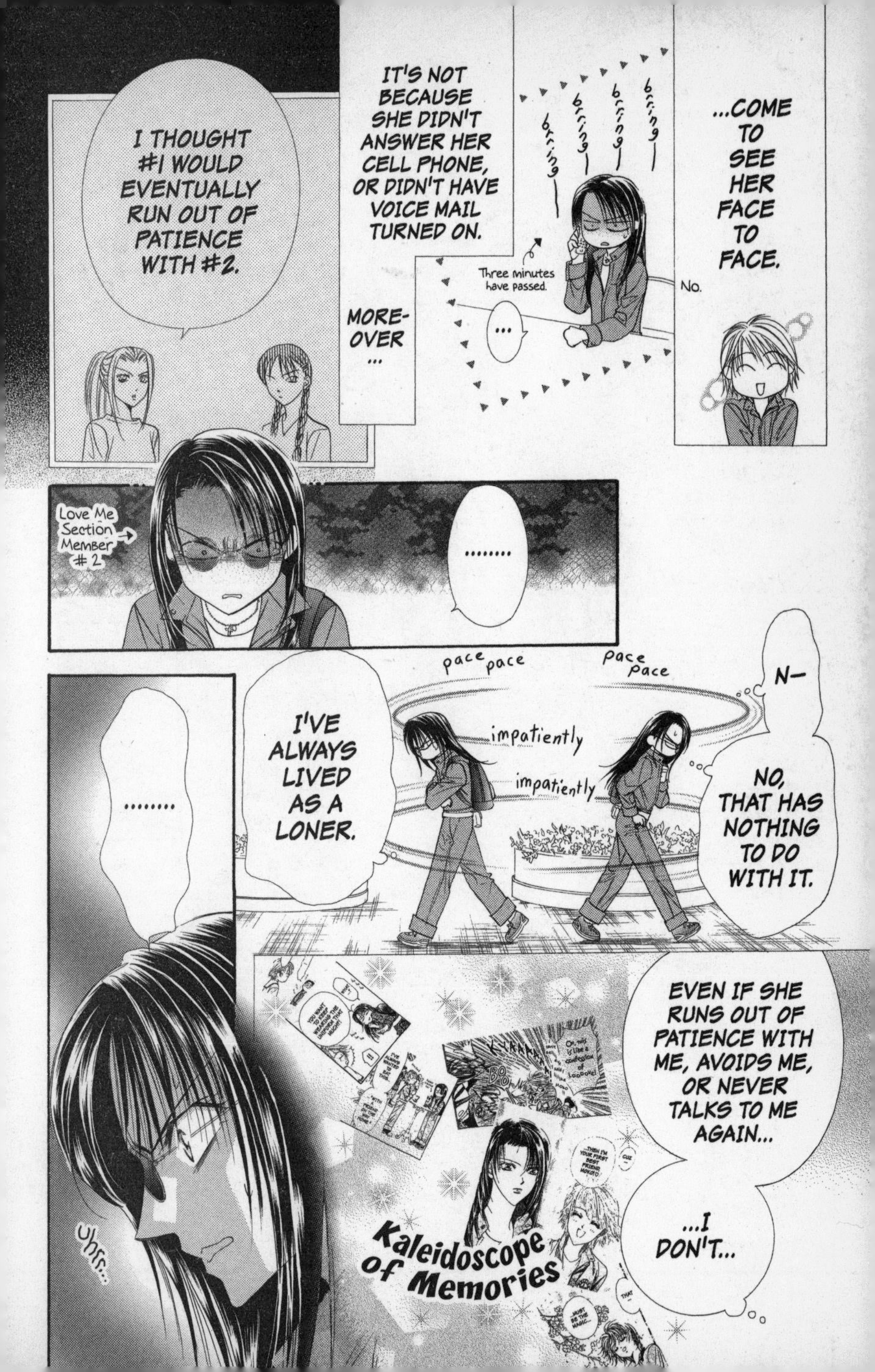
...COME TO SEE HER FACE TO FACE.
No.
IT'S NOT BECAUSE SHE DIDN'T ANSWER HER CELL PHONE, OR DIDN'T HAVE VOICE MAIL TURNED ON.
brring
brring
brring
brring
Three minutes have passed.
...
MORE-OVER...
I THOUGHT #1 WOULD EVENTUALLY RUN OUT OF PATIENCE WITH #2.
....
Love Me Section Member #2
N—
NO, THAT HAS NOTHING TO DO WITH IT.
pace pace
impatiently
pace pace
impatiently
I'VE ALWAYS LIVED AS A LONER.
EVEN IF SHE RUNS OUT OF PATIENCE WITH ME, AVOIDS ME, OR NEVER TALKS TO ME AGAIN...
...I DON'T...
Kaleidoscope of Memories
....
Uhrr...

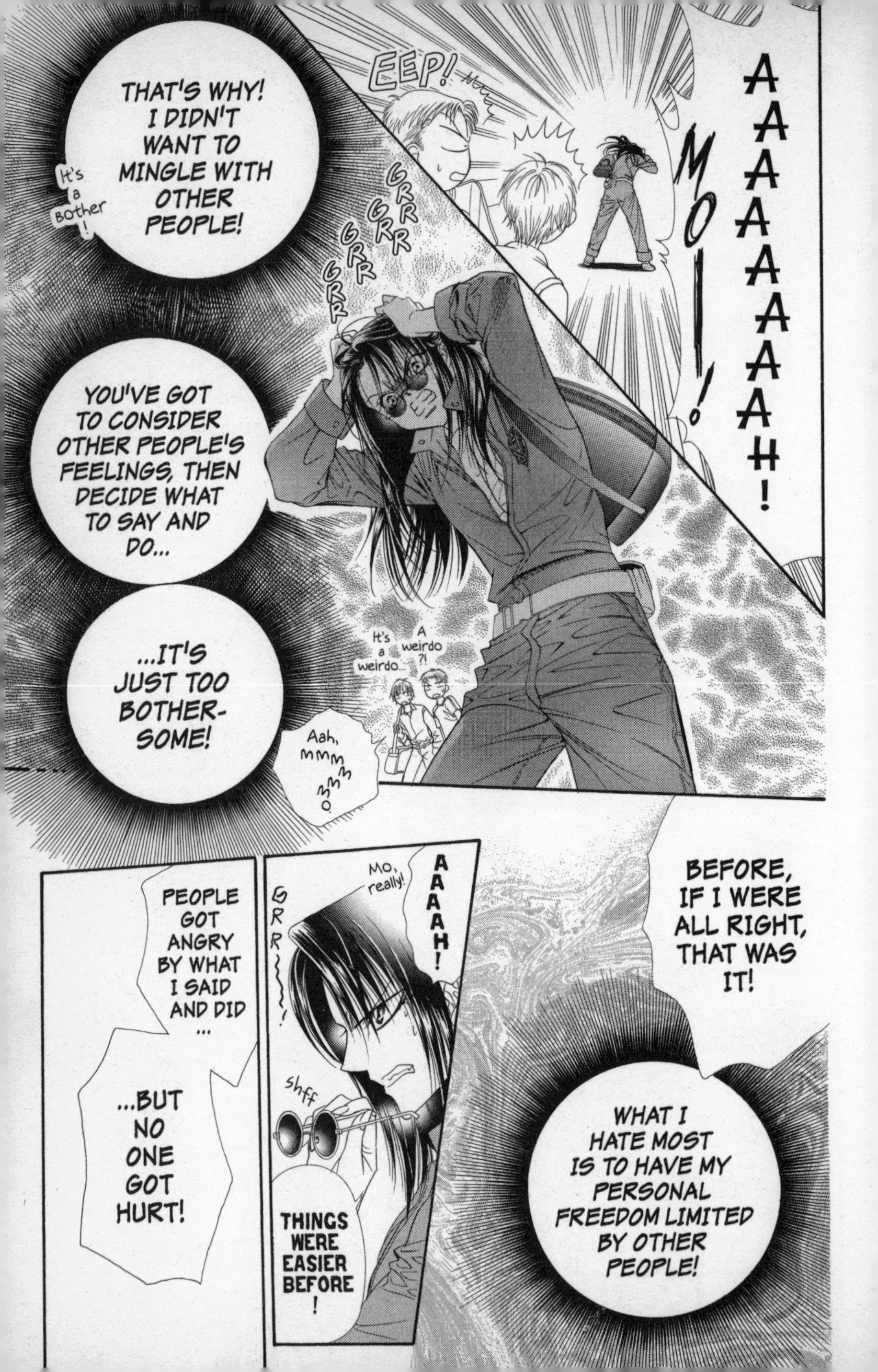
AAAAAAAAAH!
MO!!!
EEP!
GRR GRR GRR GRR
THAT'S WHY! I DIDN'T WANT TO MINGLE WITH OTHER PEOPLE!
It's a bother!
YOU'VE GOT TO CONSIDER OTHER PEOPLE'S FEELINGS, THEN DECIDE WHAT TO SAY AND DO...
...IT'S JUST TOO BOTHER-SOME!
It's a weirdo...
A weirdo?!
Aah, MMMM
BEFORE, IF I WERE ALL RIGHT, THAT WAS IT!
WHAT I HATE MOST IS TO HAVE MY PERSONAL FREEDOM LIMITED BY OTHER PEOPLE!
AAAAH!
Mo, really!
GRR~~!
shff
THINGS WERE EASIER BEFORE!
PEOPLE GOT ANGRY BY WHAT I SAID AND DID...
...BUT NO ONE GOT HURT!

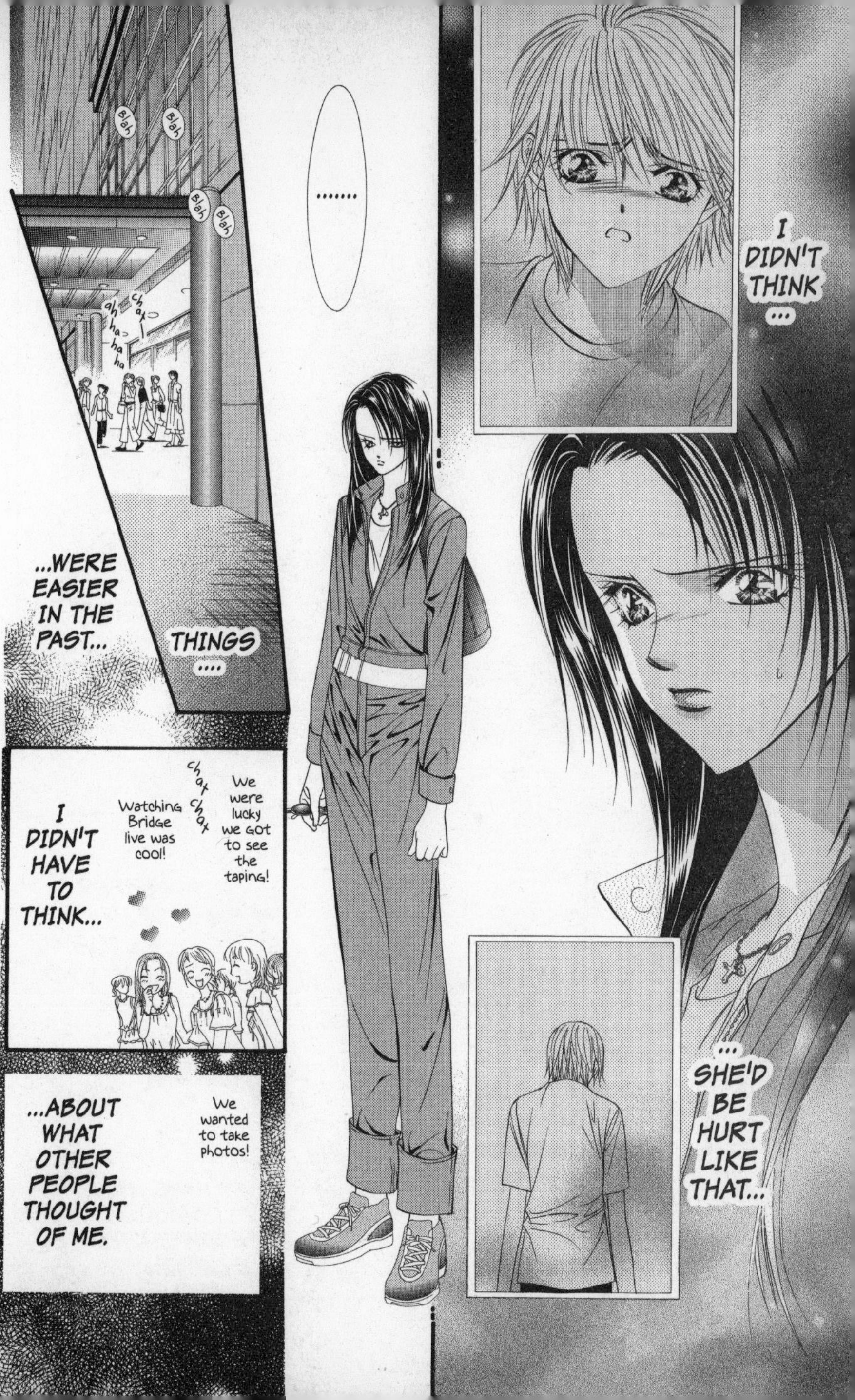
I DIDN'T THINK ...
... SHE'D BE HURT LIKE THAT...
....
Blah
Blah
Blah
Blah
chat
ah ha ha ha
THINGS ....
...WERE EASIER IN THE PAST...
I DIDN'T HAVE TO THINK...
chat chat
We were lucky we got to see the taping!
Watching Bridge live was cool!
...ABOUT WHAT OTHER PEOPLE THOUGHT OF ME.
We wanted to take photos!

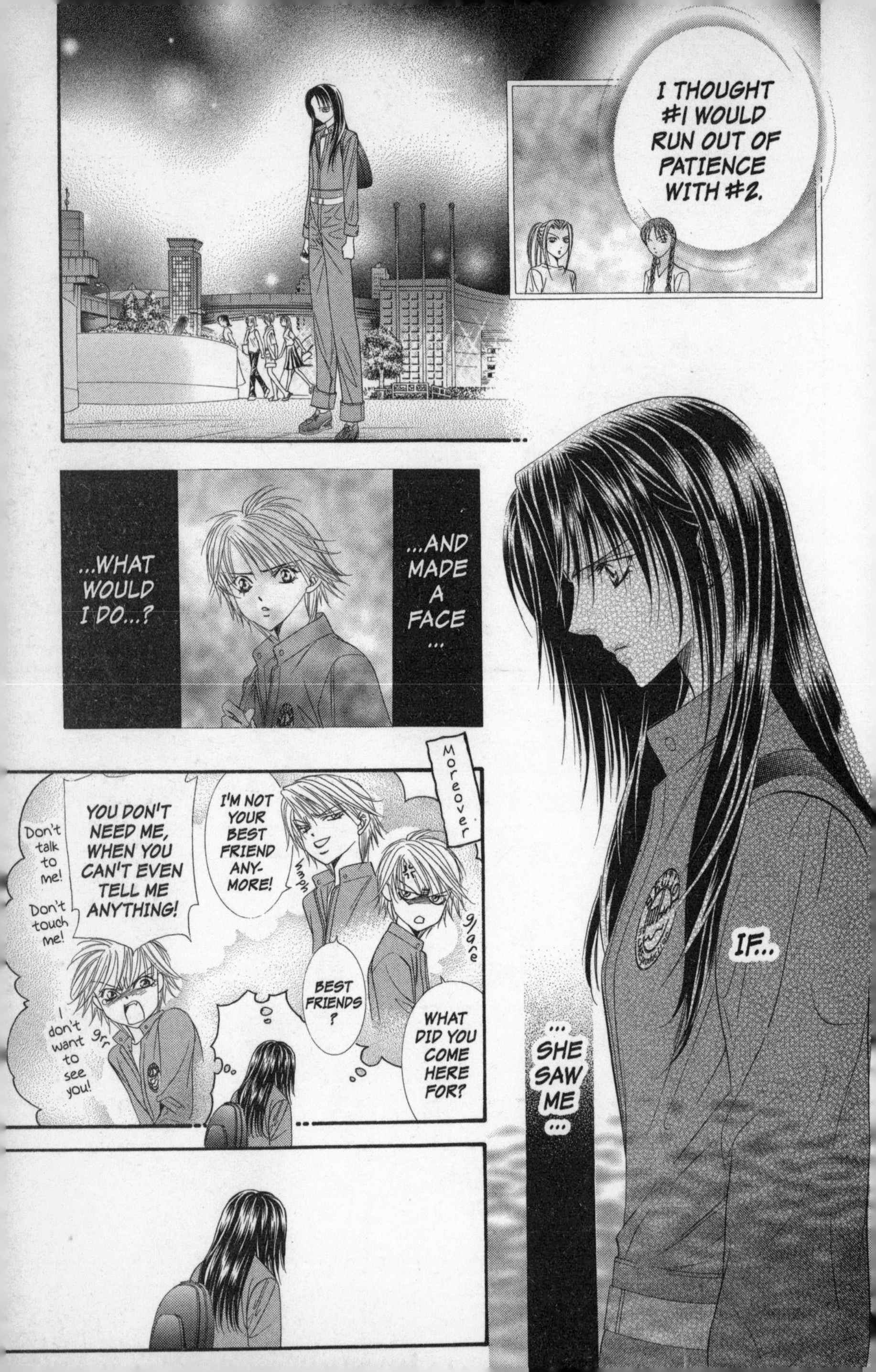
I THOUGHT #1 WOULD RUN OUT OF PATIENCE WITH #2.
IF...
...SHE SAW ME...
...AND MADE A FACE...
...WHAT WOULD I DO...?
Moreover
I'M NOT YOUR BEST FRIEND ANYMORE!
hmph
glare
WHAT DID YOU COME HERE FOR?
BEST FRIENDS?
YOU DON'T NEED ME, WHEN YOU CAN'T EVEN TELL ME ANYTHING!
Don't talk to me!
Don't touch me!
grr
I don't want to see you!

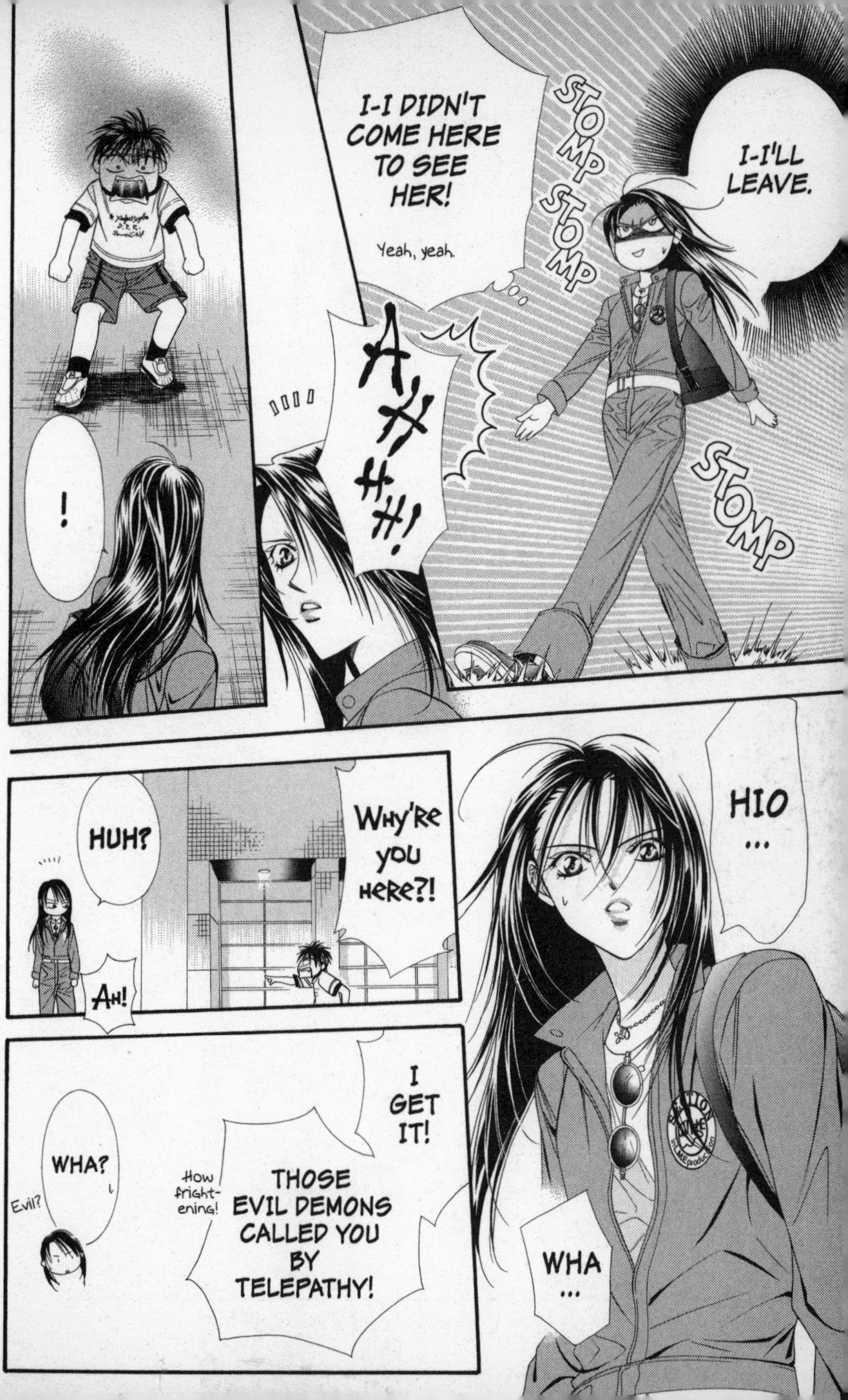
I-I'LL LEAVE.
STOMP STOMP
STOMP
I-I DIDN'T COME HERE TO SEE HER!
Yeah, yeah.
STOMP
AHHH!
!
HIO ...
WHA ...
WHY'RE YOU HERE?!
HUH?
AH!
I GET IT!
THOSE EVIL DEMONS CALLED YOU BY TELEPATHY!
How fright-ening!
WHA?
Evil?

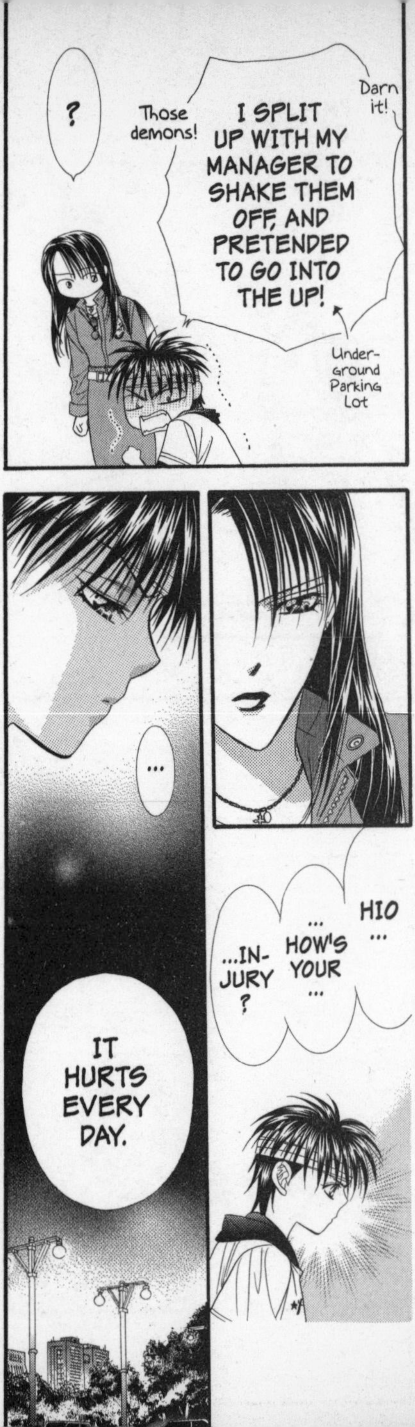
Darn it!
I SPLIT UP WITH MY MANAGER TO SHAKE THEM OFF, AND PRETENDED TO GO INTO THE UP!
Those demons!
?
Under-ground Parking Lot
...
HIO... ...HOW'S YOUR... ...IN-JURY?
IT HURTS EVERY DAY.

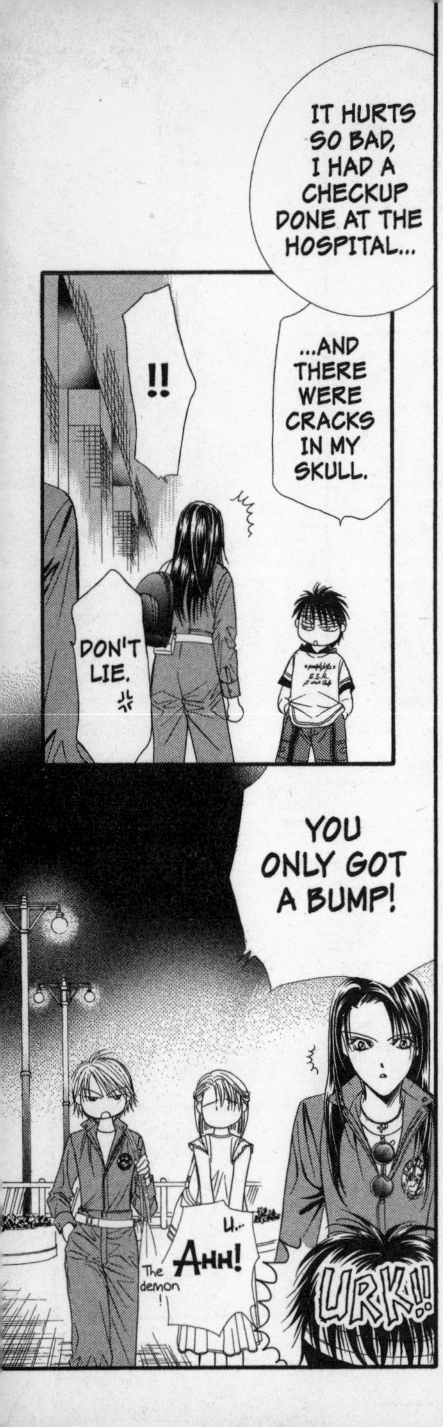
IT HURTS SO BAD, I HAD A CHECKUP DONE AT THE HOSPITAL...
...AND THERE WERE CRACKS IN MY SKULL.
!!
DON'T LIE.
YOU ONLY GOT A BUMP!
URK!!
U... AHH!
The demon!

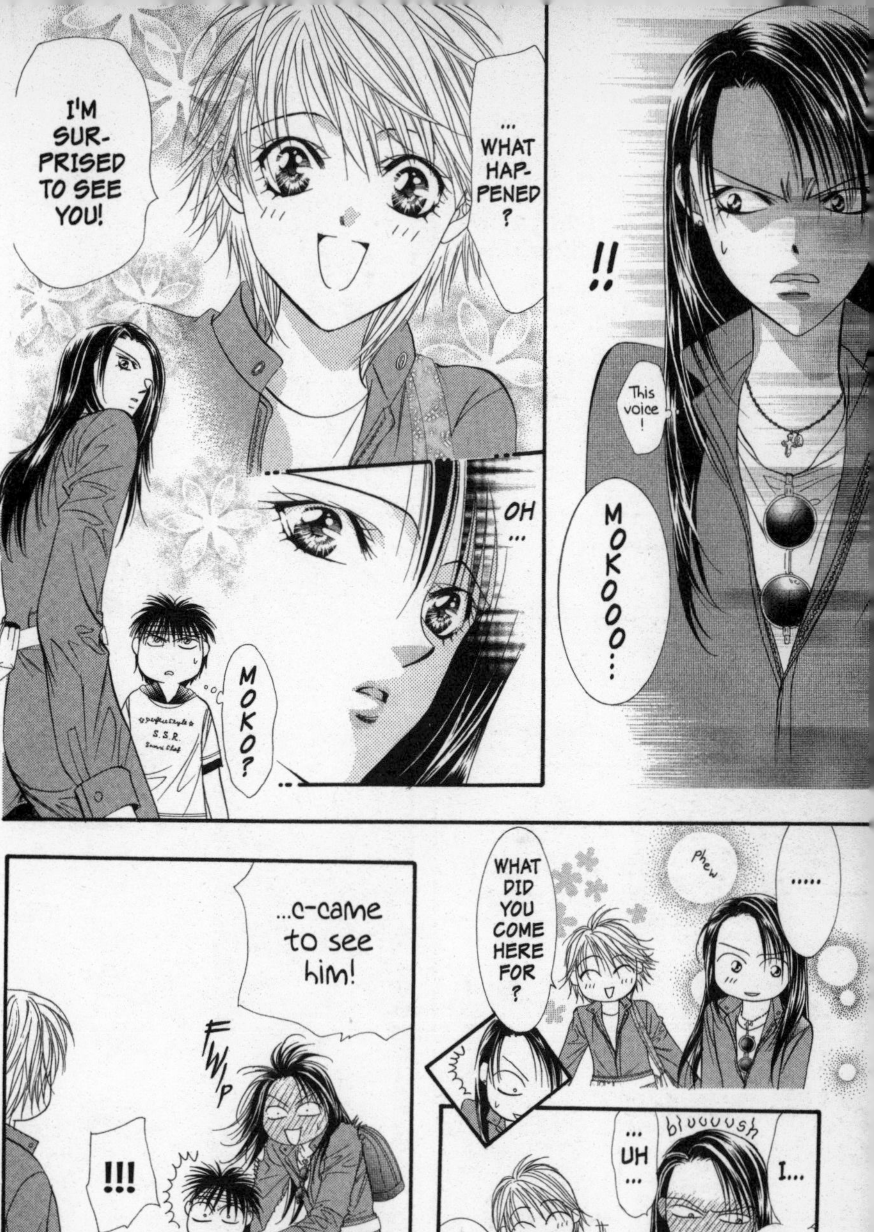
!!
This voice!
MOKOOOO...
...WHAT HAPPENED?
I'M SURPRISED TO SEE YOU!
OH...
MOKO?
.....
phew
WHAT DID YOU COME HERE FOR?
bluuuush
...UH...
I...
...UM...
YEAH YEAH?
...c-came to see him!
FWIP
!!!

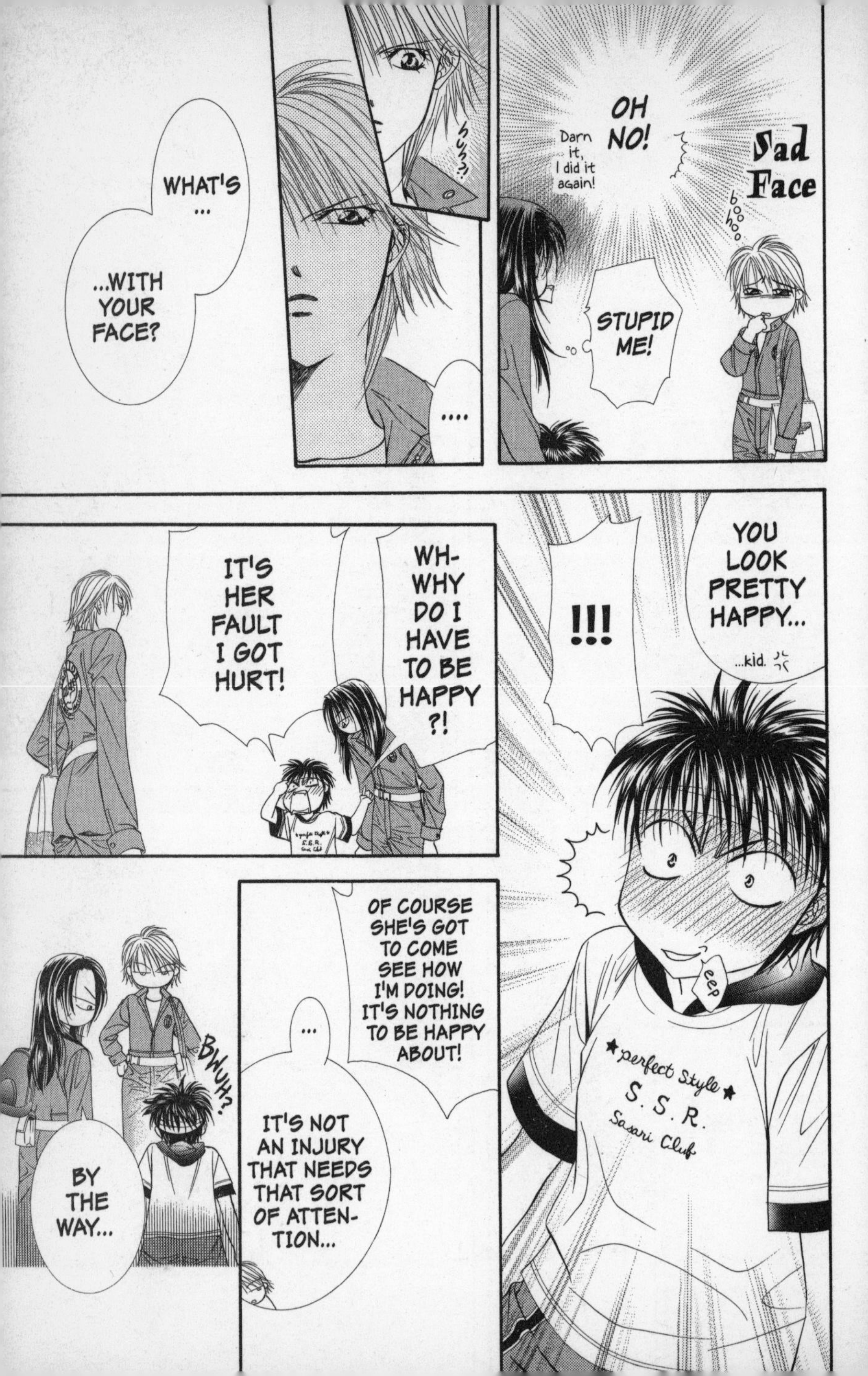
Sad Face
boo hoo
OH NO!
Darn it, I did it again!
STUPID ME!
huh?!
....
WHAT'S ...
...WITH YOUR FACE?
YOU LOOK PRETTY HAPPY...
...kid.
!!!
eep
WH- WHY DO I HAVE TO BE HAPPY ?!
IT'S HER FAULT I GOT HURT!
OF COURSE SHE'S GOT TO COME SEE HOW I'M DOING! IT'S NOTHING TO BE HAPPY ABOUT!
...
IT'S NOT AN INJURY THAT NEEDS THAT SORT OF ATTEN- TION...
BWUH?
BY THE WAY...

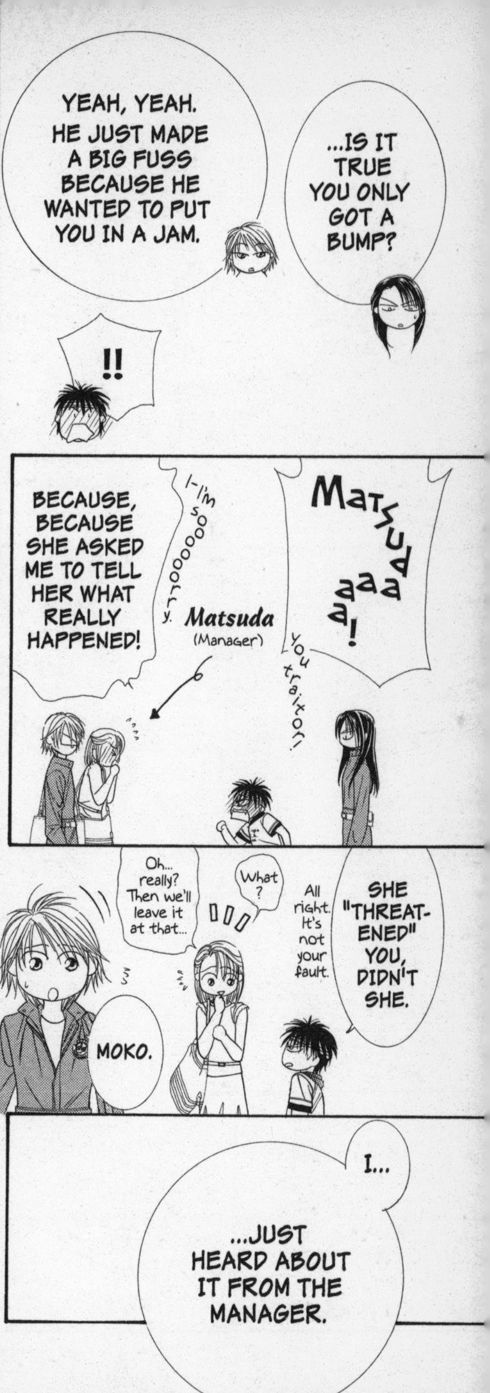
...IS IT TRUE YOU ONLY GOT A BUMP?
YEAH, YEAH. HE JUST MADE A BIG FUSS BECAUSE HE WANTED TO PUT YOU IN A JAM.
!!
Matsudaaaaa!
You traitor!
I-I'm sooooorry.
BECAUSE, BECAUSE SHE ASKED ME TO TELL HER WHAT REALLY HAPPENED!
Matsuda (Manager)
SHE "THREAT-ENED" YOU, DIDN'T SHE.
All right. It's not your fault.
What?
Oh... really? Then we'll leave it at that...
MOKO.
I...
...JUST HEARD ABOUT IT FROM THE MANAGER.
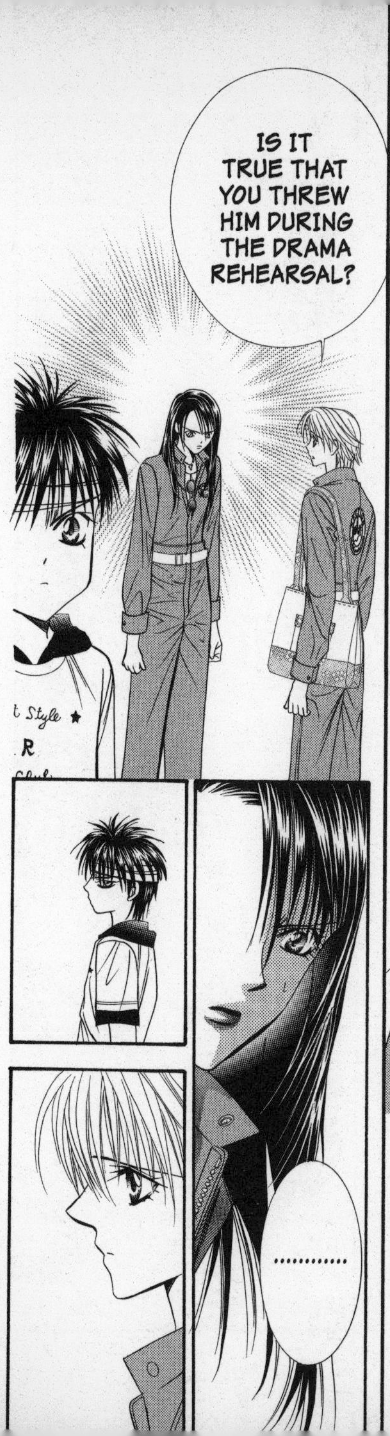
IS IT TRUE THAT YOU THREW HIM DURING THE DRAMA REHEARSAL?
....

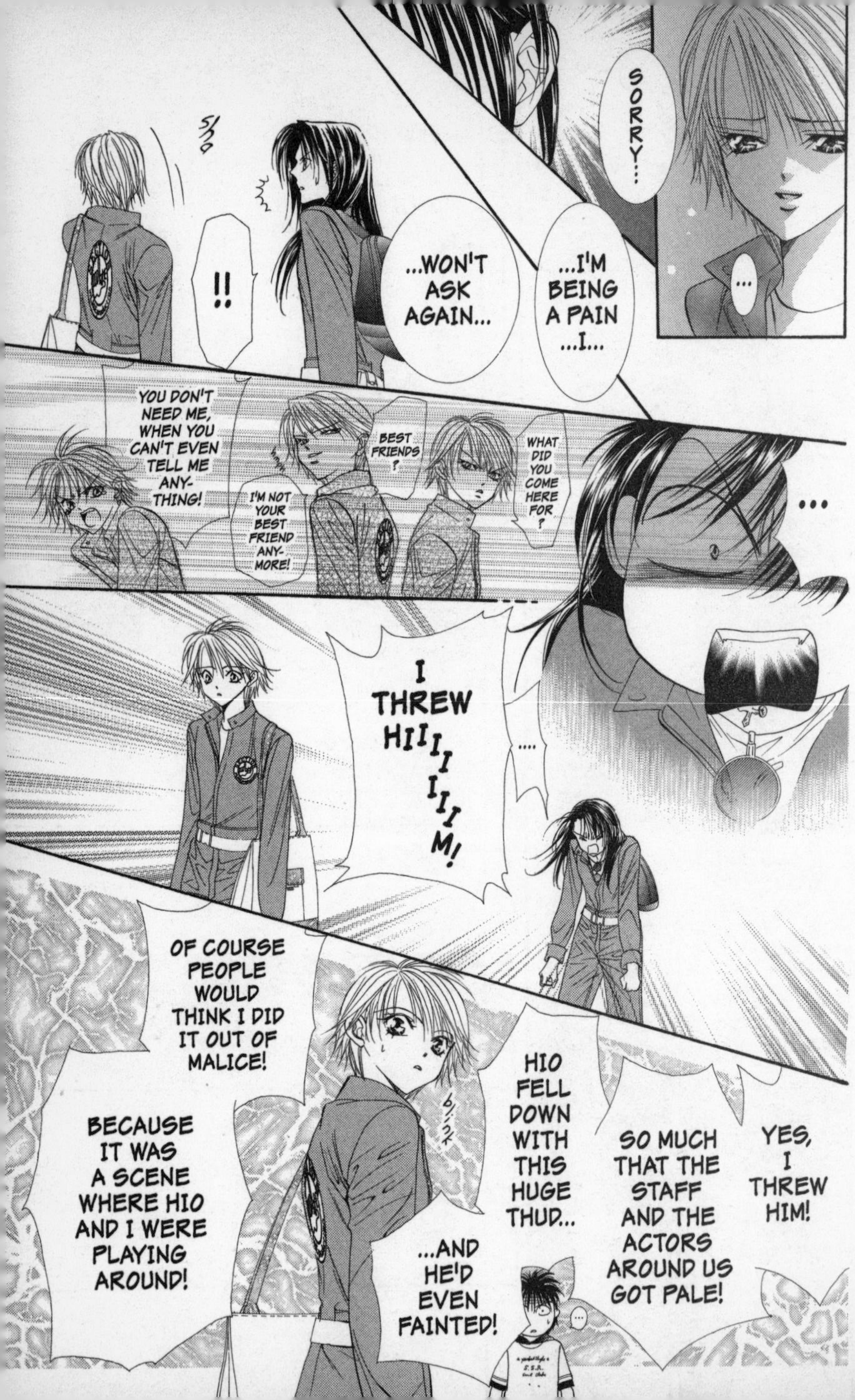
SORRY...
...
...I'M BEING A PAIN ...I...
...WON'T ASK AGAIN...
!!
...
WHAT DID YOU COME HERE FOR?
BEST FRIENDS?
I'M NOT YOUR BEST FRIEND ANYMORE!
YOU DON'T NEED ME, WHEN YOU CAN'T EVEN TELL ME ANYTHING!
...
I THREW HIIIIIIIIM!
....
YES, I THREW HIM!
SO MUCH THAT THE STAFF AND THE ACTORS AROUND US GOT PALE!
HIO FELL DOWN WITH THIS HUGE THUD...
...AND HE'D EVEN FAINTED!
...
OF COURSE PEOPLE WOULD THINK I DID IT OUT OF MALICE!
BECAUSE IT WAS A SCENE WHERE HIO AND I WERE PLAYING AROUND!

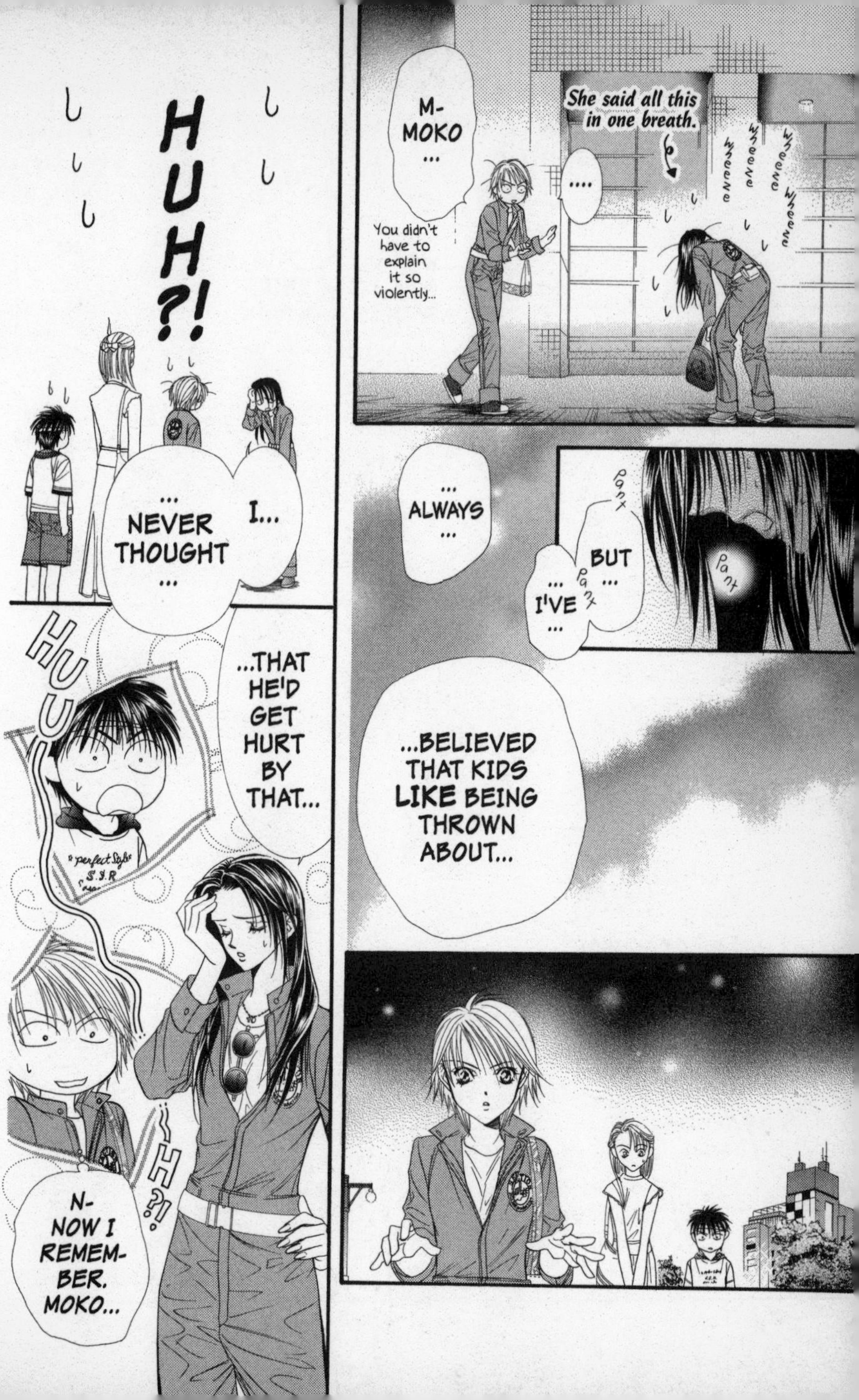

She said all this in one breath.
Wheeze wheeze
Wheeze wheeze
....
M-MOKO...
You didn't have to explain it so violently...
Pant
BUT... I'VE...
Pant Pant
...ALWAYS...
...BELIEVED THAT KIDS LIKE BEING THROWN ABOUT...
HUH?!
I...
...NEVER THOUGHT...
...THAT HE'D GET HURT BY THAT...
HUH
~H?!
N-NOW I REMEMBER. MOKO...

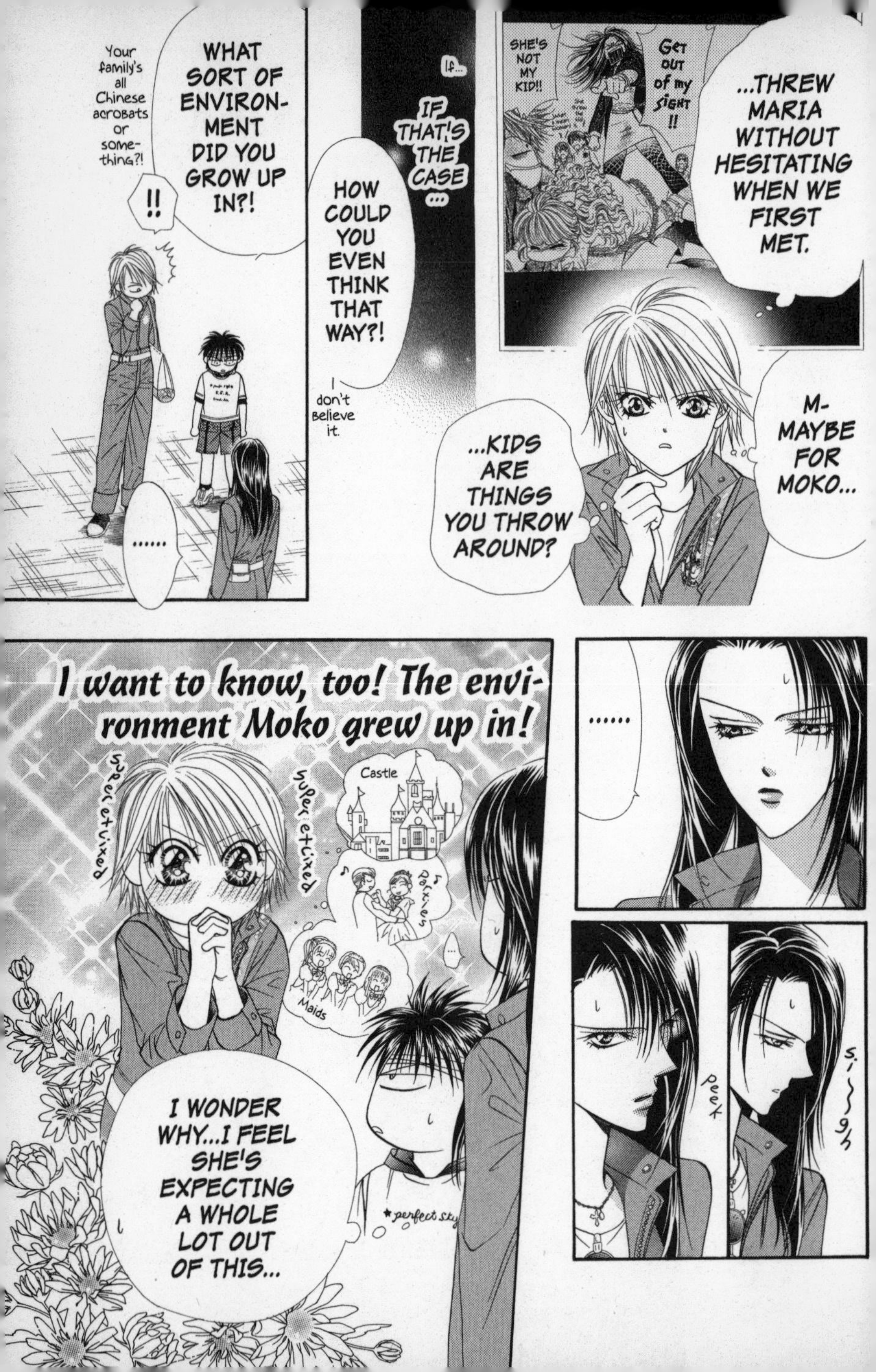
...THREW MARIA WITHOUT HESITATING WHEN WE FIRST MET.
Get out of my sight!!
SHE'S NOT MY KID!!
M-MAYBE FOR MOKO...
...KIDS ARE THINGS YOU THROW AROUND?
If...
IF THAT'S THE CASE...
HOW COULD YOU EVEN THINK THAT WAY?!
I don't believe it.
WHAT SORT OF ENVIRONMENT DID YOU GROW UP IN?!
Your family's all Chinese acrobats or something?!
!!
......
......
si~gh
Peek
I want to know, too! The environment Moko grew up in!
super excited
Castle
Pixies
Maids
super excited
...
I WONDER WHY...I FEEL SHE'S EXPECTING A WHOLE LOT OUT OF THIS...

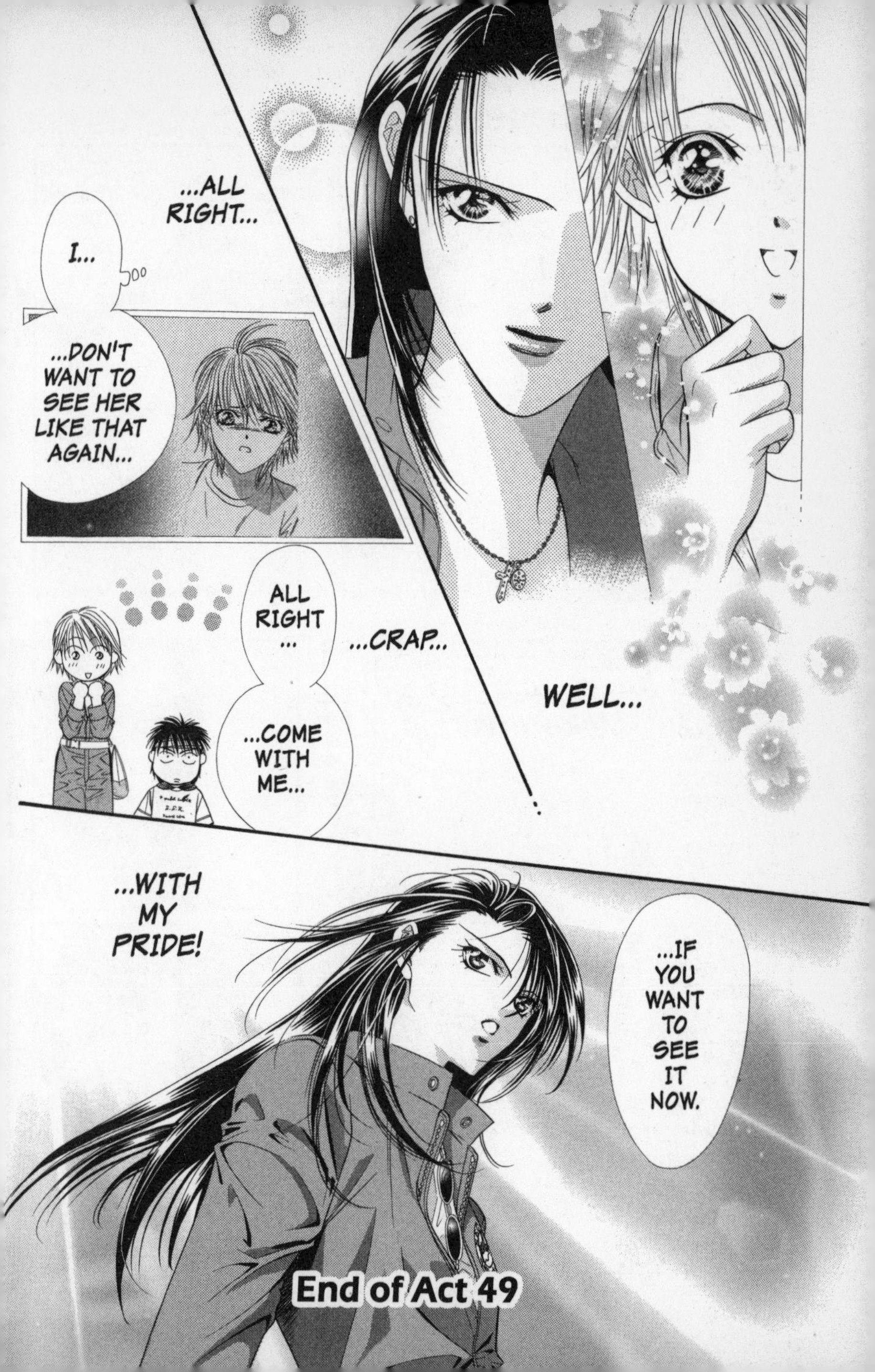
WELL...
...ALL RIGHT...
I...
...DON'T WANT TO SEE HER LIKE THAT AGAIN...
...CRAP...
ALL RIGHT ...
...COME WITH ME...
...IF YOU WANT TO SEE IT NOW.
...WITH MY PRIDE!
End of Act 49

A Little Episode: This story was an episode that was sadly cut out from the storyboard due to page constraints.

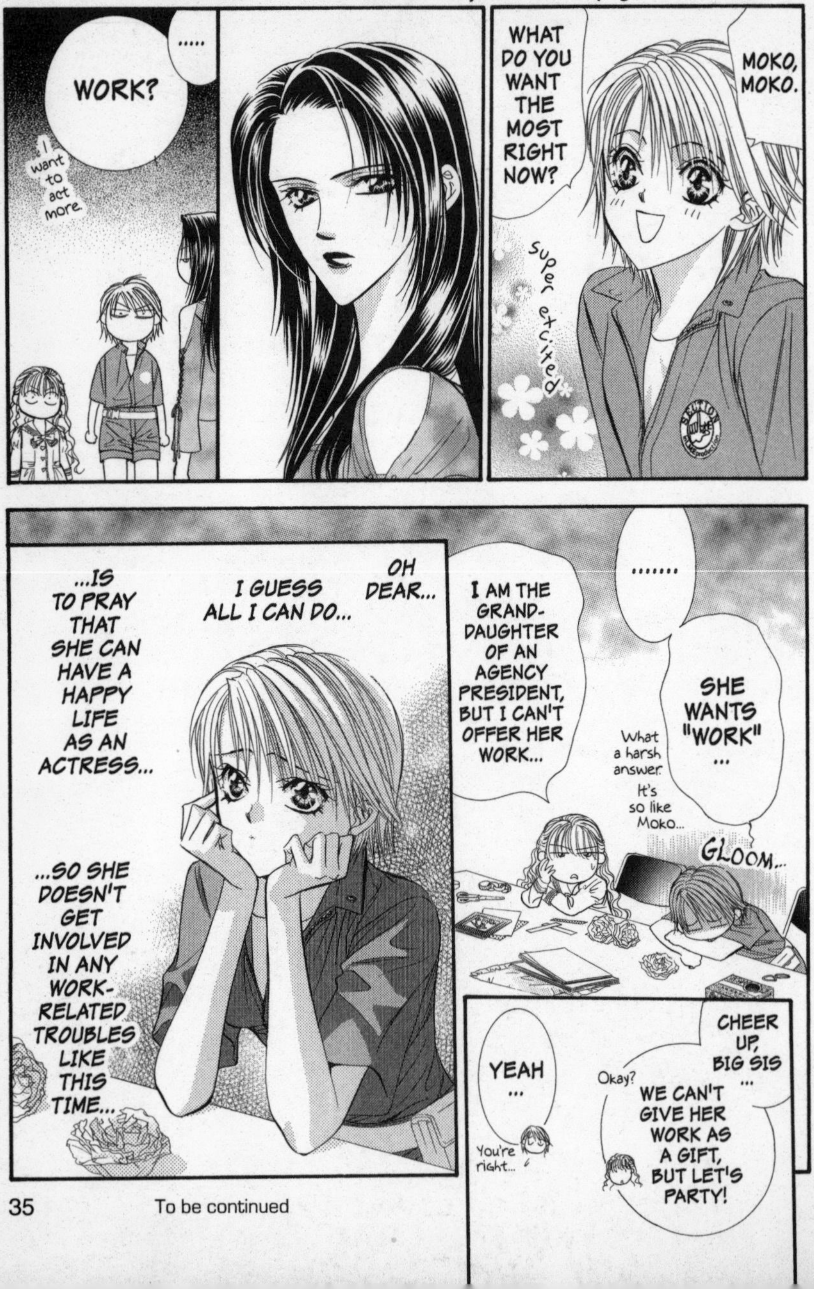
MOKO, MOKO.
WHAT DO YOU WANT THE MOST RIGHT NOW?
super excited
......
WORK?
I want to act more.
....
SHE WANTS "WORK" ...
What a harsh answer.
It's so like Moko...
I AM THE GRAND-DAUGHTER OF AN AGENCY PRESIDENT, BUT I CAN'T OFFER HER WORK...
GLOOM...
CHEER UP, BIG SIS ...
WE CAN'T GIVE HER WORK AS A GIFT, BUT LET'S PARTY!
Okay?
YEAH ...
You're right...
OH DEAR...
I GUESS ALL I CAN DO...
...IS TO PRAY THAT SHE CAN HAVE A HAPPY LIFE AS AN ACTRESS...
...SO SHE DOESN'T GET INVOLVED IN ANY WORK-RELATED TROUBLES LIKE THIS TIME...

To be continued

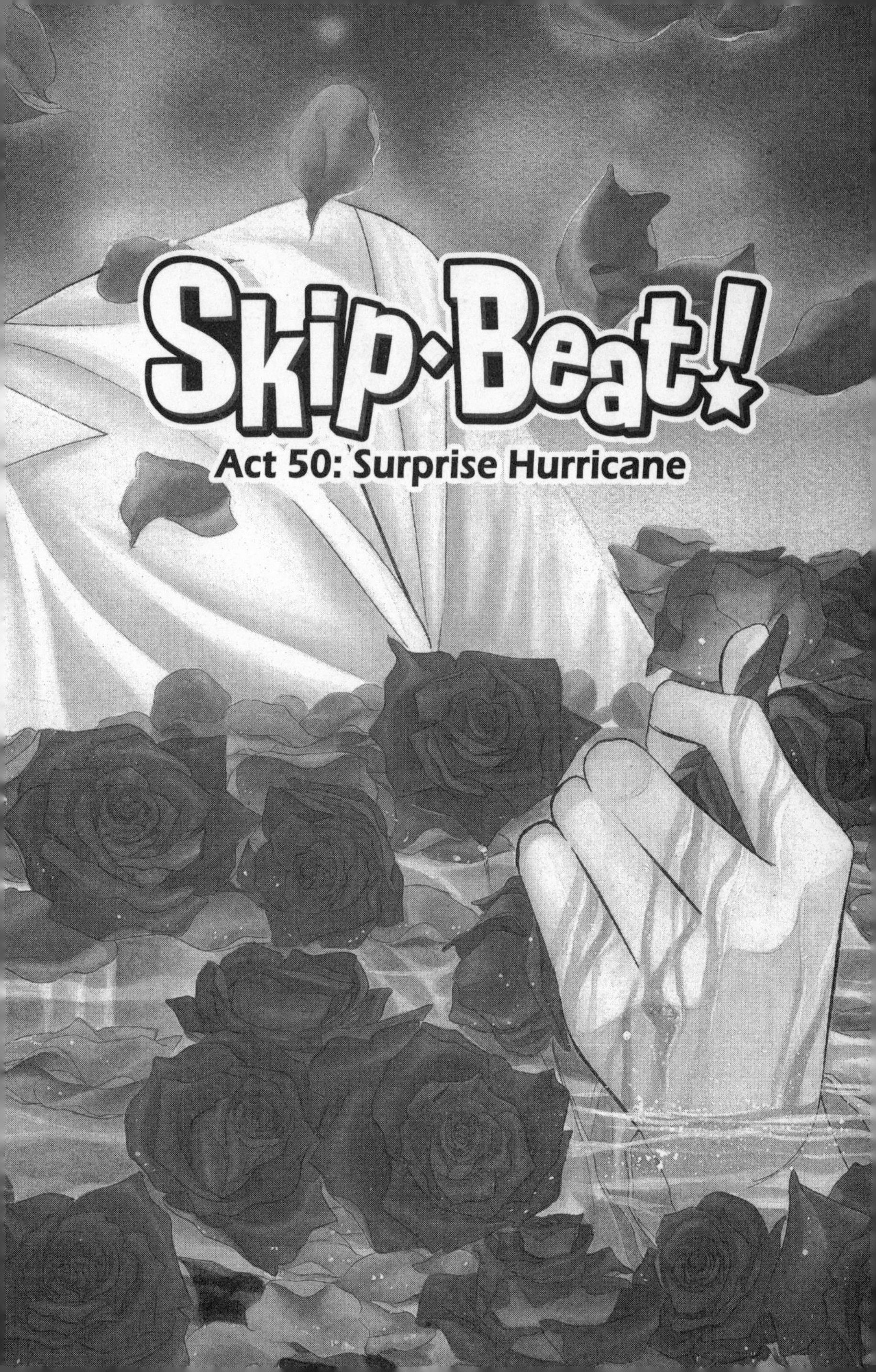
Skip·Beat!
Act 50: Surprise Hurricane

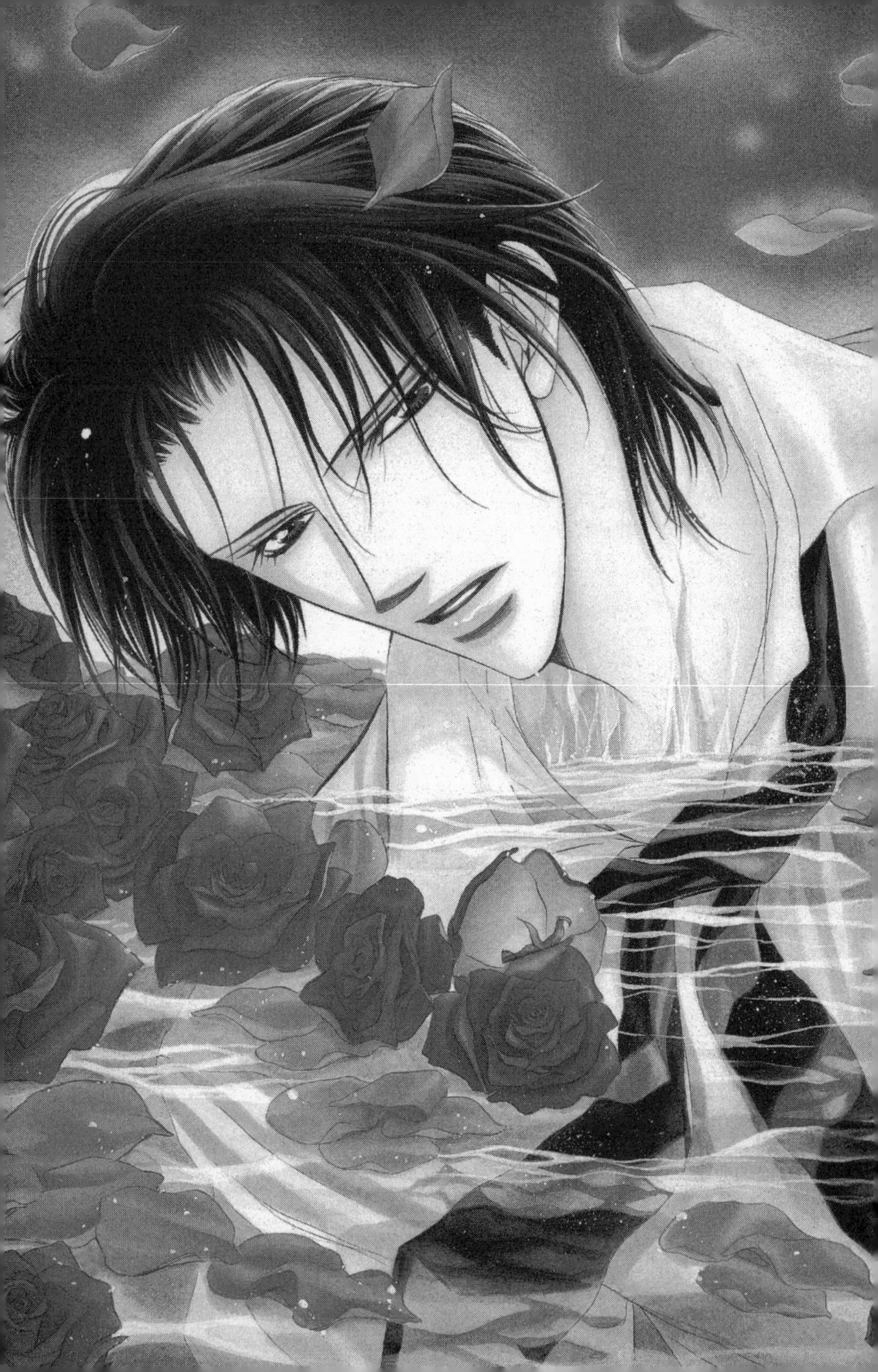

A Little Episode: Continued

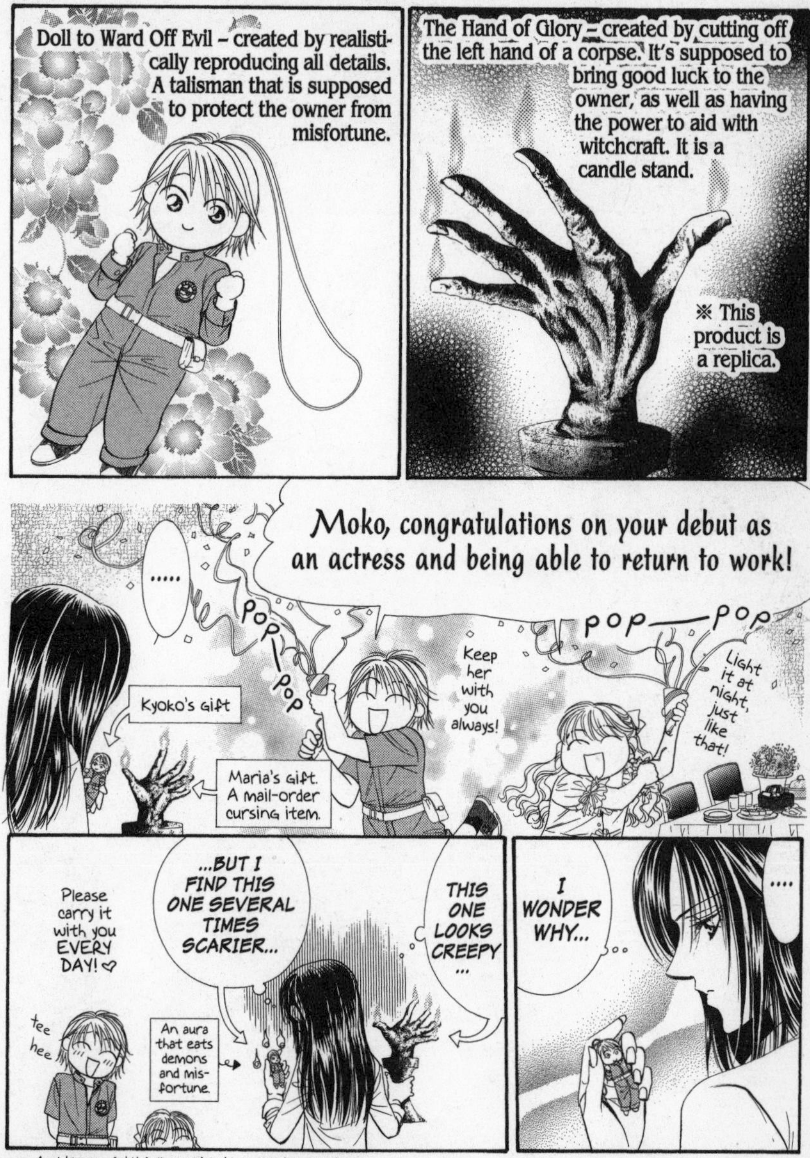
The Hand of Glory – created by cutting off the left hand of a corpse. It's supposed to bring good luck to the owner, as well as having the power to aid with witchcraft. It is a candle stand.
※ This product is a replica.
Doll to Ward Off Evil – created by realistically reproducing all details. A talisman that is supposed to protect the owner from misfortune.
Moko, congratulations on your debut as an actress and being able to return to work!
pop—pop
Light it at night, just like that!
Keep her with you always!
Pop-pop
.....
Kyoko's Gift
Maria's Gift. A mail-order cursing item.
....
I WONDER WHY...
THIS ONE LOOKS CREEPY ...
...BUT I FIND THIS ONE SEVERAL TIMES SCARIER...
Please carry it with you EVERY DAY! ♡
An aura that eats demons and misfortune.
tee hee

And Kanae faithfully carries it around every day, because she is afraid of being cursed by it...

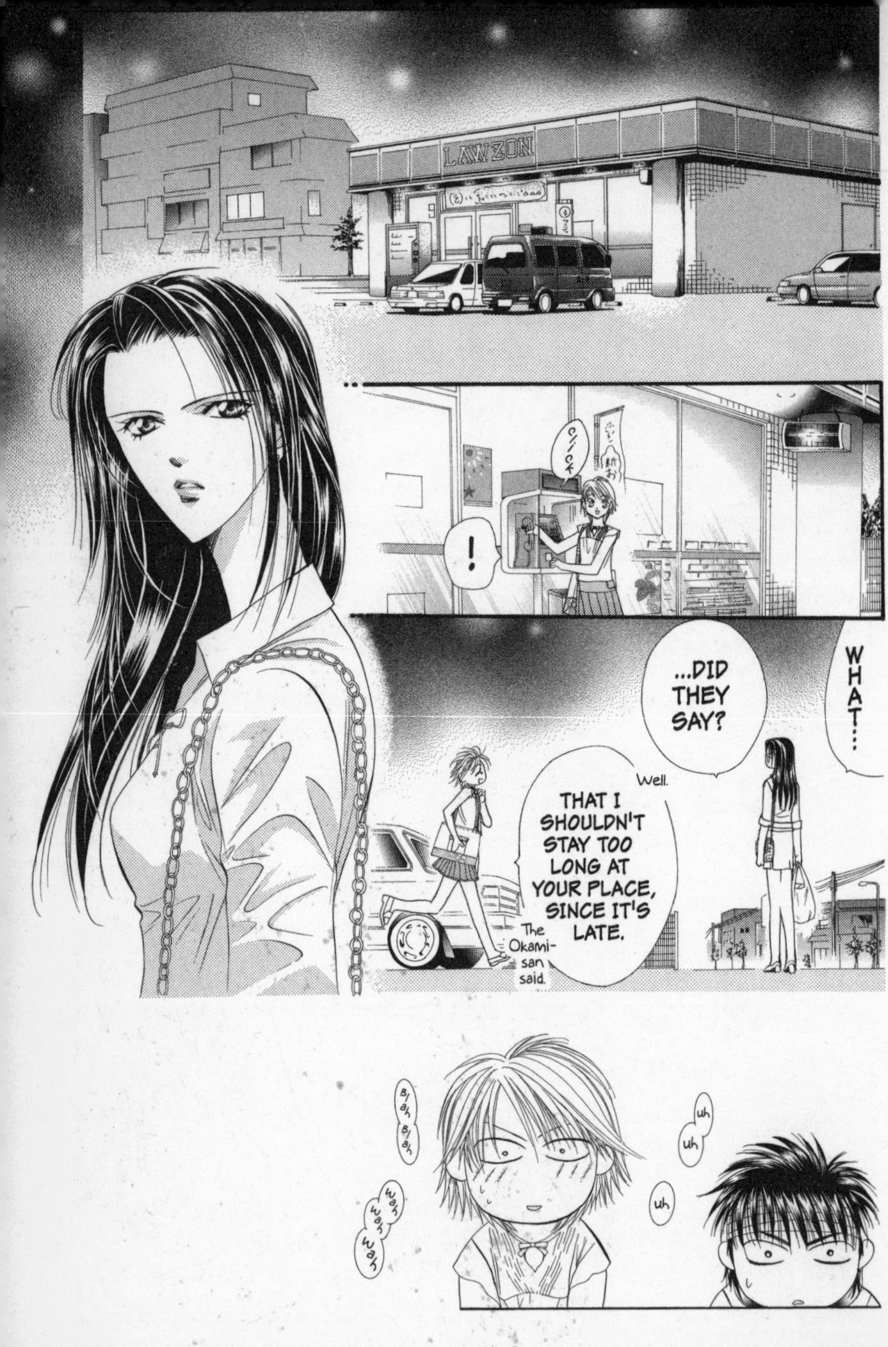
LAWZON
CLICK
!
WHAT...
...DID THEY SAY?
Well.
THAT I SHOULDN'T STAY TOO LONG AT YOUR PLACE, SINCE IT'S LATE.
The Okami-san said.
uh
uh
uh
Blah Blah Blah
wah wah wah

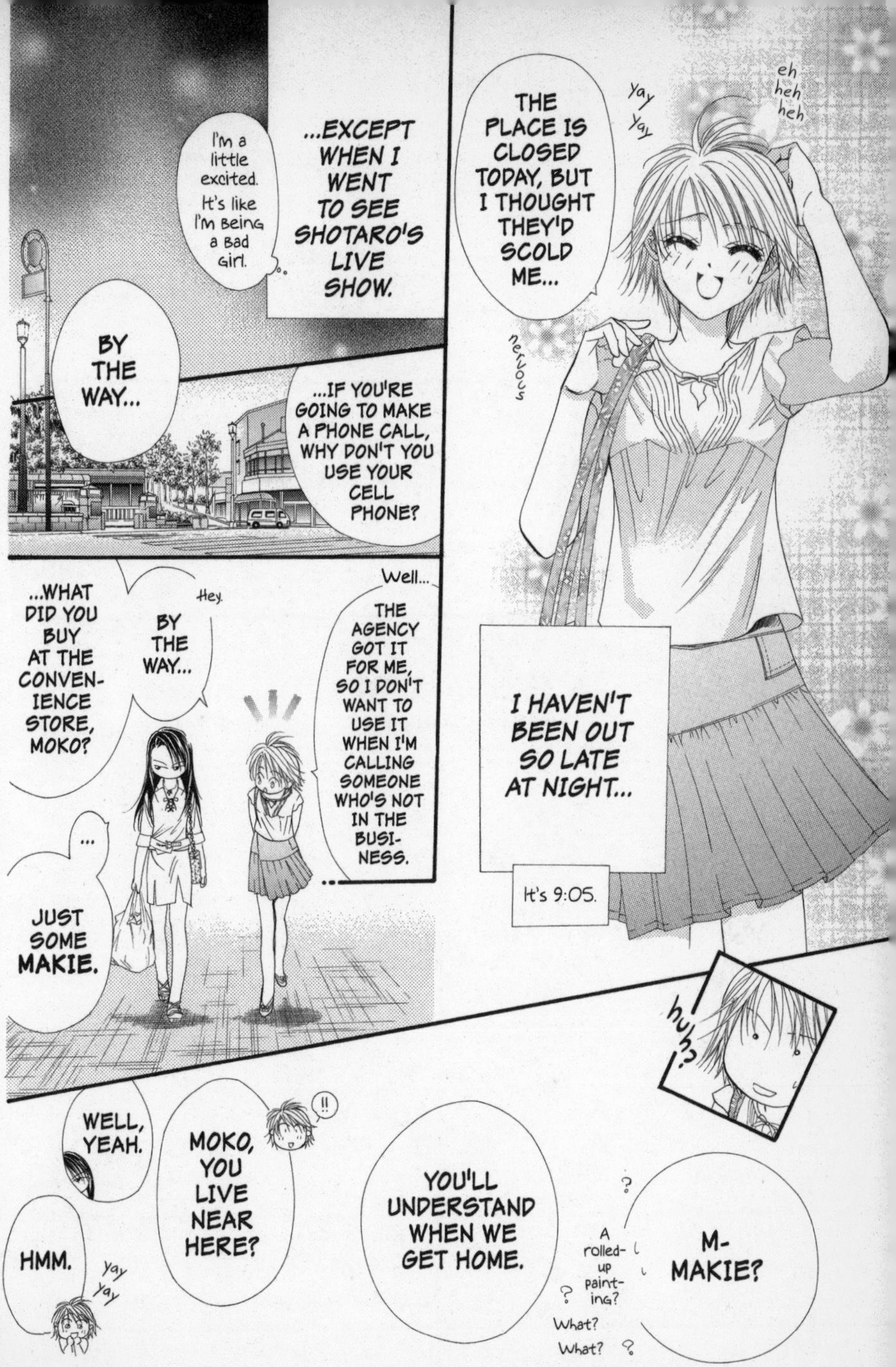

eh heh heh
yay yay
THE PLACE IS CLOSED TODAY, BUT I THOUGHT THEY'D SCOLD ME...
nervous
I HAVEN'T BEEN OUT SO LATE AT NIGHT...
It's 9:05.
...EXCEPT WHEN I WENT TO SEE SHOTARO'S LIVE SHOW.
I'm a little excited. It's like I'm being a bad girl.
BY THE WAY...
...IF YOU'RE GOING TO MAKE A PHONE CALL, WHY DON'T YOU USE YOUR CELL PHONE?
Well...
THE AGENCY GOT IT FOR ME, SO I DON'T WANT TO USE IT WHEN I'M CALLING SOMEONE WHO'S NOT IN THE BUSINESS.
Hey.
BY THE WAY...
...WHAT DID YOU BUY AT THE CONVENIENCE STORE, MOKO?
...
JUST SOME MAKIE.
huh?
M-MAKIE?
A rolled-up painting?
What?
What?
YOU'LL UNDERSTAND WHEN WE GET HOME.
MOKO, YOU LIVE NEAR HERE?
!!
WELL, YEAH.
HMM.
yay yay

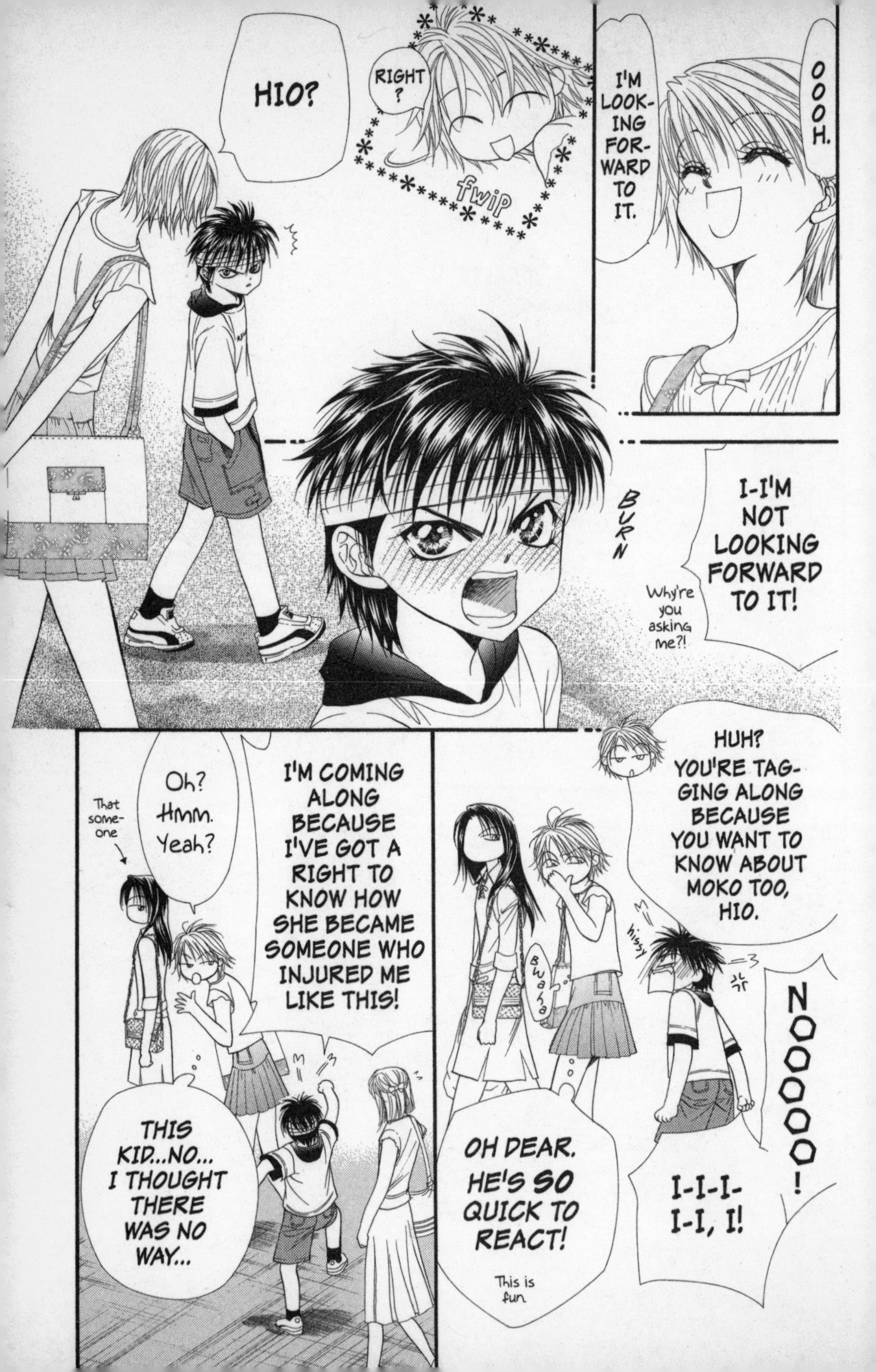
OOOH.
I'M LOOKING-ING FORWARD TO IT.
RIGHT?
fwip
HIO?
BURN
I-I'M NOT LOOKING FORWARD TO IT!
Why're you asking me?!
HUH? YOU'RE TAG-GING ALONG BECAUSE YOU WANT TO KNOW ABOUT MOKO TOO, HIO.
Bwaha
hissy
NOOOOO!
I-I-I-I-I, I!
OH DEAR. HE'S SO QUICK TO REACT!
This is fun.
I'M COMING ALONG BECAUSE I'VE GOT A RIGHT TO KNOW HOW SHE BECAME SOMEONE WHO INJURED ME LIKE THIS!
Oh? Hmm. Yeah?
That some-one
THIS KID...NO... I THOUGHT THERE WAS NO WAY...

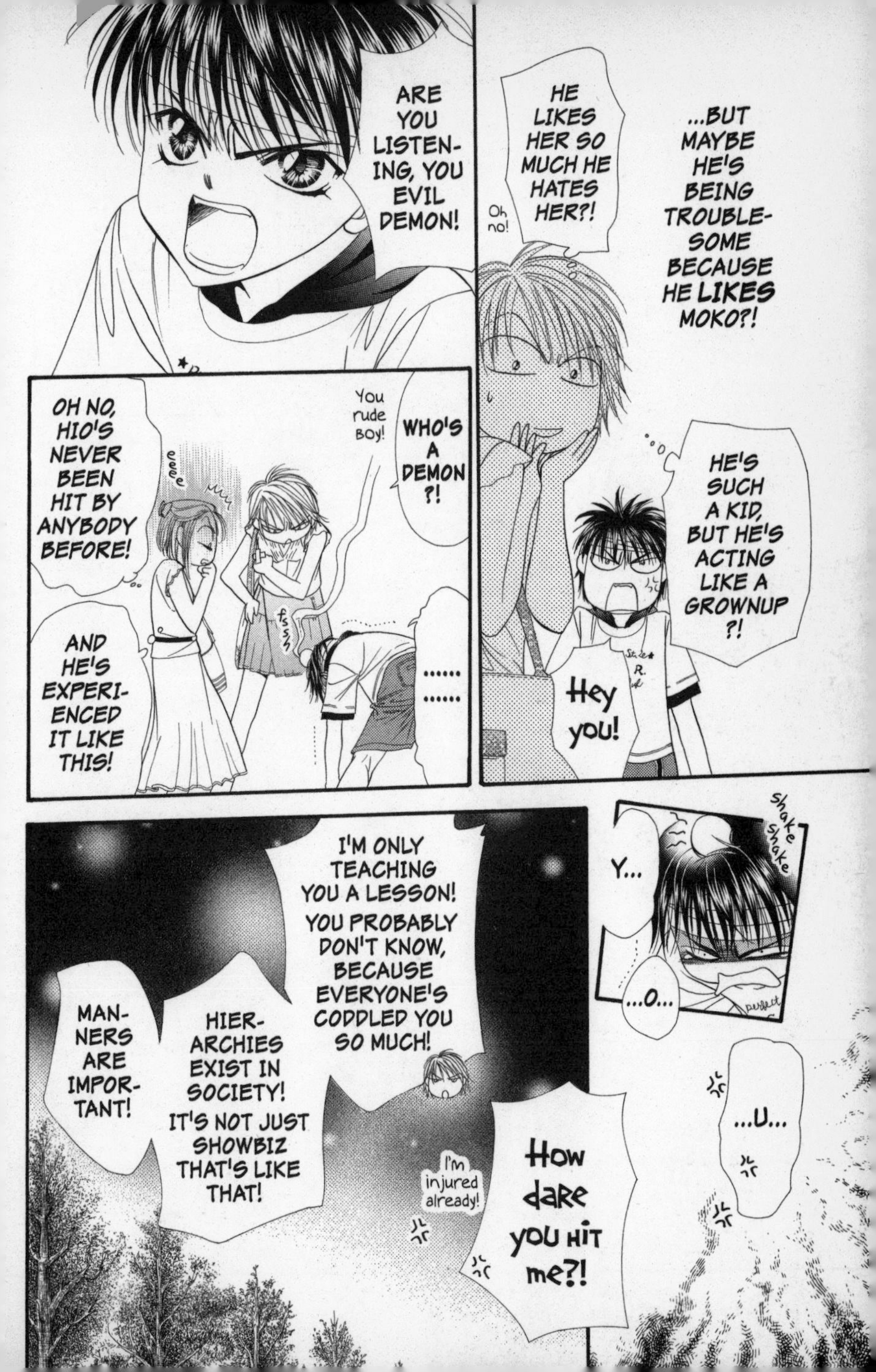
...BUT MAYBE HE'S BEING TROUBLE-SOME BECAUSE HE LIKES MOKO?!
HE LIKES HER SO MUCH HE HATES HER?!
Oh no!
HE'S SUCH A KID, BUT HE'S ACTING LIKE A GROWNUP?!
Hey you!
ARE YOU LISTEN-ING, YOU EVIL DEMON!
WHO'S A DEMON?!
You rude boy!
eeee
fsss
OH NO, HIO'S NEVER BEEN HIT BY ANYBODY BEFORE!
......
......
AND HE'S EXPERI-ENCED IT LIKE THIS!
Shake Shake
Y...
...O...
...U...
How dare you hit me?!
I'M ONLY TEACHING YOU A LESSON! YOU PROBABLY DON'T KNOW, BECAUSE EVERYONE'S CODDLED YOU SO MUCH!
I'm injured already!
HIER-ARCHIES EXIST IN SOCIETY! IT'S NOT JUST SHOWBIZ THAT'S LIKE THAT!
MAN-NERS ARE IMPOR-TANT!

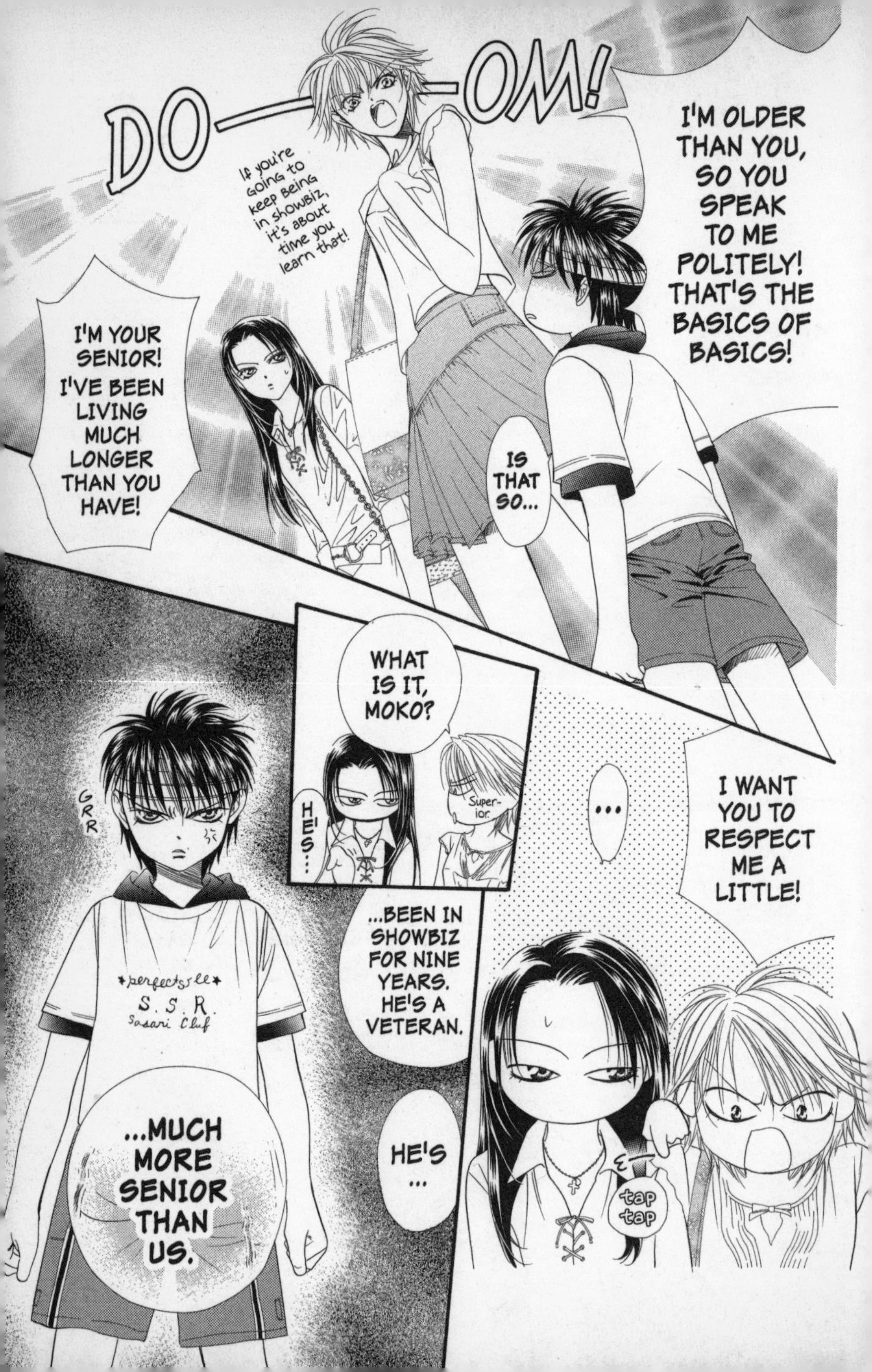
DO—OM!
I'M OLDER THAN YOU, SO YOU SPEAK TO ME POLITELY! THAT'S THE BASICS OF BASICS!
If you're going to keep being in showbiz, it's about time you learn that!
I'M YOUR SENIOR! I'VE BEEN LIVING MUCH LONGER THAN YOU HAVE!
IS THAT SO...
I WANT YOU TO RESPECT ME A LITTLE!
...
tap tap
HE'S ...
WHAT IS IT, MOKO?
HE'S...
Super-ior.
...BEEN IN SHOWBIZ FOR NINE YEARS. HE'S A VETERAN.
GRR
...MUCH MORE SENIOR THAN US.

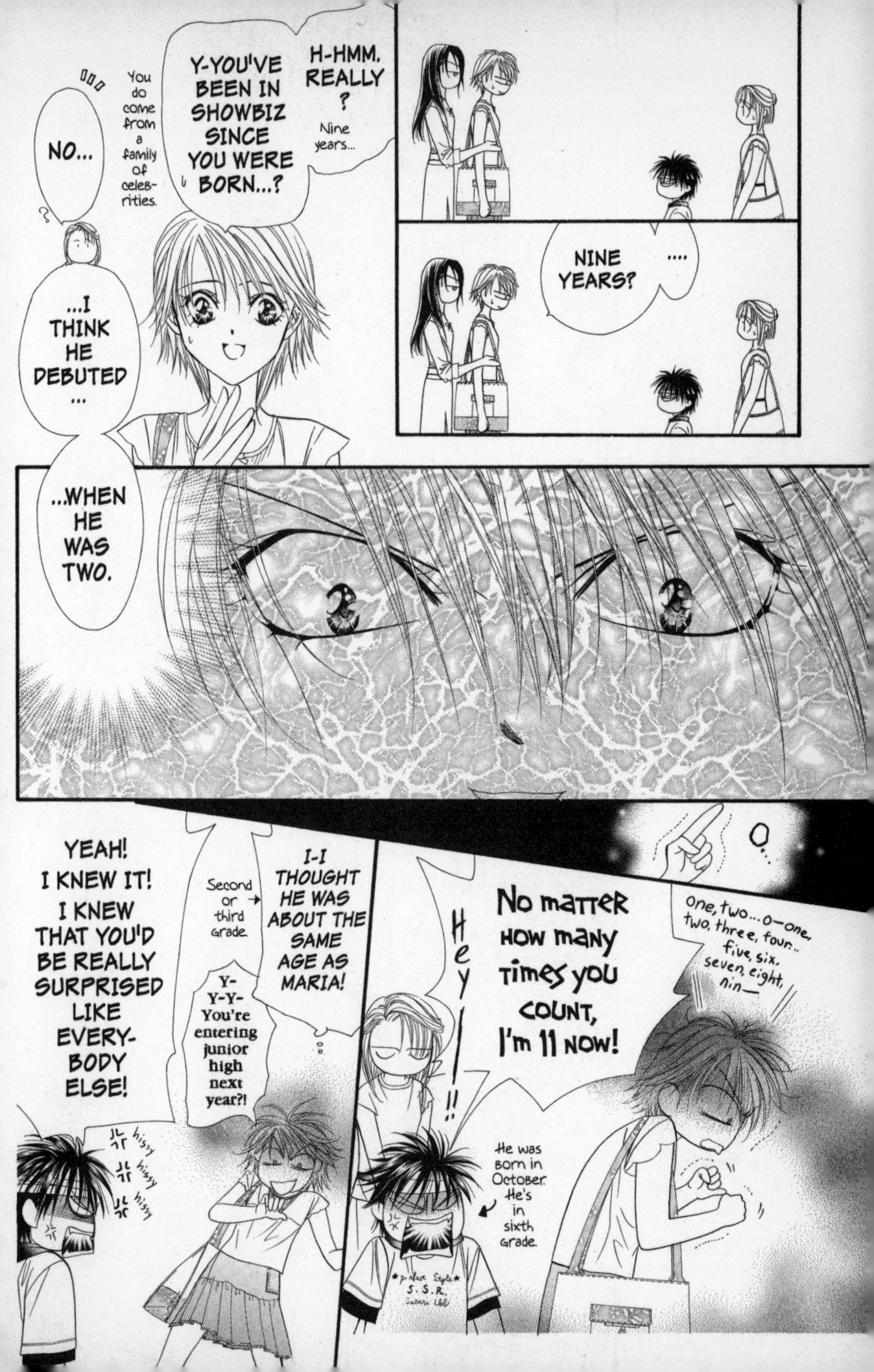
H-HMM. REALLY?
Nine years...
NINE YEARS?
....
Y-YOU'VE BEEN IN SHOWBIZ SINCE YOU WERE BORN...?
You do come from a family of celebrities.
NO...
...I THINK HE DEBUTED...
...WHEN HE WAS TWO.
O...
One, two... o-one, two, three, four... five, six, seven, eight, nin—
No matter how many times you count, I'm 11 now!
Hey!!
He was born in October. He's in sixth grade.
I-I THOUGHT HE WAS ABOUT THE SAME AGE AS MARIA!
Second or third Grade.
Y-Y-Y- You're entering junior high next year?!
YEAH! I KNEW IT! I KNEW THAT YOU'D BE REALLY SURPRISED LIKE EVERYBODY ELSE!
hissy hissy hissy

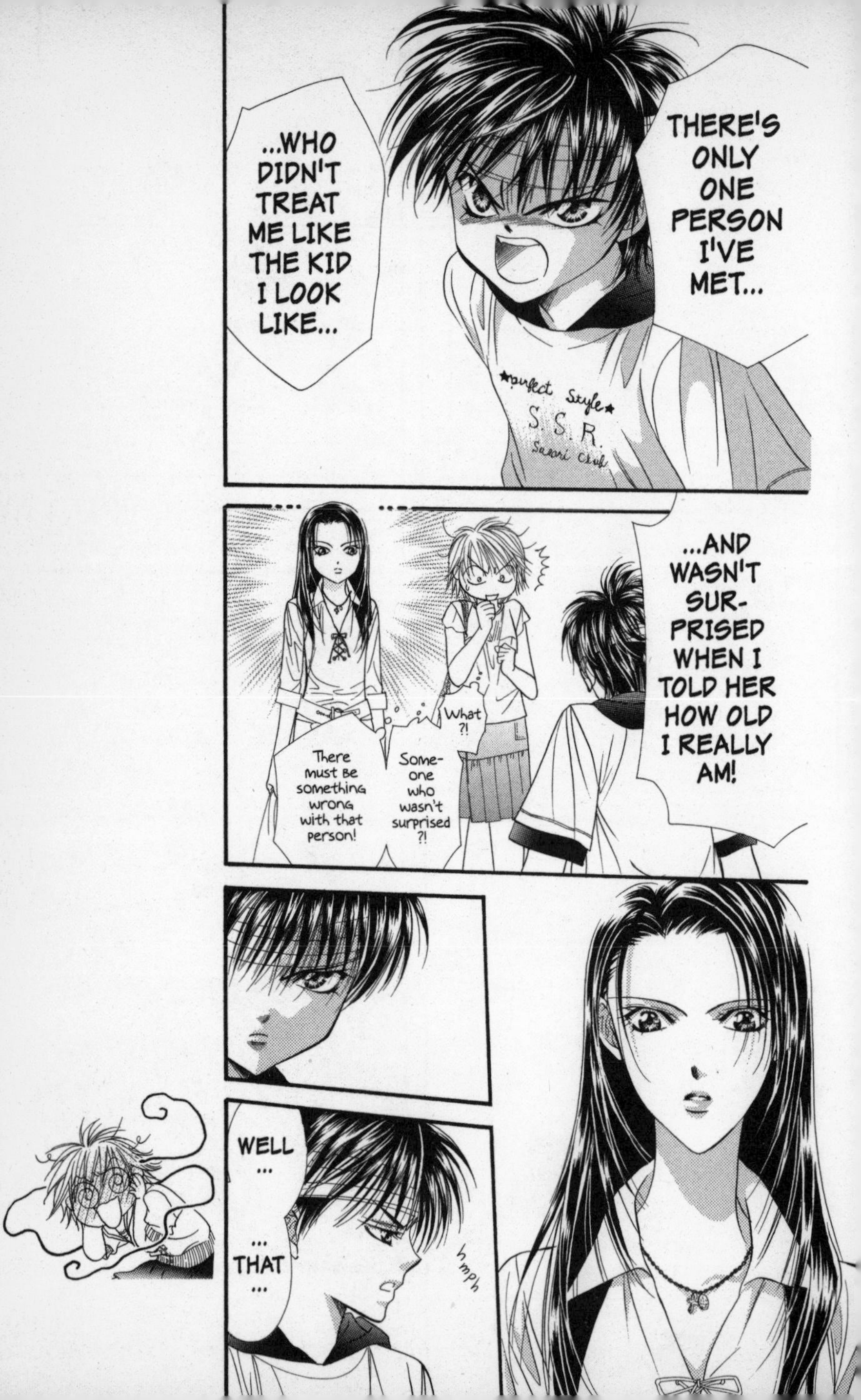

THERE'S ONLY ONE PERSON I'VE MET...
...WHO DIDN'T TREAT ME LIKE THE KID I LOOK LIKE...
★perfect Style★ S.S.R. Sasori Club
...AND WASN'T SUR-PRISED WHEN I TOLD HER HOW OLD I REALLY AM!
What ?!
Some-one who wasn't surprised ?!
There must be something wrong with that person!
WELL ...
... THAT ...
hmph

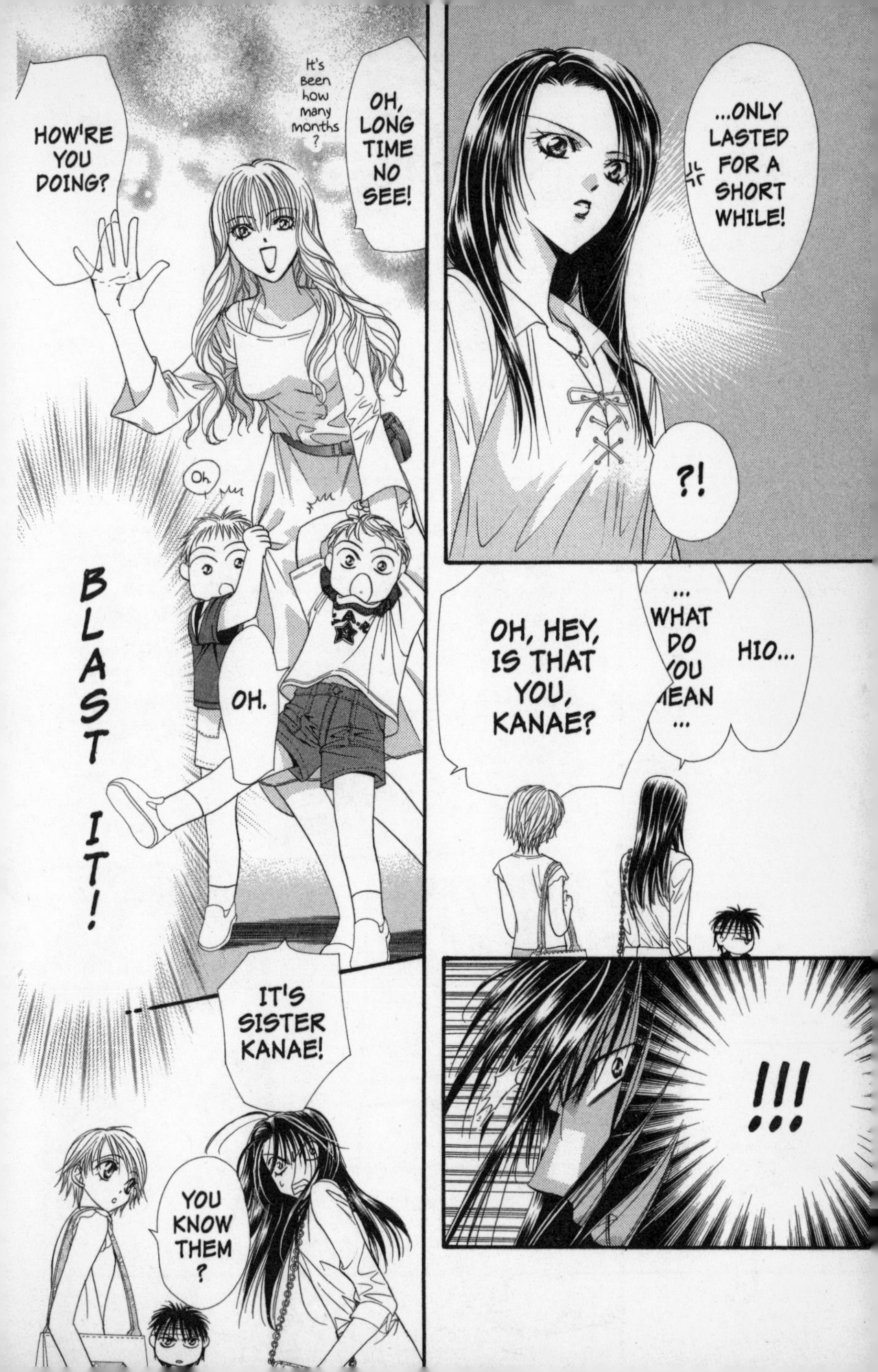
...ONLY LASTED FOR A SHORT WHILE!
?!
...WHAT DO YOU MEAN... HIO...
OH, HEY, IS THAT YOU, KANAE?
OH, LONG TIME NO SEE!
It's been how many months?
HOW'RE YOU DOING?
Oh.
BLAST IT!
OH.
!!!
IT'S SISTER KANAE!
YOU KNOW THEM?

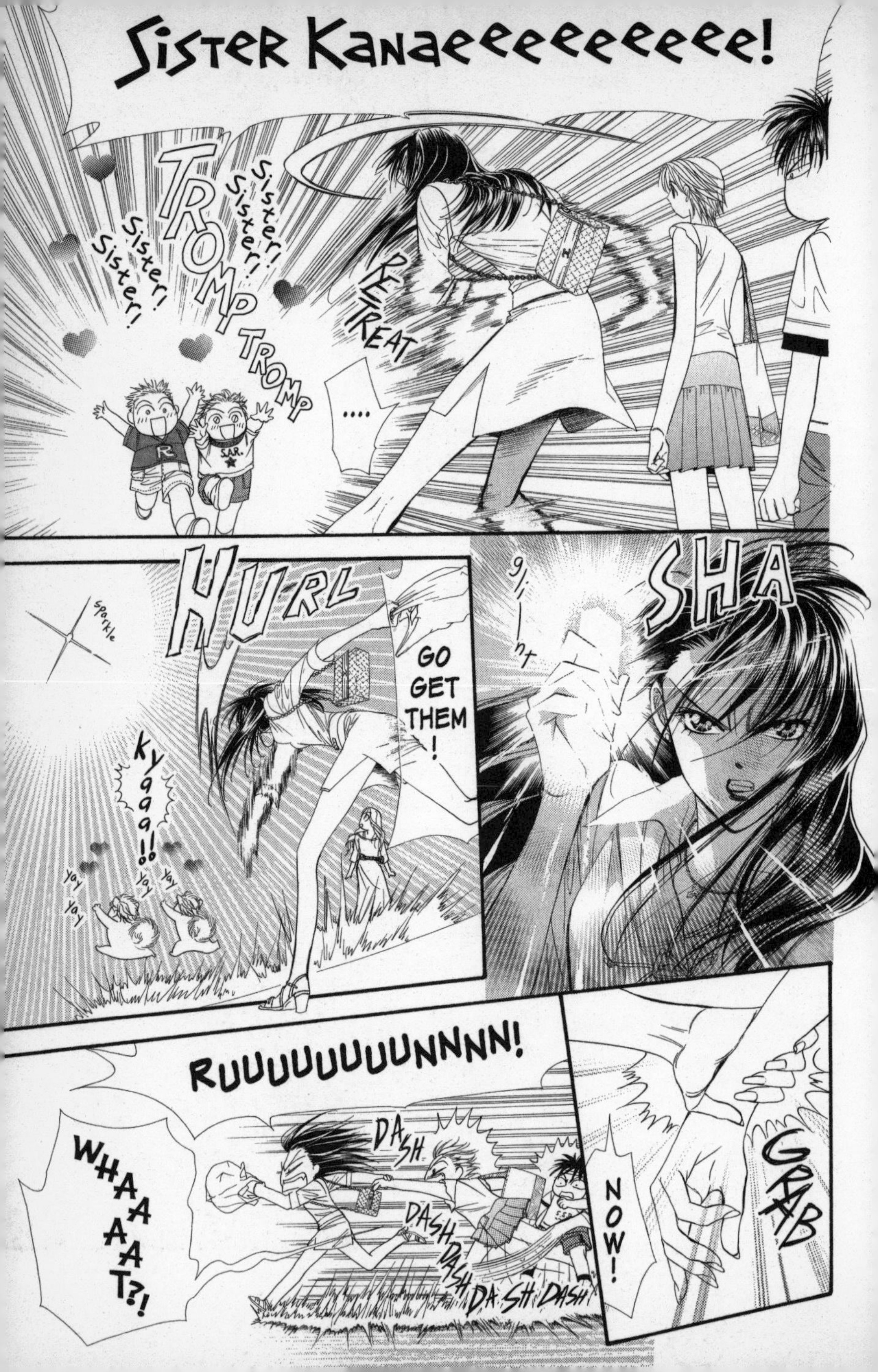
Sister Kanaeeeeeeeeee!
RETREAT
....
Sister! Sister!
Sister! Sister!
TROMP TROMP TROMP
SHA
glint
HURL
GO GET THEM!
sparkle
Kyaaa!!
yay yay yay yay
GRAB
NOW!
RUUUUUUUUUNNNN!
WHAAAAAT?!
DASH DASH DASH DASH DASH DASH

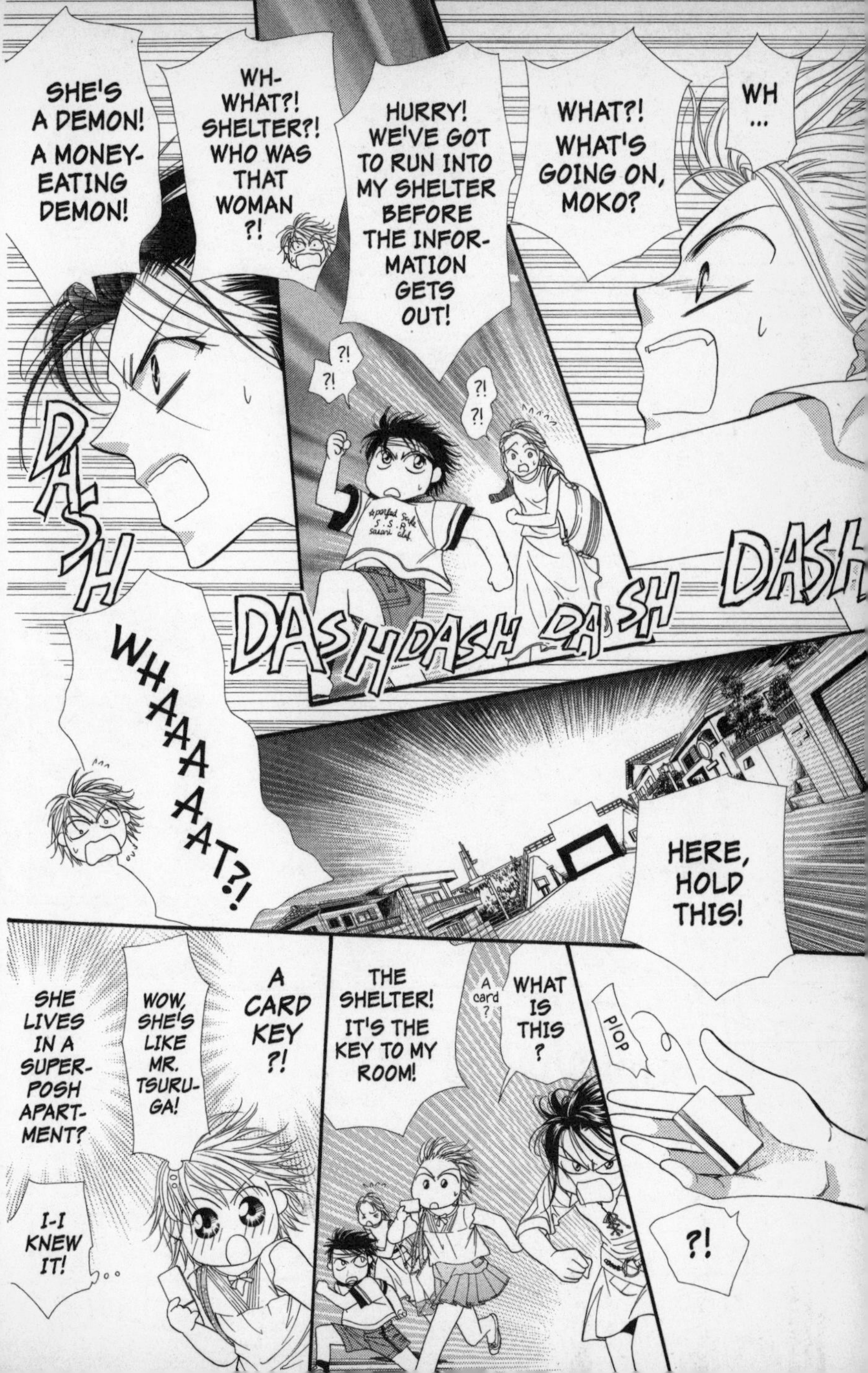
WH ...
WHAT?! WHAT'S GOING ON, MOKO?
HURRY! WE'VE GOT TO RUN INTO MY SHELTER BEFORE THE INFORMATION GETS OUT!
WH-WHAT?! SHELTER?! WHO WAS THAT WOMAN ?!
SHE'S A DEMON! A MONEY-EATING DEMON!
?! ?!
?! ?!
DASH
DASH DASH DASH DASH
DASH
HERE, HOLD THIS!
WHAAAAAAT?!
?!
PIOP
WHAT IS THIS ?
A card ?
THE SHELTER! IT'S THE KEY TO MY ROOM!
A CARD KEY ?!
WOW, SHE'S LIKE MR. TSURUGA!
SHE LIVES IN A SUPER-POSH APARTMENT?
I-I KNEW IT!

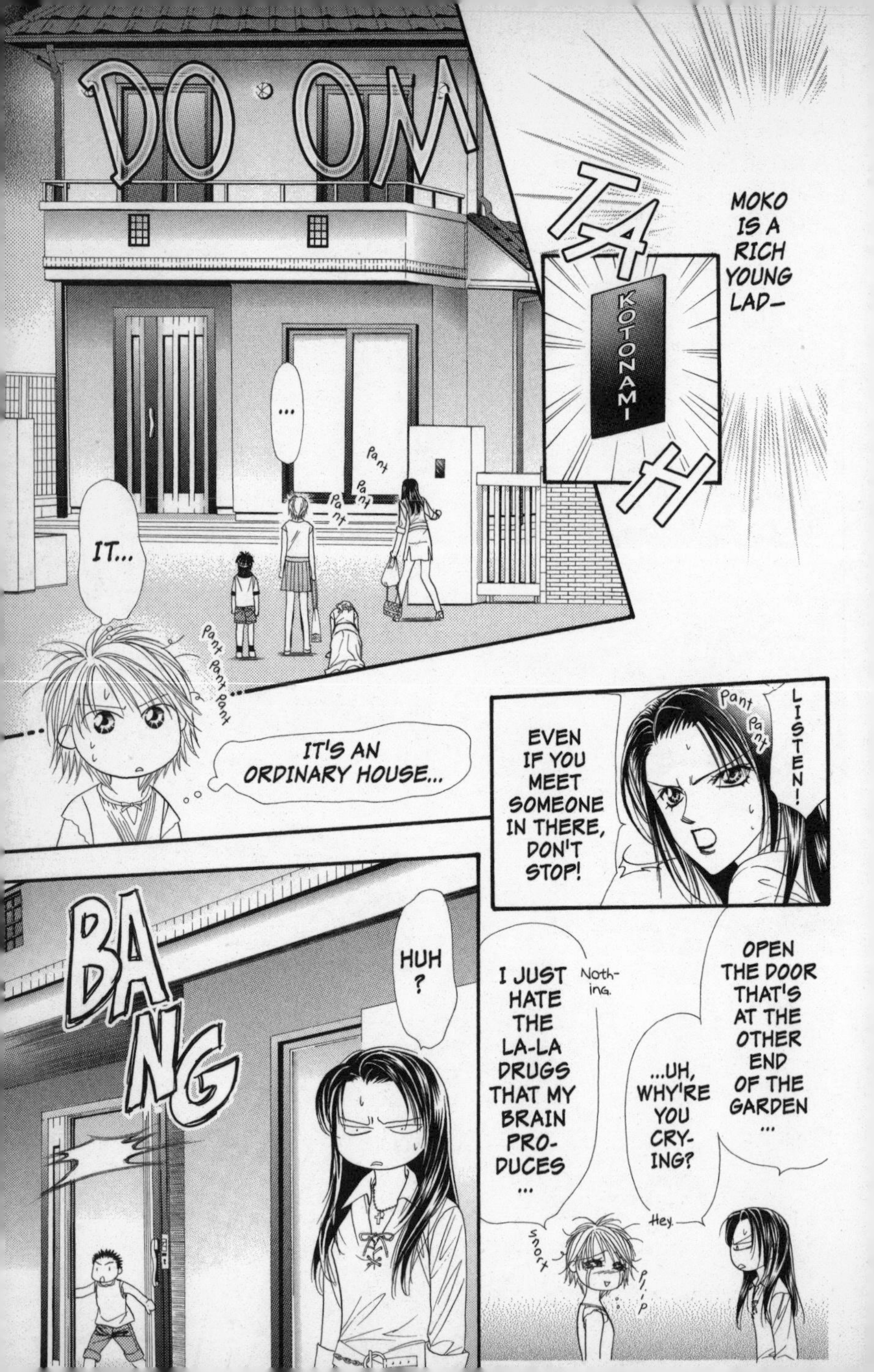
TA
H
KOTONAMI
MOKO IS A RICH YOUNG LAD—
DO OM
...
Pant Pant Pant
IT...
Pant Pant Pant
IT'S AN ORDINARY HOUSE...
LISTEN!
Pant pant
EVEN IF YOU MEET SOMEONE IN THERE, DON'T STOP!
OPEN THE DOOR THAT'S AT THE OTHER END OF THE GARDEN...
...UH, WHY'RE YOU CRY-ING?
Hey.
I JUST HATE THE LA-LA DRUGS THAT MY BRAIN PRO-DUCES...
Noth-ing.
snort
Plip
BA NG
HUH?

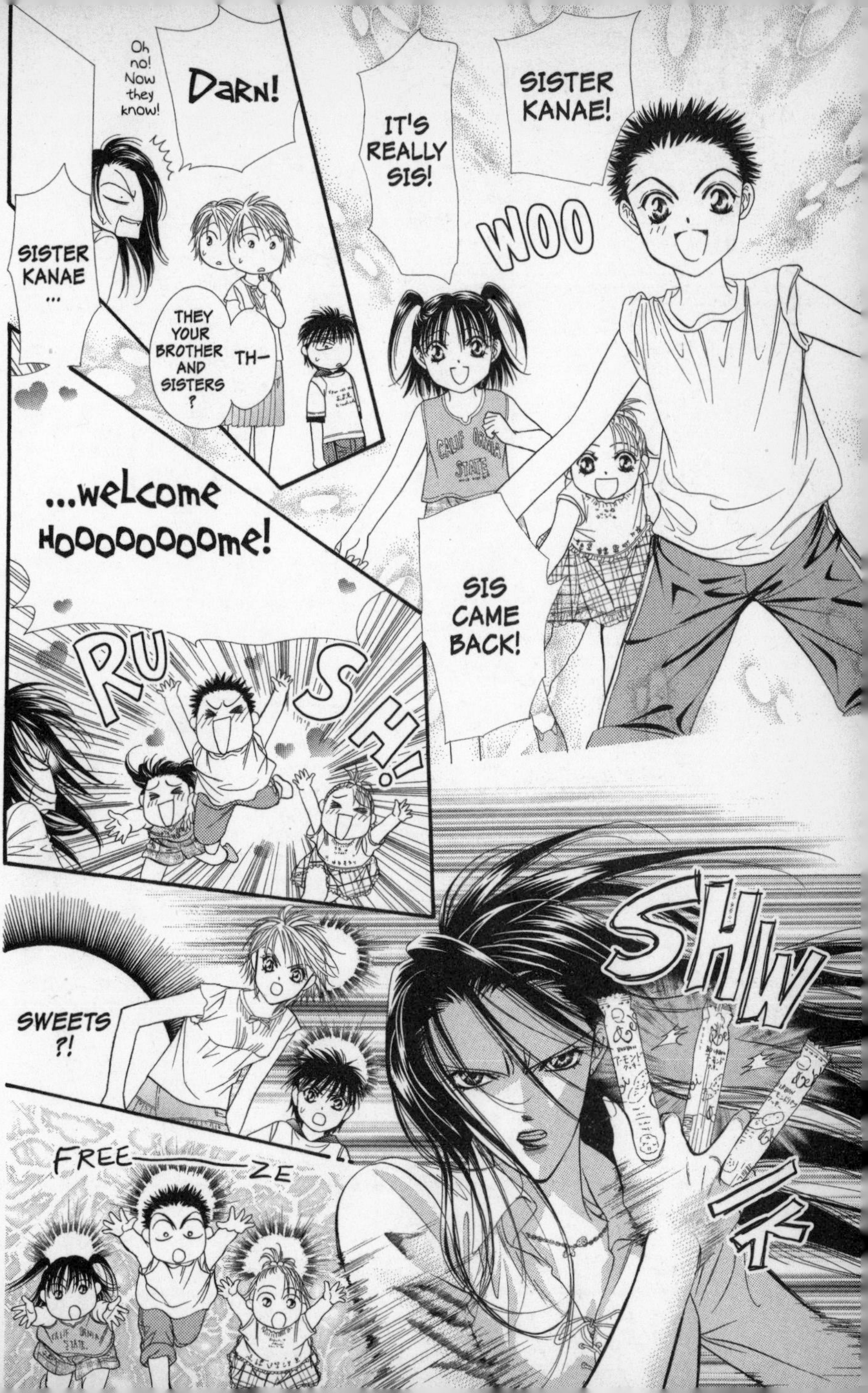
SISTER KANAE!
IT'S REALLY SIS!
WOO
SIS CAME BACK!
Darn!
Oh no! Now they know!
SISTER KANAE ...
THEY YOUR BROTHER AND SISTERS?
TH—
...welcome HOOOOOOOOme!
RUSH!
SHW
SWEETS?!
FREE—ZE

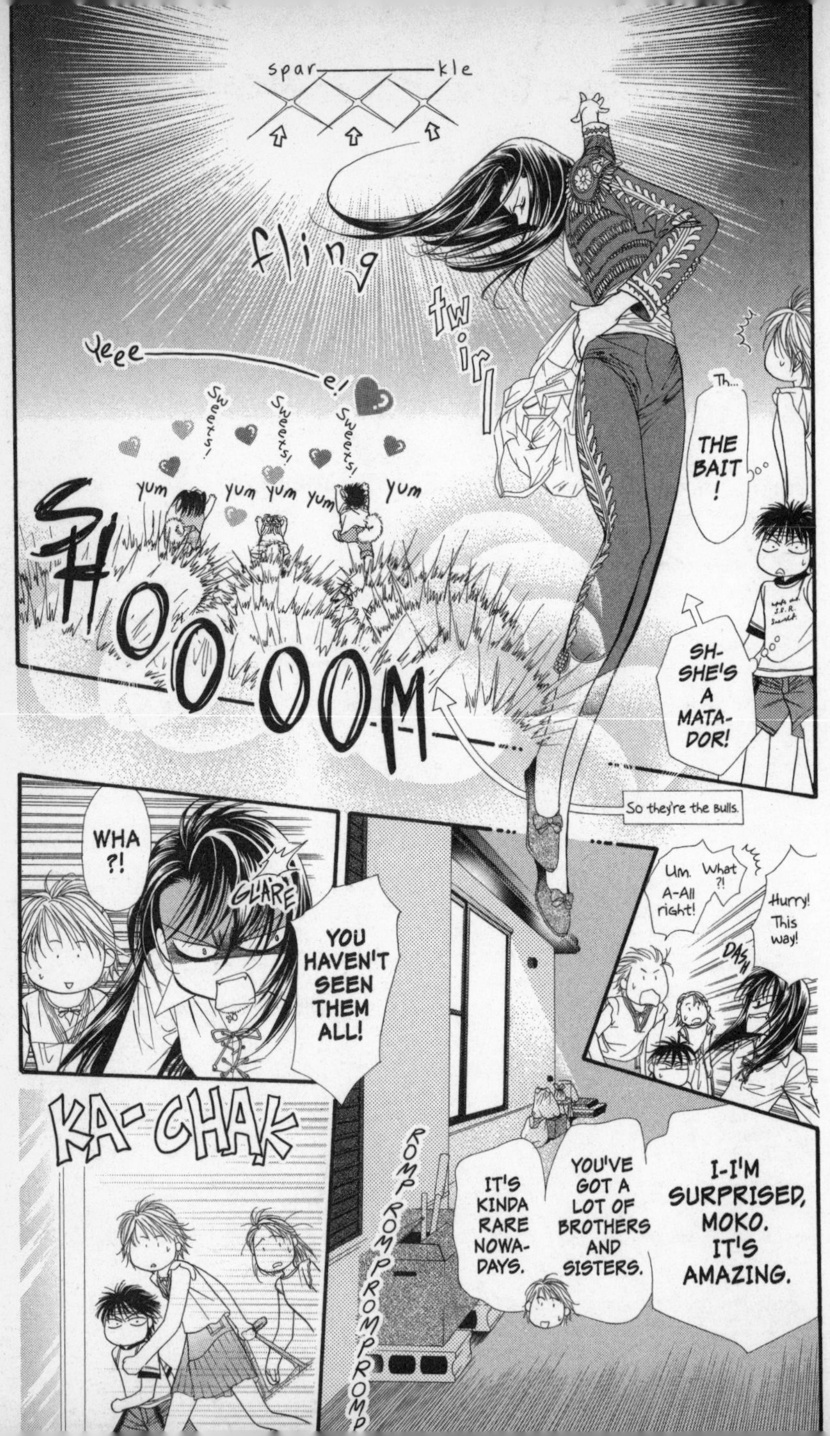
spar——kle
fling
twirl
Th...
THE BAIT!
Yeee——e!
Sweets!
Sweets!
Sweets!
yum yum yum yum yum
SHOOOOOM
SH-SHE'S A MATA-DOR!
So they're the bulls.
Hurry! This way!
What?!
Um. A-All right!
DASH
YOU HAVEN'T SEEN THEM ALL!
GLARE
WHA?!
I-I'M SURPRISED, MOKO. IT'S AMAZING.
YOU'VE GOT A LOT OF BROTHERS AND SISTERS.
IT'S KINDA RARE NOWA-DAYS.
ROMP ROMP ROMP ROMP ROMP
KA-CHAK

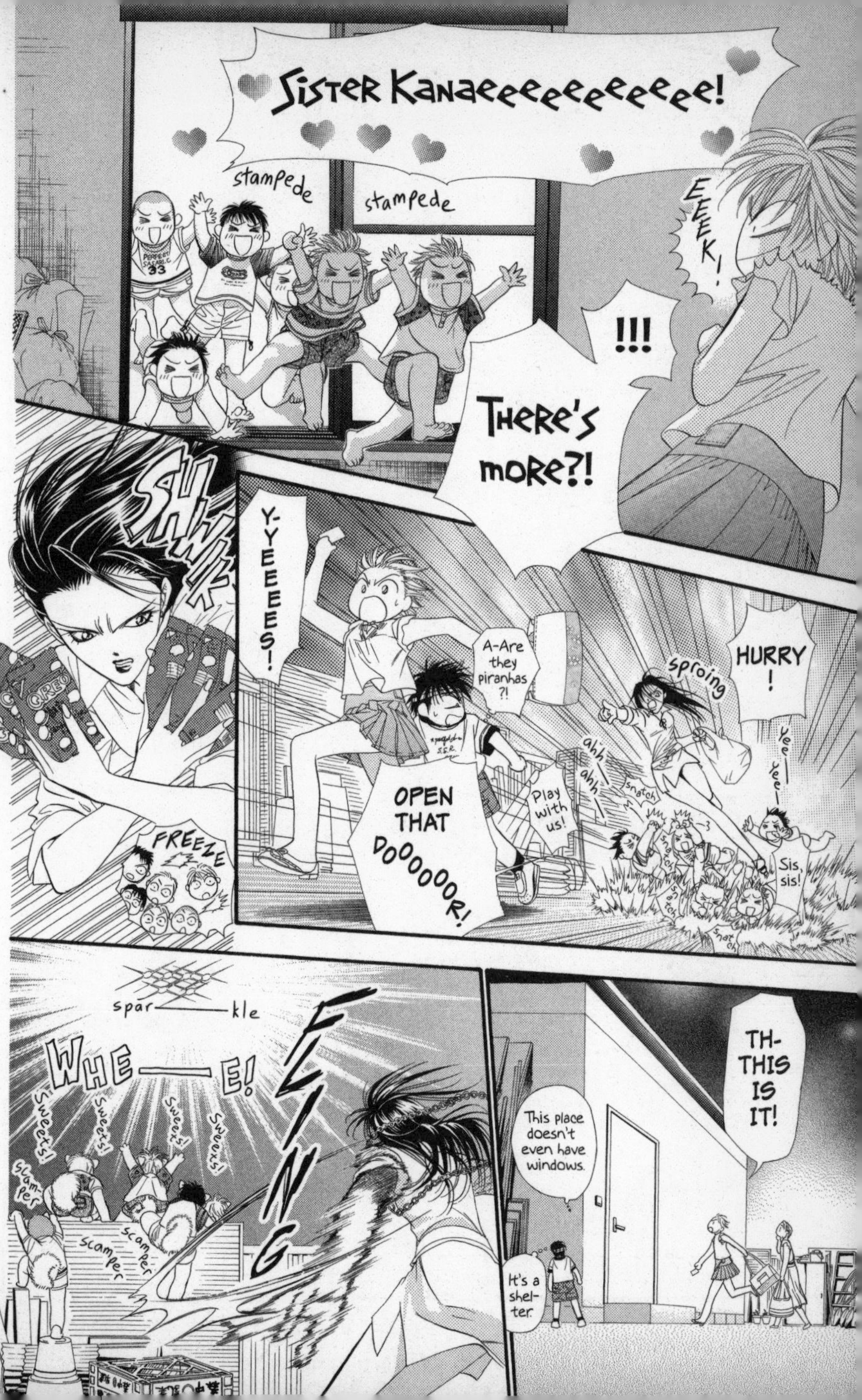
Sister Kanaeeeeeeeeeee!
stampede
stampede
EEEK!
!!!
There's more?!
HURRY!
sproing
Yee yee
Sis, sis!
A-Are they piranhas?!
Y-YEEEES!
ahh ahh
snatch
snatch
snatch
snatch
Play with us!
OPEN THAT DOOOOOOR!
SHWIK
FREEZE
TH-THIS IS IT!
This place doesn't even have windows.
It's a shelter.
spar—kle
WHE—E!
FLING
Sweets!
Sweets!
Sweets!
Sweets!
Scamper
scamper
scamper

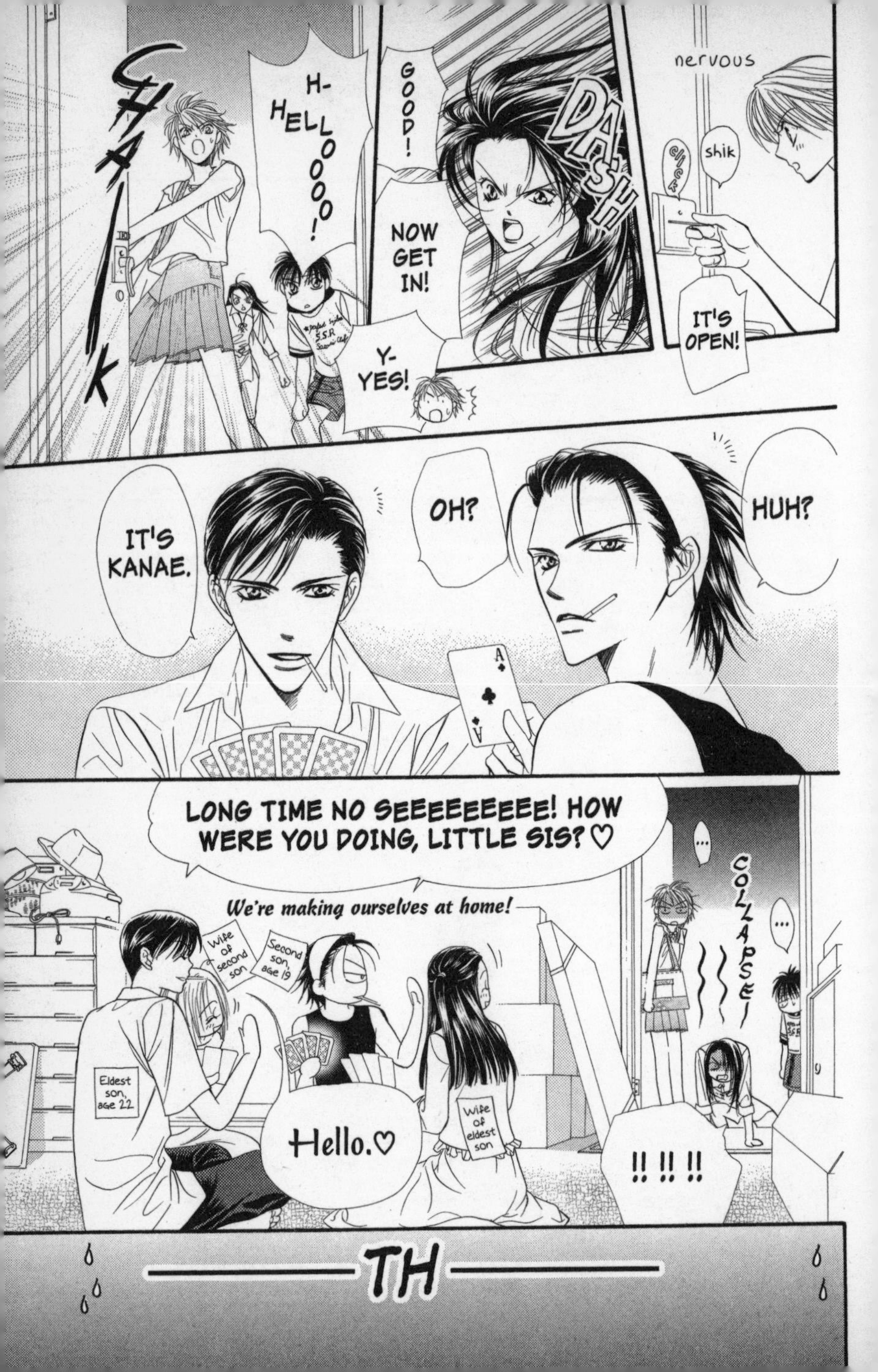
nervous
shik
click
IT'S OPEN!
DASH!
GOOD! NOW GET IN!
H-HELLOOOOO!
CHAK
Y-YES!
HUH?
OH?
IT'S KANAE.
...
COLLAPSE!
...
!! !! !!
LONG TIME NO SEEEEEEEEE! HOW WERE YOU DOING, LITTLE SIS? ♡
We're making ourselves at home!
Wife of eldest son
Second son, age 19
Wife of second son
Eldest son, age 22
Hello.♡
TH

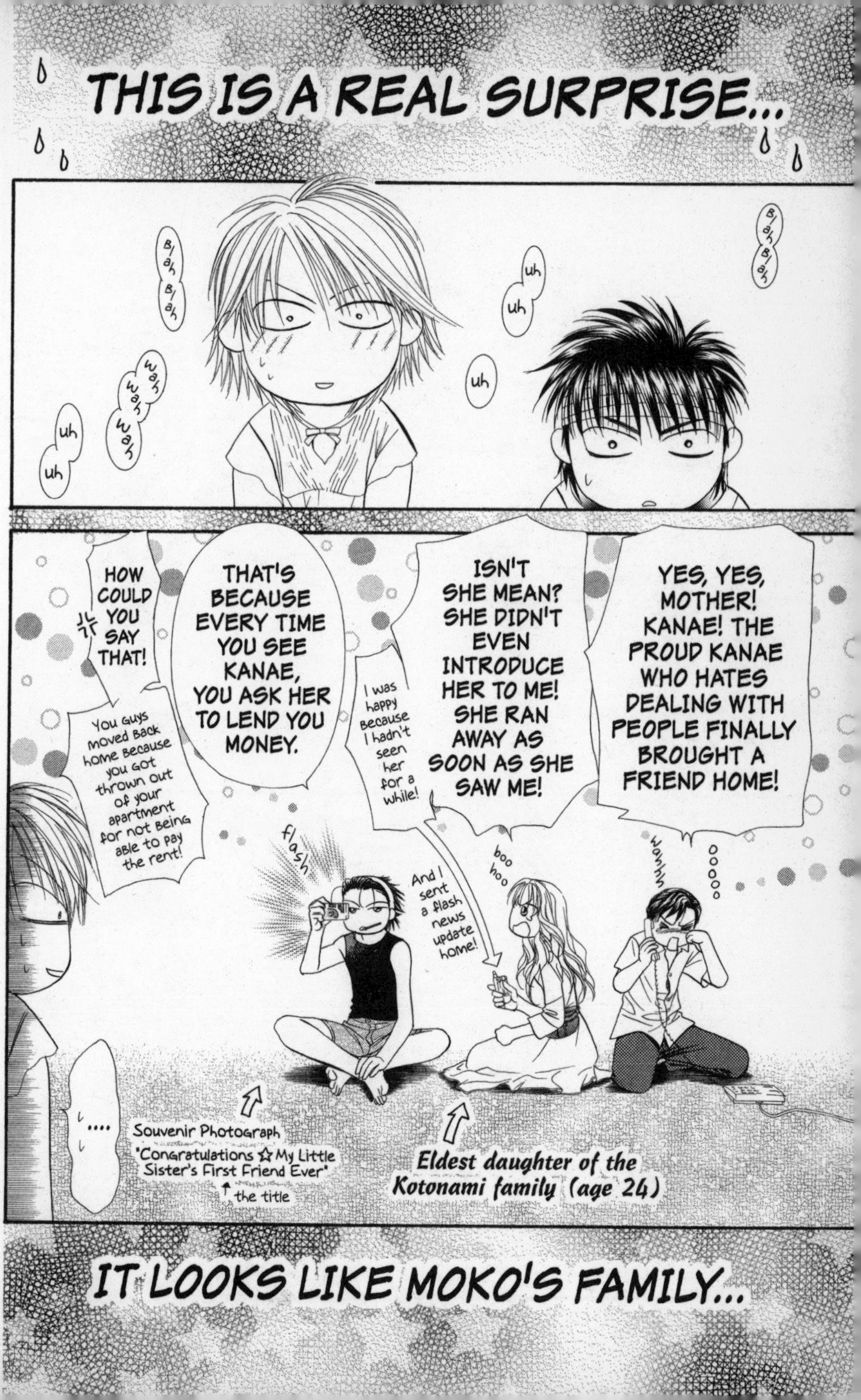
THIS IS A REAL SURPRISE...
Blah Blah
uh
uh
uh
Blah Blah
wah wah wah
uh
uh
YES, YES, MOTHER! KANAE! THE PROUD KANAE WHO HATES DEALING WITH PEOPLE FINALLY BROUGHT A FRIEND HOME!
ISN'T SHE MEAN? SHE DIDN'T EVEN INTRODUCE HER TO ME! SHE RAN AWAY AS SOON AS SHE SAW ME!
I was happy because I hadn't seen her for a while!
THAT'S BECAUSE EVERY TIME YOU SEE KANAE, YOU ASK HER TO LEND YOU MONEY.
HOW COULD YOU SAY THAT!
You guys moved back home because you got thrown out of your apartment for not being able to pay the rent!
Waahh
ooooo
boo hoo
And I sent a flash news update home!
flash
Eldest daughter of the Kotonami family (age 24)
Souvenir Photograph "Congratulations ☆ My Little Sister's First Friend Ever" ↑ the title
....
IT LOOKS LIKE MOKO'S FAMILY...

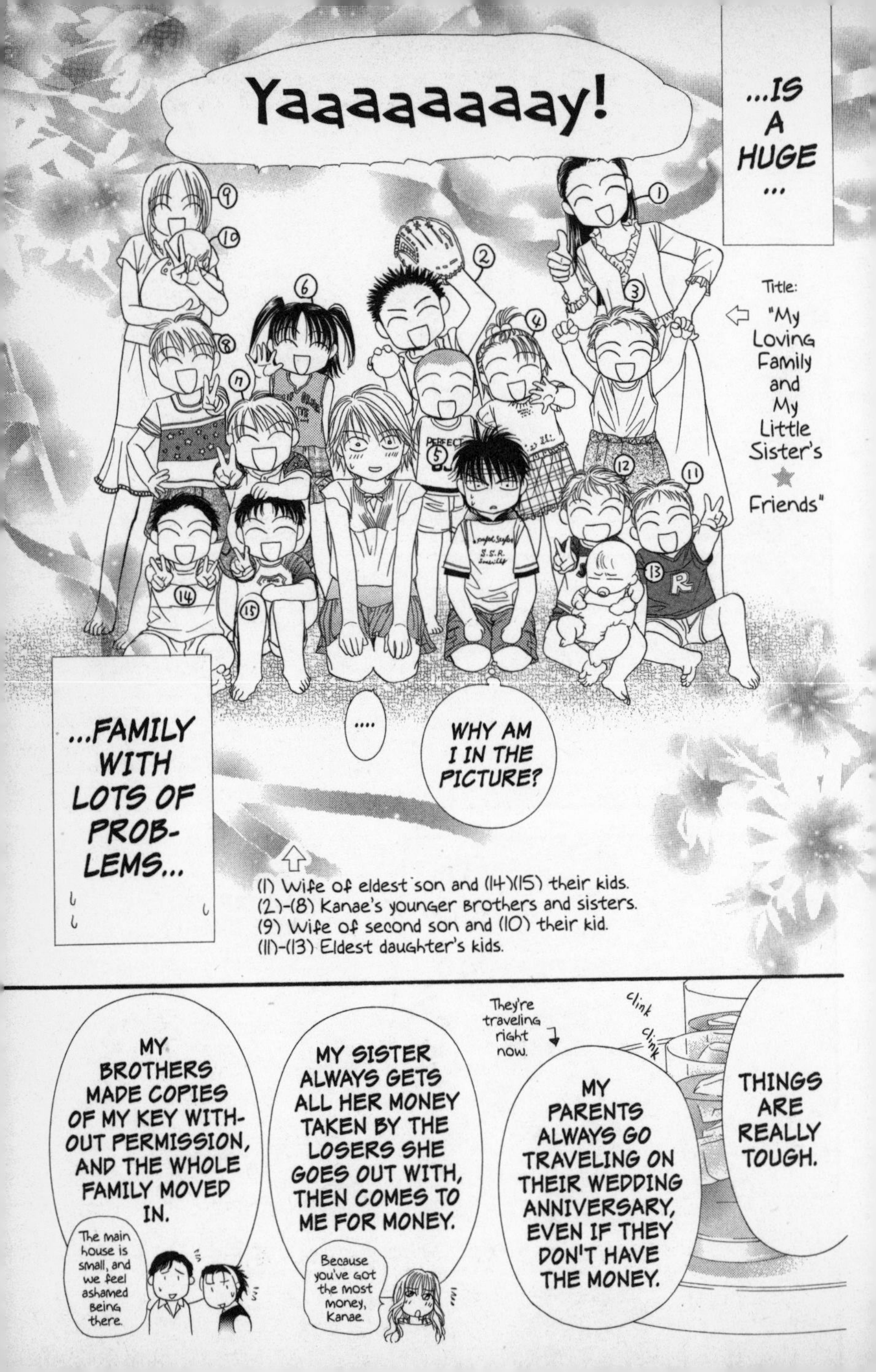
...IS A HUGE ...
Yaaaaaaaaay!
Title: "My Loving Family and My Little Sister's ★ Friends"
WHY AM I IN THE PICTURE?
....
...FAMILY WITH LOTS OF PROB-LEMS...
(1) Wife of eldest son and (14)(15) their kids.
(2)-(8) Kanae's younger brothers and sisters.
(9) Wife of second son and (10) their kid.
(11)-(13) Eldest daughter's kids.
THINGS ARE REALLY TOUGH.
clink
clink
They're traveling right now.
MY PARENTS ALWAYS GO TRAVELING ON THEIR WEDDING ANNIVERSARY, EVEN IF THEY DON'T HAVE THE MONEY.
MY SISTER ALWAYS GETS ALL HER MONEY TAKEN BY THE LOSERS SHE GOES OUT WITH, THEN COMES TO ME FOR MONEY.
Because you've got the most money, Kanae.
MY BROTHERS MADE COPIES OF MY KEY WITH-OUT PERMISSION, AND THE WHOLE FAMILY MOVED IN.
The main house is small, and we feel ashamed being there.

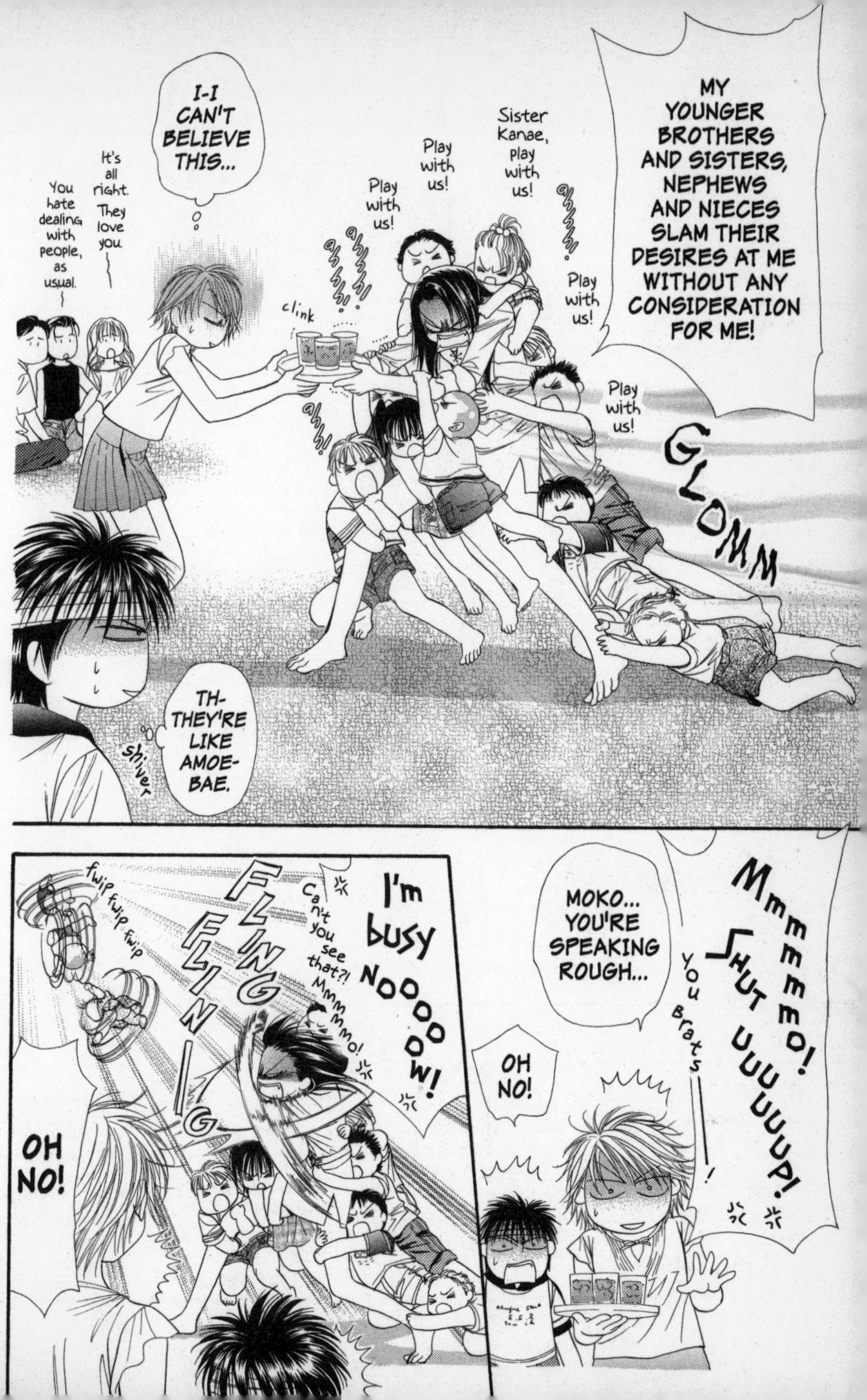
MY YOUNGER BROTHERS AND SISTERS, NEPHEWS AND NIECES SLAM THEIR DESIRES AT ME WITHOUT ANY CONSIDERATION FOR ME!
Sister Kanae, play with us!
Play with us!
Play with us!
ahhhh!
ahhhhh!
Play with us!
Play with us!
GLOMM
I-I CAN'T BELIEVE THIS...
It's all right. They love you.
You hate dealing with people, as usual.
clink
ahh!
TH-THEY'RE LIKE AMOEBAE.
shiver
Mmmmmmo! SHUT UUUUUUP!
You brats—!
MOKO... YOU'RE SPEAKING ROUGH...
OH NO!
I'm busy NOOOOOW!
Can't you see that?! Mmmmmo!
FLING FLING
fwip fwip fwip
OH NO!

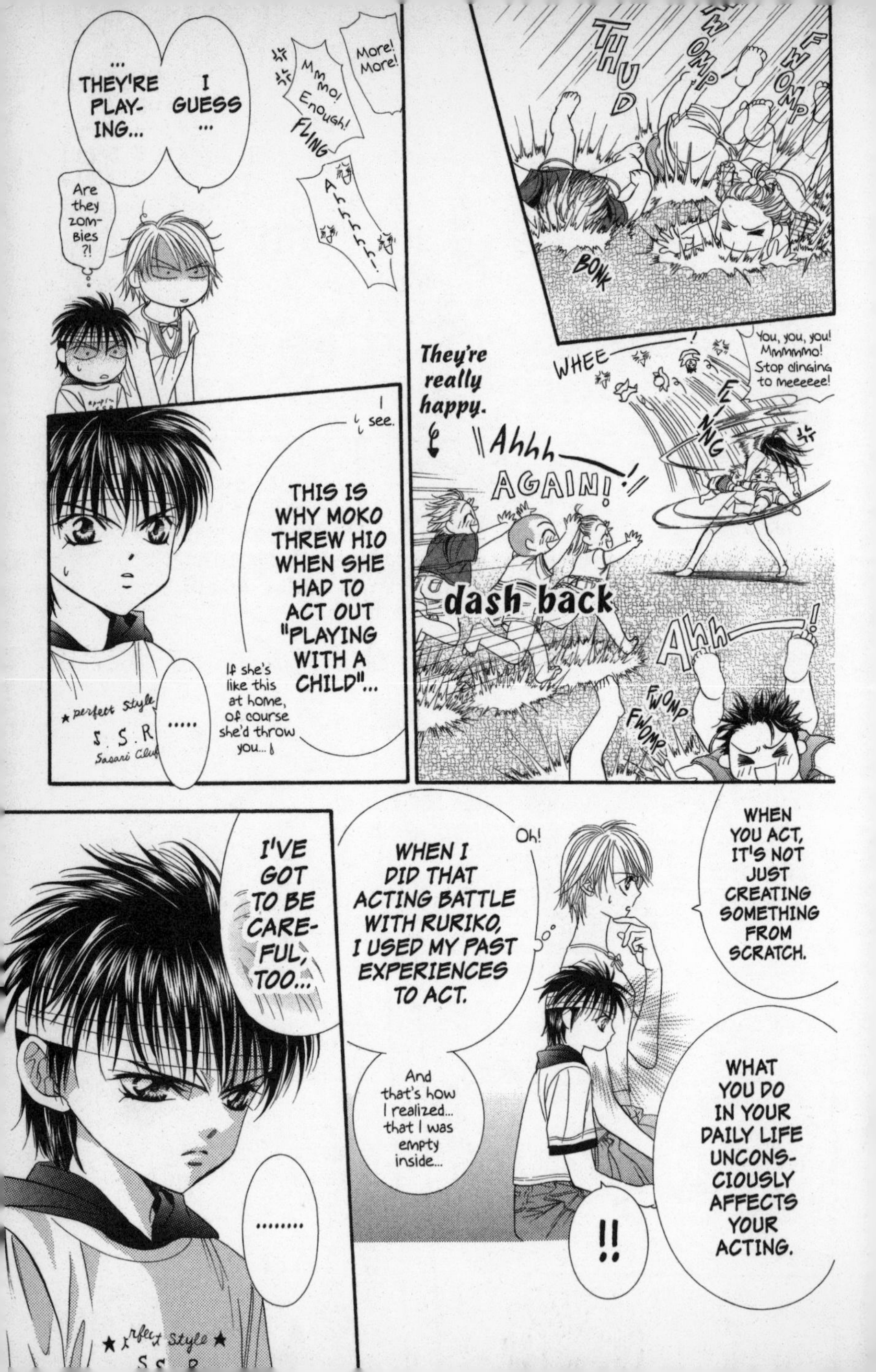
THUD
FWOMP
FWOMP
BONK
More! More!
Mmmo! Enough!
FLING
Ahhhhh!
... THEY'RE PLAYING...
I GUESS ...
Are they zombies?!
You, you, you! Mmmmmo! Stop clinging to meeeeee!
WHEE
FLING
They're really happy.
Ahhh AGAIN!
dash back
Ahh!
FWOMP
FWOMP
I see.
THIS IS WHY MOKO THREW HIO WHEN SHE HAD TO ACT OUT "PLAYING WITH A CHILD"...
If she's like this at home, of course she'd throw you...
.....
WHEN YOU ACT, IT'S NOT JUST CREATING SOMETHING FROM SCRATCH.
WHAT YOU DO IN YOUR DAILY LIFE UNCONSCIOUSLY AFFECTS YOUR ACTING.
!!
Oh!
WHEN I DID THAT ACTING BATTLE WITH RURIKO, I USED MY PAST EXPERIENCES TO ACT.
And that's how I realized... that I was empty inside...
I'VE GOT TO BE CAREFUL, TOO...
....

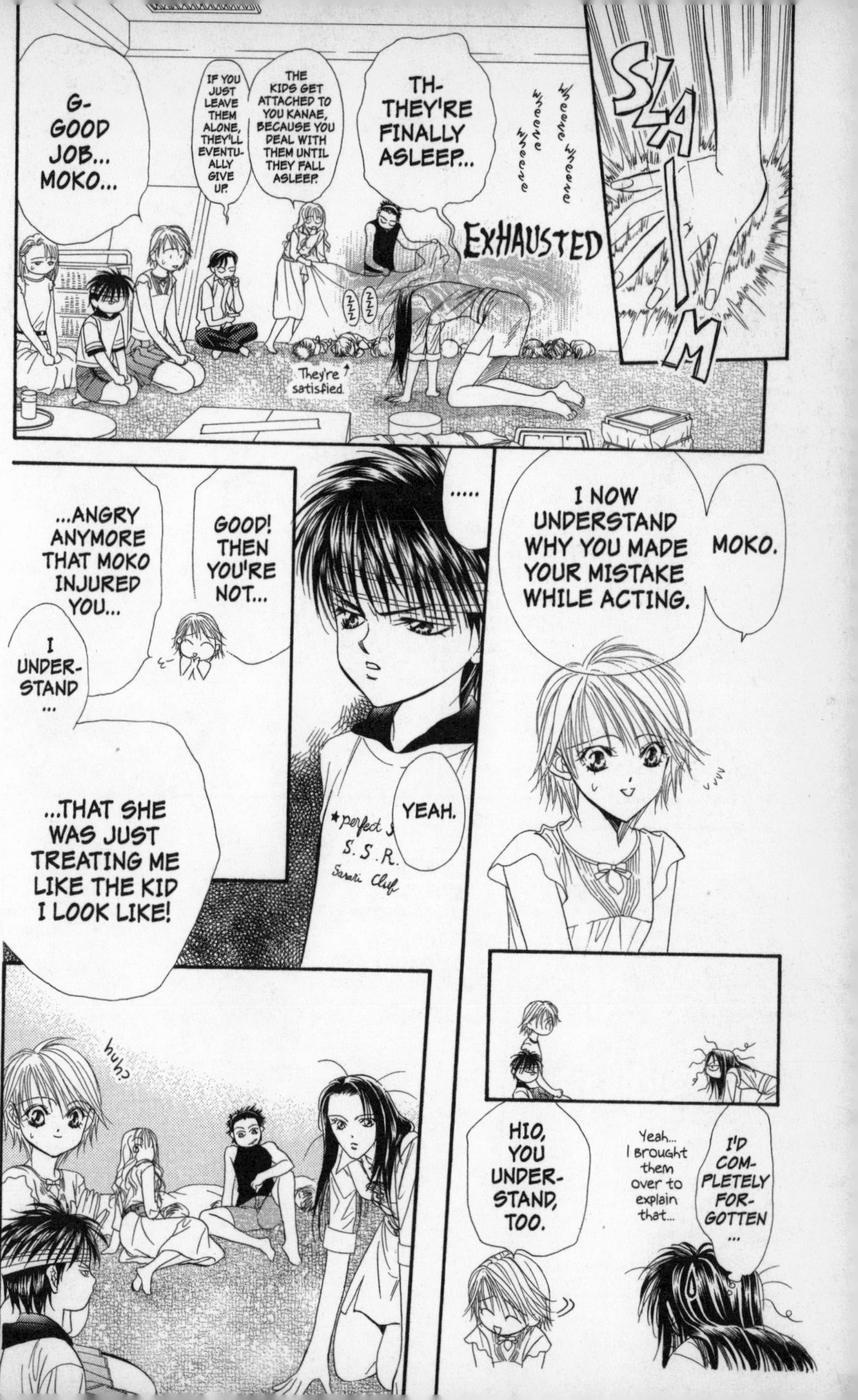
SLAM
Wheeze wheeze
Wheeze wheeze
EXHAUSTED
TH-THEY'RE FINALLY ASLEEP...
THE KIDS GET ATTACHED TO YOU KANAE, BECAUSE YOU DEAL WITH THEM UNTIL THEY FALL ASLEEP.
IF YOU JUST LEAVE THEM ALONE, THEY'LL EVENTUALLY GIVE UP.
G-GOOD JOB... MOKO...
They're satisfied.
MOKO.
I NOW UNDERSTAND WHY YOU MADE YOUR MISTAKE WHILE ACTING.
.....
YEAH.
GOOD! THEN YOU'RE NOT...
...ANGRY ANYMORE THAT MOKO INJURED YOU...
I UNDERSTAND...
...THAT SHE WAS JUST TREATING ME LIKE THE KID I LOOK LIKE!
I'D COMPLETELY FORGOTTEN...
Yeah... I brought them over to explain that...
HIO, YOU UNDERSTAND, TOO.
huh?

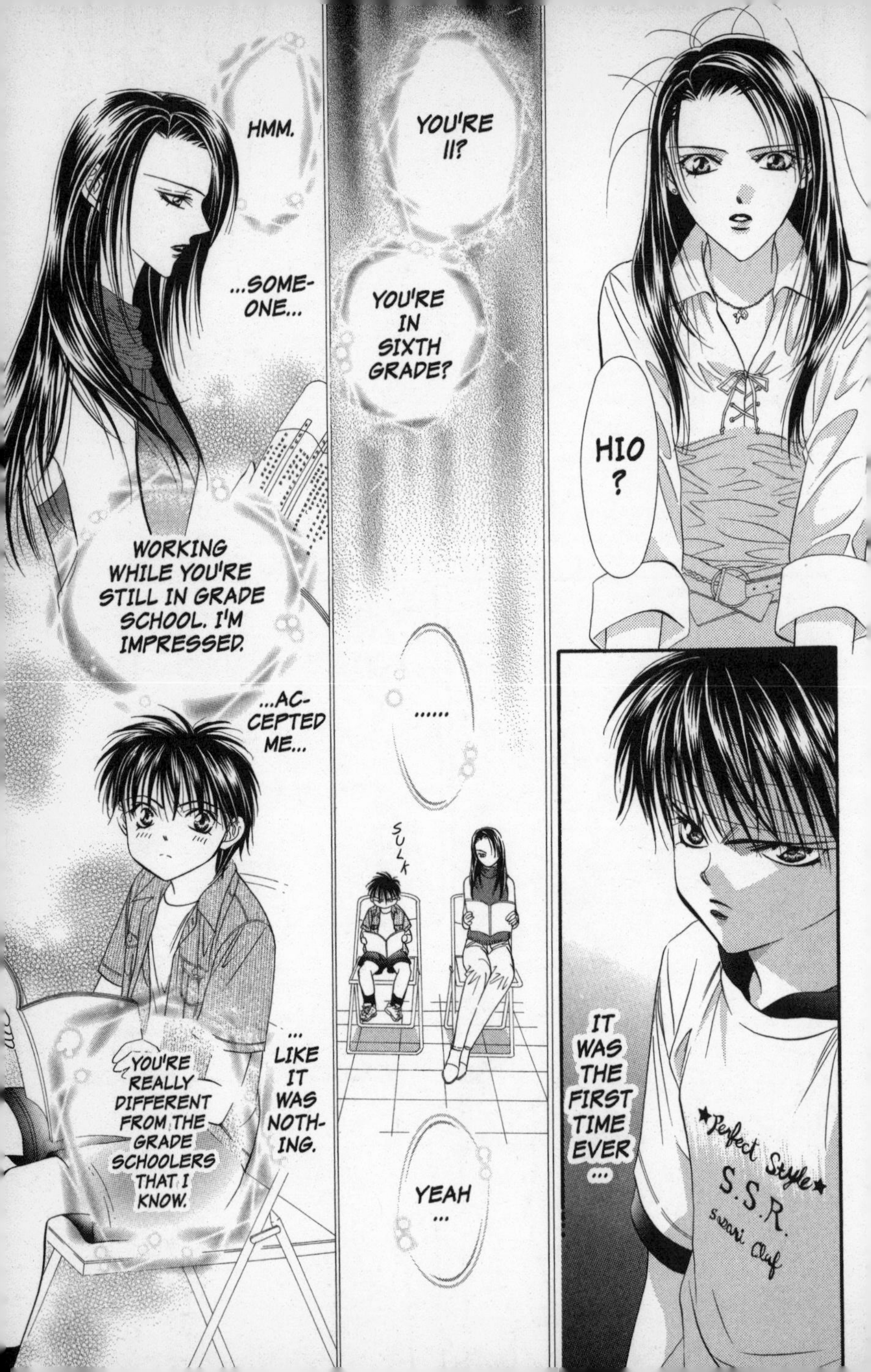
HIO ?
IT WAS THE FIRST TIME EVER ...
★Perfect Style★
S.S.R.
YOU'RE 11?
YOU'RE IN SIXTH GRADE?
......
SULK
YEAH ...
HMM.
...SOME-ONE...
WORKING WHILE YOU'RE STILL IN GRADE SCHOOL. I'M IMPRESSED.
...AC-CEPTED ME...
... LIKE IT WAS NOTH-ING.
YOU'RE REALLY DIFFERENT FROM THE GRADE SCHOOLERS THAT I KNOW.

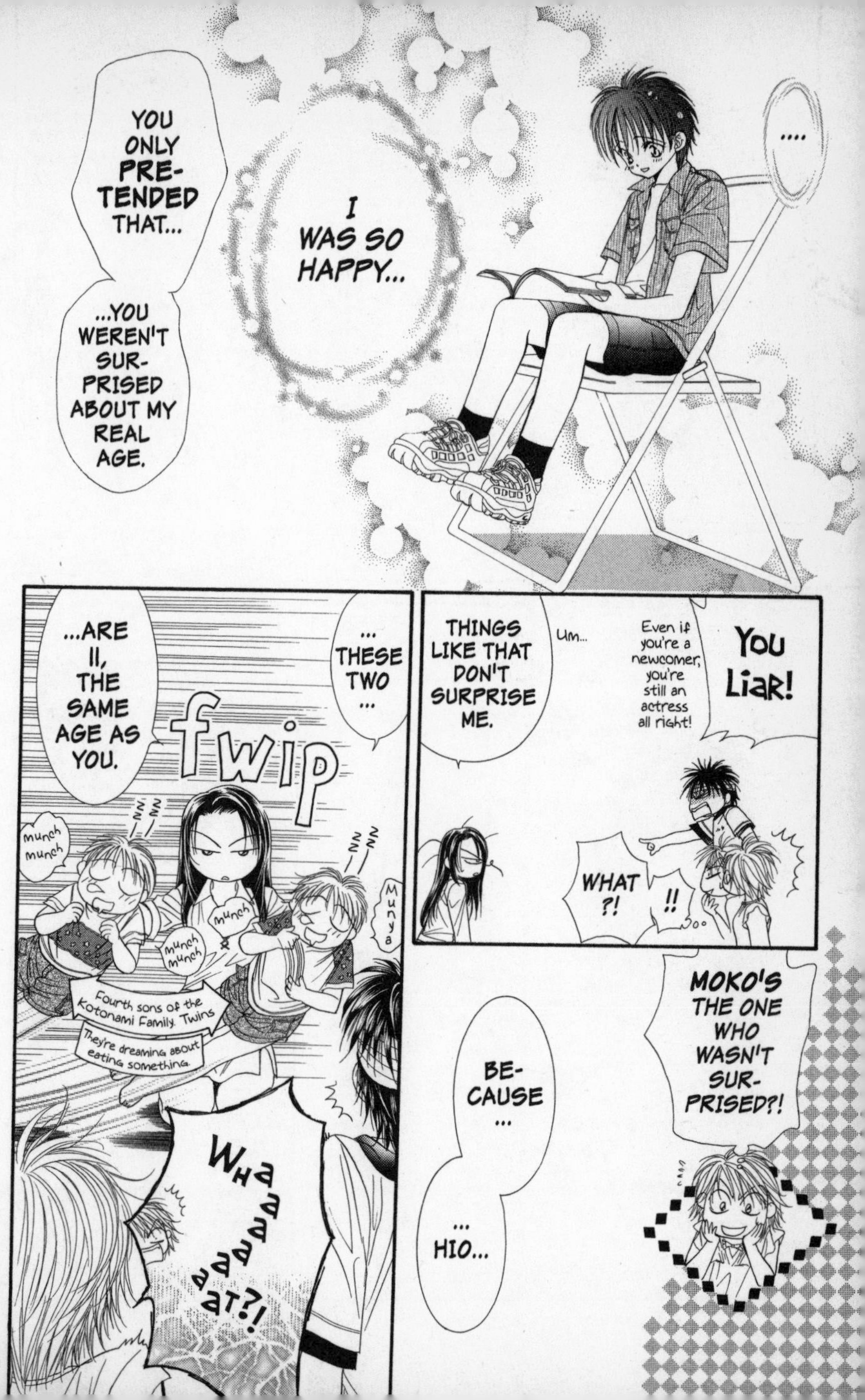
....
I WAS SO HAPPY...
YOU ONLY PRE-TENDED THAT...
...YOU WEREN'T SUR-PRISED ABOUT MY REAL AGE.
YOU LIAR!
Even if you're a newcomer, you're still an actress all right!
Um...
THINGS LIKE THAT DON'T SURPRISE ME.
WHAT?!
!!
MOKO'S THE ONE WHO WASN'T SUR-PRISED?!
BE-CAUSE...
...HIO...
...THESE TWO...
...ARE 11, THE SAME AGE AS YOU.
fwip
Munya
munch munch
munch
munch munch
Fourth sons of the Kotonami Family. Twins
They're dreaming about eating something.
WHAAAAAAAAT?!

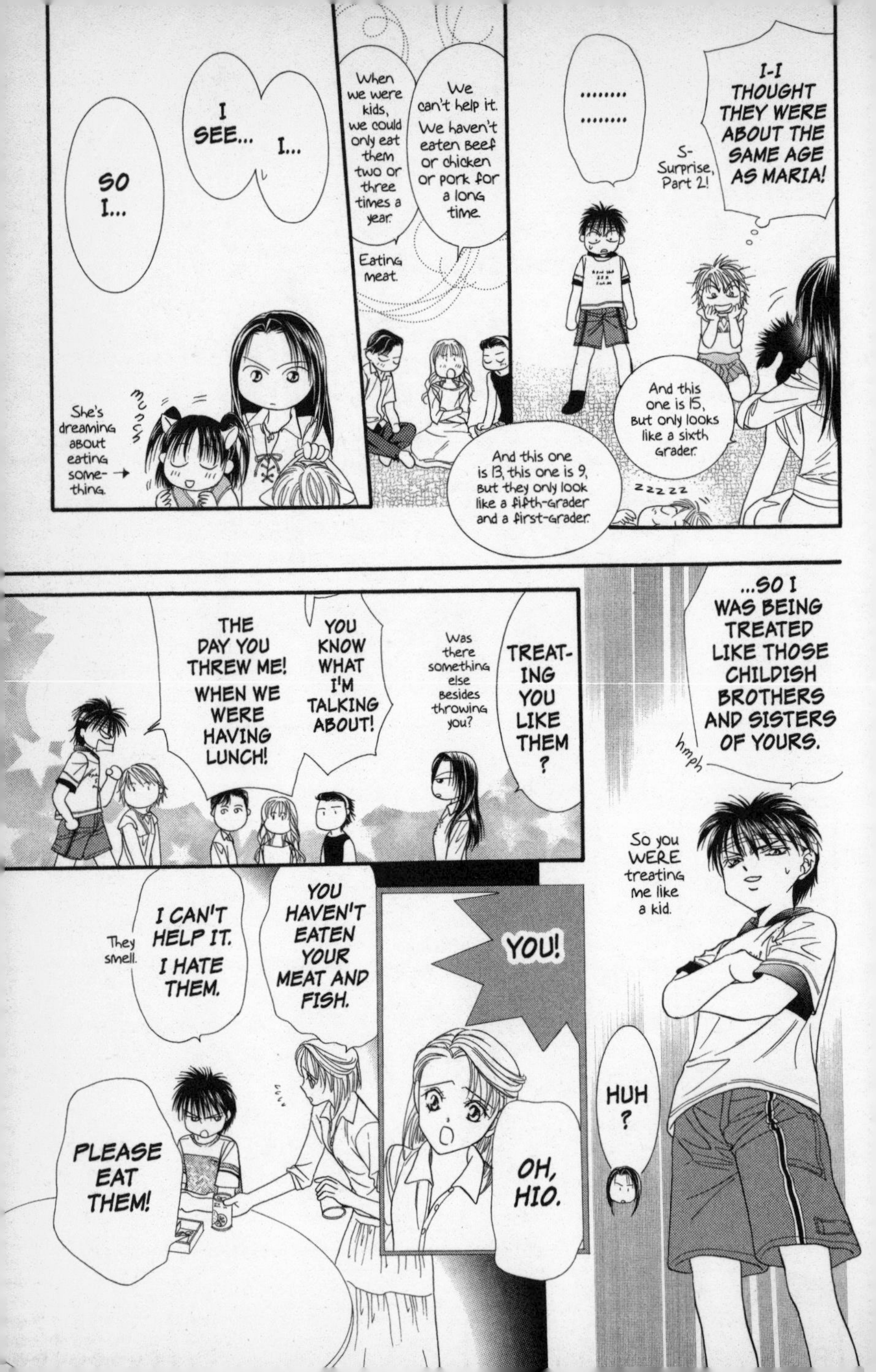
I-I THOUGHT THEY WERE ABOUT THE SAME AGE AS MARIA!
....
S-Surprise, Part 2!
And this one is 15, but only looks like a sixth grader.
And this one is 13, this one is 9, but they only look like a fifth-grader and a first-grader.
zzzzz
We can't help it. We haven't eaten beef or chicken or pork for a long time.
When we were kids, we could only eat them two or three times a year.
Eating meat.
I SEE... I...
SO I...
She's dreaming about eating some-thing.
munch
...SO I WAS BEING TREATED LIKE THOSE CHILDISH BROTHERS AND SISTERS OF YOURS.
hmph
So you WERE treating me like a kid.
HUH?
TREAT-ING YOU LIKE THEM?
Was there something else besides throwing you?
YOU KNOW WHAT I'M TALKING ABOUT!
THE DAY YOU THREW ME! WHEN WE WERE HAVING LUNCH!
YOU!
OH, HIO.
YOU HAVEN'T EATEN YOUR MEAT AND FISH.
I CAN'T HELP IT. I HATE THEM.
They smell.
PLEASE EAT THEM!

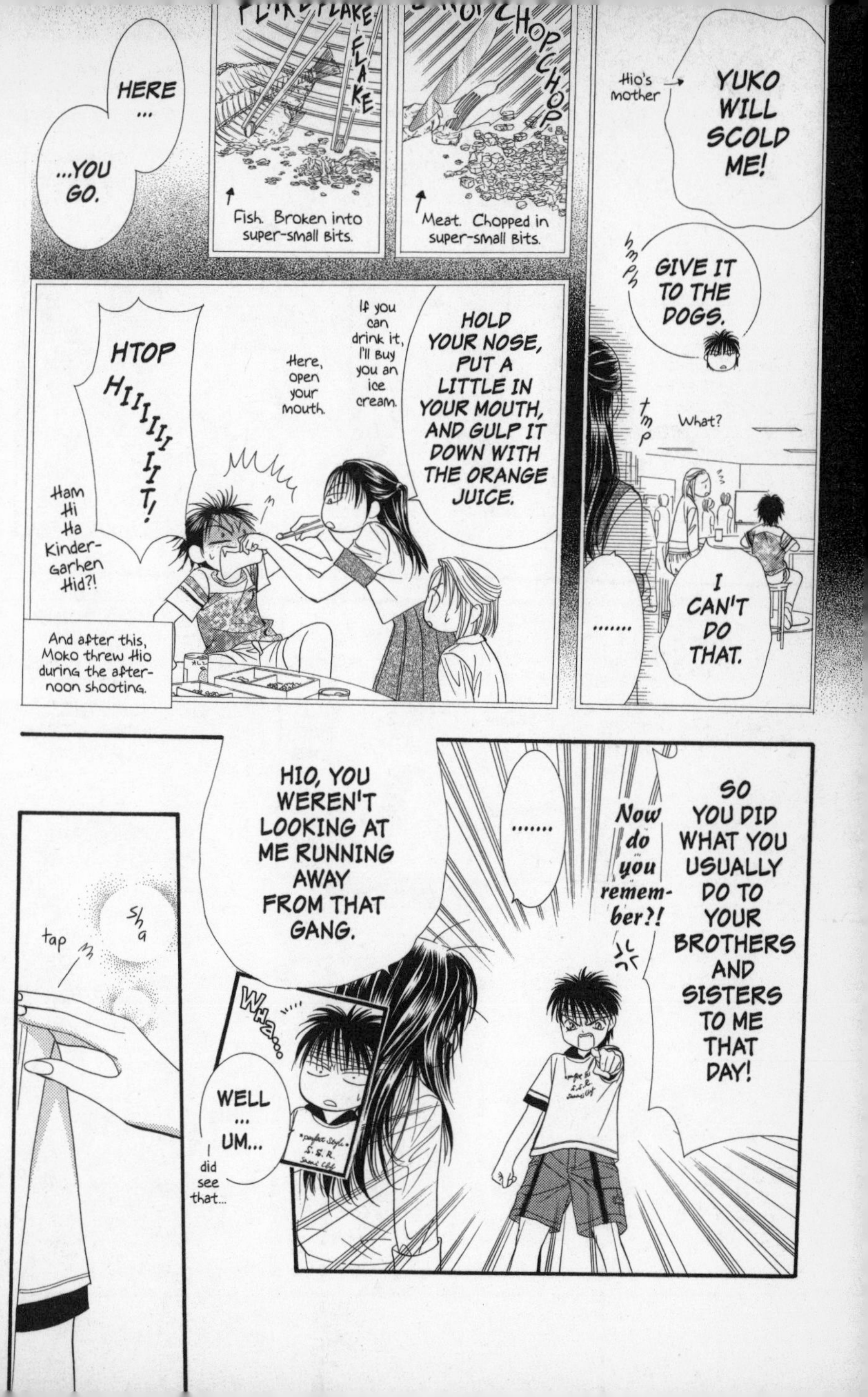

Hio's mother
YUKO WILL SCOLD ME!
hmph
GIVE IT TO THE DOGS.
tmp
What?
....
I CAN'T DO THAT.
CHOP CHOP
Meat. Chopped in super-small bits.
FLAKE FLAKE
Fish. Broken into super-small bits.
HERE ...
...YOU GO.
HOLD YOUR NOSE, PUT A LITTLE IN YOUR MOUTH, AND GULP IT DOWN WITH THE ORANGE JUICE.
If you can drink it, I'll buy you an ice cream.
Here, open your mouth.
HTOP HIIIIIIIT!
Ham Hi Ha Kinder-garhen Hid?!
And after this, Moko threw Hio during the after-noon shooting.
SO YOU DID WHAT YOU USUALLY DO TO YOUR BROTHERS AND SISTERS TO ME THAT DAY!
Now do you remem-ber?!
....
HIO, YOU WEREN'T LOOKING AT ME RUNNING AWAY FROM THAT GANG.
Wha...
WELL ... UM...
I did see that...
sha
tap

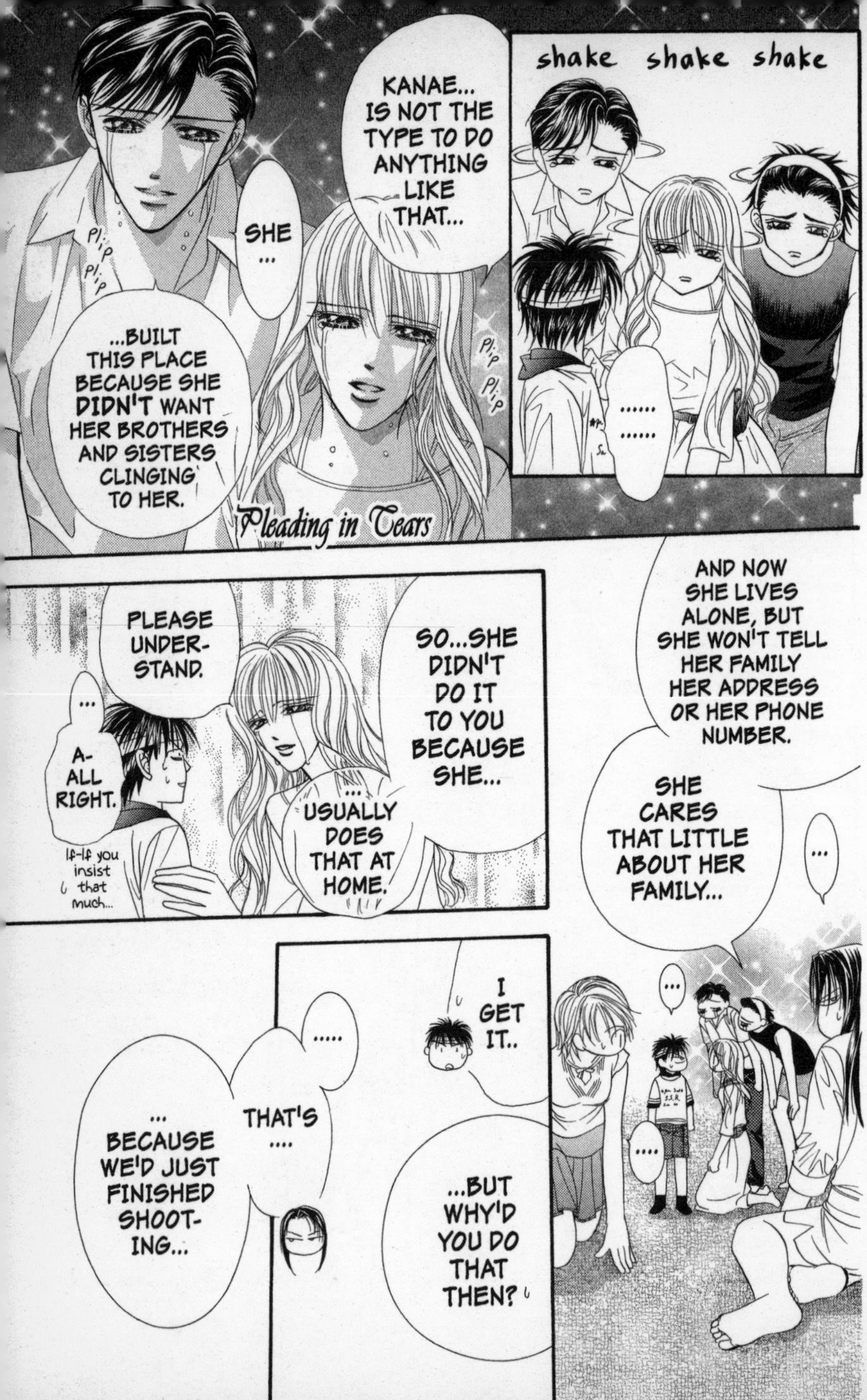
shake shake shake
......
......
KANAE... IS NOT THE TYPE TO DO ANYTHING LIKE THAT...
SHE ...
...BUILT THIS PLACE BECAUSE SHE DIDN'T WANT HER BROTHERS AND SISTERS CLINGING TO HER.
Plip Plip
Plip Plip
Pleading in Tears
AND NOW SHE LIVES ALONE, BUT SHE WON'T TELL HER FAMILY HER ADDRESS OR HER PHONE NUMBER.
SHE CARES THAT LITTLE ABOUT HER FAMILY...
...
SO...SHE DIDN'T DO IT TO YOU BECAUSE SHE...
...USUALLY DOES THAT AT HOME.
PLEASE UNDER-STAND.
...
A-ALL RIGHT.
If-If you insist that much...
...
....
I GET IT..
...BUT WHY'D YOU DO THAT THEN?
......
THAT'S ....
... BECAUSE WE'D JUST FINISHED SHOOT-ING...

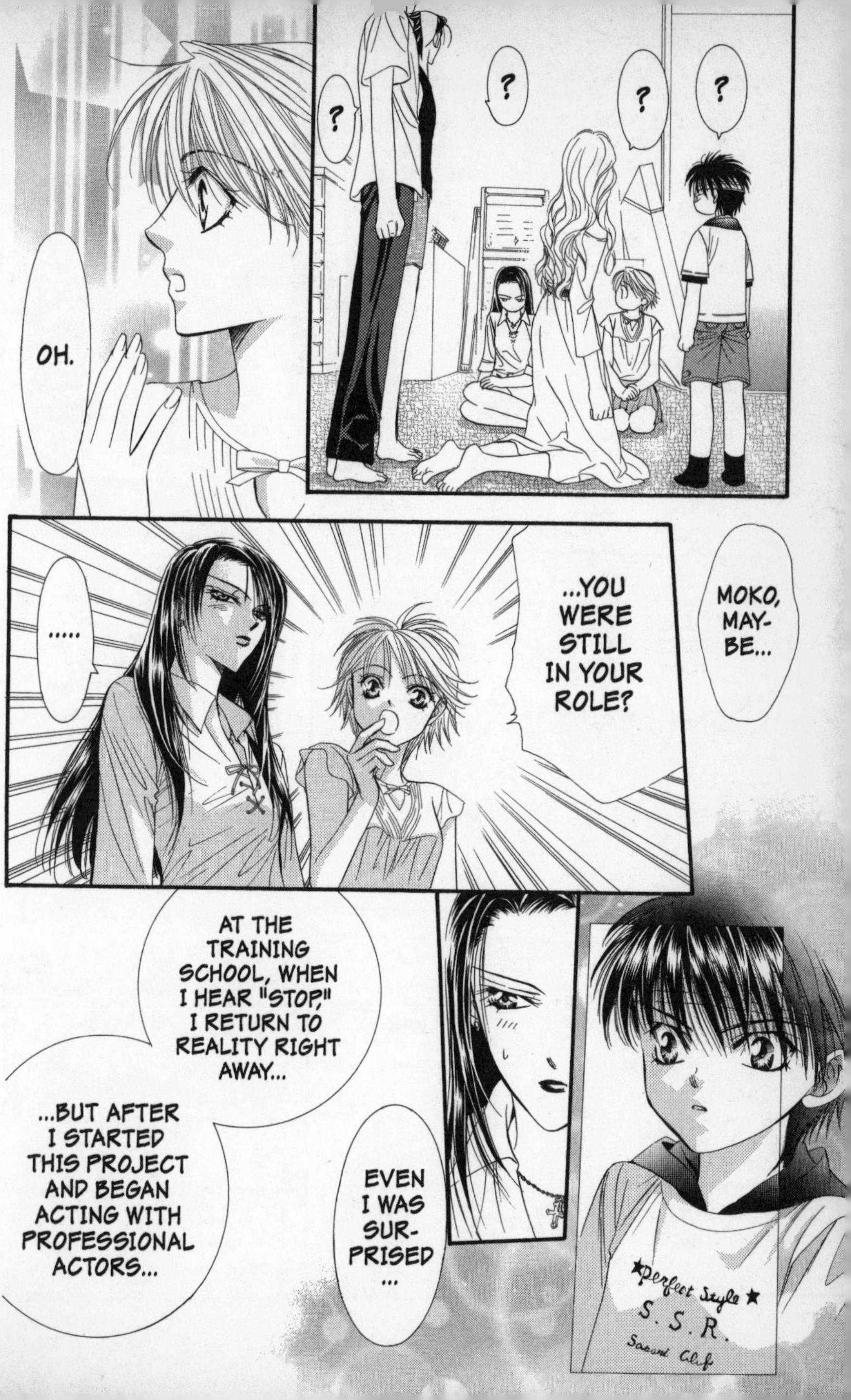
?
?
?
?
OH.
MOKO, MAY-BE...
...YOU WERE STILL IN YOUR ROLE?
.....
★Perfect Style★ S.S.R. Second Clif
EVEN I WAS SUR-PRISED...
AT THE TRAINING SCHOOL, WHEN I HEAR "STOP," I RETURN TO REALITY RIGHT AWAY...
...BUT AFTER I STARTED THIS PROJECT AND BEGAN ACTING WITH PROFESSIONAL ACTORS...

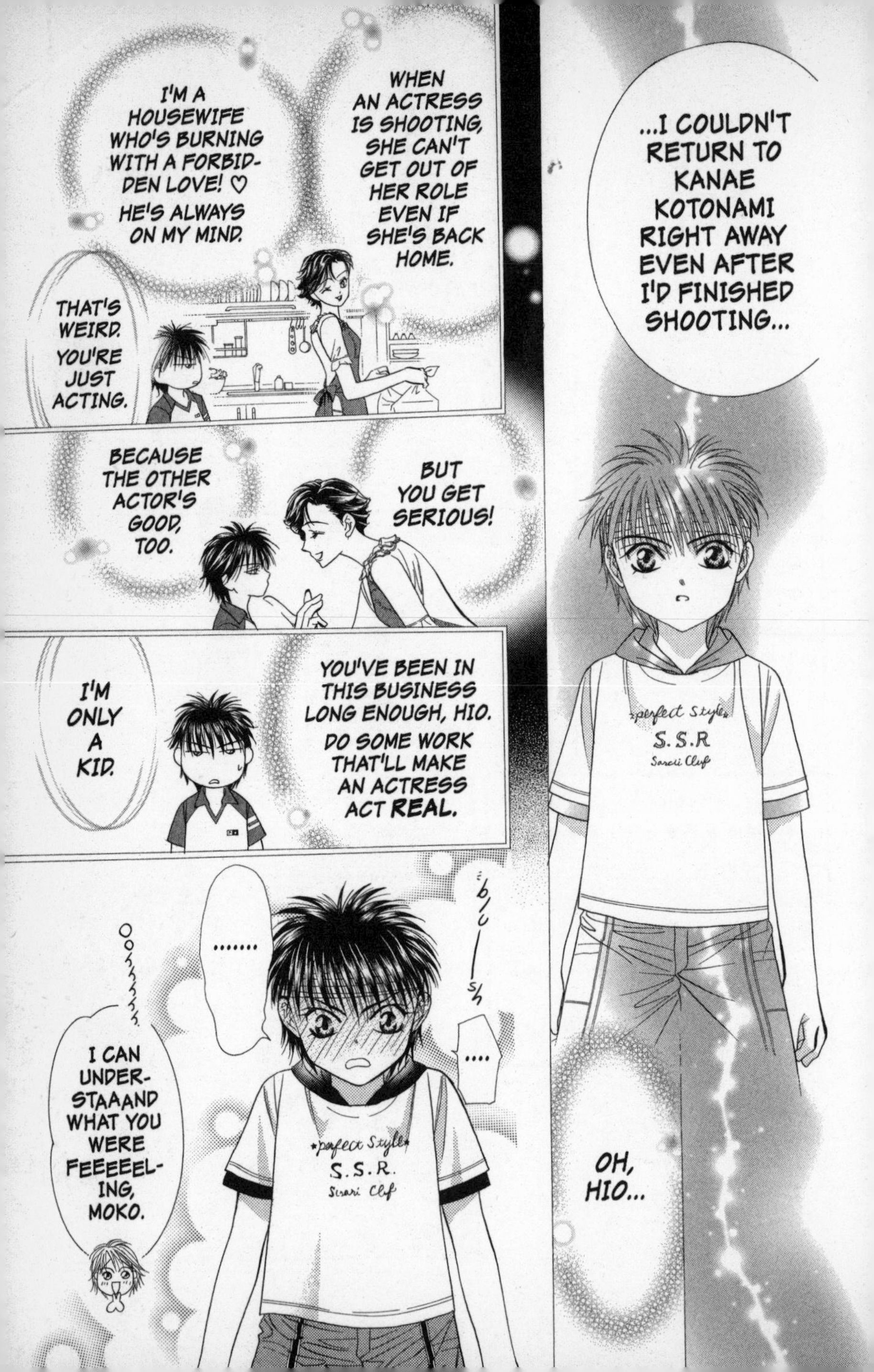
...I COULDN'T RETURN TO KANAE KOTONAMI RIGHT AWAY EVEN AFTER I'D FINISHED SHOOTING...
OH, HIO...
WHEN AN ACTRESS IS SHOOTING, SHE CAN'T GET OUT OF HER ROLE EVEN IF SHE'S BACK HOME.
I'M A HOUSEWIFE WHO'S BURNING WITH A FORBID-DEN LOVE! ♡ HE'S ALWAYS ON MY MIND.
THAT'S WEIRD. YOU'RE JUST ACTING.
BUT YOU GET SERIOUS!
BECAUSE THE OTHER ACTOR'S GOOD, TOO.
YOU'VE BEEN IN THIS BUSINESS LONG ENOUGH, HIO. DO SOME WORK THAT'LL MAKE AN ACTRESS ACT REAL.
I'M ONLY A KID.
blush
....
....
Oohhhhh
I CAN UNDER-STAAAND WHAT YOU WERE FEEEEEL-ING, MOKO.

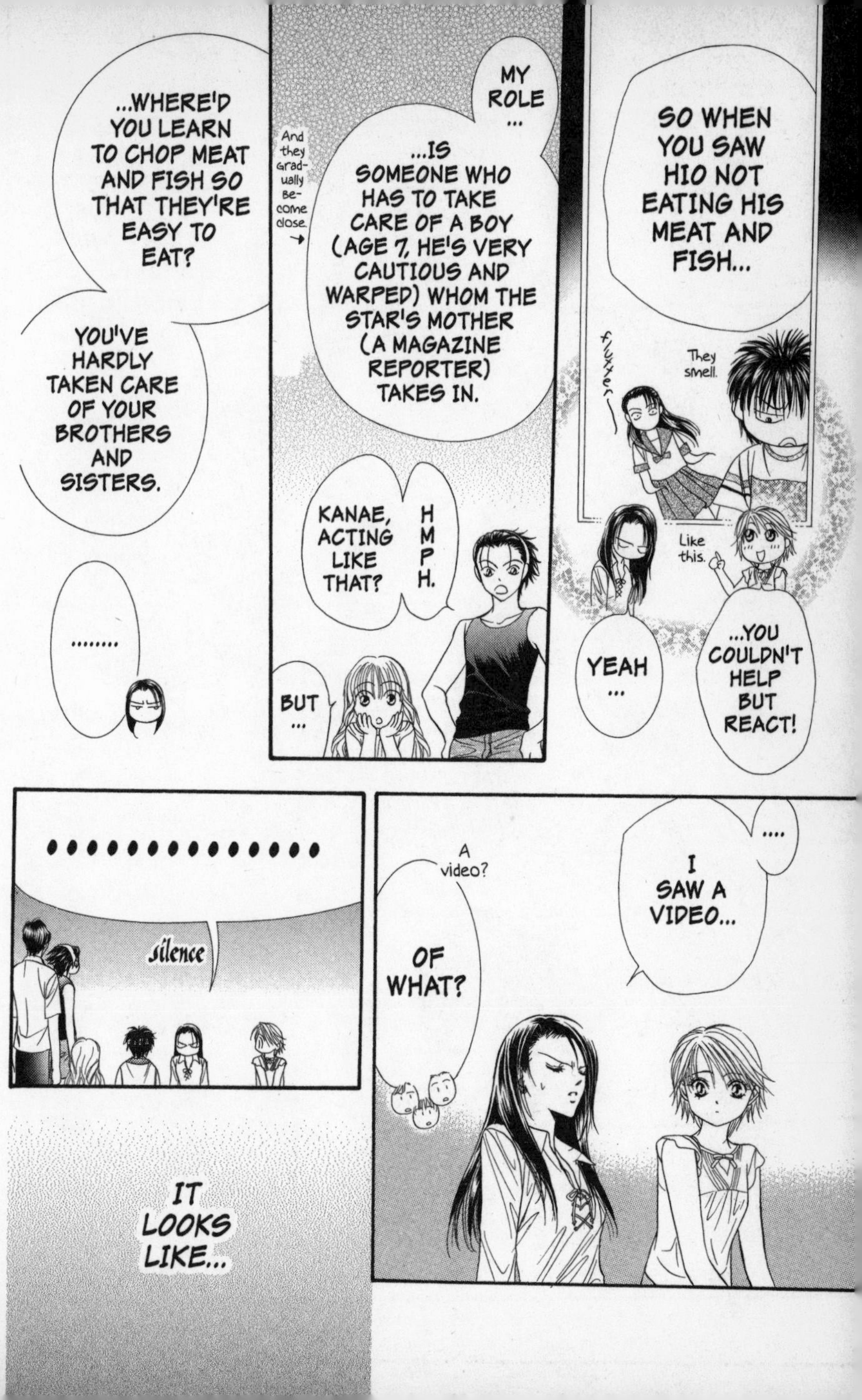
SO WHEN YOU SAW HIO NOT EATING HIS MEAT AND FISH...
fluxxer
They smell.
Like this.
YEAH...
...YOU COULDN'T HELP BUT REACT!
MY ROLE...
...IS SOMEONE WHO HAS TO TAKE CARE OF A BOY (AGE 7, HE'S VERY CAUTIOUS AND WARPED) WHOM THE STAR'S MOTHER (A MAGAZINE REPORTER) TAKES IN.
And they Grad-ually be-come close.
KANAE, ACTING LIKE THAT?
HMPH.
BUT...
...WHERE'D YOU LEARN TO CHOP MEAT AND FISH SO THAT THEY'RE EASY TO EAT?
YOU'VE HARDLY TAKEN CARE OF YOUR BROTHERS AND SISTERS.
....
....
I SAW A VIDEO...
A video?
OF WHAT?
....
silence
IT LOOKS LIKE...

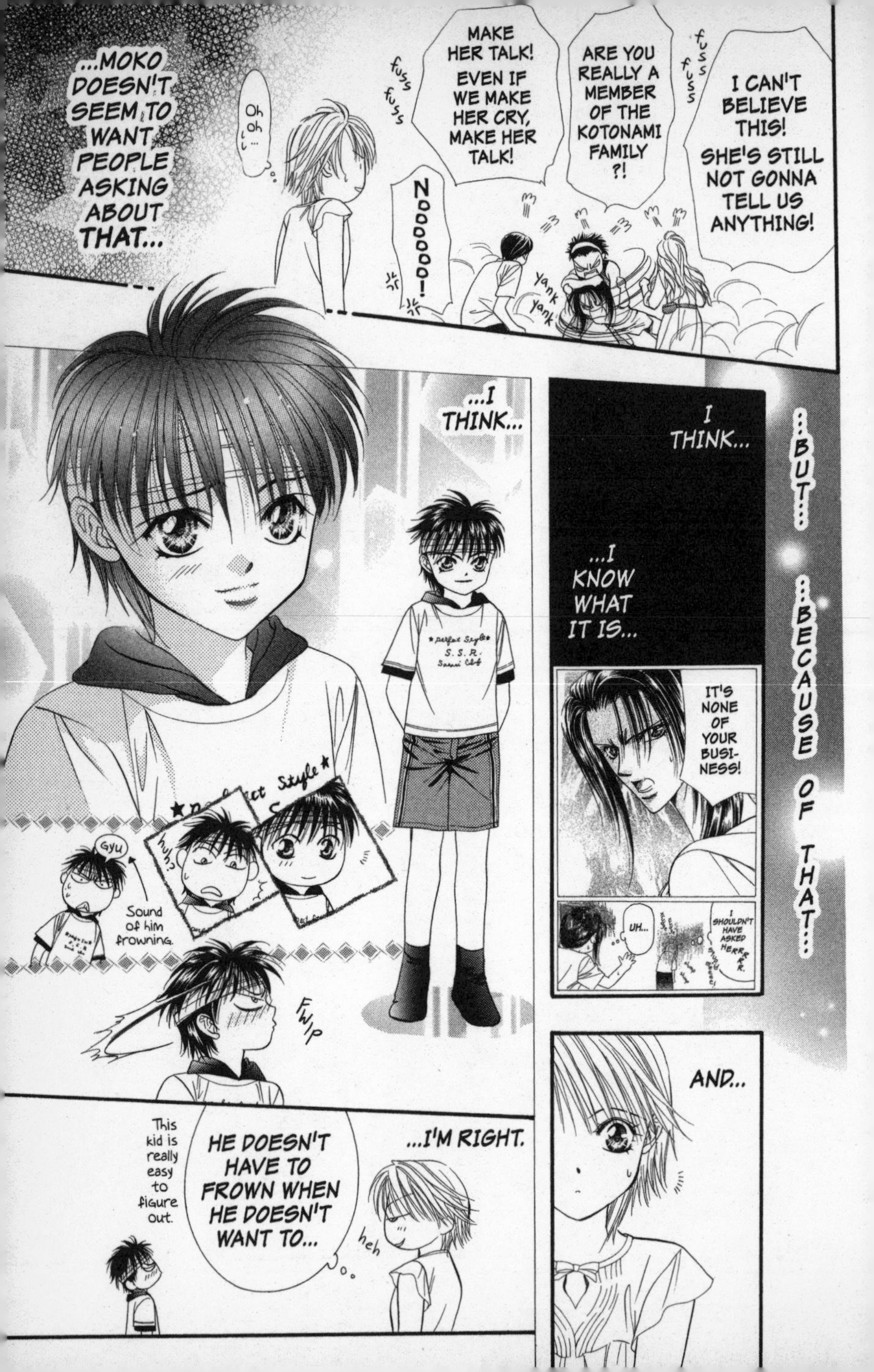
I CAN'T BELIEVE THIS! SHE'S STILL NOT GONNA TELL US ANYTHING!
fuss fuss
ARE YOU REALLY A MEMBER OF THE KOTONAMI FAMILY?!
MAKE HER TALK! EVEN IF WE MAKE HER CRY, MAKE HER TALK!
fuss fuss
yank yank
NOOOOOOO!
Oh oh...
...MOKO DOESN'T SEEM TO WANT PEOPLE ASKING ABOUT THAT...
...BUT... ...BECAUSE OF THAT...
I THINK...
...I KNOW WHAT IT IS...
IT'S NONE OF YOUR BUSINESS!
UH...
I SHOULDN'T HAVE ASKED HERRRR.
...I THINK...
huh?
Gyu
Sound of him frowning.
FWIP
AND...
...I'M RIGHT.
heh
HE DOESN'T HAVE TO FROWN WHEN HE DOESN'T WANT TO...
This kid is really easy to figure out.

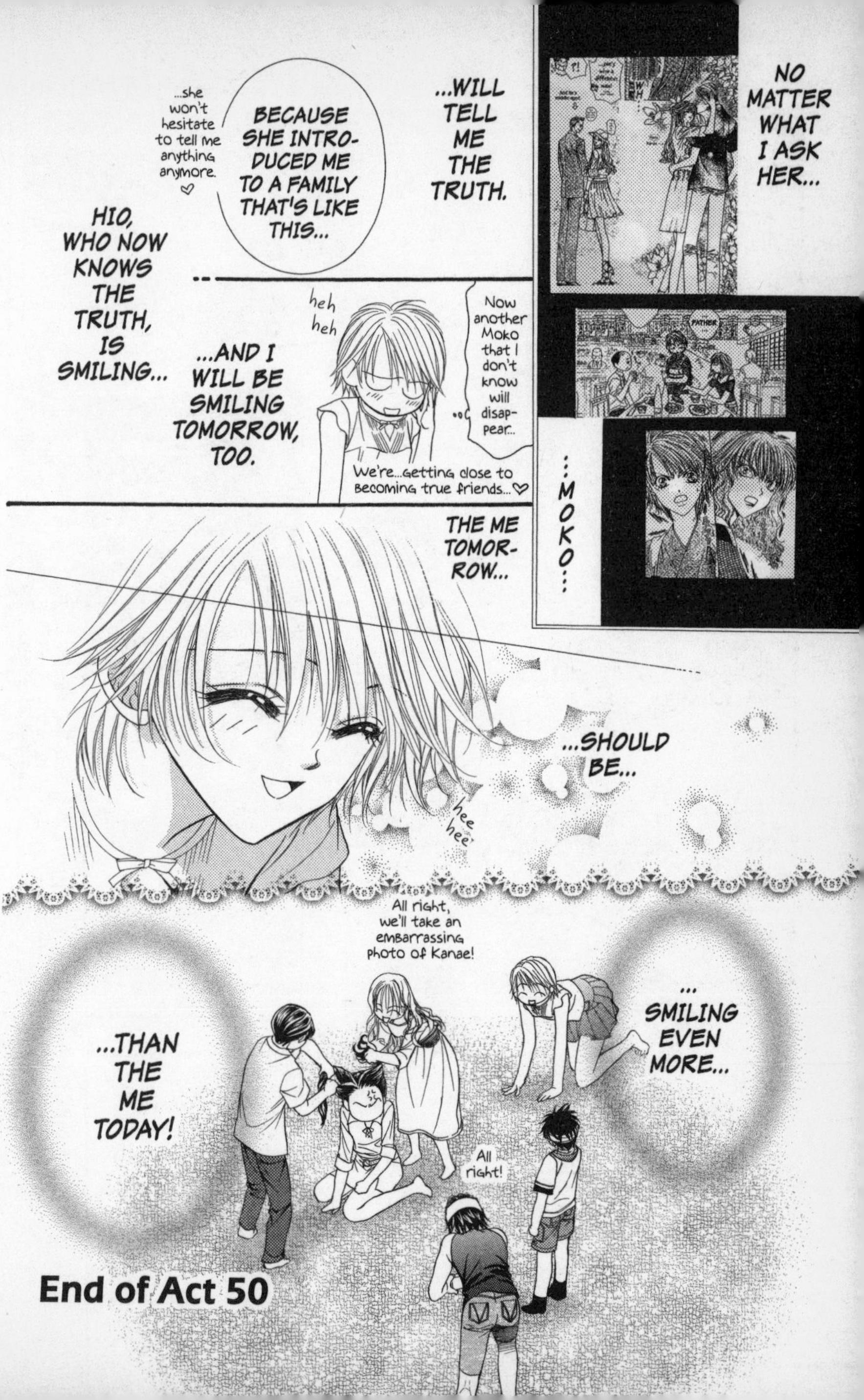
NO MATTER WHAT I ASK HER...
FATHER
...MOKO...
...WILL TELL ME THE TRUTH.
BECAUSE SHE INTRODUCED ME TO A FAMILY THAT'S LIKE THIS...
...she won't hesitate to tell me anything anymore.♡
HIO, WHO NOW KNOWS THE TRUTH, IS SMILING...
Now another Moko that I don't know will disappear...
heh heh
...AND I WILL BE SMILING TOMORROW, TOO.
We're...getting close to becoming true friends...♡
THE ME TOMORROW...
...SHOULD BE...
hee hee
...SMILING EVEN MORE...
All right, we'll take an embarrassing photo of Kanae!
...THAN THE ME TODAY!
All right!
End of Act 50

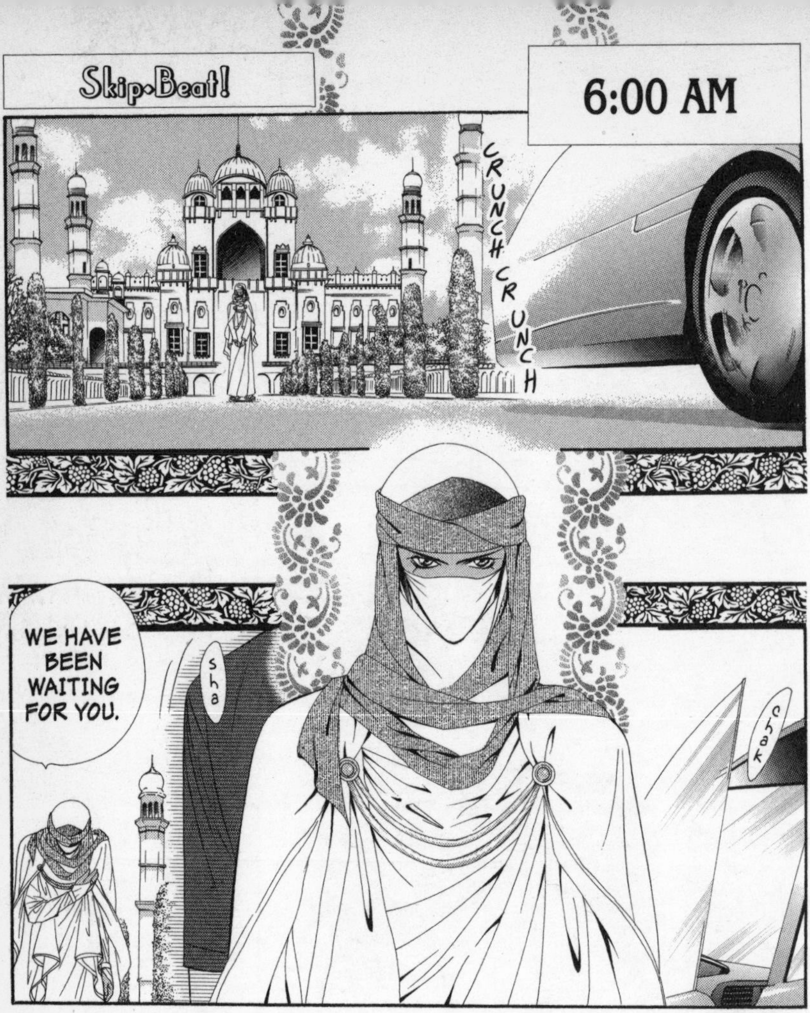
Skip-Beat!
6:00 AM
CRUNCH CRUNCH
CRUNCH
chak
sha
WE HAVE BEEN WAITING FOR YOU.

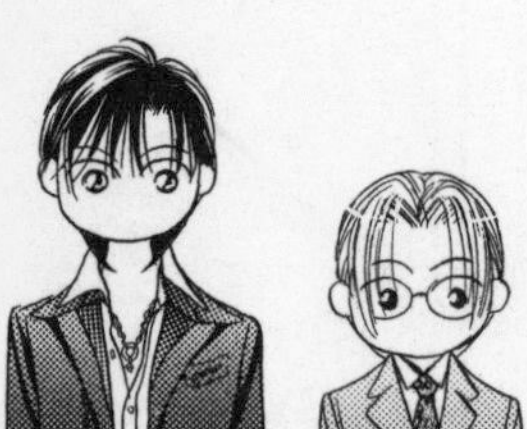

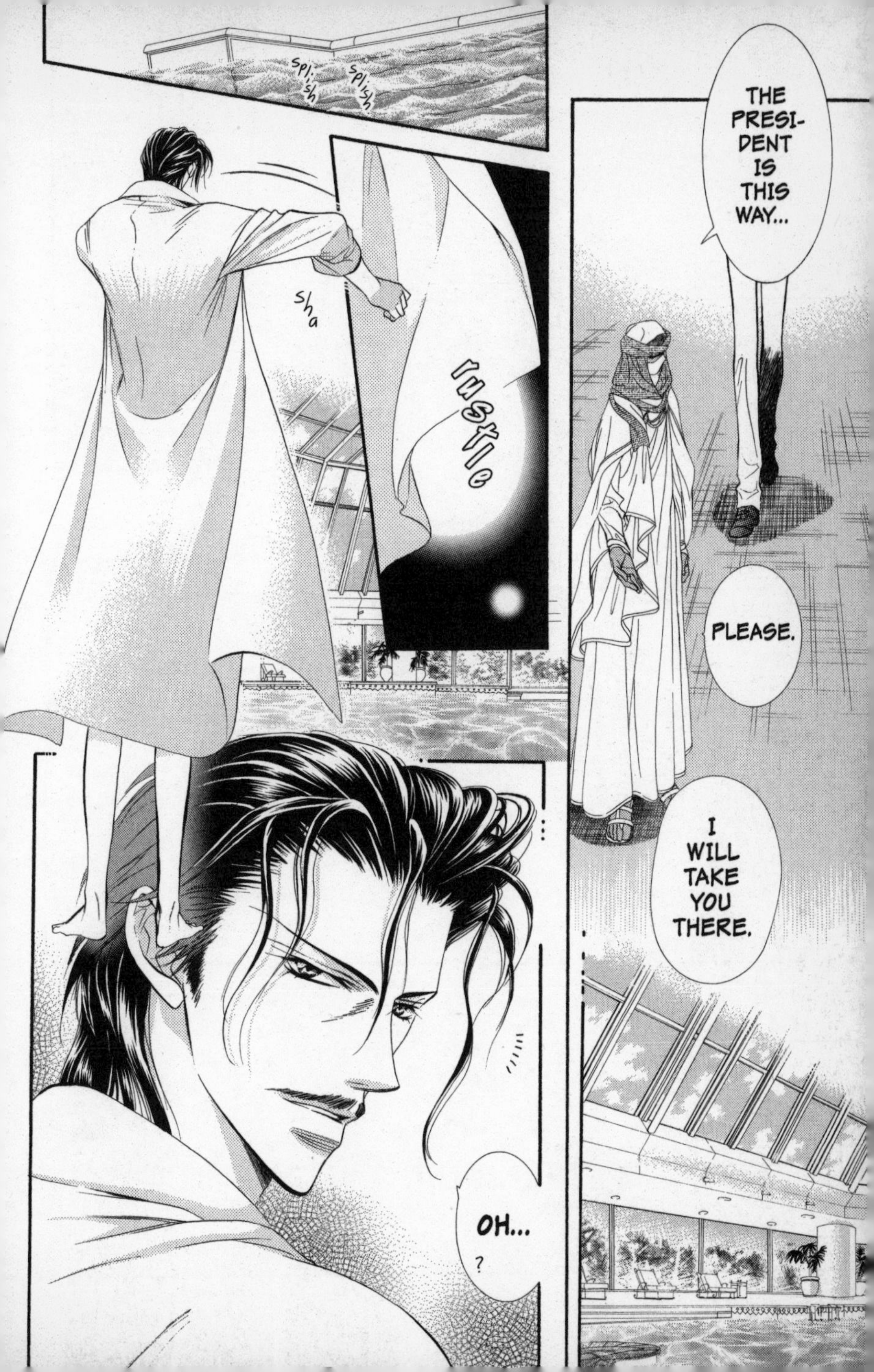
THE PRESIDENT IS THIS WAY...
PLEASE.
I WILL TAKE YOU THERE.
splish
splish
sha
rustle
...
OH...
?

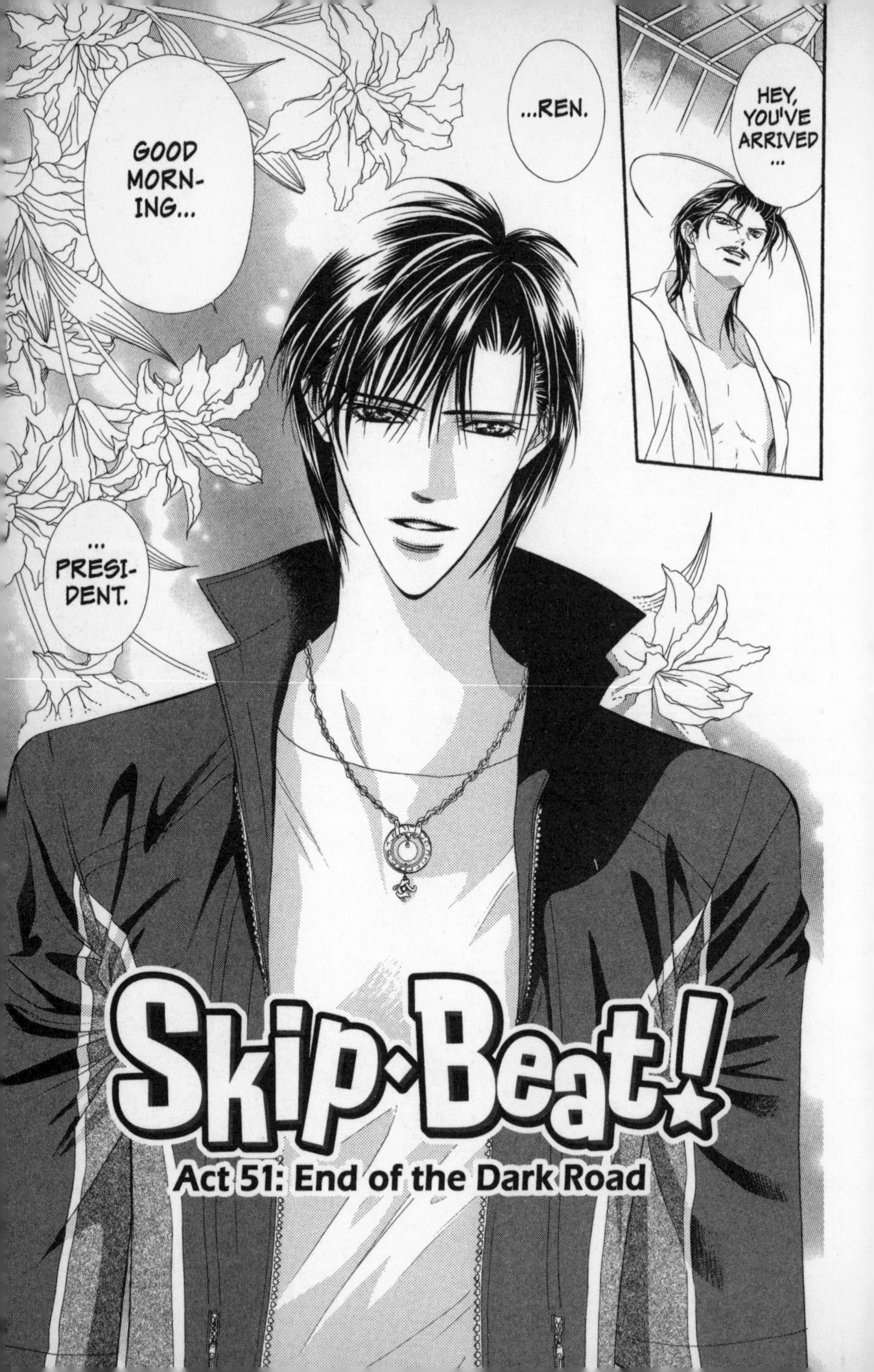
HEY, YOU'VE ARRIVED ...
...REN.
GOOD MORN-ING...
... PRESI-DENT.
Skip·Beat!
Act 51: End of the Dark Road

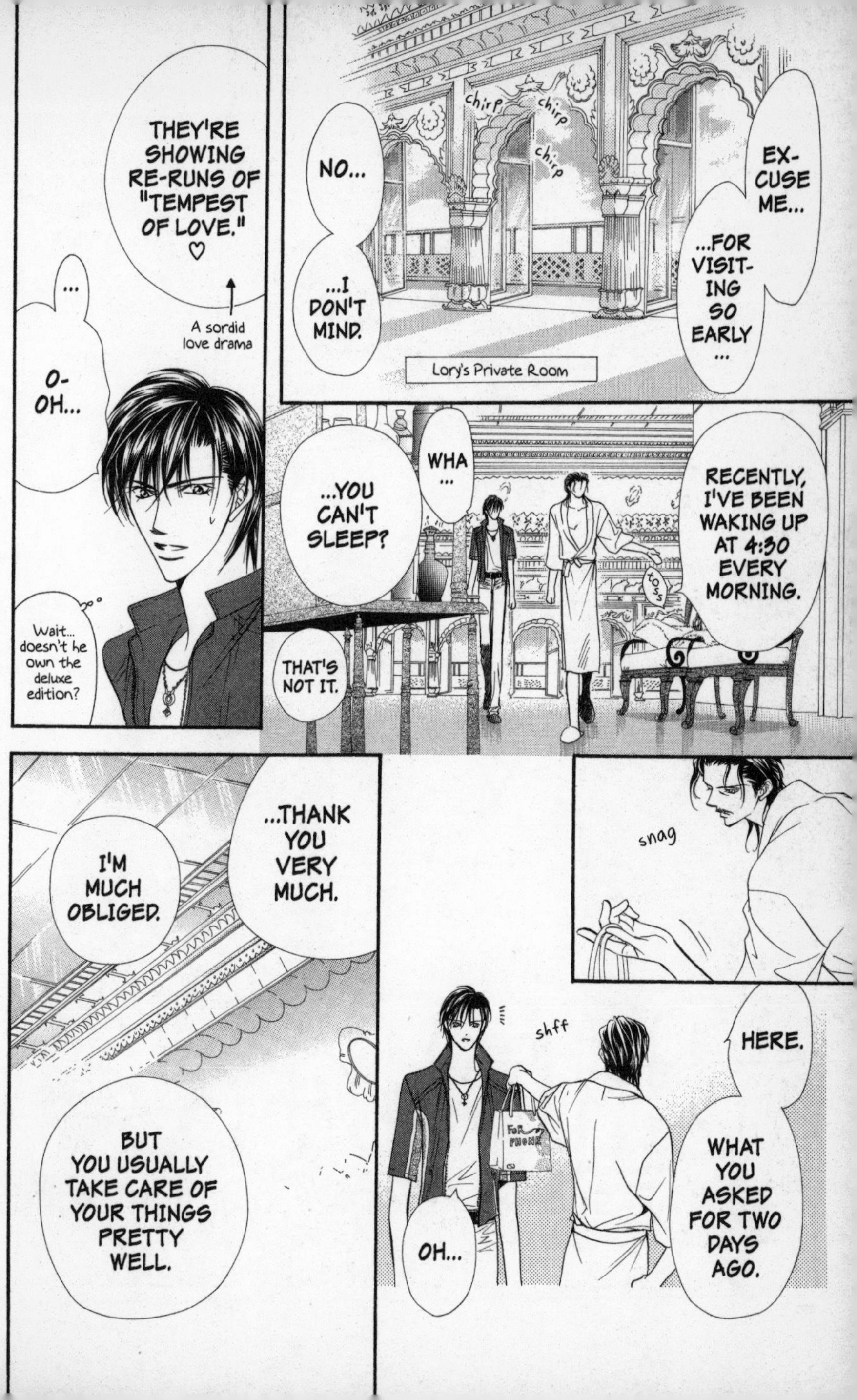
EX-CUSE ME...
...FOR VISIT-ING SO EARLY...
chirp chirp chirp
NO...
...I DON'T MIND.
Lory's Private Room
RECENTLY, I'VE BEEN WAKING UP AT 4:30 EVERY MORNING.
toss
WHA...
...YOU CAN'T SLEEP?
THAT'S NOT IT.
THEY'RE SHOWING RE-RUNS OF "TEMPEST OF LOVE." ♡
A sordid love drama
...
O-OH...
Wait... doesn't he own the deluxe edition?
snag
HERE.
WHAT YOU ASKED FOR TWO DAYS AGO.
shff
OH...
...THANK YOU VERY MUCH.
I'M MUCH OBLIGED.
BUT YOU USUALLY TAKE CARE OF YOUR THINGS PRETTY WELL.

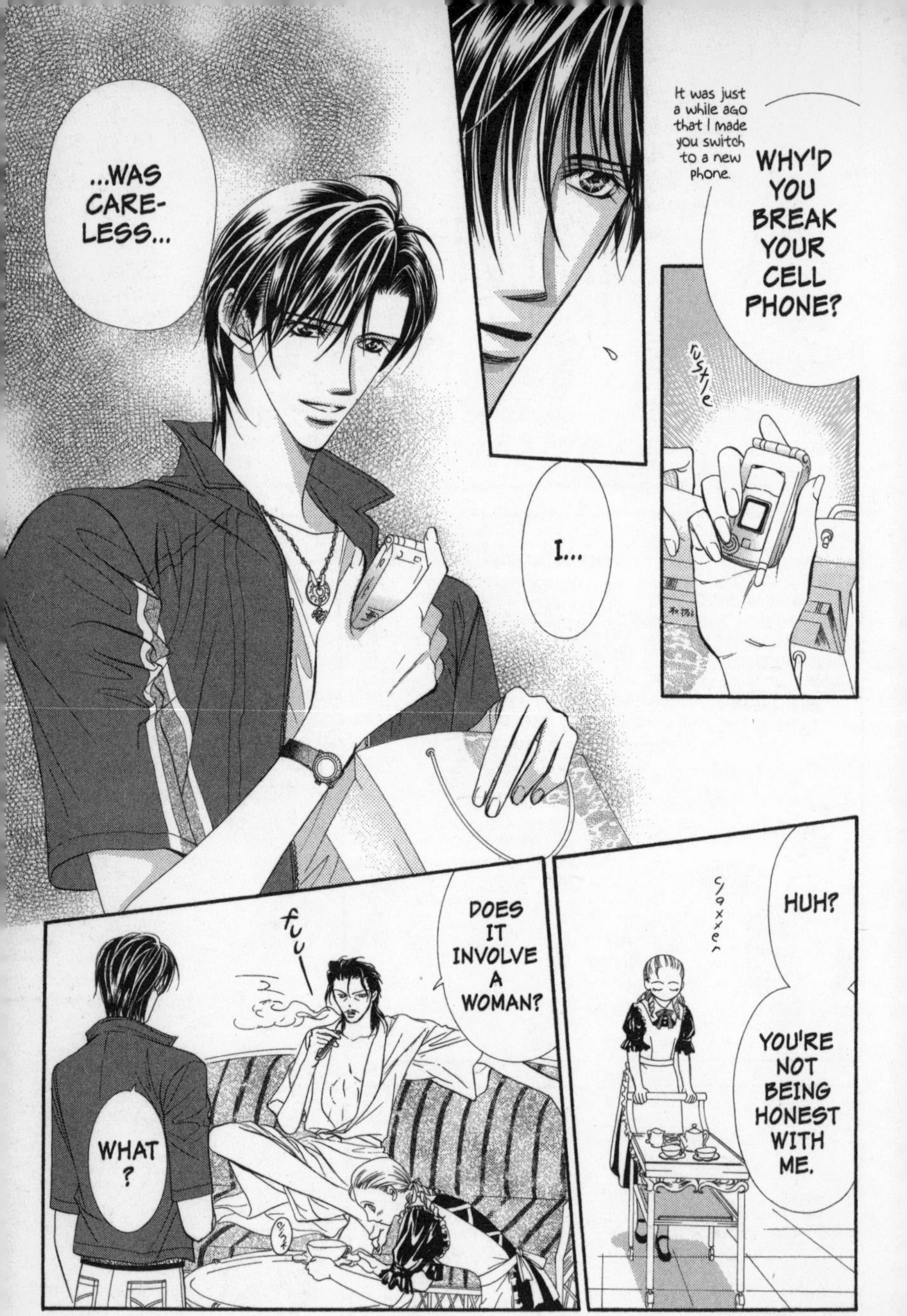
WHY'D YOU BREAK YOUR CELL PHONE?
It was just a while ago that I made you switch to a new phone.
rustle
I...
...WAS CARELESS...
HUH?
clatter
YOU'RE NOT BEING HONEST WITH ME.
DOES IT INVOLVE A WOMAN?
fuu
WHAT?

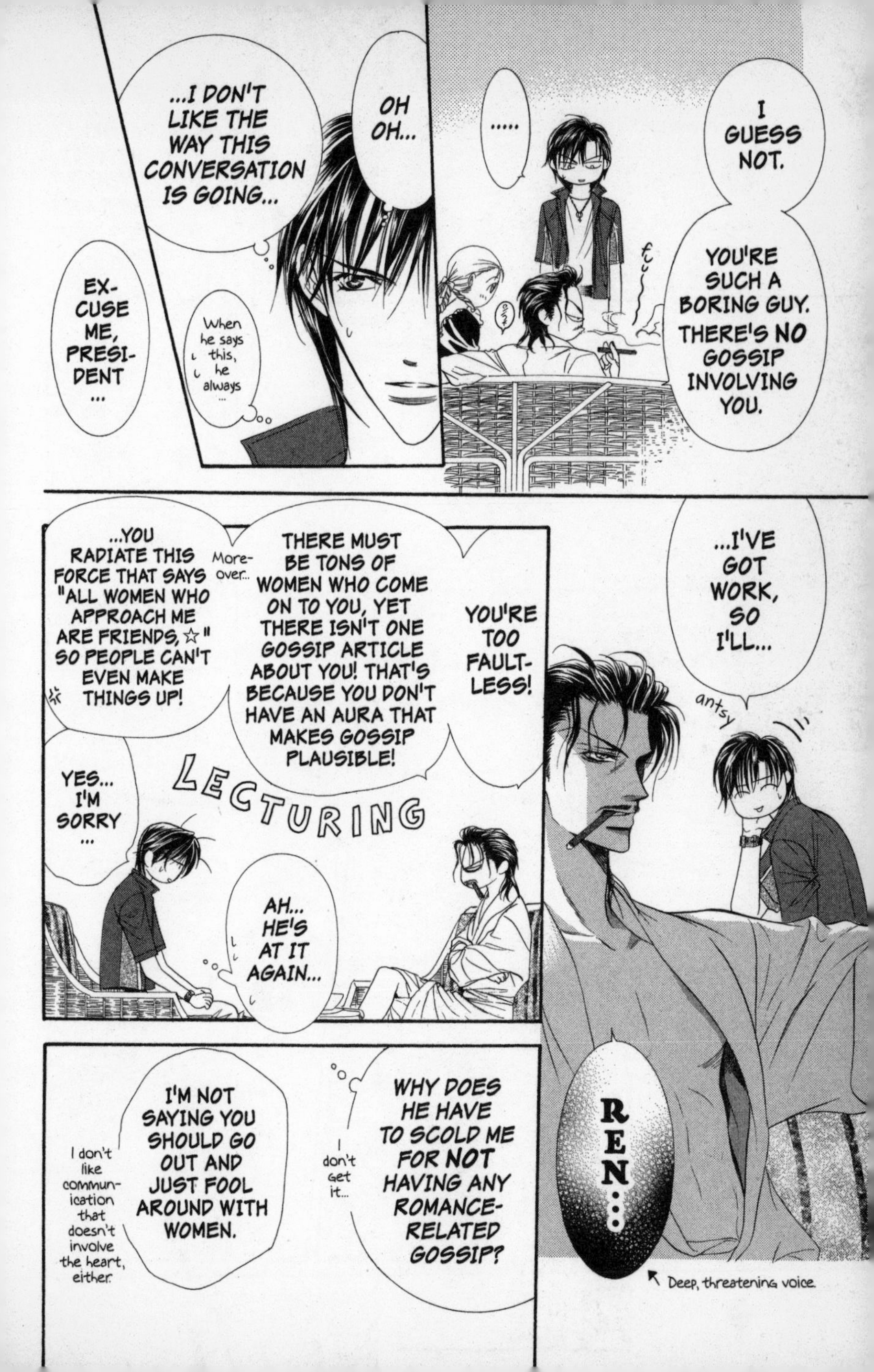
I GUESS NOT.
YOU'RE SUCH A BORING GUY. THERE'S NO GOSSIP INVOLVING YOU.
.....
OH OH...
...I DON'T LIKE THE WAY THIS CONVERSATION IS GOING...
When he says this, he always ...
EX-CUSE ME, PRESI-DENT ...
...I'VE GOT WORK, SO I'LL...
antsy
REN...
Deep, threatening voice.
YOU'RE TOO FAULT-LESS!
THERE MUST BE TONS OF WOMEN WHO COME ON TO YOU, YET THERE ISN'T ONE GOSSIP ARTICLE ABOUT YOU! THAT'S BECAUSE YOU DON'T HAVE AN AURA THAT MAKES GOSSIP PLAUSIBLE!
More-over...
...YOU RADIATE THIS FORCE THAT SAYS "ALL WOMEN WHO APPROACH ME ARE FRIENDS,☆" SO PEOPLE CAN'T EVEN MAKE THINGS UP!
LECTURING
YES... I'M SORRY ...
AH... HE'S AT IT AGAIN...
WHY DOES HE HAVE TO SCOLD ME FOR NOT HAVING ANY ROMANCE-RELATED GOSSIP?
I don't get it...
I'M NOT SAYING YOU SHOULD GO OUT AND JUST FOOL AROUND WITH WOMEN.
I don't like commun-ication that doesn't involve the heart, either.

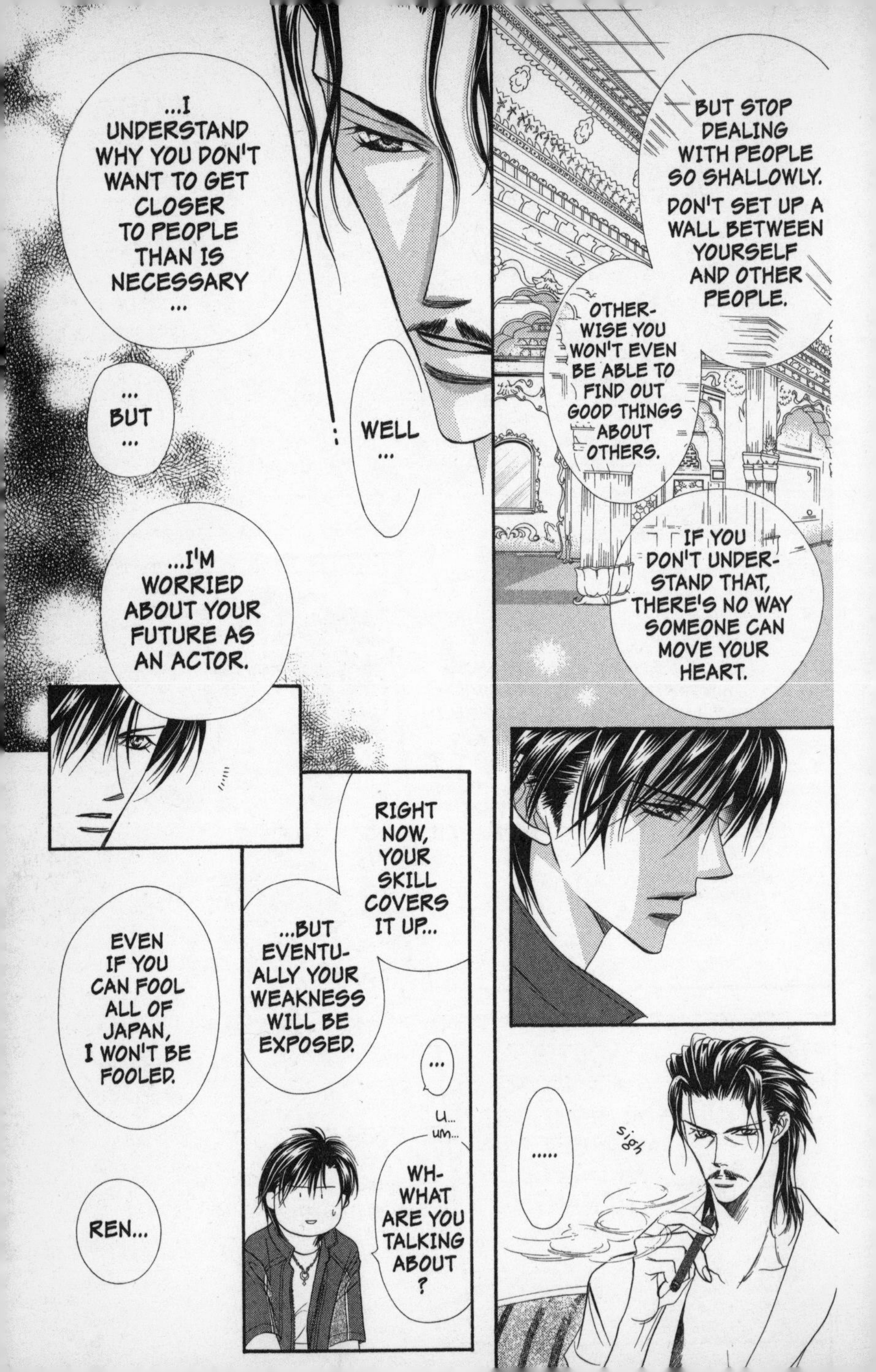
WELL ...
...I UNDERSTAND WHY YOU DON'T WANT TO GET CLOSER TO PEOPLE THAN IS NECESSARY ...
... BUT ...
...I'M WORRIED ABOUT YOUR FUTURE AS AN ACTOR.
RIGHT NOW, YOUR SKILL COVERS IT UP...
...BUT EVENTU-ALLY YOUR WEAKNESS WILL BE EXPOSED.
EVEN IF YOU CAN FOOL ALL OF JAPAN, I WON'T BE FOOLED.
REN...
...
U... um...
WH-WHAT ARE YOU TALKING ABOUT ?
BUT STOP DEALING WITH PEOPLE SO SHALLOWLY. DON'T SET UP A WALL BETWEEN YOURSELF AND OTHER PEOPLE.
OTHER-WISE YOU WON'T EVEN BE ABLE TO FIND OUT GOOD THINGS ABOUT OTHERS.
IF YOU DON'T UNDER-STAND THAT, THERE'S NO WAY SOMEONE CAN MOVE YOUR HEART.
.....
sigh

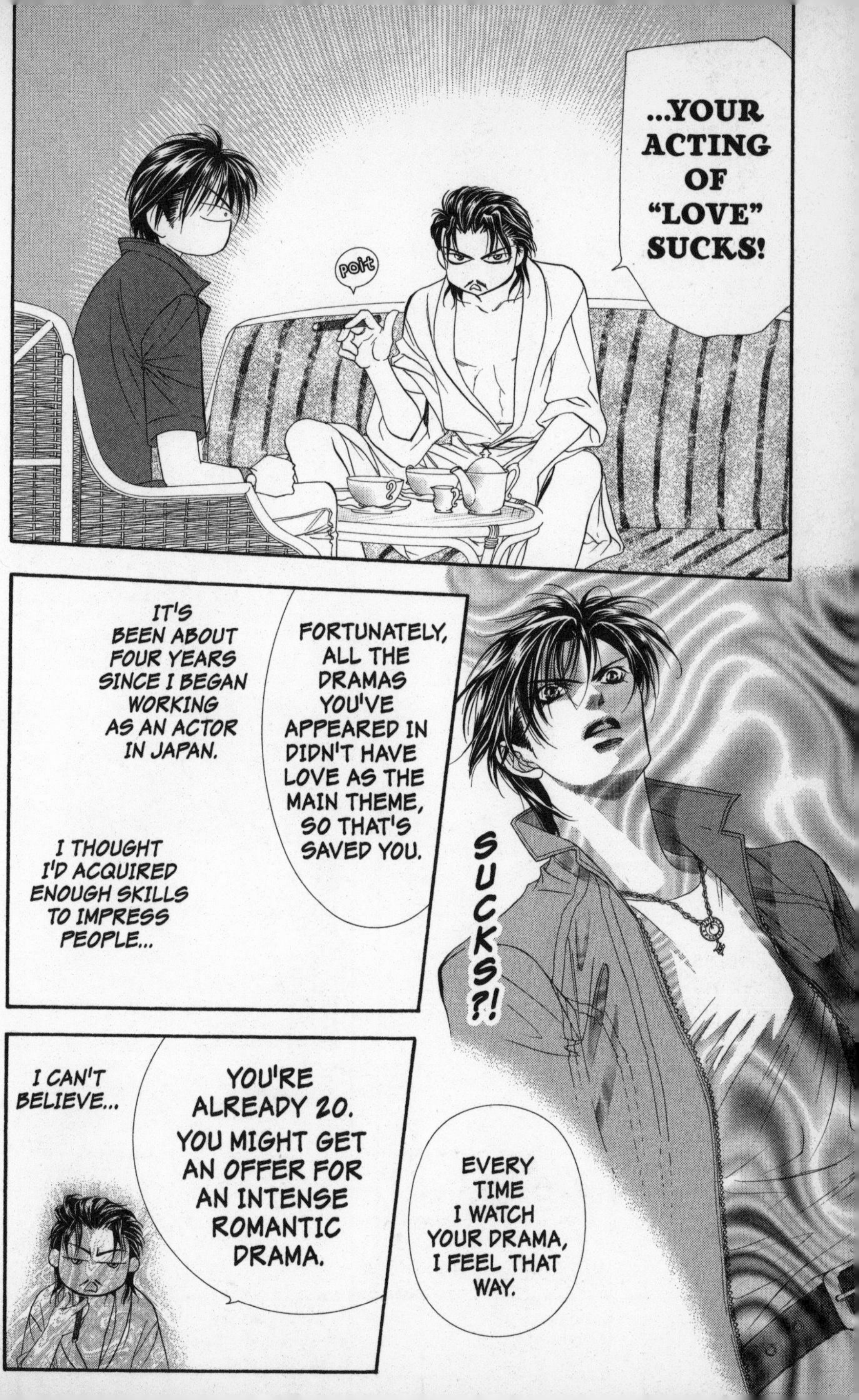
...YOUR ACTING OF "LOVE" SUCKS!
poit
SUCKS?!
EVERY TIME I WATCH YOUR DRAMA, I FEEL THAT WAY.
FORTUNATELY, ALL THE DRAMAS YOU'VE APPEARED IN DIDN'T HAVE LOVE AS THE MAIN THEME, SO THAT'S SAVED YOU.
IT'S BEEN ABOUT FOUR YEARS SINCE I BEGAN WORKING AS AN ACTOR IN JAPAN.
I THOUGHT I'D ACQUIRED ENOUGH SKILLS TO IMPRESS PEOPLE...
YOU'RE ALREADY 20. YOU MIGHT GET AN OFFER FOR AN INTENSE ROMANTIC DRAMA.
I CAN'T BELIEVE...

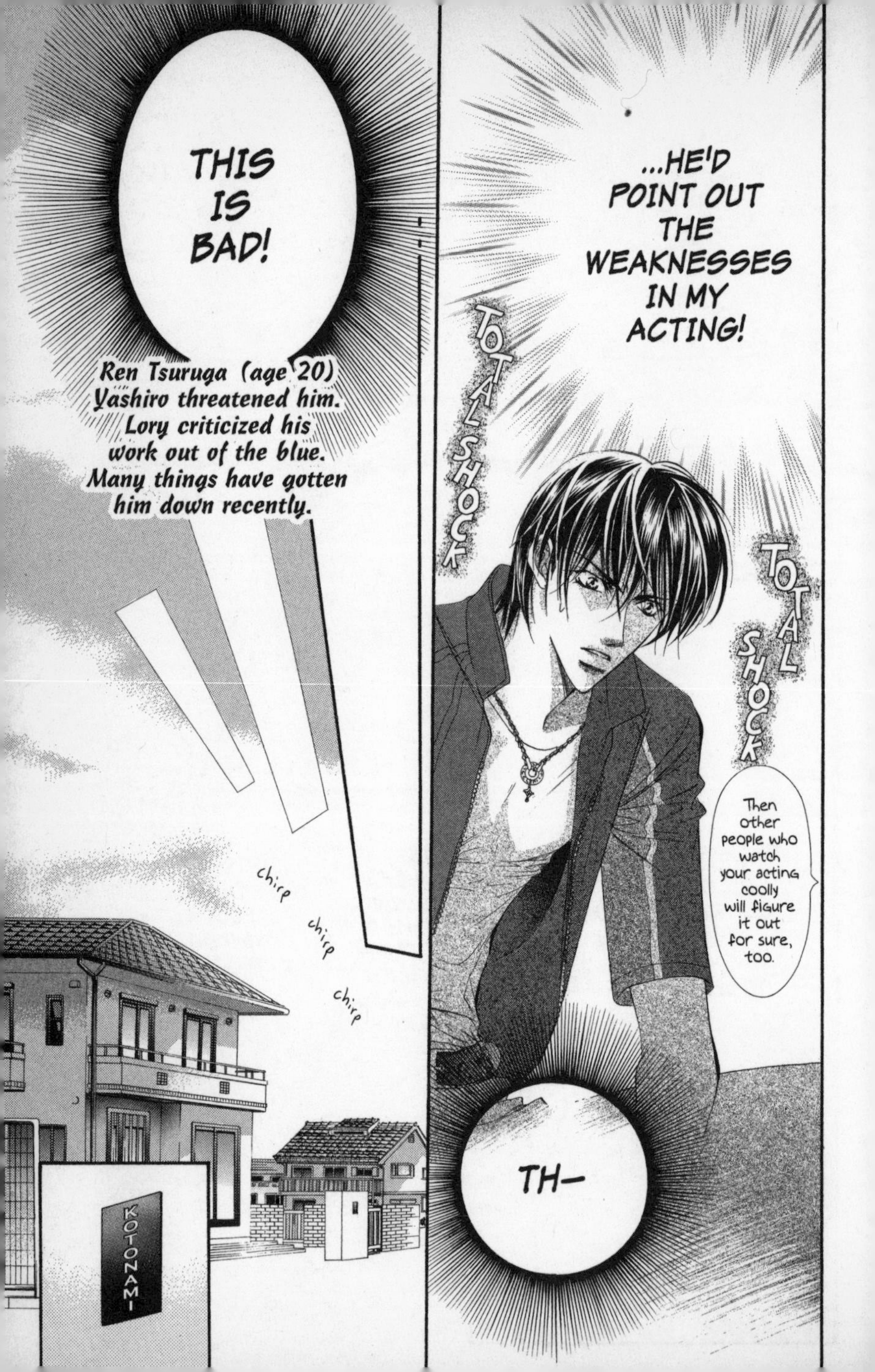
...HE'D POINT OUT THE WEAKNESSES IN MY ACTING!
TOTAL SHOCK
TOTAL SHOCK
Then other people who watch your acting coolly will figure it out for sure, too.
TH-
THIS IS BAD!
Ren Tsuruga (age 20) Yashiro threatened him. Lory criticized his work out of the blue. Many things have gotten him down recently.
chirp
chirp
chirp
KOTONAMI

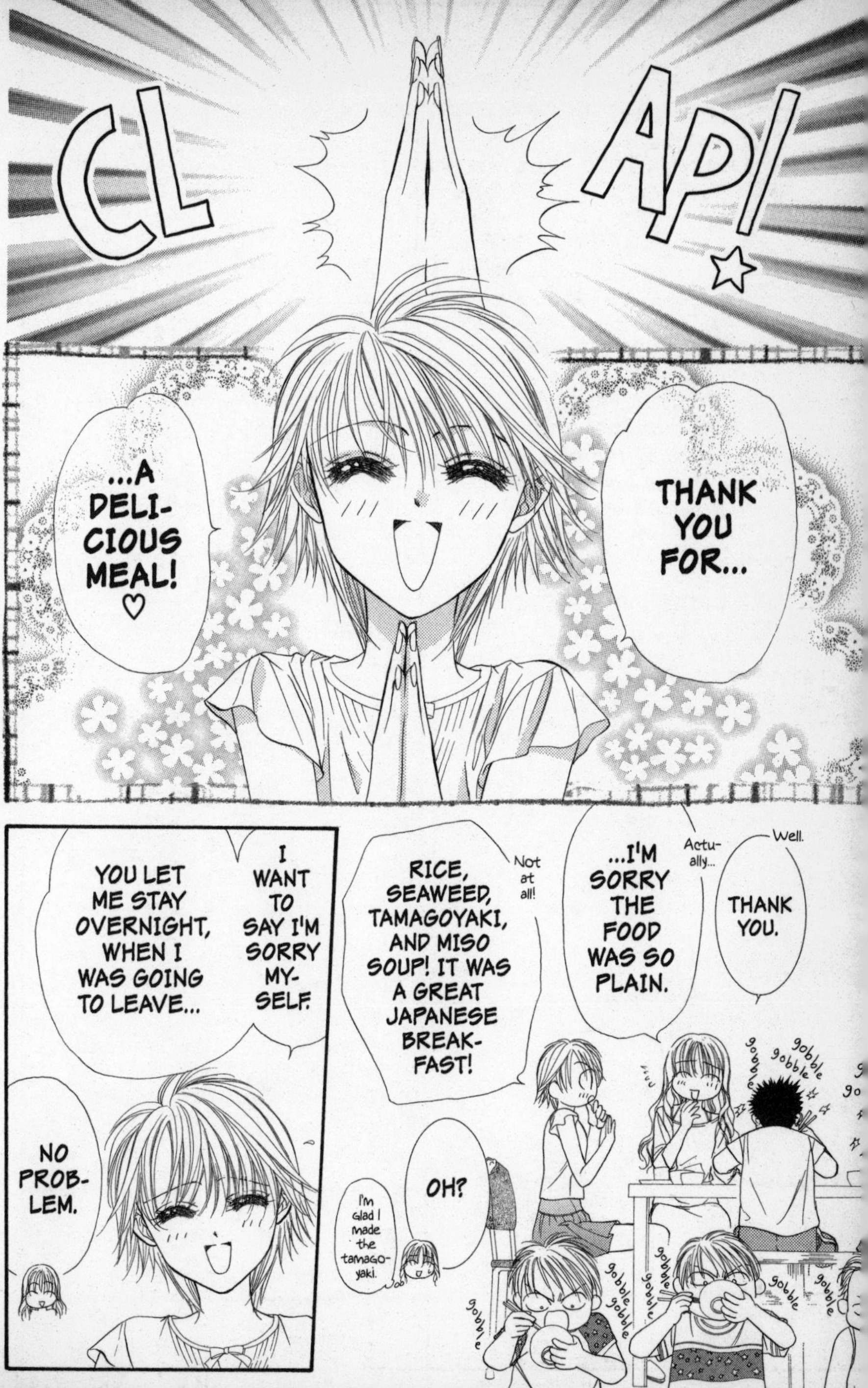
CLAP!
THANK YOU FOR...
...A DELICIOUS MEAL! ♡
Well.
THANK YOU.
Actually...
...I'M SORRY THE FOOD WAS SO PLAIN.
Not at all!
RICE, SEAWEED, TAMAGOYAKI, AND MISO SOUP! IT WAS A GREAT JAPANESE BREAKFAST!
gobble gobble
gobble gobble
gobble gobble
gobble
OH?
I'm Glad I made the tamagoyaki.
I WANT TO SAY I'M SORRY MYSELF.
YOU LET ME STAY OVERNIGHT, WHEN I WAS GOING TO LEAVE...
NO PROBLEM.

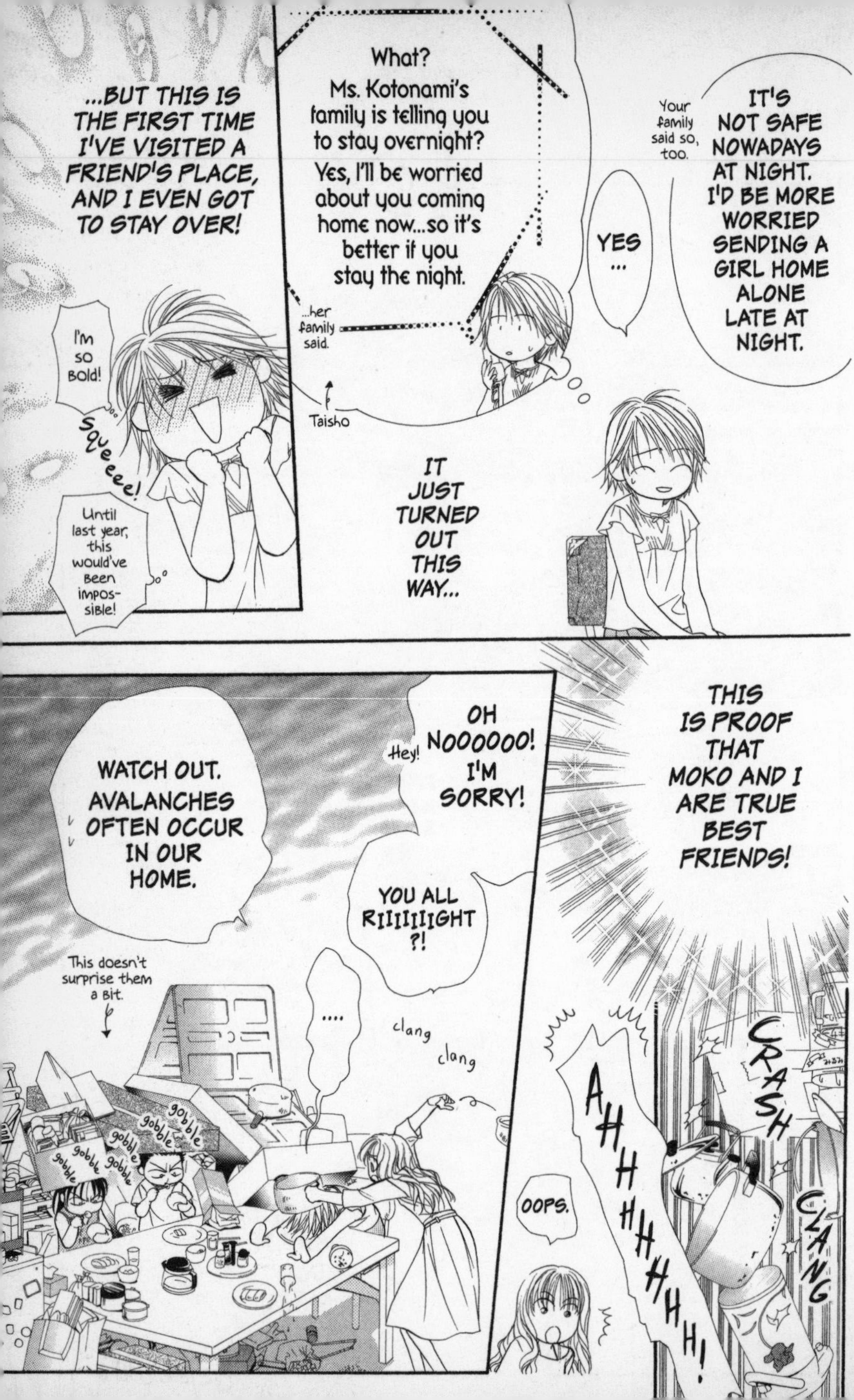
IT'S NOT SAFE NOWADAYS AT NIGHT. I'D BE MORE WORRIED SENDING A GIRL HOME ALONE LATE AT NIGHT.
Your family said so, too.
YES ...
What? Ms. Kotonami's family is telling you to stay overnight? Yes, I'll be worried about you coming home now...so it's better if you stay the night.
...her family said.
Taisho
IT JUST TURNED OUT THIS WAY...
...BUT THIS IS THE FIRST TIME I'VE VISITED A FRIEND'S PLACE, AND I EVEN GOT TO STAY OVER!
Squeeeee!
I'm so Bold!
Until last year, this would've Been impos-sible!
THIS IS PROOF THAT MOKO AND I ARE TRUE BEST FRIENDS!
CRASH
AHHHHHHHH!
CLANG
OOPS.
OH NOOOOOO! I'M SORRY!
Hey!
WATCH OUT. AVALANCHES OFTEN OCCUR IN OUR HOME.
YOU ALL RIIIIIIGHT ?!
....
clang
clang
gobble
gobble
gobble
gobble
gobble
This doesn't surprise them a Bit.

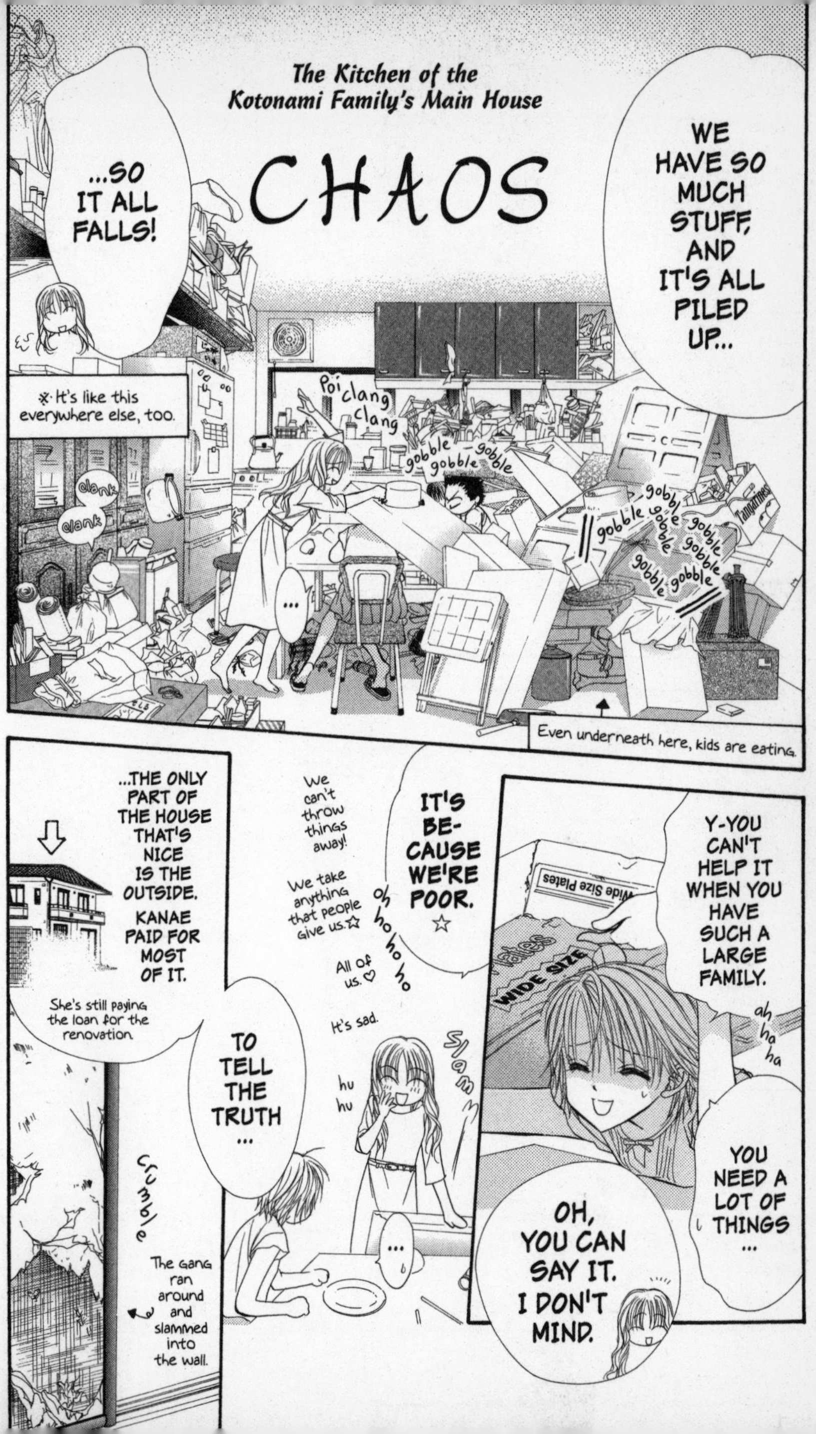

WE HAVE SO MUCH STUFF, AND IT'S ALL PILED UP...
The Kitchen of the Kotonami Family's Main House
CHAOS
...SO IT ALL FALLS!
※ It's like this everywhere else, too.
Poi
clang clang
gobble gobble gobble
gobble gobble gobble gobble gobble gobble gobble gobble
clank clank
...
Even underneath here, kids are eating.
Y-YOU CAN'T HELP IT WHEN YOU HAVE SUCH A LARGE FAMILY.
ah ha ha
YOU NEED A LOT OF THINGS ...
OH, YOU CAN SAY IT. I DON'T MIND.
IT'S BE-CAUSE WE'RE POOR. ☆
oh ho ho ho
We can't throw things away!
We take anything that people give us.☆
All of us.♡
It's sad.
Slam
hu hu
TO TELL THE TRUTH ...
...
...THE ONLY PART OF THE HOUSE THAT'S NICE IS THE OUTSIDE. KANAE PAID FOR MOST OF IT.
She's still paying the loan for the renovation.
crumble
The gang ran around and slammed into the wall.

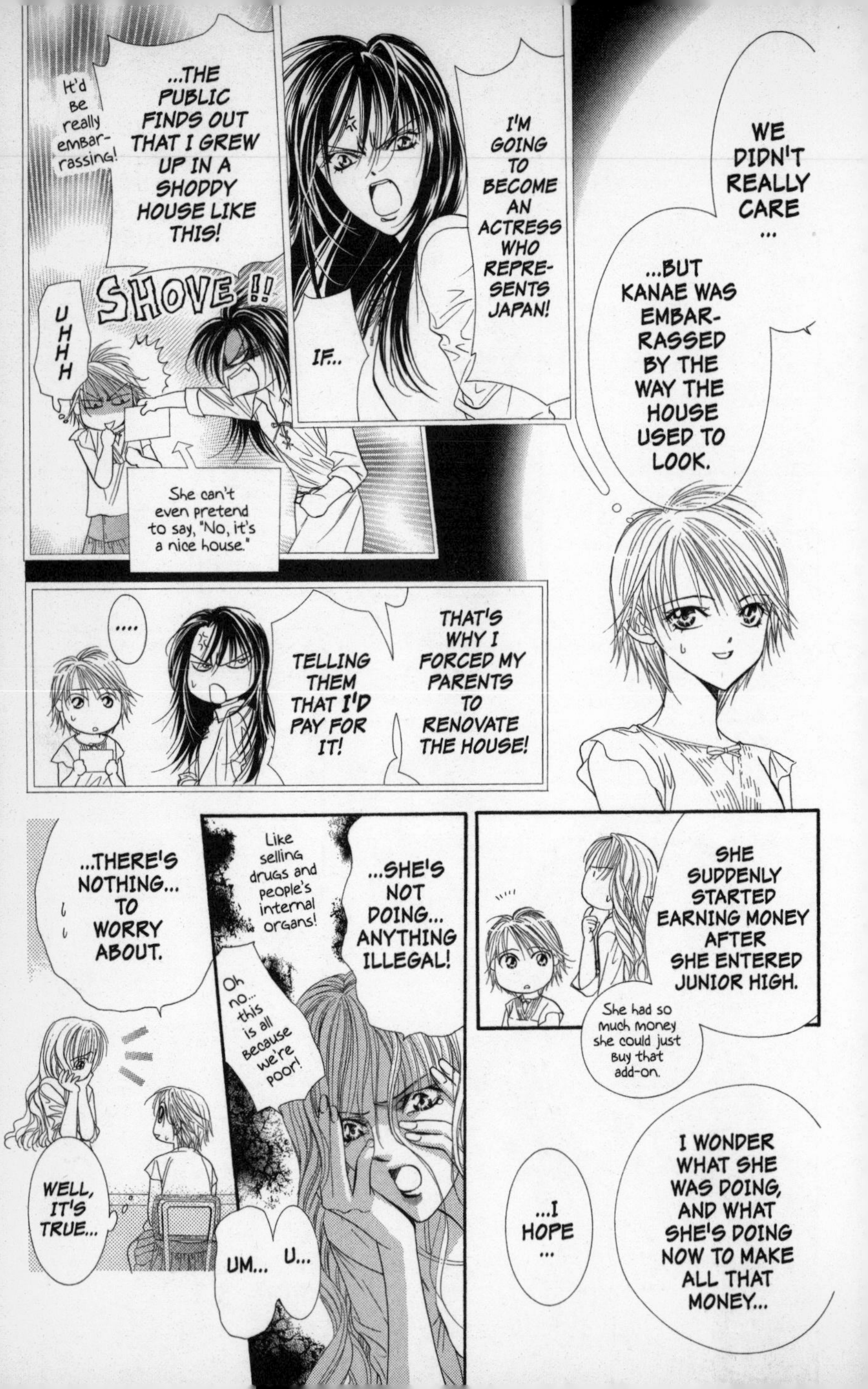
WE DIDN'T REALLY CARE ...
...BUT KANAE WAS EMBARRASSED BY THE WAY THE HOUSE USED TO LOOK.
I'M GOING TO BECOME AN ACTRESS WHO REPRESENTS JAPAN!
IF...
...THE PUBLIC FINDS OUT THAT I GREW UP IN A SHODDY HOUSE LIKE THIS!
It'd be really embarrassing!
SHOVE!!
UHHH
She can't even pretend to say, "No, it's a nice house."
THAT'S WHY I FORCED MY PARENTS TO RENOVATE THE HOUSE!
TELLING THEM THAT I'D PAY FOR IT!
....
SHE SUDDENLY STARTED EARNING MONEY AFTER SHE ENTERED JUNIOR HIGH.
She had so much money she could just buy that add-on.
I WONDER WHAT SHE WAS DOING, AND WHAT SHE'S DOING NOW TO MAKE ALL THAT MONEY...
...I HOPE ...
...SHE'S NOT DOING... ANYTHING ILLEGAL!
Like selling drugs and people's internal organs!
Oh no... this is all because we're poor!
UM... U...
...THERE'S NOTHING... TO WORRY ABOUT.
WELL, IT'S TRUE...

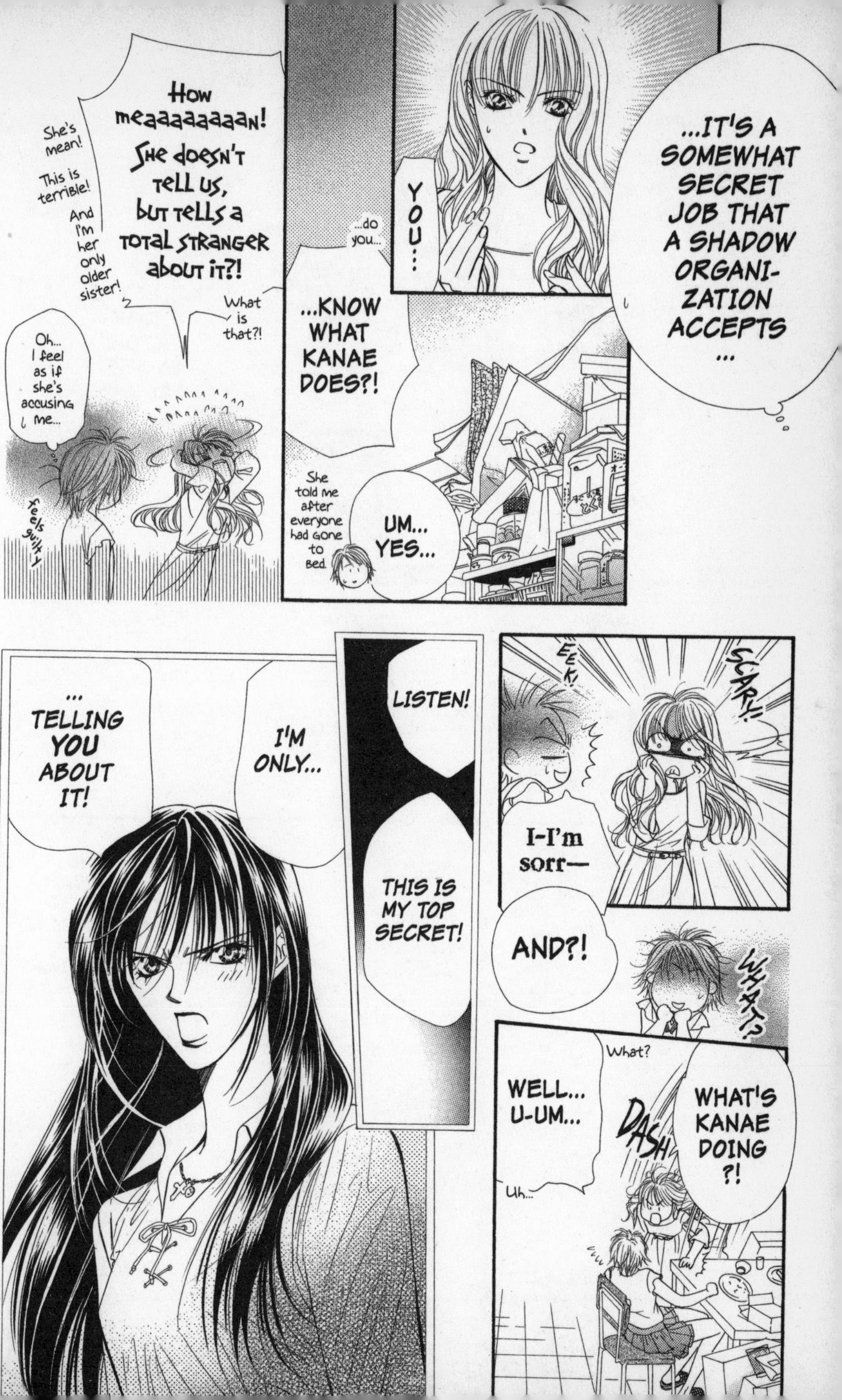
...IT'S A SOMEWHAT SECRET JOB THAT A SHADOW ORGANIZATION ACCEPTS...
YOU...
...do you...
...KNOW WHAT KANAE DOES?!
UM... YES...
She told me after everyone had gone to bed.
How meaaaaaaaaan! She doesn't tell us, but tells a total stranger about it?!
What is that?!
She's mean! This is terrible! And I'm her only older sister!
Oh... I feel as if she's accusing me...
feels guilty
SCARY!
EEK!
I-I'm sorr—
AND?!
WHAT?!
What?
WHAT'S KANAE DOING?!
WELL... U-UM...
DASH
Uh...
LISTEN!
THIS IS MY TOP SECRET!
I'M ONLY...
...TELLING YOU ABOUT IT!

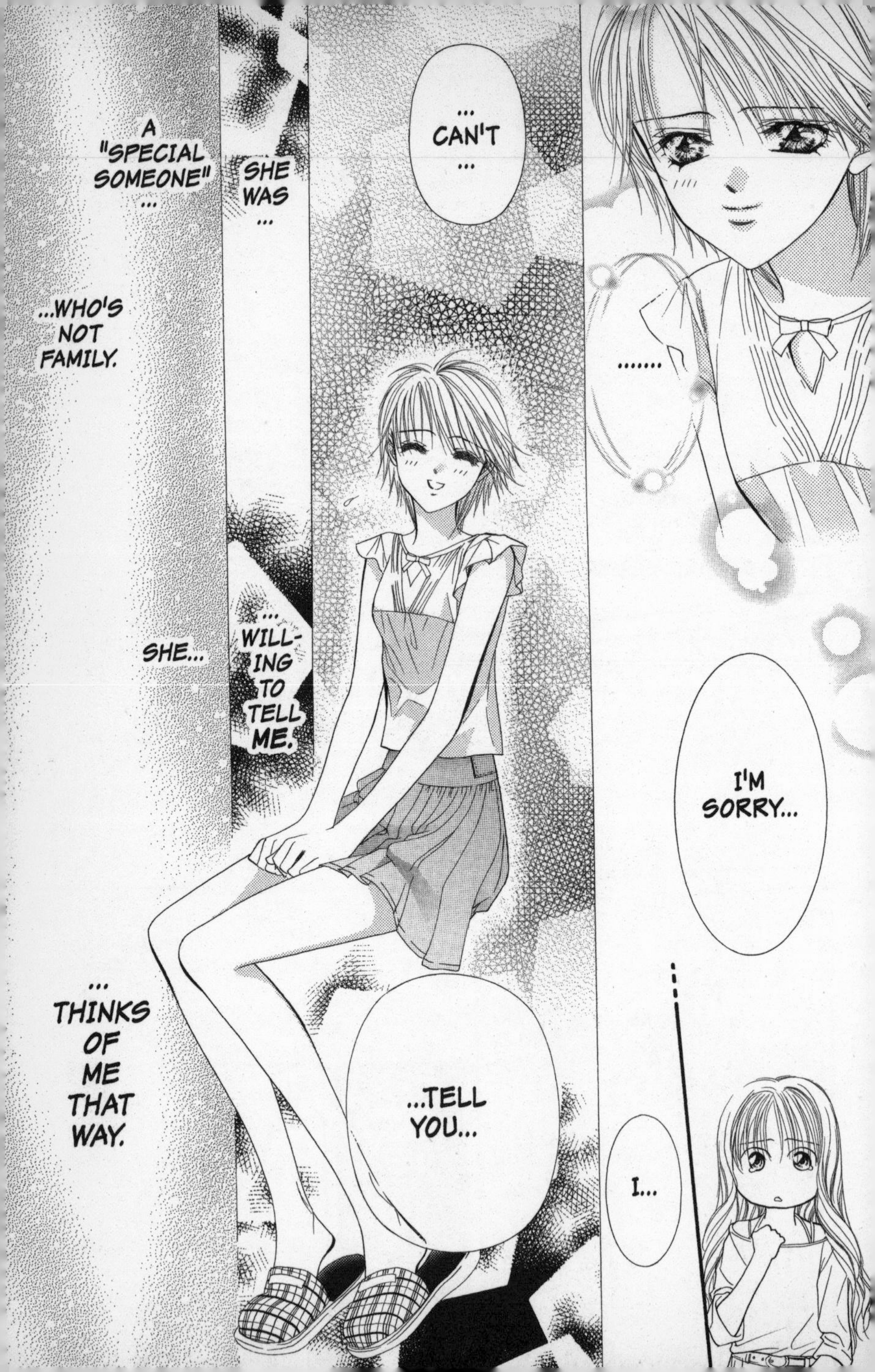

......
I'M SORRY...
I...
...CAN'T...
...TELL YOU...
SHE WAS...
...WILLING TO TELL ME.
A "SPECIAL SOMEONE"...
...WHO'S NOT FAMILY.
SHE...
...THINKS OF ME THAT WAY.

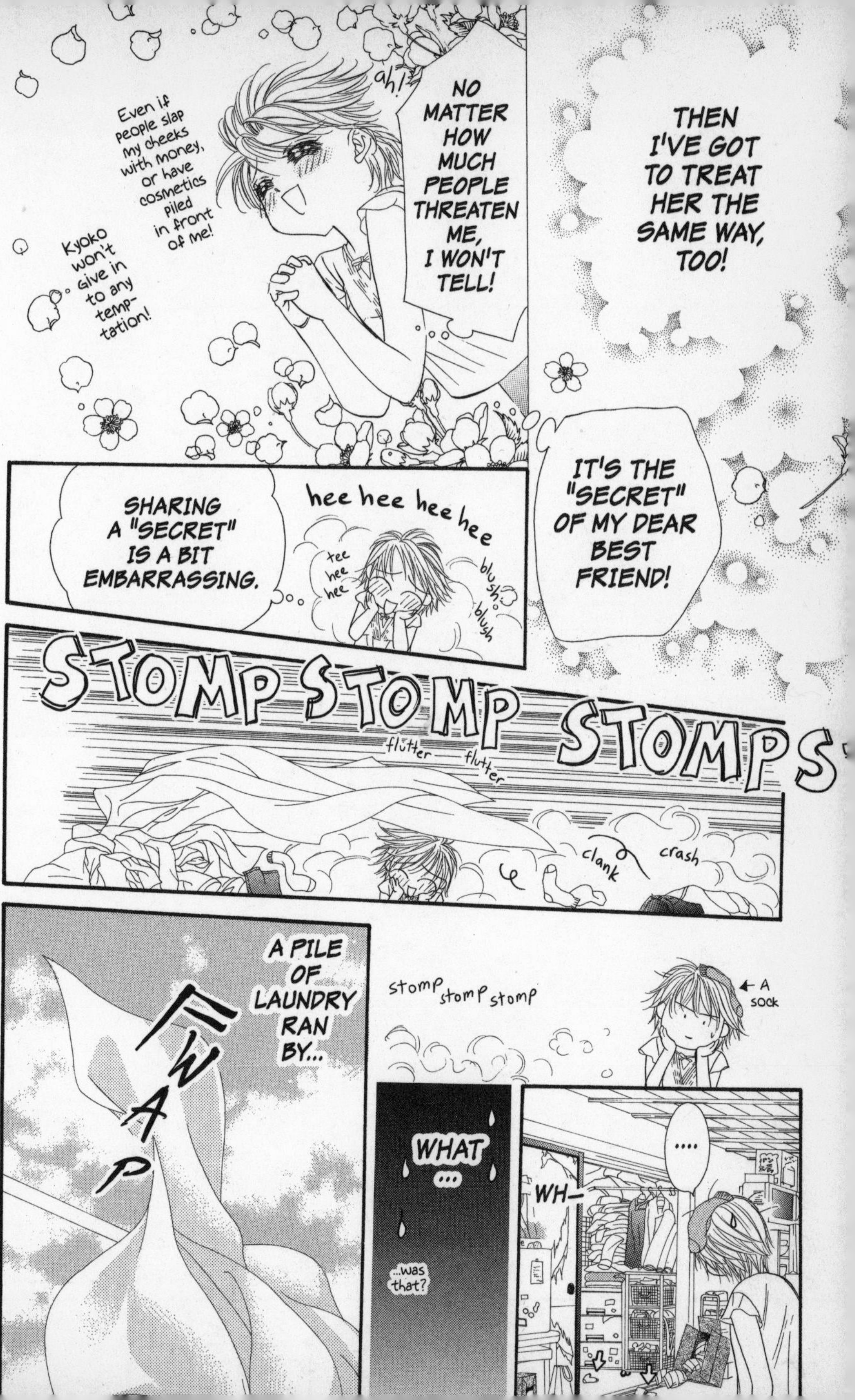

THEN I'VE GOT TO TREAT HER THE SAME WAY, TOO!
IT'S THE "SECRET" OF MY DEAR BEST FRIEND!
ah!
NO MATTER HOW MUCH PEOPLE THREATEN ME, I WON'T TELL!
Even if people slap my cheeks with money, or have cosmetics piled in front of me!
Kyoko won't give in to any temptation!
hee hee hee hee
tee hee hee
blush blush
SHARING A "SECRET" IS A BIT EMBARRASSING.
STOMP STOMP STOMPS
flutter flutter
clank
crash
stomp stomp stomp
← A sock
....
WH-
WHAT ...
...was that?
A PILE OF LAUNDRY RAN BY...
FWAP

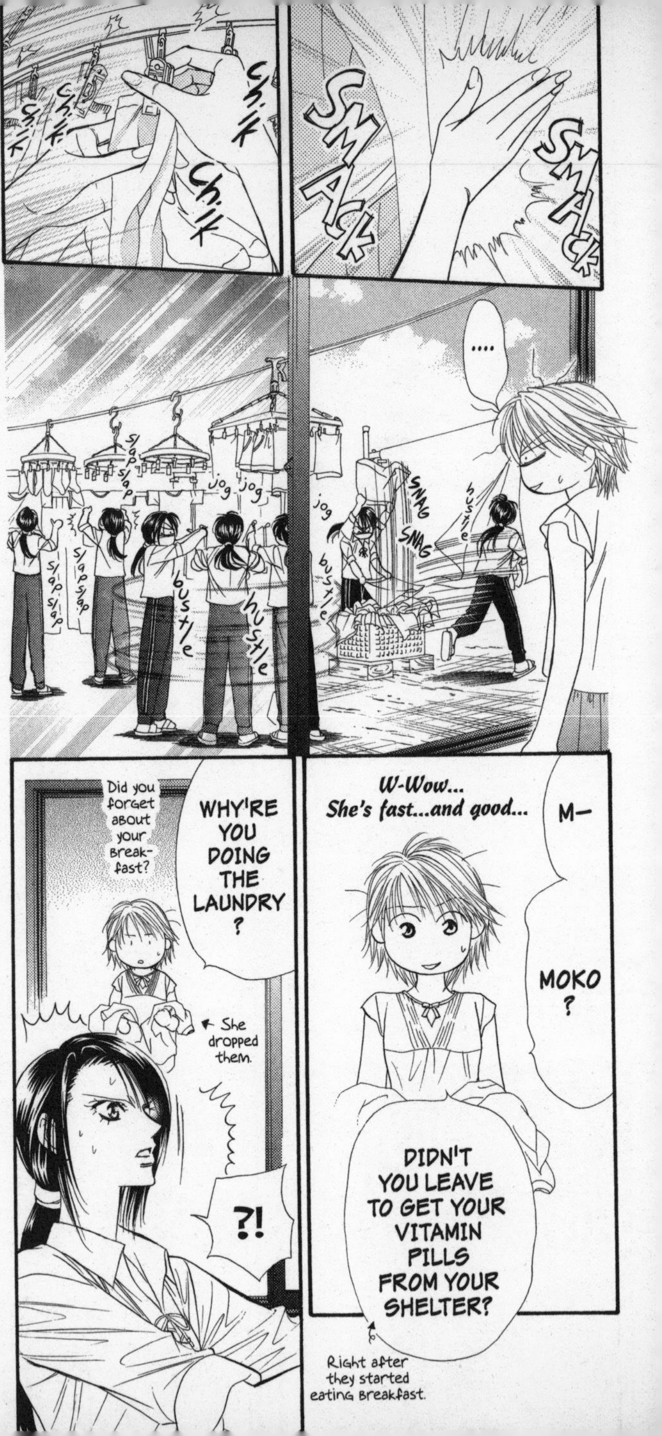
SMACK
SMACK
chik
chik
chik
chik
chik
....
SNAG
SNAG
hustle
bustle
bustle
jog
slap
slap
slap
jog
jog
slap slap
slap slap
slap slap
bustle
hustle
W-Wow... She's fast...and good...
M—
MOKO?
DIDN'T YOU LEAVE TO GET YOUR VITAMIN PILLS FROM YOUR SHELTER?
Right after they started eating breakfast.
WHY'RE YOU DOING THE LAUNDRY?
Did you forget about your breakfast?
She dropped them.
?!

Hio Uesugi

The last time, I wrote that I would just draw stuff that come out naturally...But I'd forgotten... that there was a chapter where he appears... (And the reason is the same one I mentioned in the Greeting this time... I like having the Hio+Kanae pair and the Hio+Kyoko pair interacting quite a bit, so I'd like to have him appear again if possible...

The hawk cowers at the chicken...

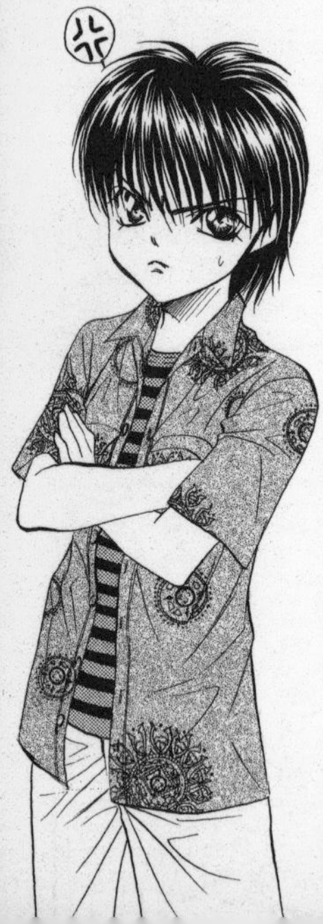

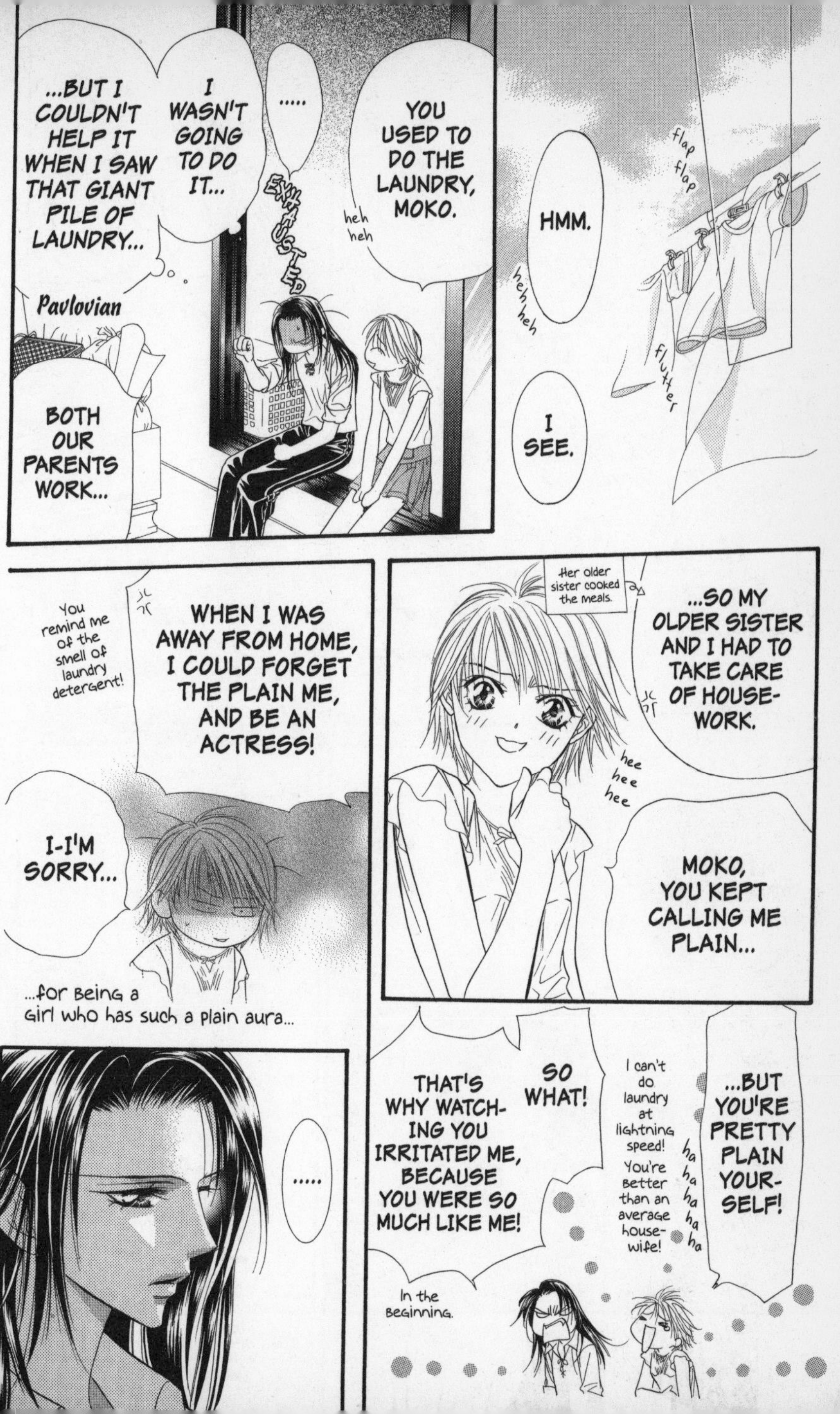
flap flap
HMM.
heh heh
flutter
I SEE.
YOU USED TO DO THE LAUNDRY, MOKO.
heh heh
.....
EXHAUSTED
I WASN'T GOING TO DO IT...
...BUT I COULDN'T HELP IT WHEN I SAW THAT GIANT PILE OF LAUNDRY...
Pavlovian
BOTH OUR PARENTS WORK...
Her older sister cooked the meals.
...SO MY OLDER SISTER AND I HAD TO TAKE CARE OF HOUSE-WORK.
hee hee hee
MOKO, YOU KEPT CALLING ME PLAIN...
WHEN I WAS AWAY FROM HOME, I COULD FORGET THE PLAIN ME, AND BE AN ACTRESS!
You remind me of the smell of laundry detergent!
I-I'M SORRY...
...for being a girl who has such a plain aura...
...BUT YOU'RE PRETTY PLAIN YOUR-SELF!
ha ha ha ha ha ha
I can't do laundry at lightning speed!
You're better than an average house-wife!
SO WHAT!
THAT'S WHY WATCH-ING YOU IRRITATED ME, BECAUSE YOU WERE SO MUCH LIKE ME!
In the beginning.
.....

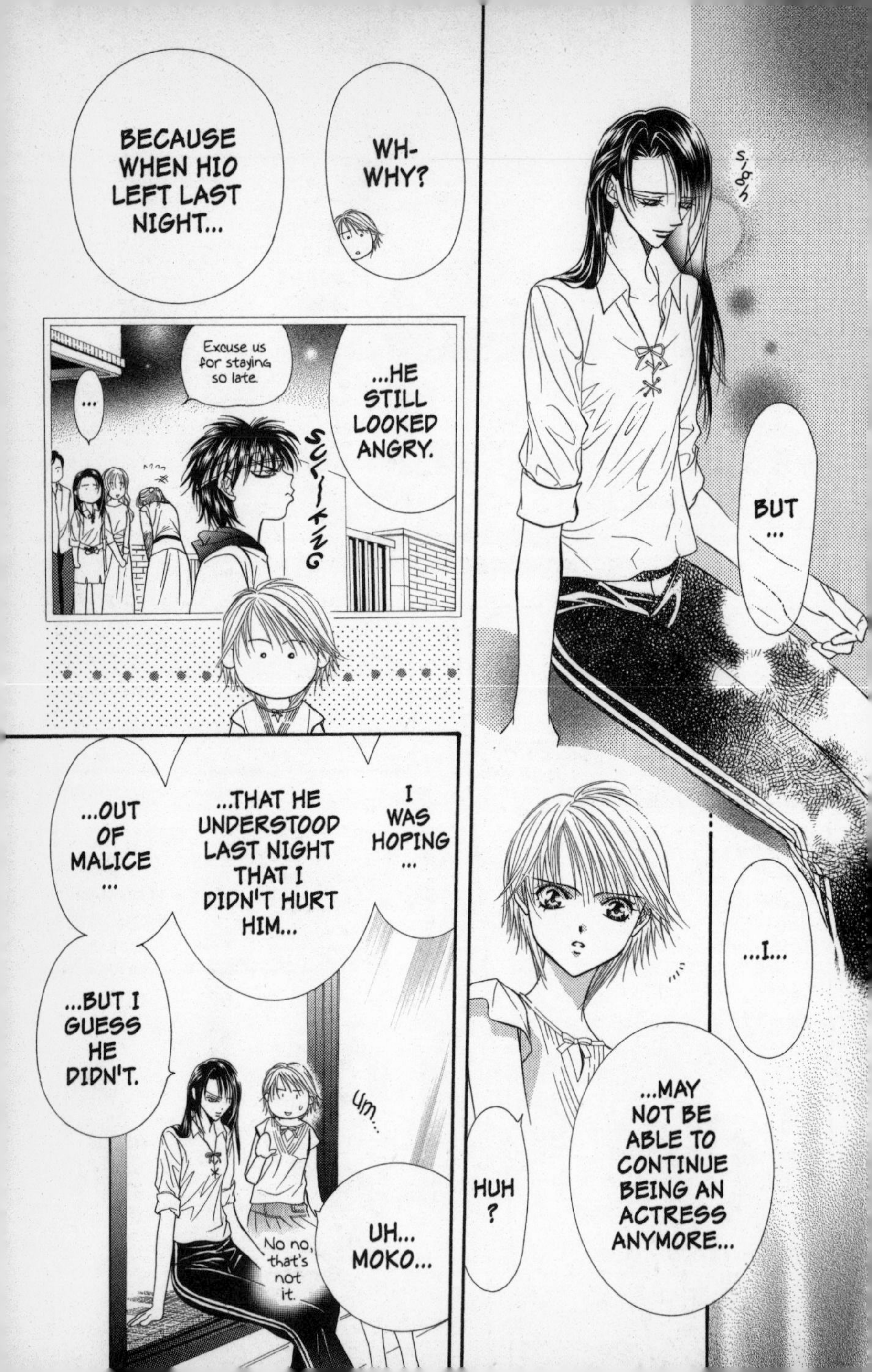
sigh
BUT ...
...I...
...MAY NOT BE ABLE TO CONTINUE BEING AN ACTRESS ANYMORE...
HUH ?
WH- WHY?
BECAUSE WHEN HIO LEFT LAST NIGHT...
...HE STILL LOOKED ANGRY.
Excuse us for staying so late.
...
SULKING
I WAS HOPING ...
...THAT HE UNDERSTOOD LAST NIGHT THAT I DIDN'T HURT HIM...
...OUT OF MALICE ...
...BUT I GUESS HE DIDN'T.
Um...
UH... MOKO...
No no, that's not it.

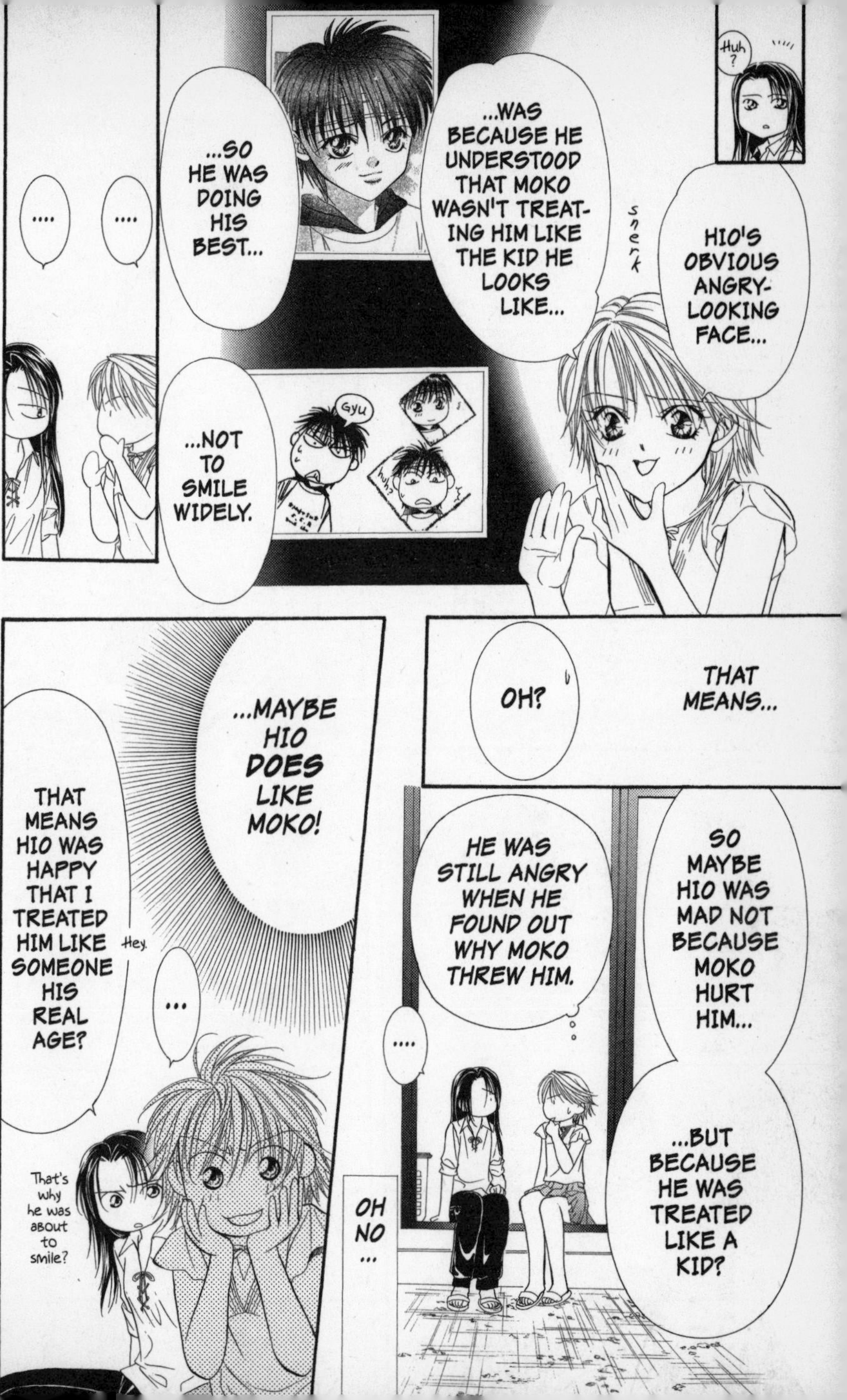
Huh?
HIO'S OBVIOUS ANGRY-LOOKING FACE...
snerk
...WAS BECAUSE HE UNDERSTOOD THAT MOKO WASN'T TREATING HIM LIKE THE KID HE LOOKS LIKE...
...SO HE WAS DOING HIS BEST...
...NOT TO SMILE WIDELY.
Gyu
huh?
....
....
THAT MEANS...
OH?
SO MAYBE HIO WAS MAD NOT BECAUSE MOKO HURT HIM...
...BUT BECAUSE HE WAS TREATED LIKE A KID?
HE WAS STILL ANGRY WHEN HE FOUND OUT WHY MOKO THREW HIM.
....
OH NO ...
...MAYBE HIO DOES LIKE MOKO!
THAT MEANS HIO WAS HAPPY THAT I TREATED HIM LIKE SOMEONE HIS REAL AGE?
Hey.
...
That's why he was about to smile?

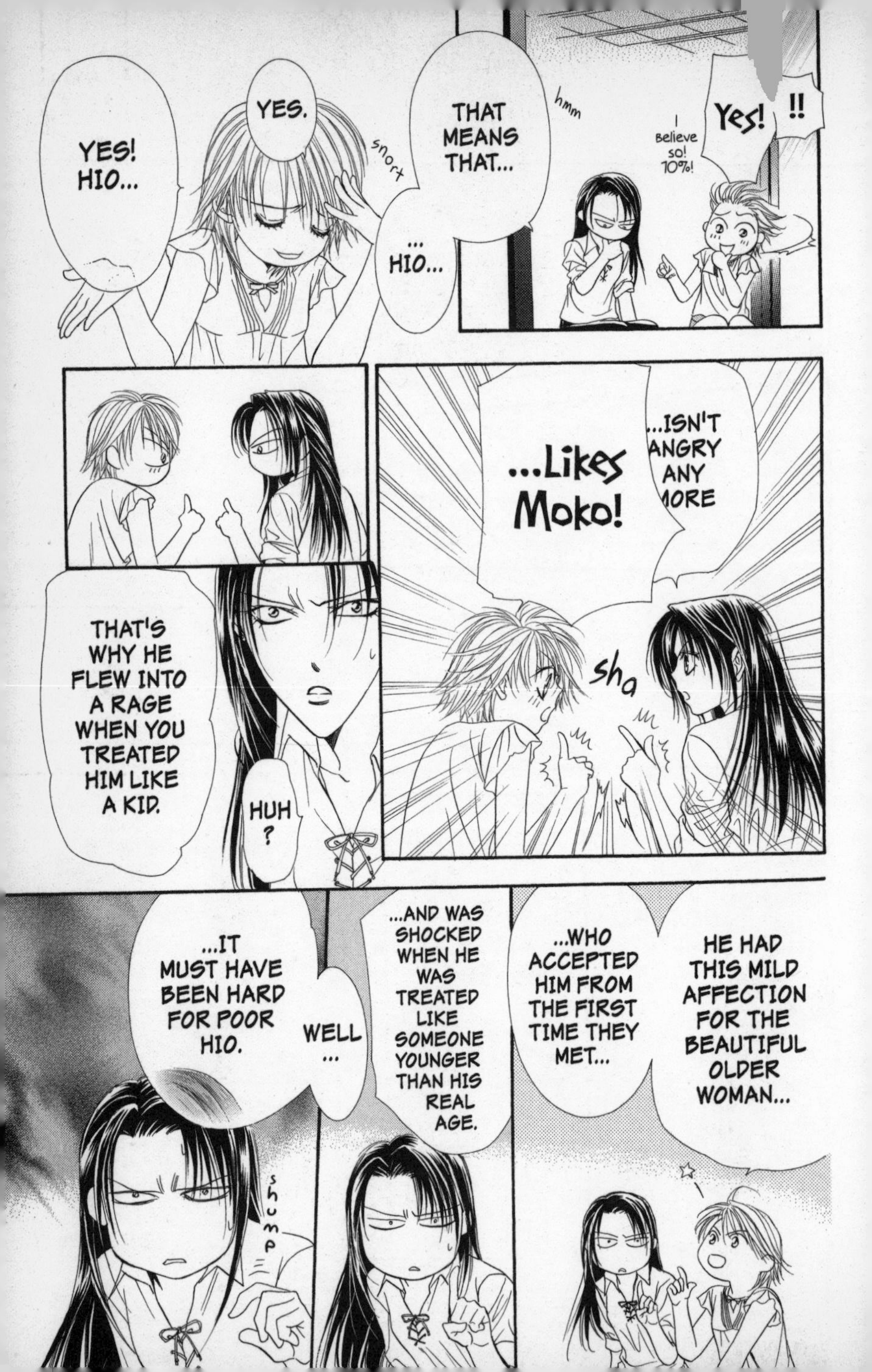

Yes! !!
I Believe so! 70%!
hmm
THAT MEANS THAT...
... HIO...
snort
YES.
YES! HIO...
...ISN'T ANGRY ANY MORE
...Likes Moko!
sha
HUH?
THAT'S WHY HE FLEW INTO A RAGE WHEN YOU TREATED HIM LIKE A KID.
HE HAD THIS MILD AFFECTION FOR THE BEAUTIFUL OLDER WOMAN...
...WHO ACCEPTED HIM FROM THE FIRST TIME THEY MET...
...AND WAS SHOCKED WHEN HE WAS TREATED LIKE SOMEONE YOUNGER THAN HIS REAL AGE.
WELL ...
...IT MUST HAVE BEEN HARD FOR POOR HIO.
shump

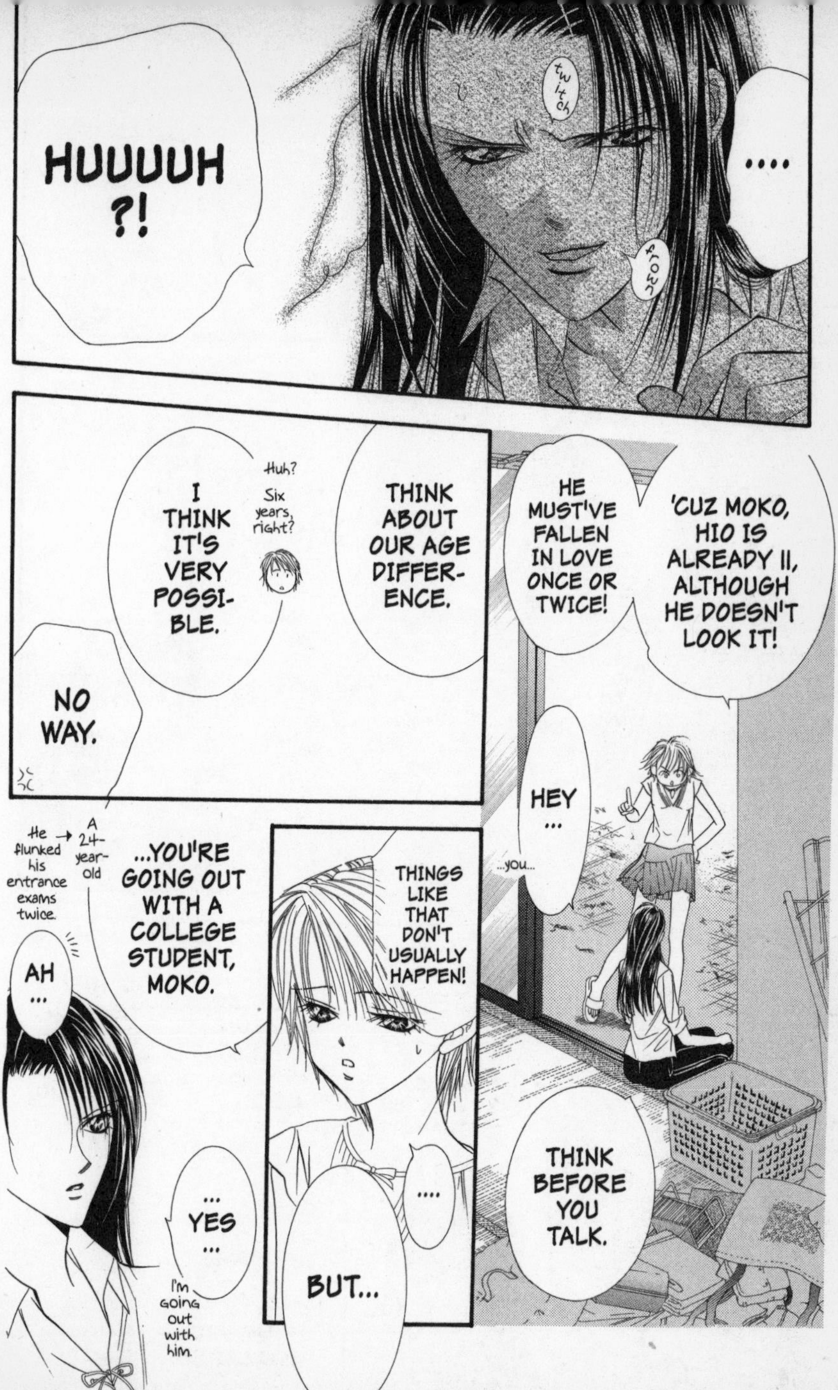
....
twitch
frown
HUUUUH ?!
'CUZ MOKO, HIO IS ALREADY 11, ALTHOUGH HE DOESN'T LOOK IT!
HE MUST'VE FALLEN IN LOVE ONCE OR TWICE!
HEY ...
...you...
THINK BEFORE YOU TALK.
THINK ABOUT OUR AGE DIFFERENCE.
Huh? Six years, right?
I THINK IT'S VERY POSSIBLE.
NO WAY.
THINGS LIKE THAT DON'T USUALLY HAPPEN!
....
BUT...
...YOU'RE GOING OUT WITH A COLLEGE STUDENT, MOKO.
A 24-year-old
He flunked his entrance exams twice.
AH ...
... YES ...
I'm going out with him.

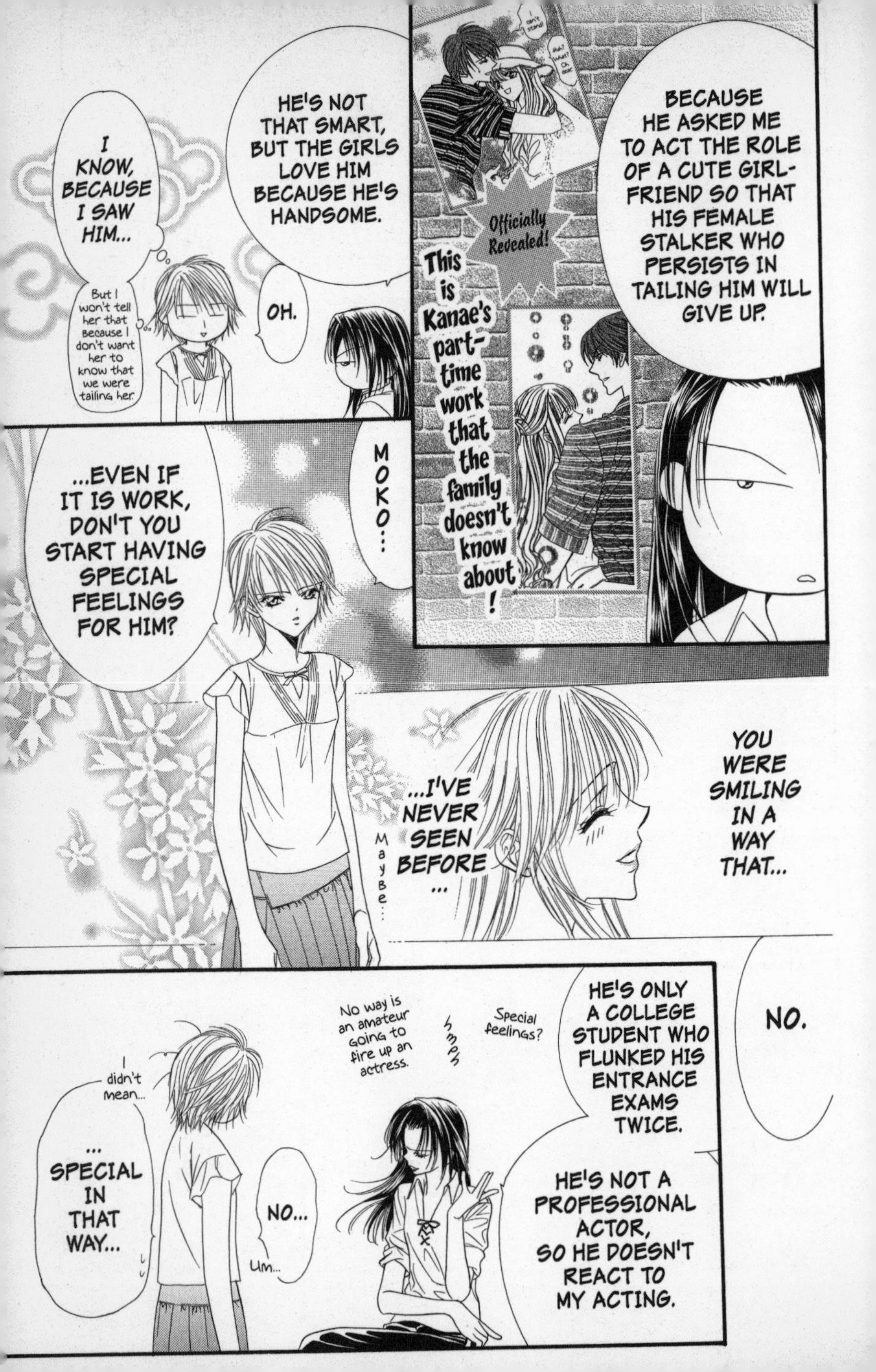
BECAUSE HE ASKED ME TO ACT THE ROLE OF A CUTE GIRL-FRIEND SO THAT HIS FEMALE STALKER WHO PERSISTS IN TAILING HIM WILL GIVE UP.
I can't stand!
Huh? What? Oh dear.
Officially Revealed!
This is Kanae's part-time work that the family doesn't know about!
HE'S NOT THAT SMART, BUT THE GIRLS LOVE HIM BECAUSE HE'S HANDSOME.
OH.
I KNOW, BECAUSE I SAW HIM...
But I won't tell her that because I don't want her to know that we were tailing her.
MOKO...
...EVEN IF IT IS WORK, DON'T YOU START HAVING SPECIAL FEELINGS FOR HIM?
YOU WERE SMILING IN A WAY THAT...
...I'VE NEVER SEEN BEFORE...
Maybe...
NO.
HE'S ONLY A COLLEGE STUDENT WHO FLUNKED HIS ENTRANCE EXAMS TWICE.
HE'S NOT A PROFESSIONAL ACTOR, SO HE DOESN'T REACT TO MY ACTING.
Special feelings?
hmph
No way is an amateur going to fire up an actress.
NO...
Um...
I didn't mean...
...SPECIAL IN THAT WAY...

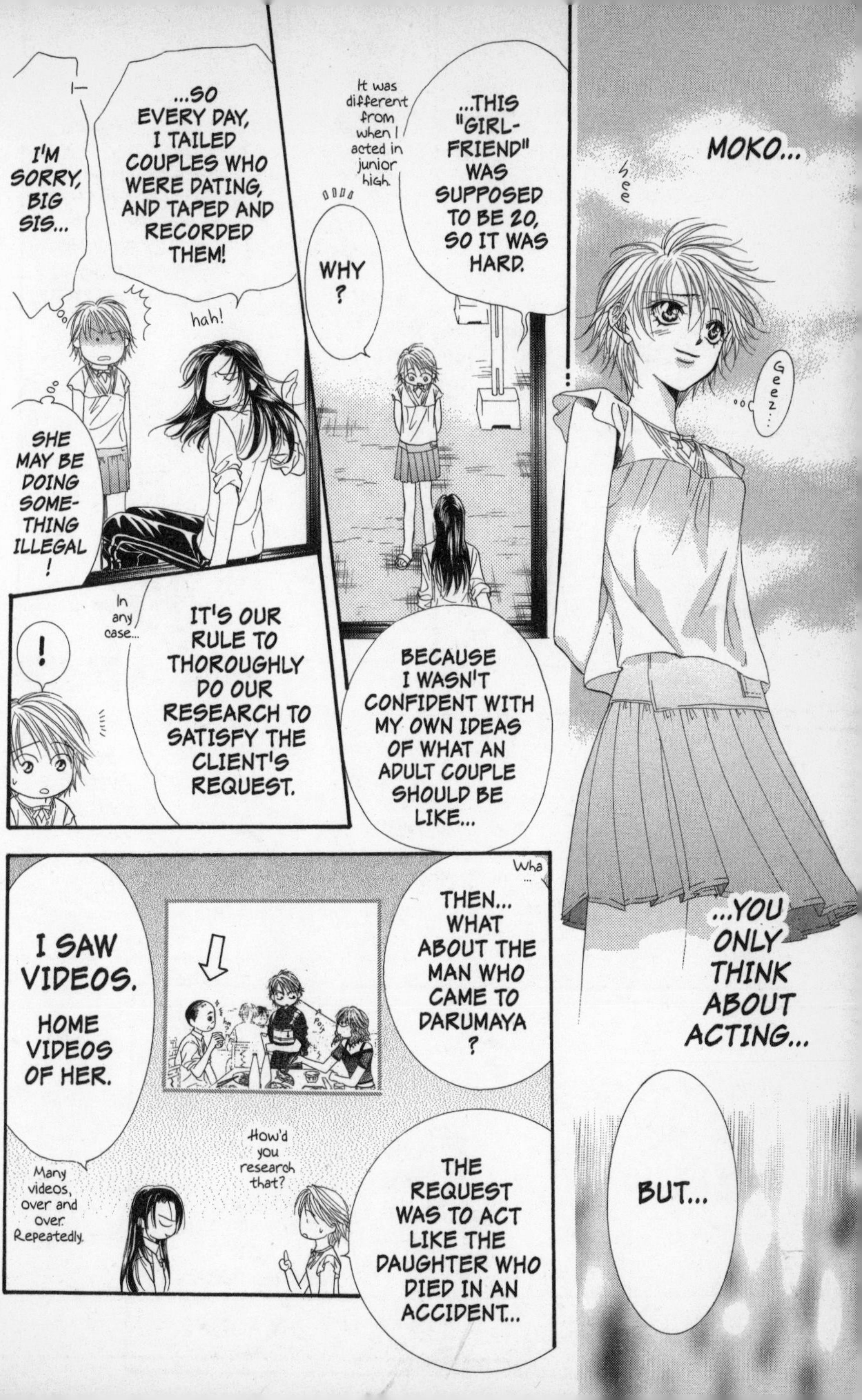
MOKO...
hee
Geez...
...YOU ONLY THINK ABOUT ACTING...
BUT...
It was different from when I acted in junior high.
...THIS "GIRL-FRIEND" WAS SUPPOSED TO BE 20, SO IT WAS HARD.
WHY?
BECAUSE I WASN'T CONFIDENT WITH MY OWN IDEAS OF WHAT AN ADULT COUPLE SHOULD BE LIKE...
...SO EVERY DAY, I TAILED COUPLES WHO WERE DATING, AND TAPED AND RECORDED THEM!
I'M SORRY, BIG SIS...
hah!
SHE MAY BE DOING SOME-THING ILLEGAL!
In any case...
IT'S OUR RULE TO THOROUGHLY DO OUR RESEARCH TO SATISFY THE CLIENT'S REQUEST.
!
Wha...
THEN... WHAT ABOUT THE MAN WHO CAME TO DARUMAYA?
THE REQUEST WAS TO ACT LIKE THE DAUGHTER WHO DIED IN AN ACCIDENT...
How'd you research that?
I SAW VIDEOS.
HOME VIDEOS OF HER.
Many videos, over and over. Repeatedly.

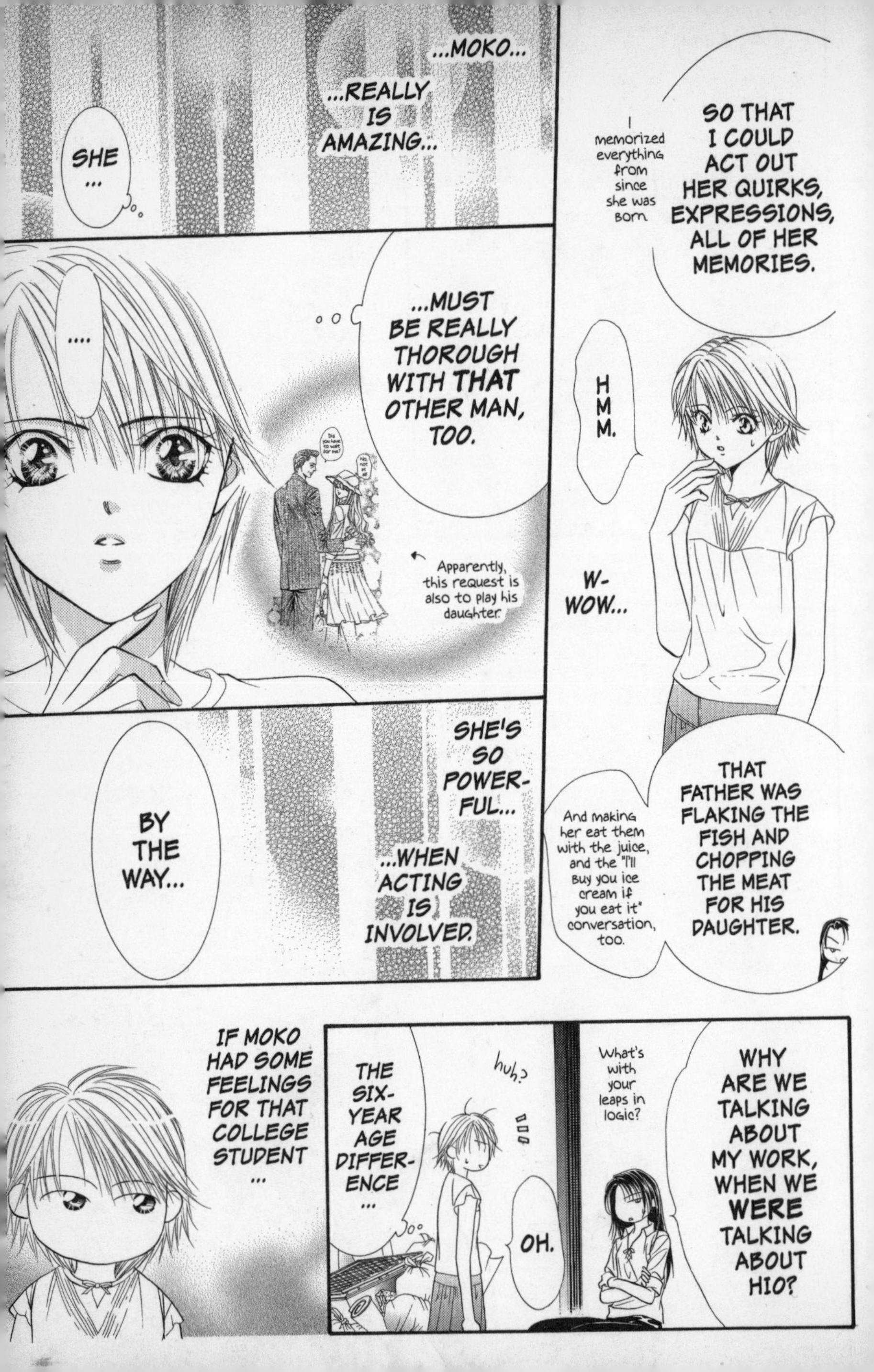
SO THAT I COULD ACT OUT HER QUIRKS, EXPRESSIONS, ALL OF HER MEMORIES.
I memorized everything from since she was born.
HMM.
W-WOW...
THAT FATHER WAS FLAKING THE FISH AND CHOPPING THE MEAT FOR HIS DAUGHTER.
And making her eat them with the juice, and the "I'll buy you ice cream if you eat it" conversation, too.
...MOKO...
...REALLY IS AMAZING...
SHE ...
...MUST BE REALLY THOROUGH WITH THAT OTHER MAN, TOO.
....
Apparently, this request is also to play his daughter.
SHE'S SO POWERFUL...
...WHEN ACTING IS INVOLVED.
BY THE WAY...
WHY ARE WE TALKING ABOUT MY WORK, WHEN WE WERE TALKING ABOUT HIO?
What's with your leaps in logic?
OH.
huh?
THE SIX-YEAR AGE DIFFERENCE ...
IF MOKO HAD SOME FEELINGS FOR THAT COLLEGE STUDENT ...

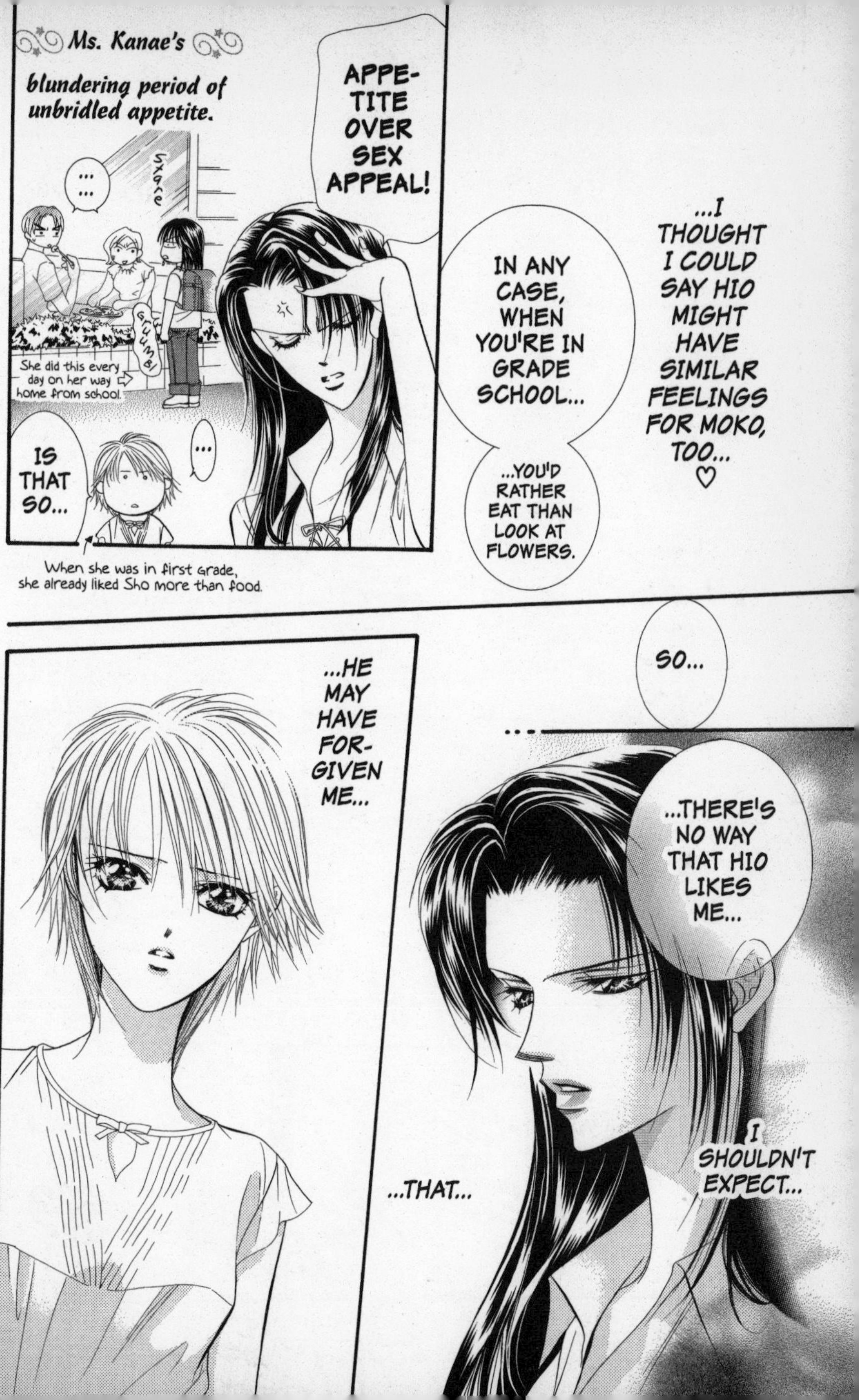

...I THOUGHT I COULD SAY HIO MIGHT HAVE SIMILAR FEELINGS FOR MOKO, TOO... ♡
IN ANY CASE, WHEN YOU'RE IN GRADE SCHOOL...
...YOU'D RATHER EAT THAN LOOK AT FLOWERS.
APPE-TITE OVER SEX APPEAL!
Ms. Kanae's blundering period of unbridled appetite.
...
...
Stare
GRUUMB!
She did this every day on her way home from school.
IS THAT SO...
...
When she was in first grade, she already liked Sho more than food.
SO...
...THERE'S NO WAY THAT HIO LIKES ME...
I SHOULDN'T EXPECT...
...THAT...
...HE MAY HAVE FOR-GIVEN ME...

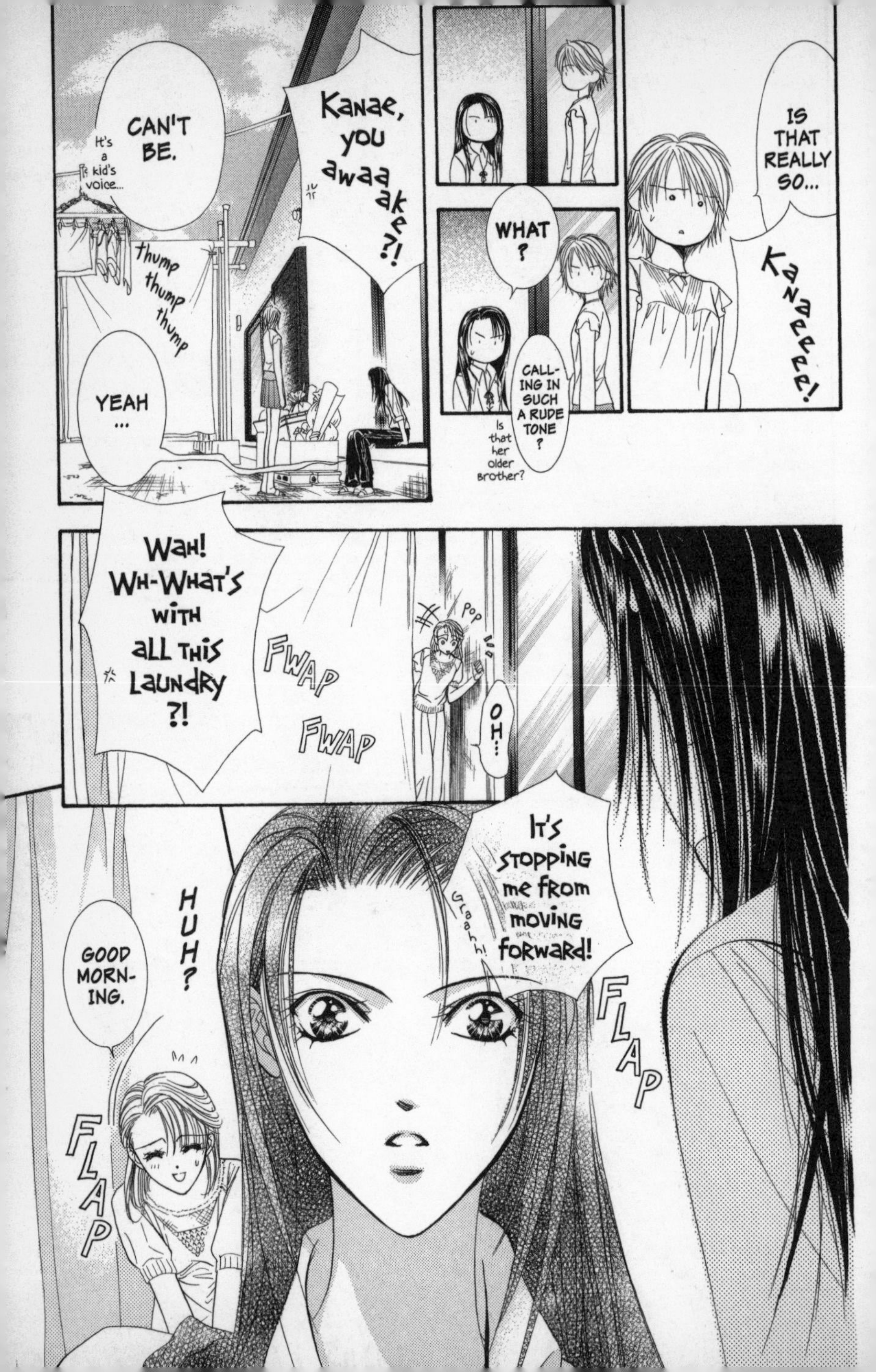

IS THAT REALLY SO...
Kanaeee!
WHAT?
CALLING IN SUCH A RUDE TONE?
Is that her older brother?
Kanae, you awaaake?!
CAN'T BE.
It's a kid's voice...
thump thump thump
YEAH...
pop
OH...
FWAP
FWAP
Wah! Wh-What's with all this laundry?!
It's stopping me from moving forward!
Graahh!
FLAP
HUH?
GOOD MORNING.
FLAP

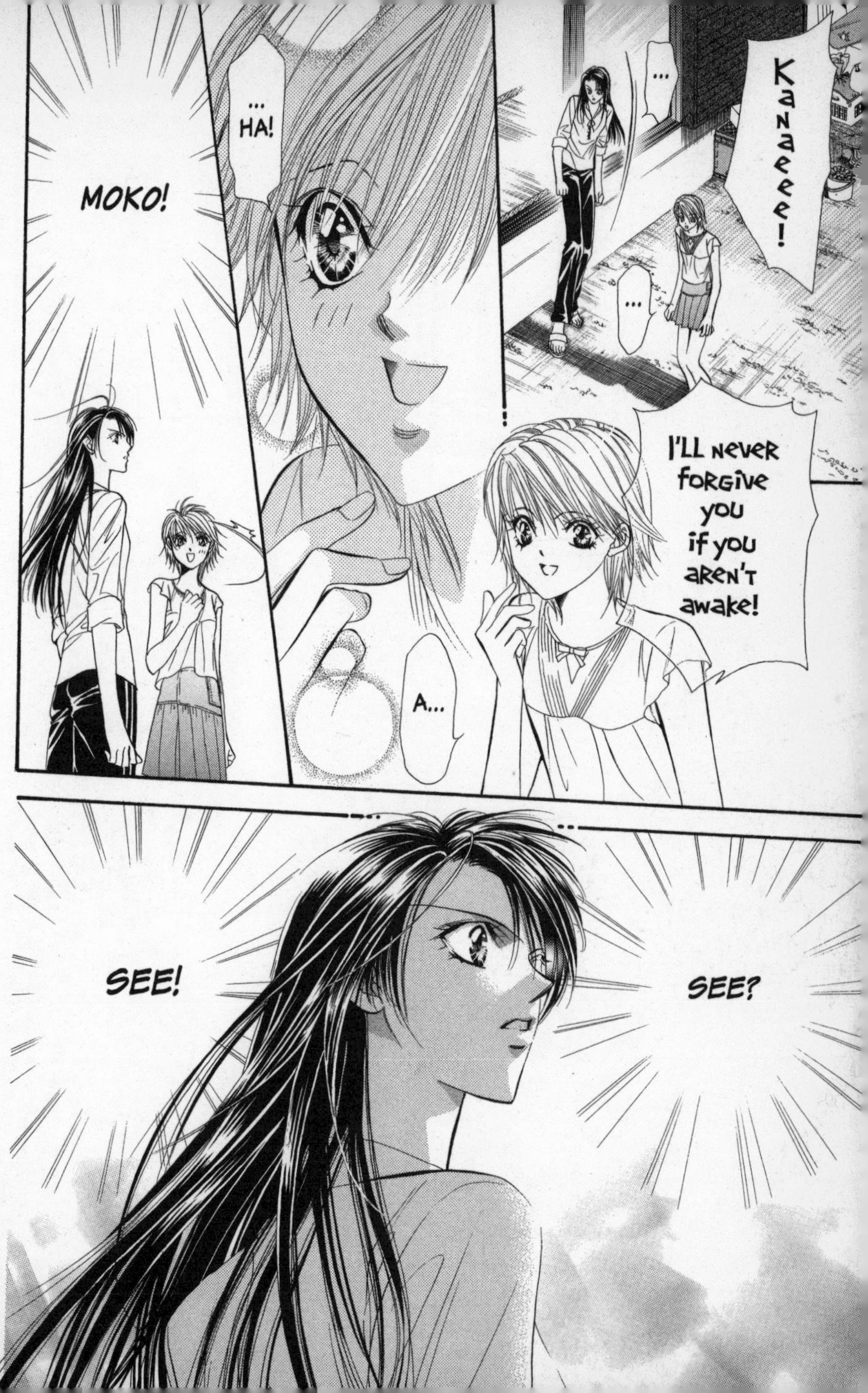
Kanaeee!
...
...
I'll never forgive you if you aren't awake!
A...
...HA!
MOKO!
SEE?
SEE!

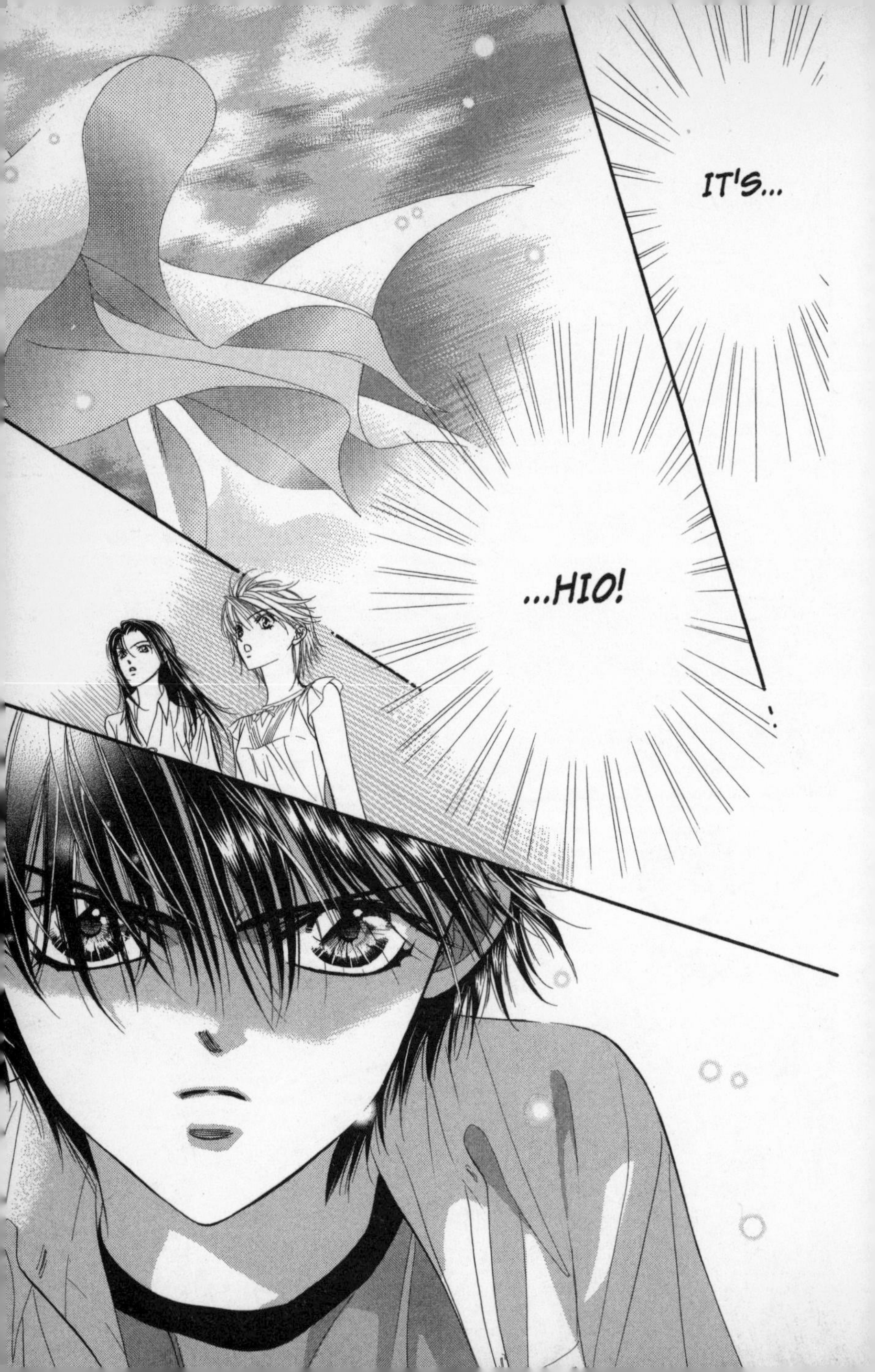
IT'S...
...HIO!

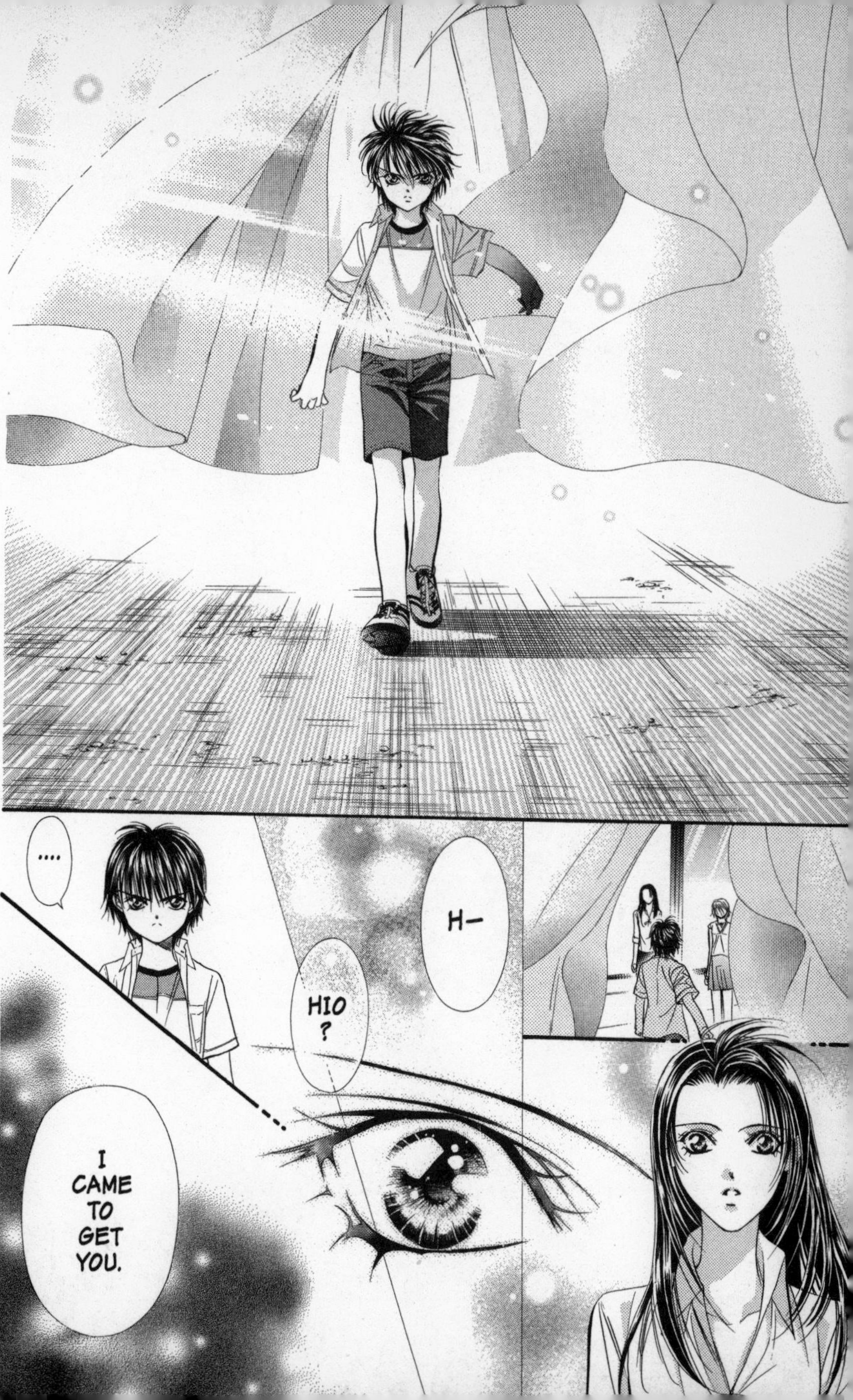
H-
HIO?
....
I CAME TO GET YOU.

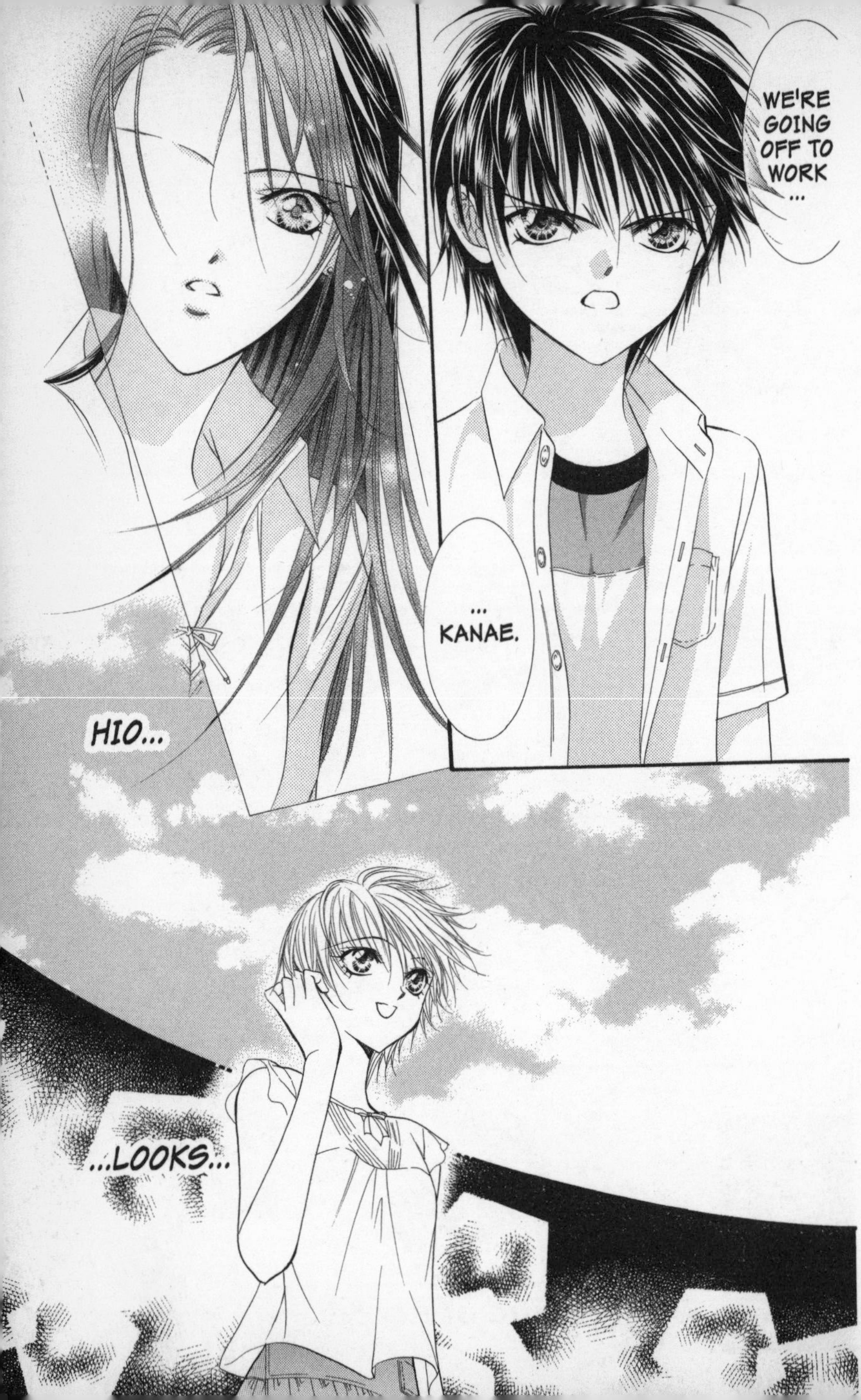
WE'RE GOING OFF TO WORK ...
... KANAE.
HIO...
...LOOKS...

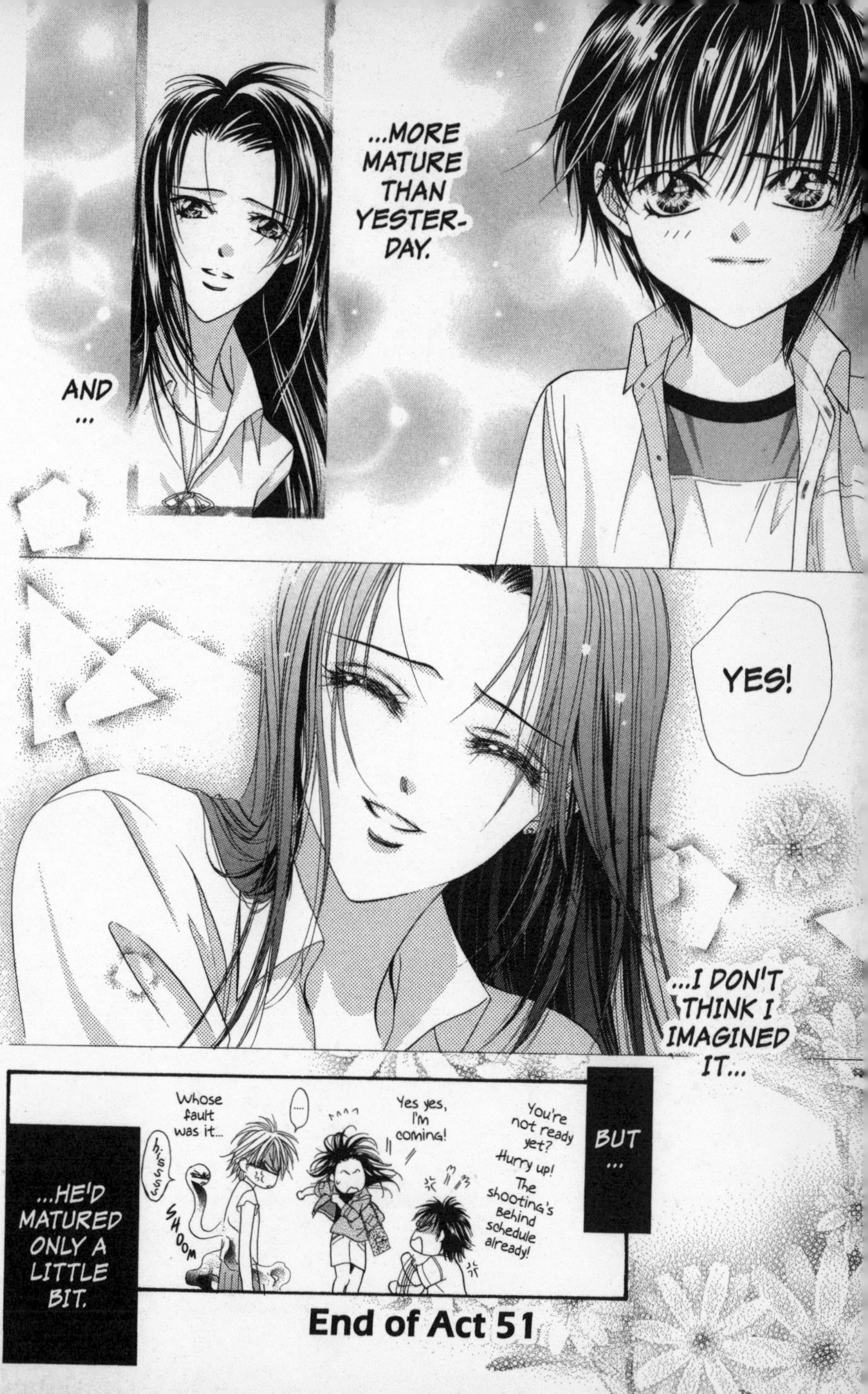
...MORE MATURE THAN YESTER-DAY.
AND ...
YES!
...I DON'T THINK I IMAGINED IT...
BUT ...
You're not ready yet? Hurry up! The shooting's behind schedule already!
Yes yes, I'm coming!
....
Whose fault was it...
hissss
SHOOM
...HE'D MATURED ONLY A LITTLE BIT.

End of Act 51

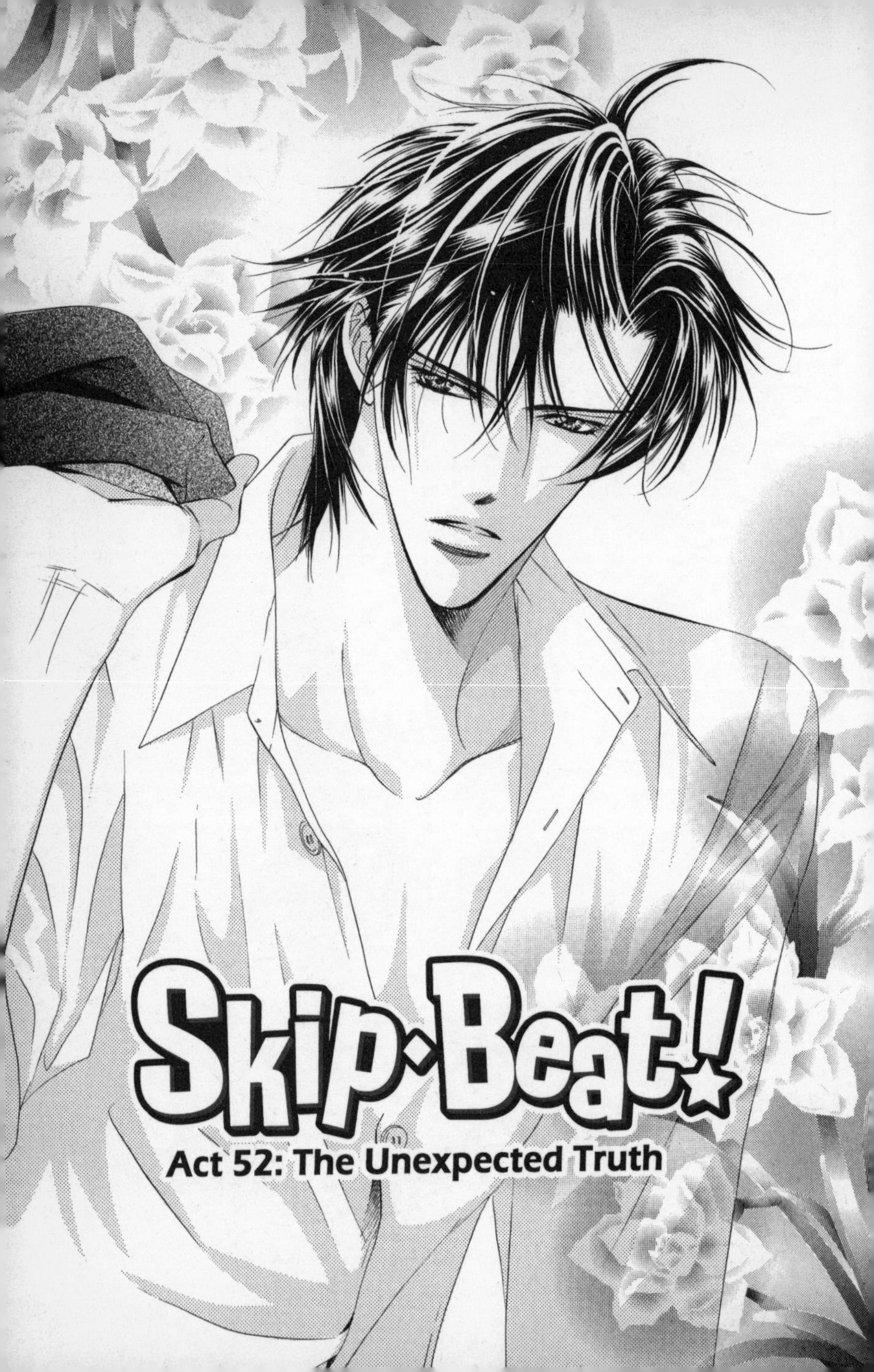
Skip·Beat!
Act 52: The Unexpected Truth

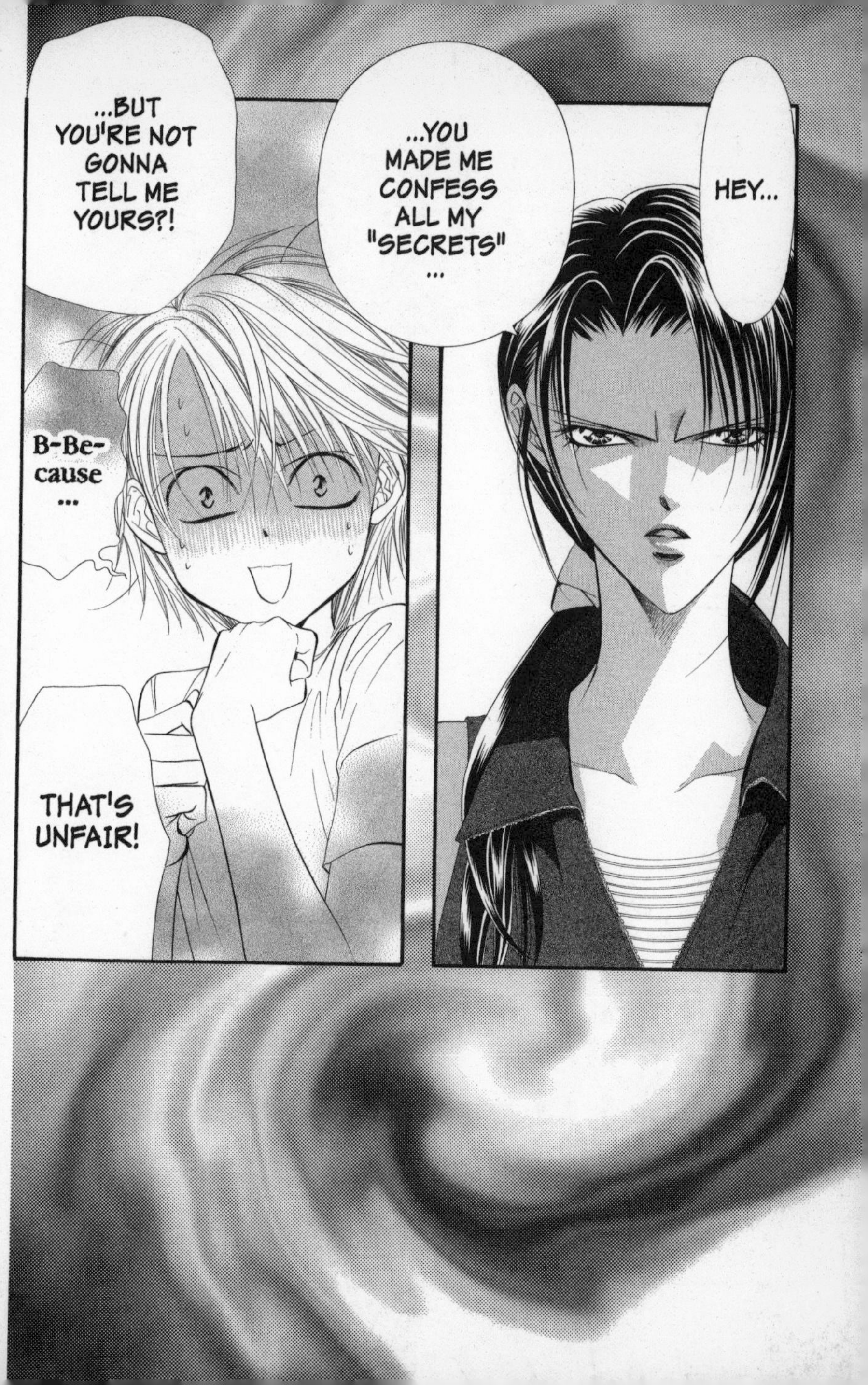
HEY...
...YOU MADE ME CONFESS ALL MY "SECRETS" ...
...BUT YOU'RE NOT GONNA TELL ME YOURS?!
B-Be-cause ...
THAT'S UNFAIR!

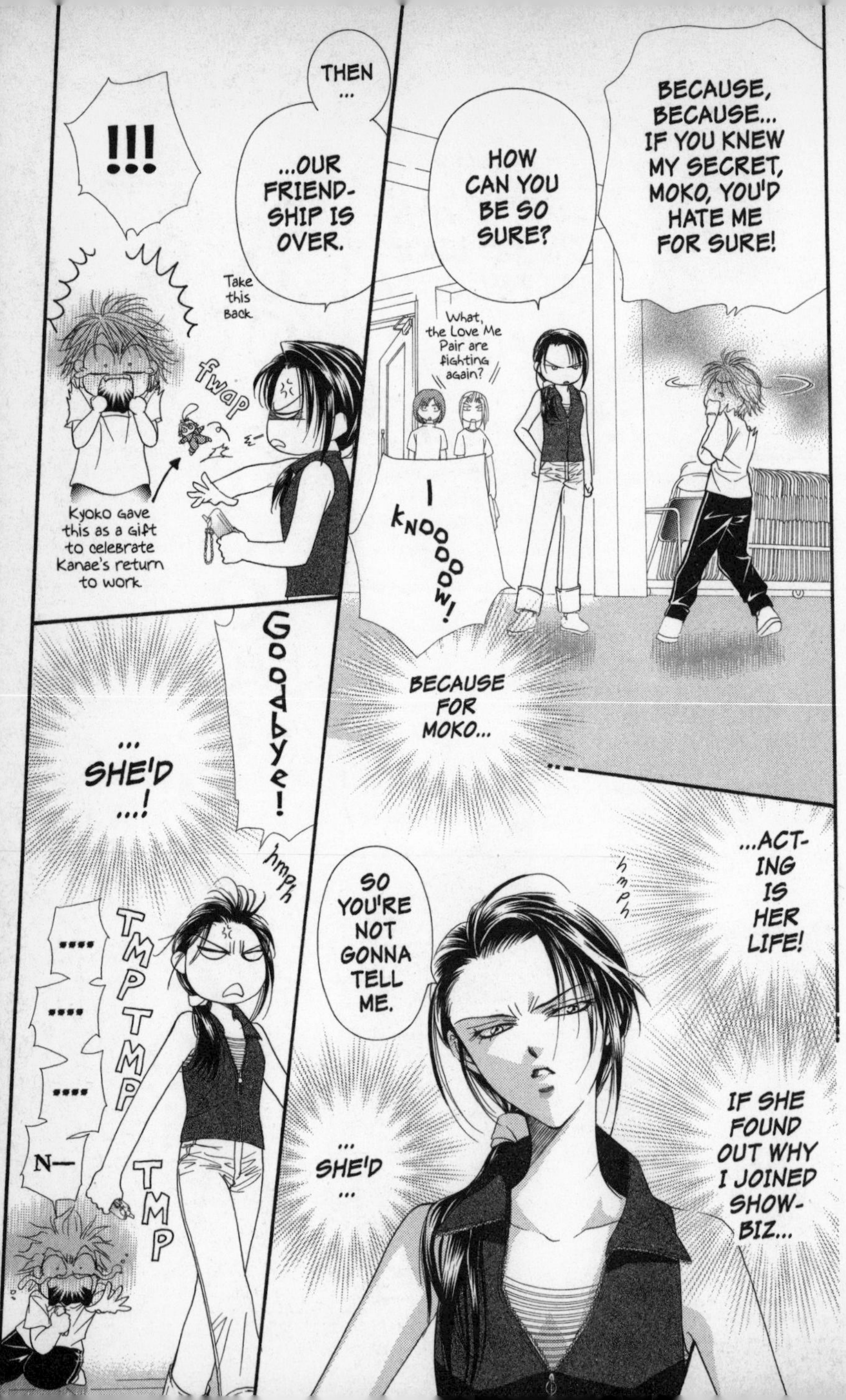
BECAUSE, BECAUSE... IF YOU KNEW MY SECRET, MOKO, YOU'D HATE ME FOR SURE!
HOW CAN YOU BE SO SURE?
What, the Love Me Pair are fighting again?
I KNOOOOOOW!
BECAUSE FOR MOKO...
THEN...
...OUR FRIEND-SHIP IS OVER.
!!!
Take this Back
fwap
Kyoko Gave this as a Gift to celebrate Kanae's return to work.
...ACT-ING IS HER LIFE!
hmph
SO YOU'RE NOT GONNA TELL ME.
IF SHE FOUND OUT WHY I JOINED SHOW-BIZ...
...SHE'D...
Goodbye!
...SHE'D...!
hmph
TMPTMP
....
....
....
N—
TMP

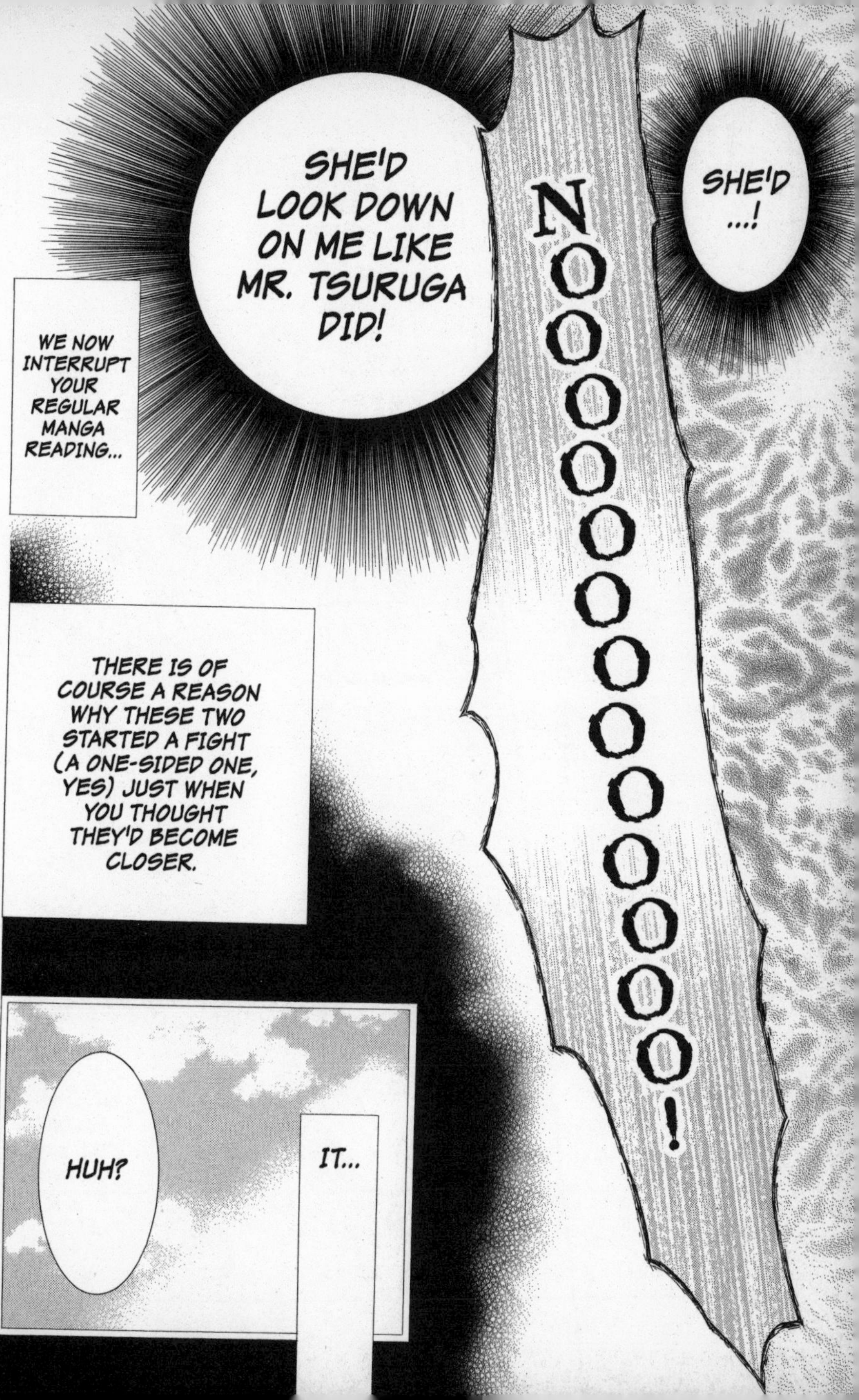
SHE'D ...!
NOOOOOOOOOOOOOOOOOO!
SHE'D LOOK DOWN ON ME LIKE MR. TSURUGA DID!
WE NOW INTERRUPT YOUR REGULAR MANGA READING...
THERE IS OF COURSE A REASON WHY THESE TWO STARTED A FIGHT (A ONE-SIDED ONE, YES) JUST WHEN YOU THOUGHT THEY'D BECOME CLOSER.
IT...
HUH?

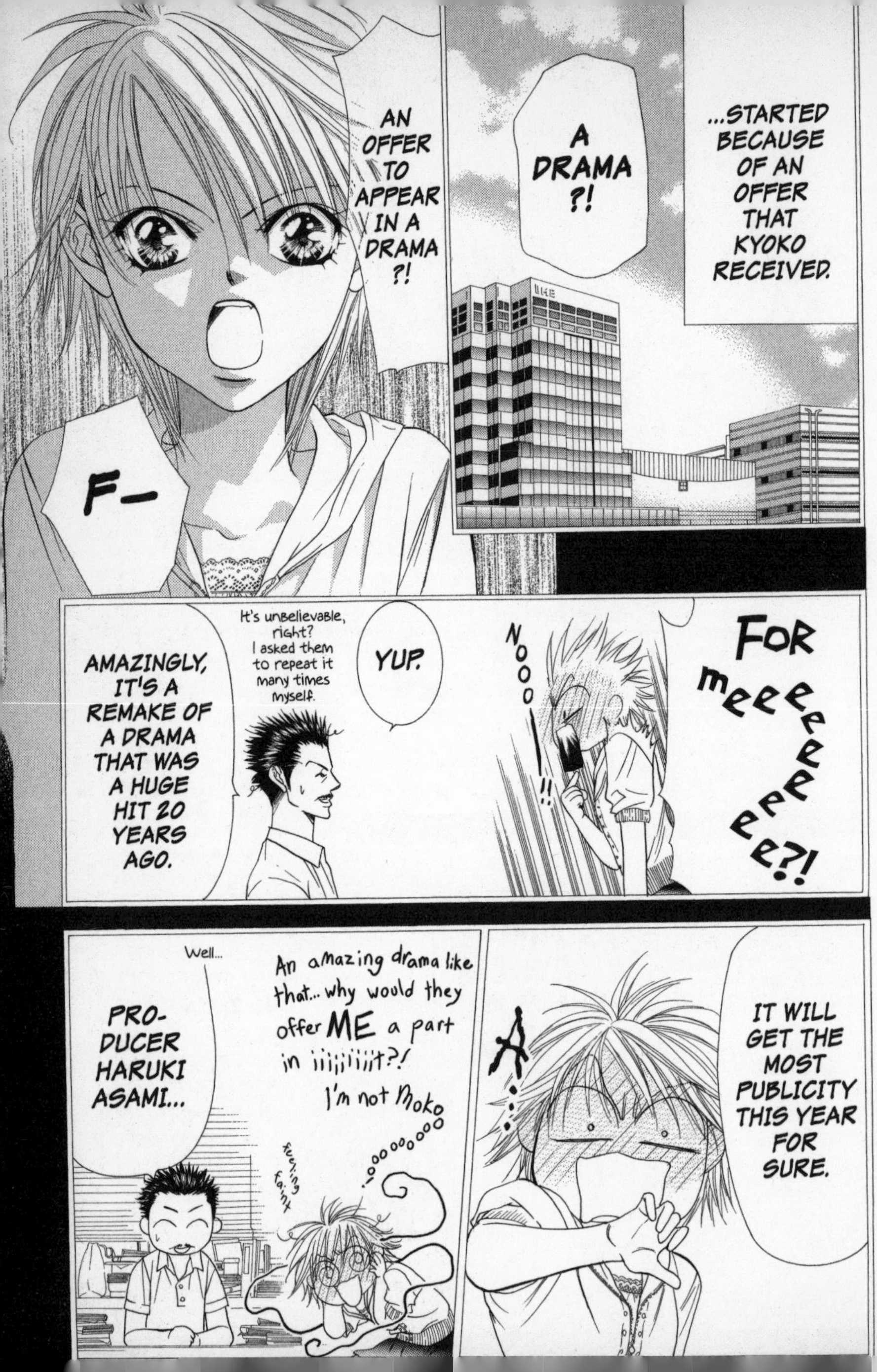
...STARTED BECAUSE OF AN OFFER THAT KYOKO RECEIVED.
A DRAMA ?!
AN OFFER TO APPEAR IN A DRAMA ?!
F—
FOR meeeeeeeeee?!
Nooo—!!
YUP.
It's unbelievable, right? I asked them to repeat it many times myself.
AMAZINGLY, IT'S A REMAKE OF A DRAMA THAT WAS A HUGE HIT 20 YEARS AGO.
IT WILL GET THE MOST PUBLICITY THIS YEAR FOR SURE.
A
An amazing drama like that... why would they offer ME a part in iiiiiiiiit?!
I'm not Moko-oooooooo
feeling faint
Well...
PRO-DUCER HARUKI ASAMI...

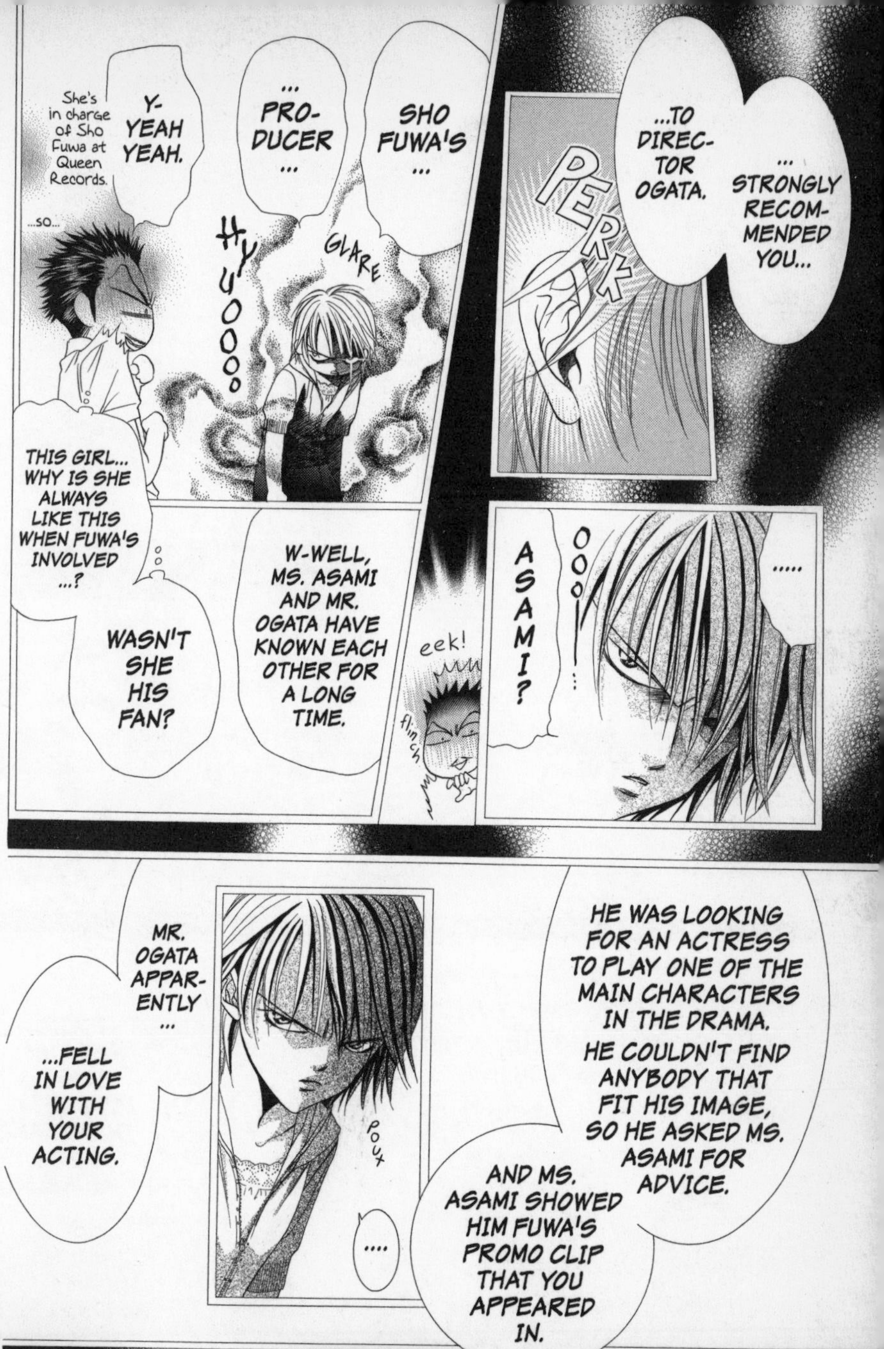

... STRONGLY RECOMMENDED YOU...
...TO DIRECTOR OGATA.
PERK
SHO FUWA'S ...
... PRODUCER ...
Y-YEAH YEAH.
She's in charge of Sho Fuwa at Queen Records.
...so...
GLARE
HYUOOOO
THIS GIRL... WHY IS SHE ALWAYS LIKE THIS WHEN FUWA'S INVOLVED ...?
.....
ASAMI?
OOO!...
eek!
flinch
W-WELL, MS. ASAMI AND MR. OGATA HAVE KNOWN EACH OTHER FOR A LONG TIME.
WASN'T SHE HIS FAN?
HE WAS LOOKING FOR AN ACTRESS TO PLAY ONE OF THE MAIN CHARACTERS IN THE DRAMA.
HE COULDN'T FIND ANYBODY THAT FIT HIS IMAGE, SO HE ASKED MS. ASAMI FOR ADVICE.
AND MS. ASAMI SHOWED HIM FUWA'S PROMO CLIP THAT YOU APPEARED IN.
....
POUT
MR. OGATA APPARENTLY ...
...FELL IN LOVE WITH YOUR ACTING.

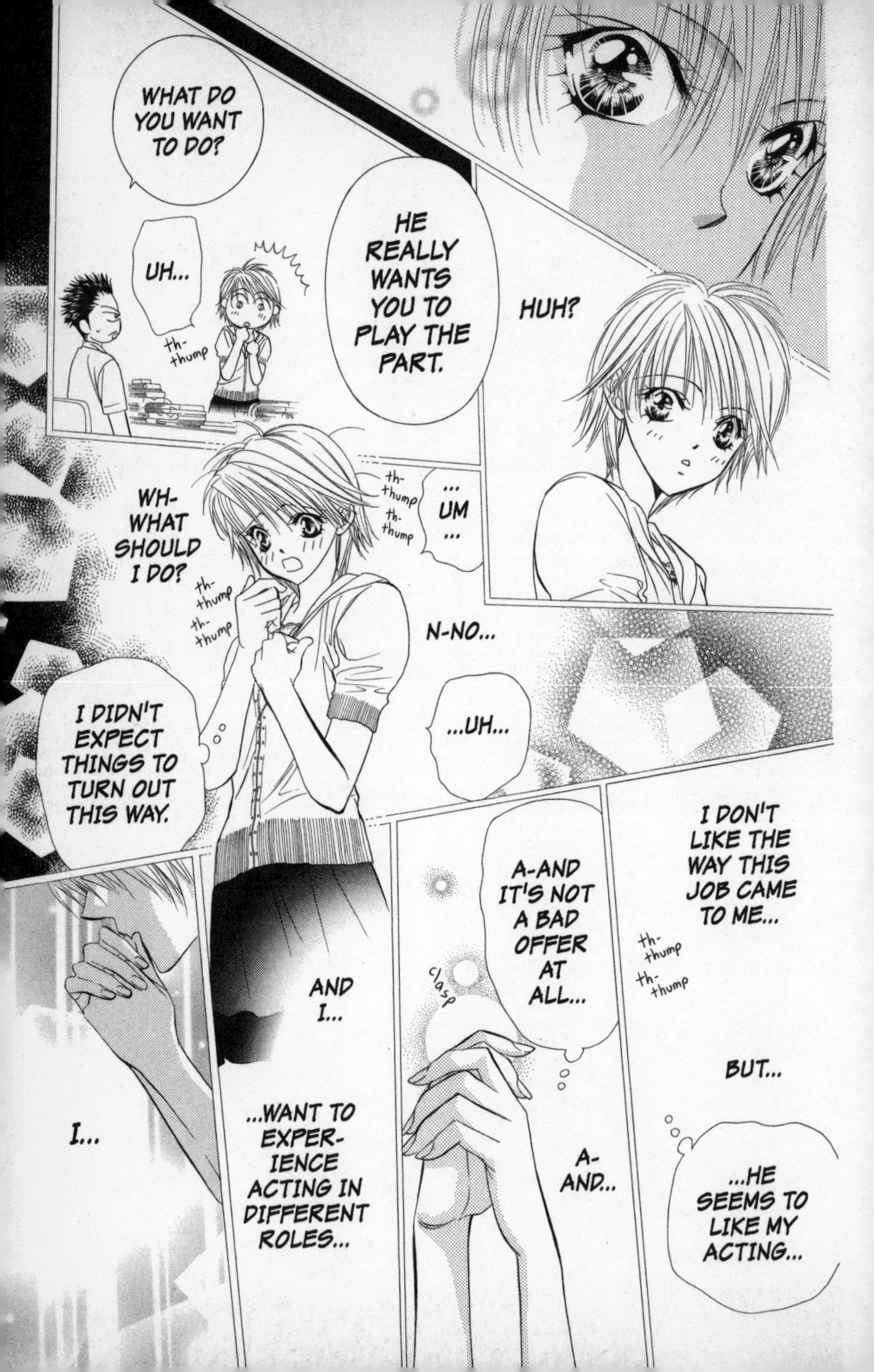
WHAT DO YOU WANT TO DO?
UH...
th-thump
MUU
HE REALLY WANTS YOU TO PLAY THE PART.
HUH?
... UM ...
th-thump th-thump
WH-WHAT SHOULD I DO?
th-thump th-thump
N-NO...
...UH...
I DIDN'T EXPECT THINGS TO TURN OUT THIS WAY.
I DON'T LIKE THE WAY THIS JOB CAME TO ME...
th-thump th-thump
BUT...
...HE SEEMS TO LIKE MY ACTING...
A-AND IT'S NOT A BAD OFFER AT ALL...
clasp
A-AND...
AND I...
...WANT TO EXPERIENCE ACTING IN DIFFERENT ROLES...
I...

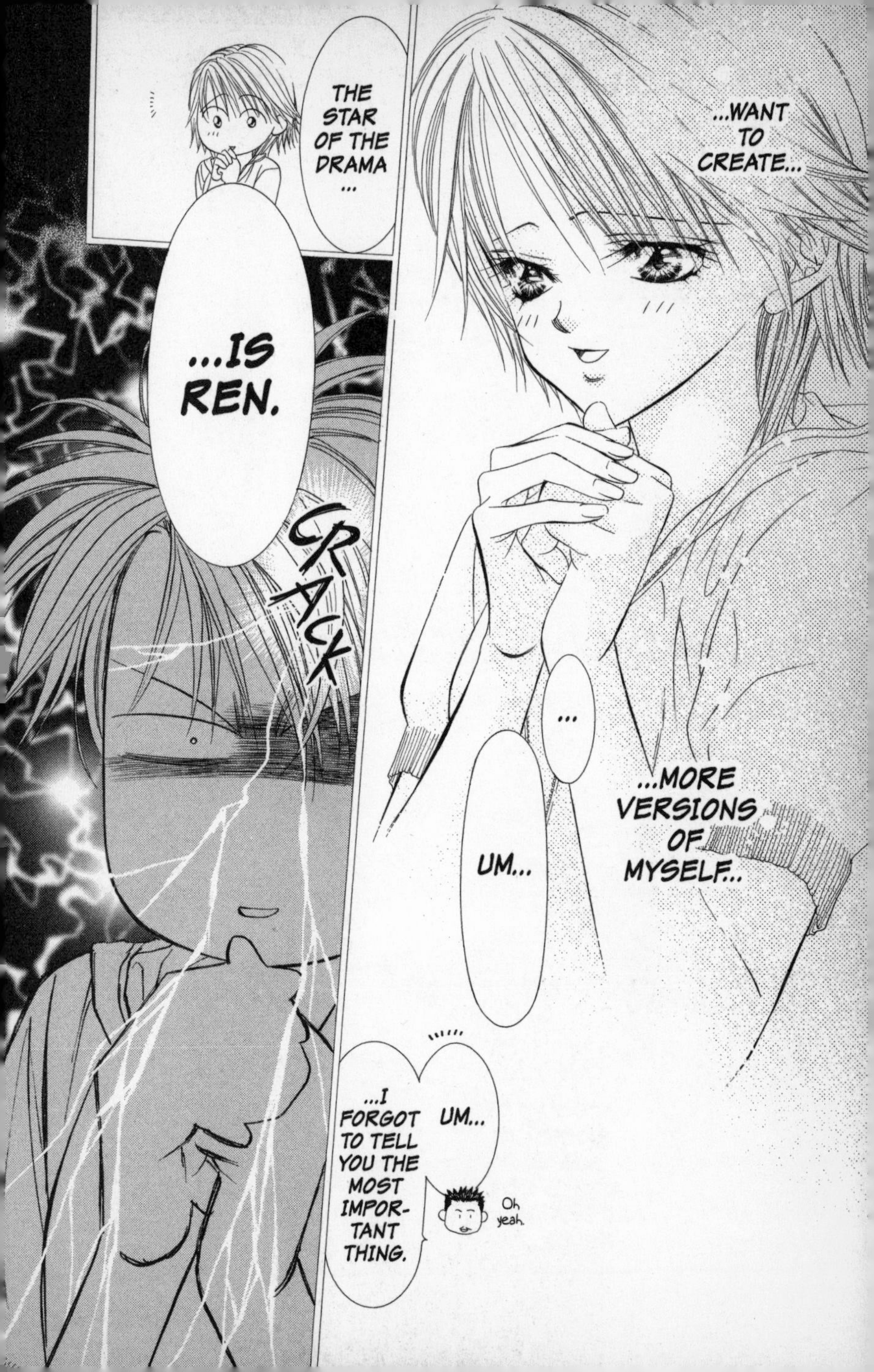

...WANT TO CREATE...
...MORE VERSIONS OF MYSELF...
...
UM...
UM...
...I FORGOT TO TELL YOU THE MOST IMPOR-TANT THING.
Oh yeah.
THE STAR OF THE DRAMA...
...IS REN.
CRACK

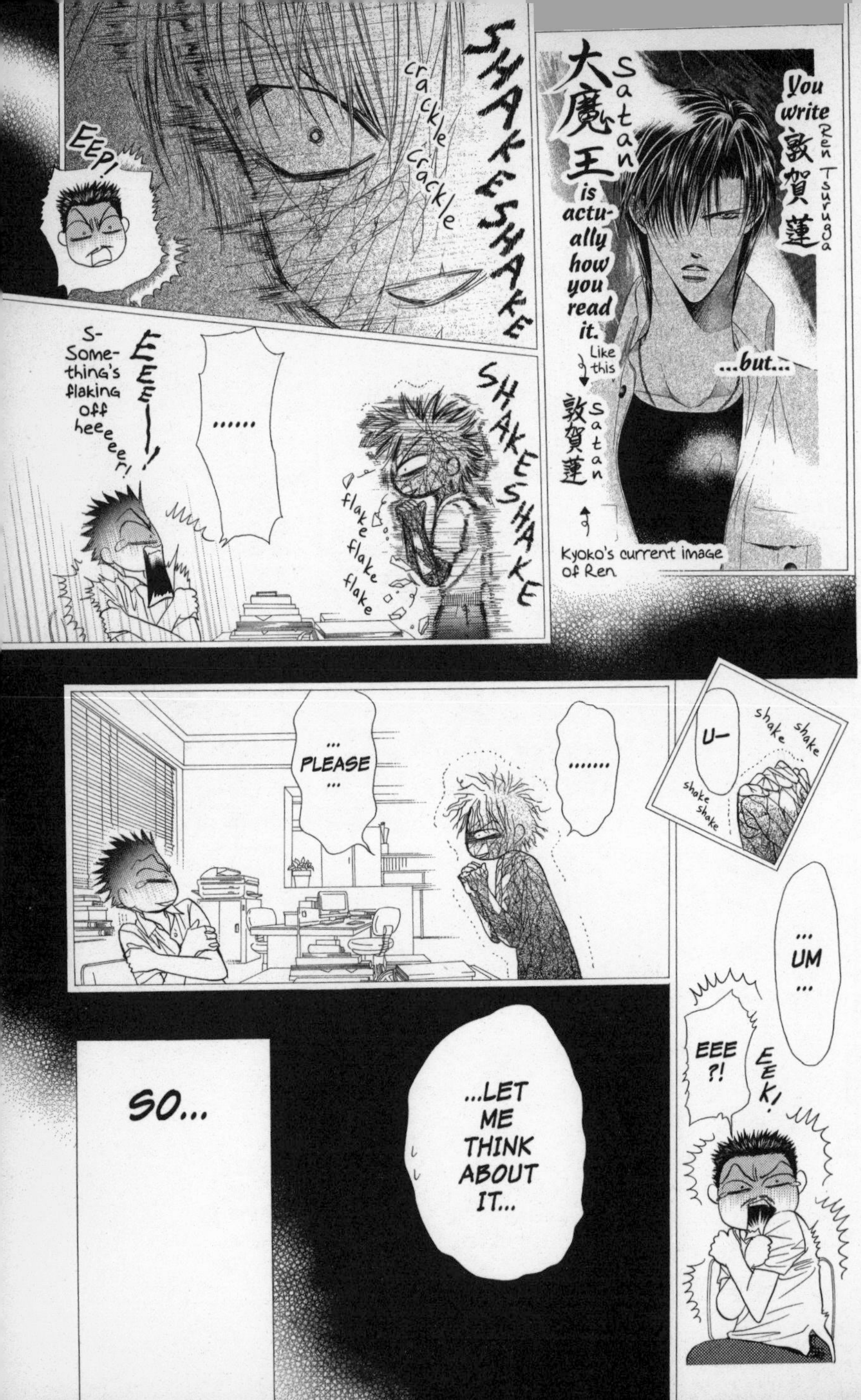
You write 敦賀蓮 Ren Tsuruga
...but...
大魔王 Satan is actually how you read it.
Like this
敦賀蓮 Satan
Kyoko's current image of Ren
SHAKESHAKESHAKE
crackle crackle
EEP!
SHAKESHAKESHAKE
......
EEE—!
S-Some-thing's flaking off heeeeer!
flake flake flake flake
U–
shake shake
shake shake
... PLEASE ...
....
... UM ...
EEE?!
EEK!
...LET ME THINK ABOUT IT...
SO...

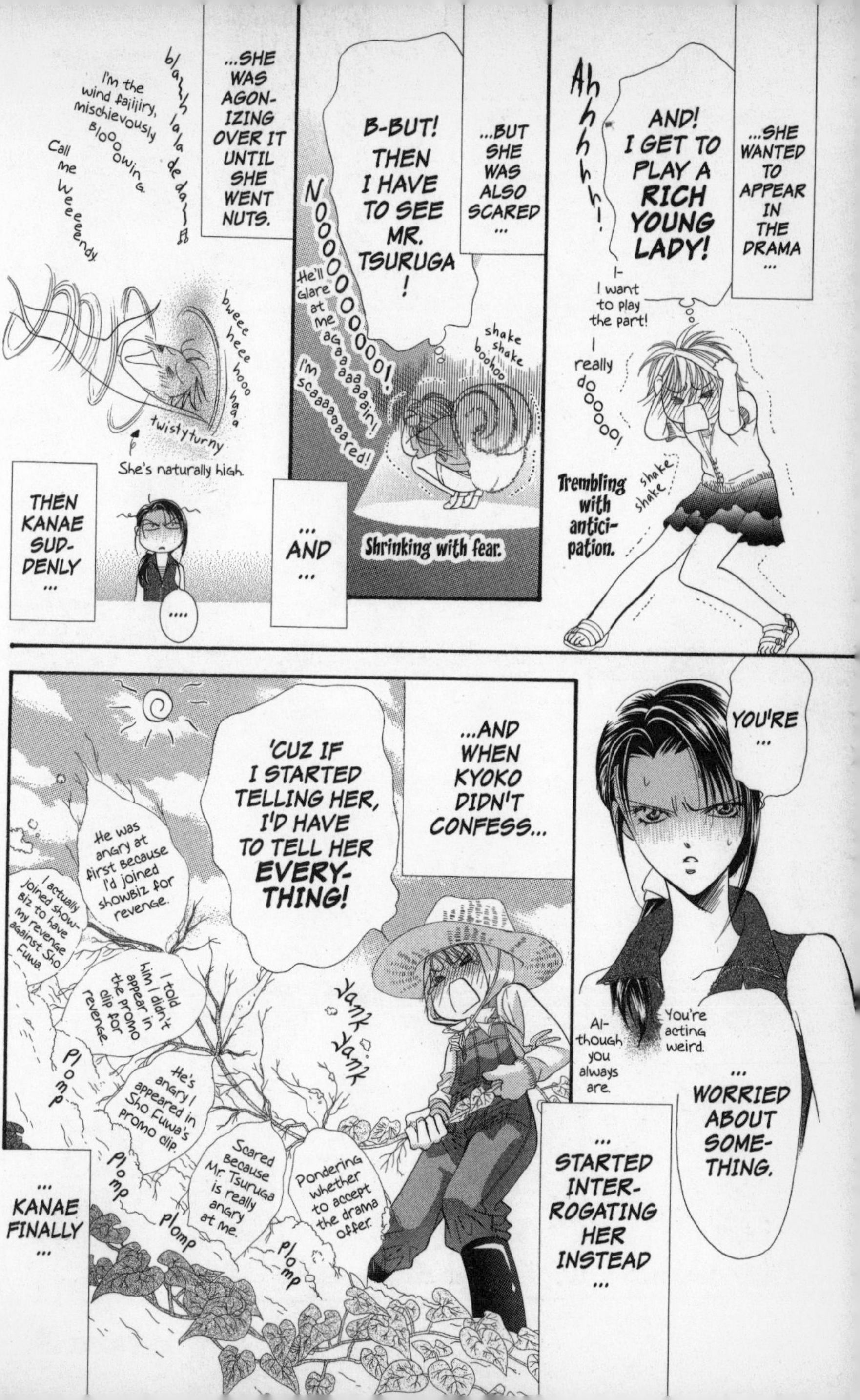

...SHE WANTED TO APPEAR IN THE DRAMA ...
AND! I GET TO PLAY A RICH YOUNG LADY!
Ahhhhh!
I- I want to play the part!
I really doooooo!
shake shake
Trembling with antici-pation.
...BUT SHE WAS ALSO SCARED ...
B-BUT! THEN I HAVE TO SEE MR. TSURUGA!
Noooooooooooo!
He'll glare at me agaaaaaaain!
I'm scaaaaaaaared!
shake shake boohoo
Shrinking with fear.
... AND ...
...SHE WAS AGONIZING OVER IT UNTIL SHE WENT NUTS.
blaaah lala de da♪
I'm the wind faiiiiiry, mischievously blooooowing.
Call me Weeeeendy
bweee heee hooo haaa
twistyturny
She's naturally high.
THEN KANAE SUDDENLY ...
....
YOU'RE ...
... WORRIED ABOUT SOMETHING.
You're acting weird.
Although you always are.
... STARTED INTERROGATING HER INSTEAD ...
...AND WHEN KYOKO DIDN'T CONFESS...
'CUZ IF I STARTED TELLING HER, I'D HAVE TO TELL HER EVERYTHING!
yank yank
Pondering whether to accept the drama offer.
Scared because Mr. Tsuruga is really angry at me.
He's angry I appeared in Sho Fuwa's promo clip.
I told him I didn't appear in the promo clip for revenge.
He was angry at first because I'd joined showbiz for revenge.
I actually joined showbiz to have my revenge against Sho Fuwa.
plomp
plomp
plomp
plomp
plomp
... KANAE FINALLY ...

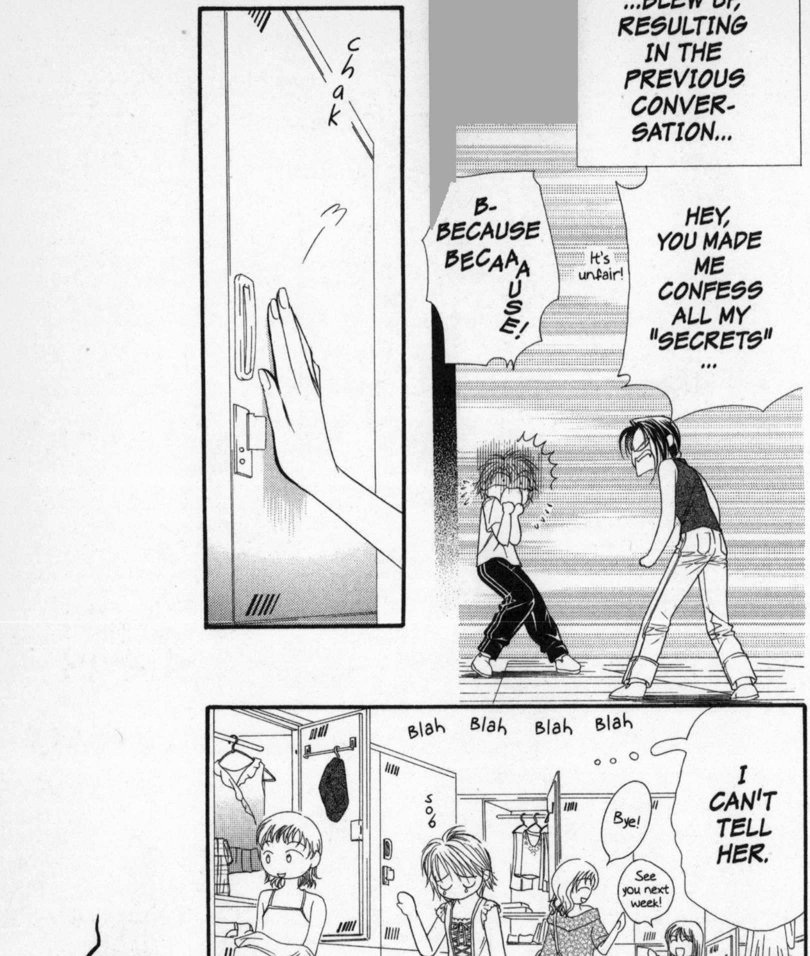
...BLEW UP, RESULTING IN THE PREVIOUS CONVER-SATION...
HEY, YOU MADE ME CONFESS ALL MY "SECRETS" ...
It's unfair!
B- BECAUSE BECAAAUSE!
chak
I CAN'T TELL HER.
See you next week!
Bye!
sob
Blah Blah Blah Blah

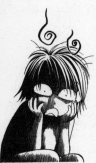

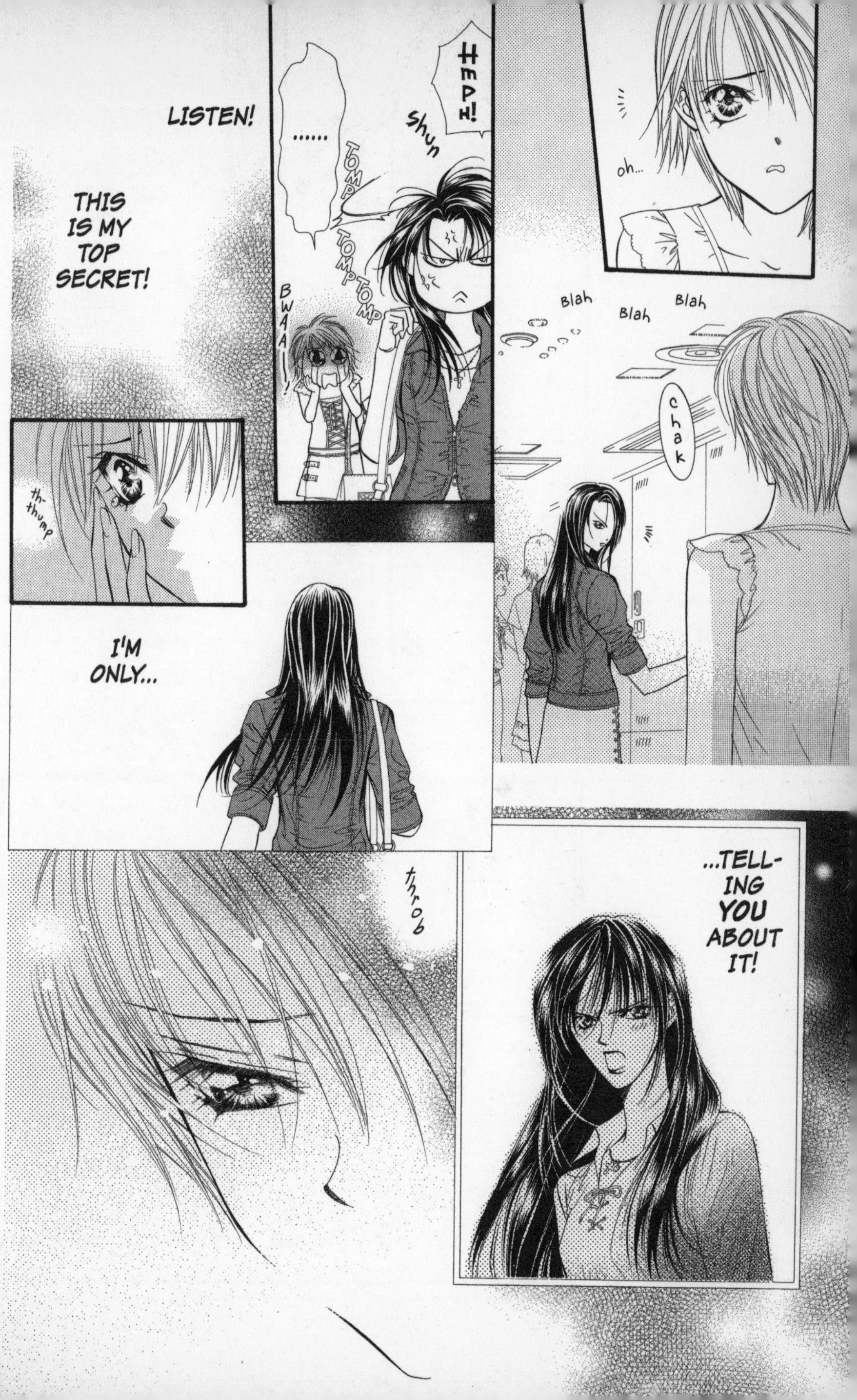
oh...
Blah Blah Blah
Chak
HMPH!
......
Shun
TOMP TOMPTOMPTOMP
BWAA~!
LISTEN!
THIS IS MY TOP SECRET!
th-thump
I'M ONLY...
...TELL-ING YOU ABOUT IT!
throb

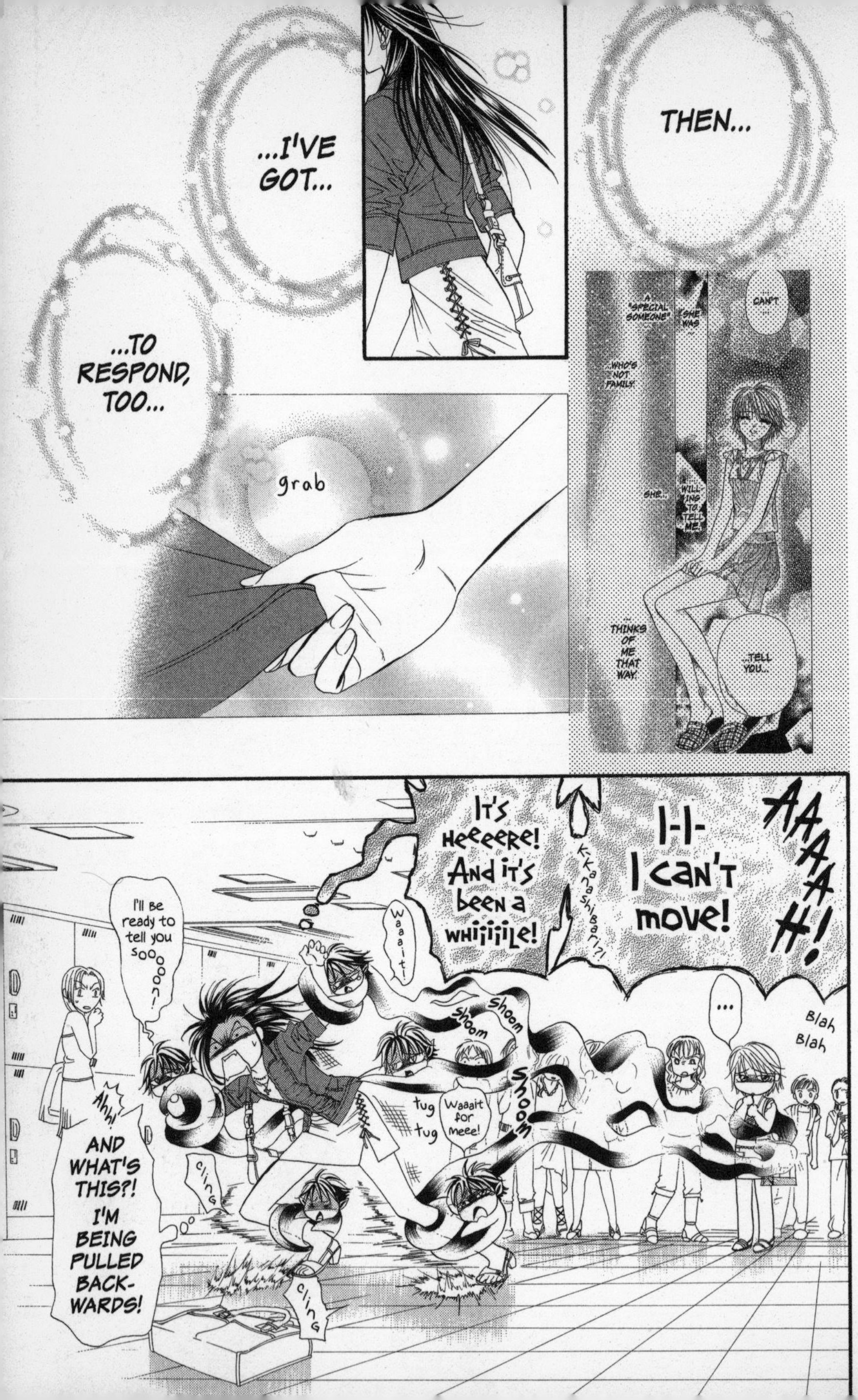
THEN...
...CAN'T...
A "SPECIAL SOMEONE"
SHE WAS
...WHO'S NOT FAMILY
...TELL YOU...
SHE...
WILLING TO TELL ME.
...THINKS OF ME THAT WAY.
...I'VE GOT...
...TO RESPOND, TOO...
grab
AAAAH!
I-I- I can't move!
K-kanashibari?!
It's heeeere! And it's been a whiiiiile!
Waaait!
I'll be ready to tell you soooooon!
Shoom
Shoom
...
Blah Blah
Shoom
Waaait for meee!
tug tug
Ahh!
AND WHAT'S THIS?! I'M BEING PULLED BACKWARDS!
cling
cling

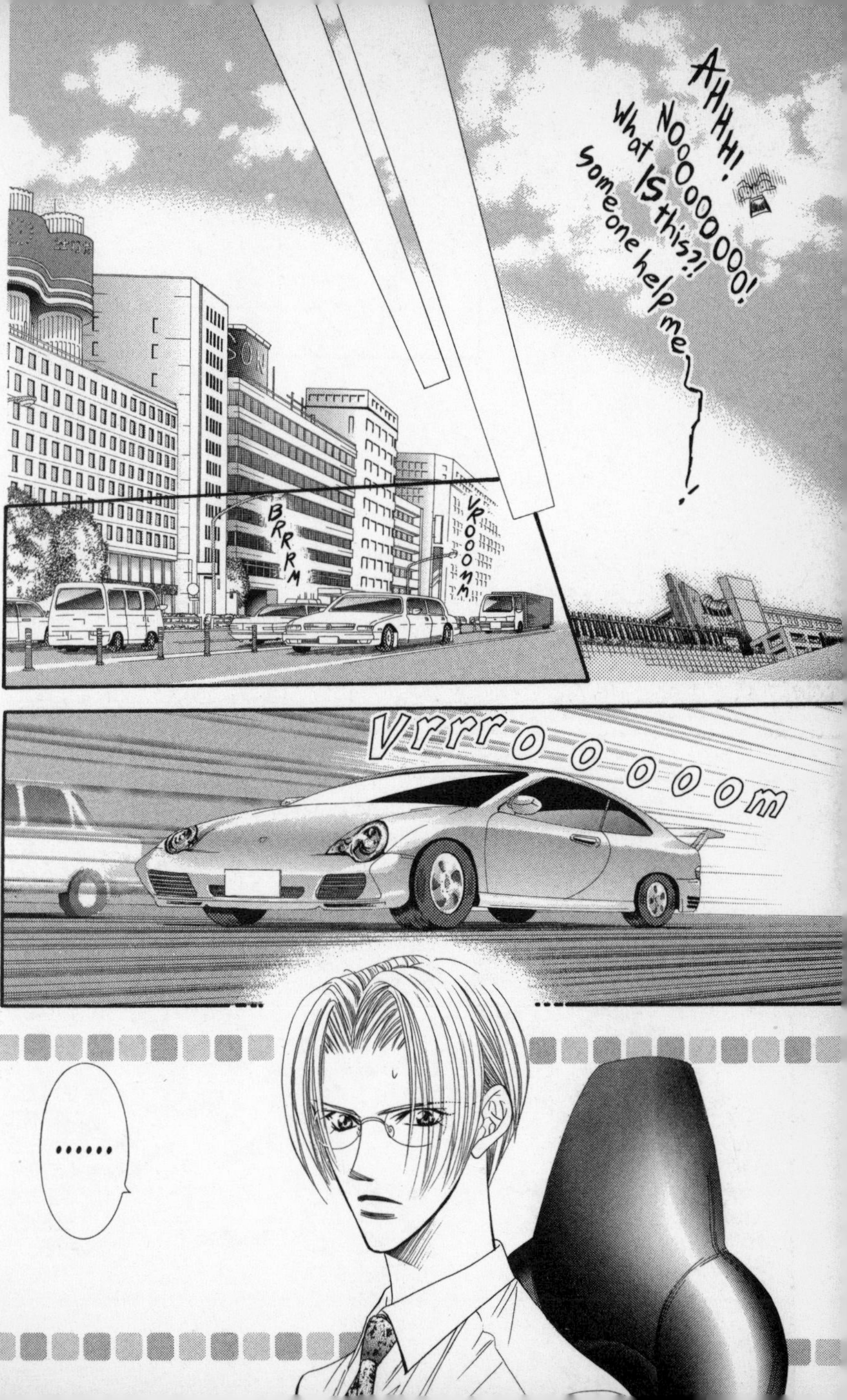
AHHH! NOooOOOOOOO! What IS this?! Someone help me~~~!
BRRRM
VROOOOMM
Vrrrooooom
......

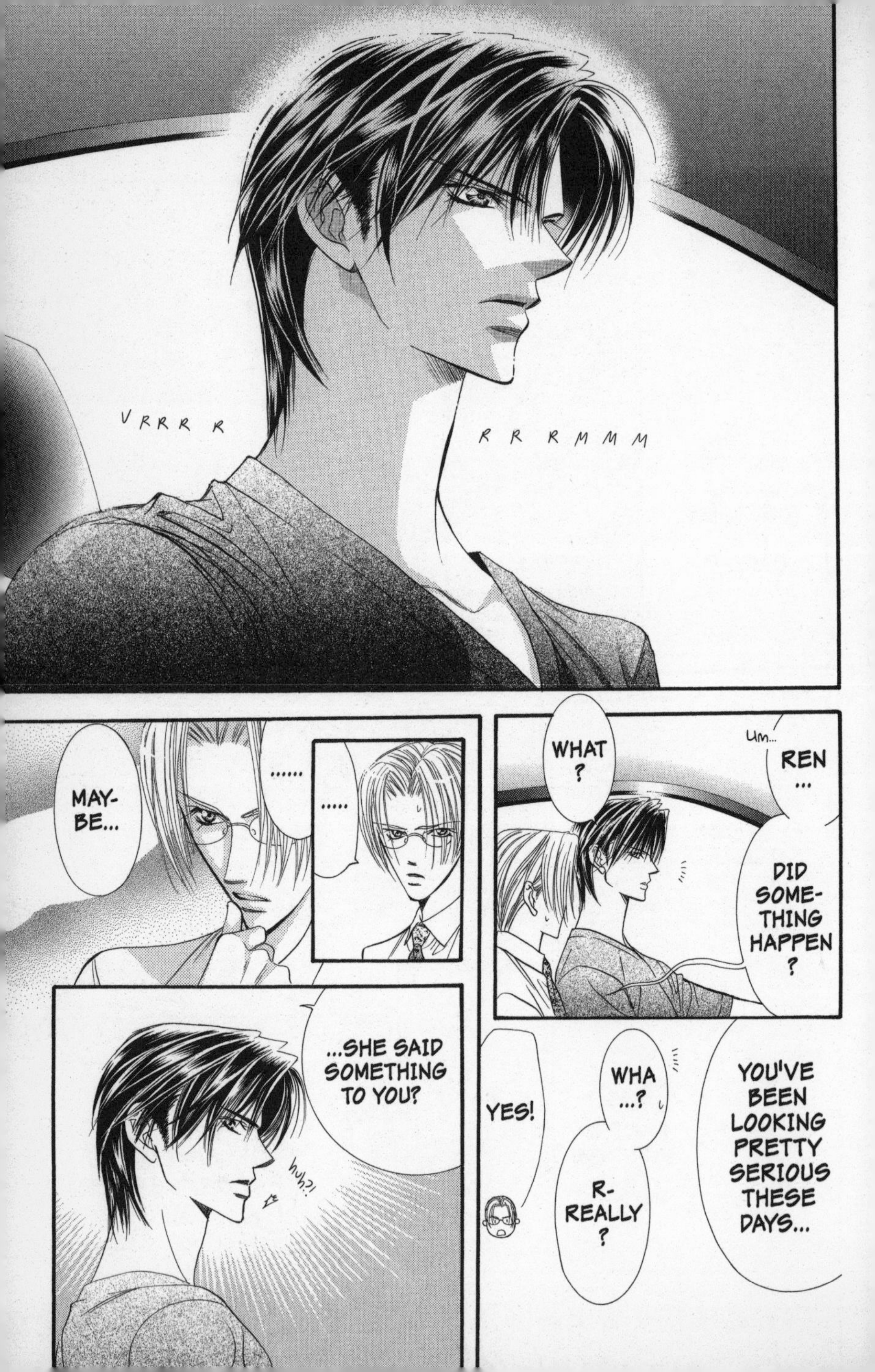
R R RMMM
VRRRR R
Um...
REN ...
DID SOMETHING HAPPEN ?
WHAT ?
......
......
MAY-BE...
YOU'VE BEEN LOOKING PRETTY SERIOUS THESE DAYS...
WHA ...?
R-REALLY ?
YES!
...SHE SAID SOMETHING TO YOU?
huh?!

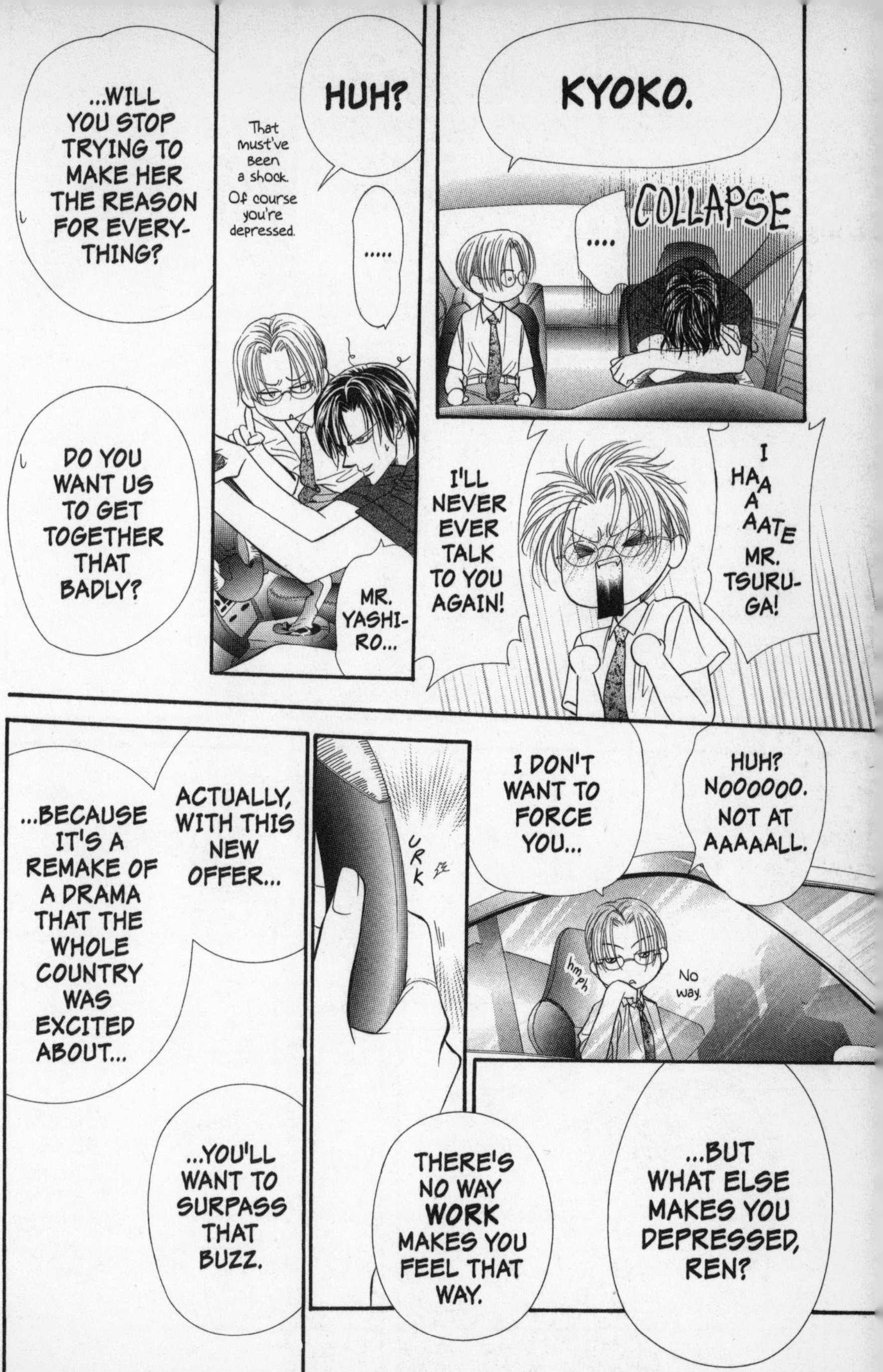
KYOKO.
....
COLLAPSE
I HAAAAATE MR. TSURUGA!
I'LL NEVER EVER TALK TO YOU AGAIN!
HUH?
That must've been a shock. Of course you're depressed.
.....
MR. YASHIRO...
...WILL YOU STOP TRYING TO MAKE HER THE REASON FOR EVERY-THING?
DO YOU WANT US TO GET TOGETHER THAT BADLY?
HUH? NOOOOOO. NOT AT AAAAALL.
I DON'T WANT TO FORCE YOU...
hmph
No way.
...BUT WHAT ELSE MAKES YOU DEPRESSED, REN?
THERE'S NO WAY WORK MAKES YOU FEEL THAT WAY.
URK
ACTUALLY, WITH THIS NEW OFFER...
...BECAUSE IT'S A REMAKE OF A DRAMA THAT THE WHOLE COUNTRY WAS EXCITED ABOUT...
...YOU'LL WANT TO SURPASS THAT BUZZ.

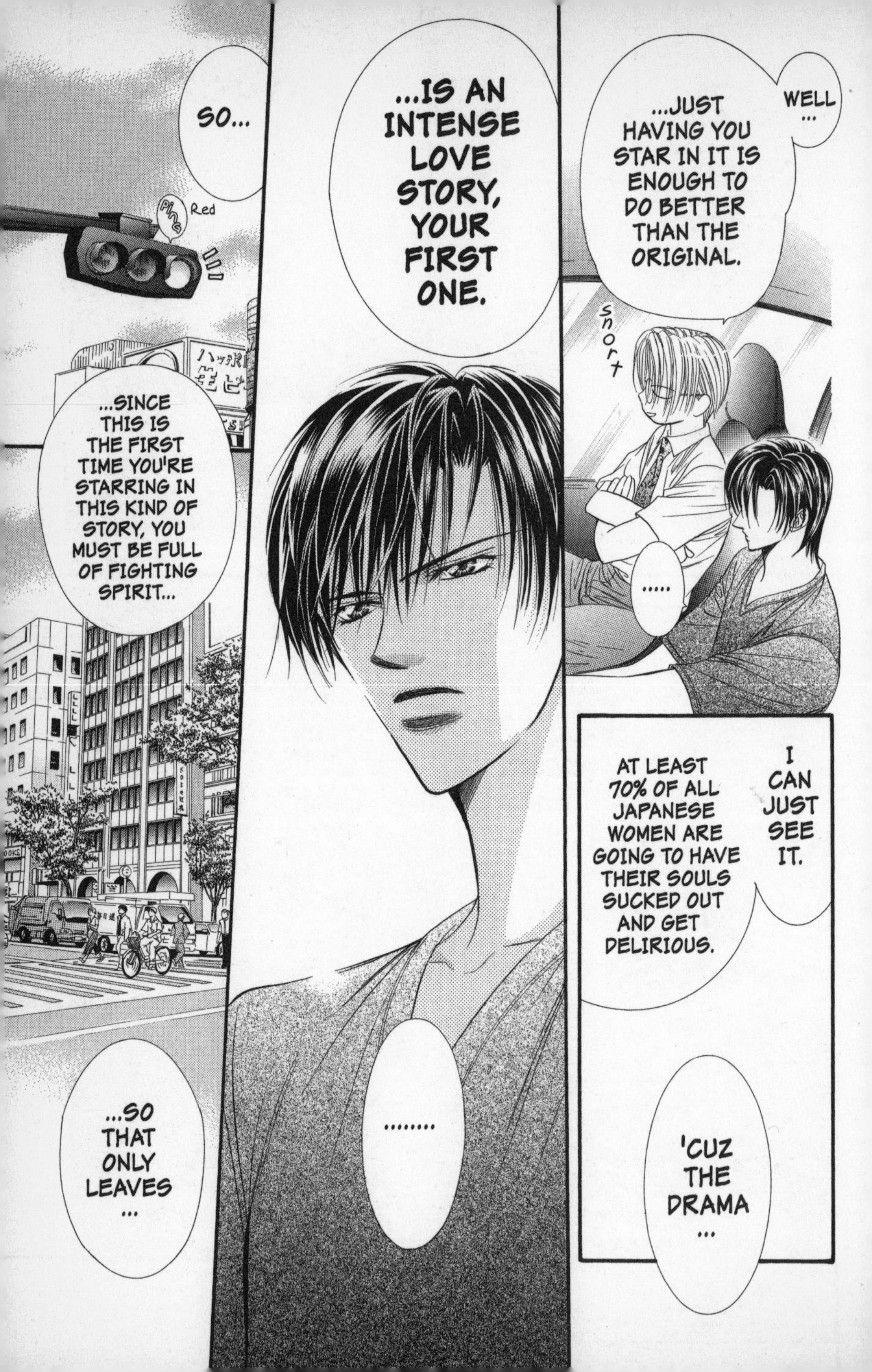
WELL ...
...JUST HAVING YOU STAR IN IT IS ENOUGH TO DO BETTER THAN THE ORIGINAL.
snort
.....
I CAN JUST SEE IT.
AT LEAST 70% OF ALL JAPANESE WOMEN ARE GOING TO HAVE THEIR SOULS SUCKED OUT AND GET DELIRIOUS.
'CUZ THE DRAMA ...
...IS AN INTENSE LOVE STORY, YOUR FIRST ONE.
....
SO...
Ping
Red
...SINCE THIS IS THE FIRST TIME YOU'RE STARRING IN THIS KIND OF STORY, YOU MUST BE FULL OF FIGHTING SPIRIT...
...SO THAT ONLY LEAVES ...

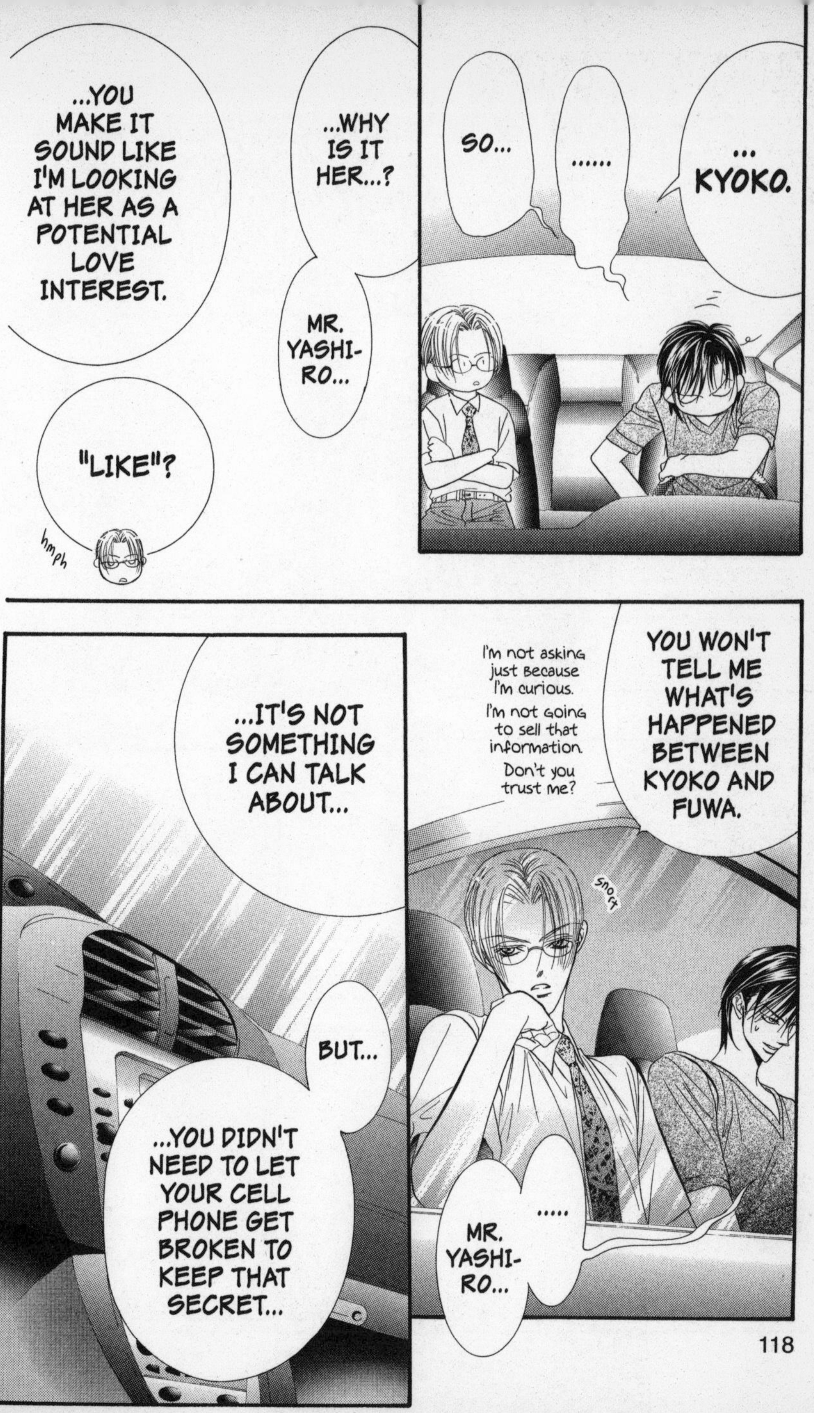
... KYOKO.
......
SO...
...WHY IS IT HER...?
MR. YASHIRO...
...YOU MAKE IT SOUND LIKE I'M LOOKING AT HER AS A POTENTIAL LOVE INTEREST.
"LIKE"?
hmph
YOU WON'T TELL ME WHAT'S HAPPENED BETWEEN KYOKO AND FUWA.
I'm not asking just because I'm curious.
I'm not going to sell that information.
Don't you trust me?
snort
.....
MR. YASHIRO...
...IT'S NOT SOMETHING I CAN TALK ABOUT...
BUT...
...YOU DIDN'T NEED TO LET YOUR CELL PHONE GET BROKEN TO KEEP THAT SECRET...

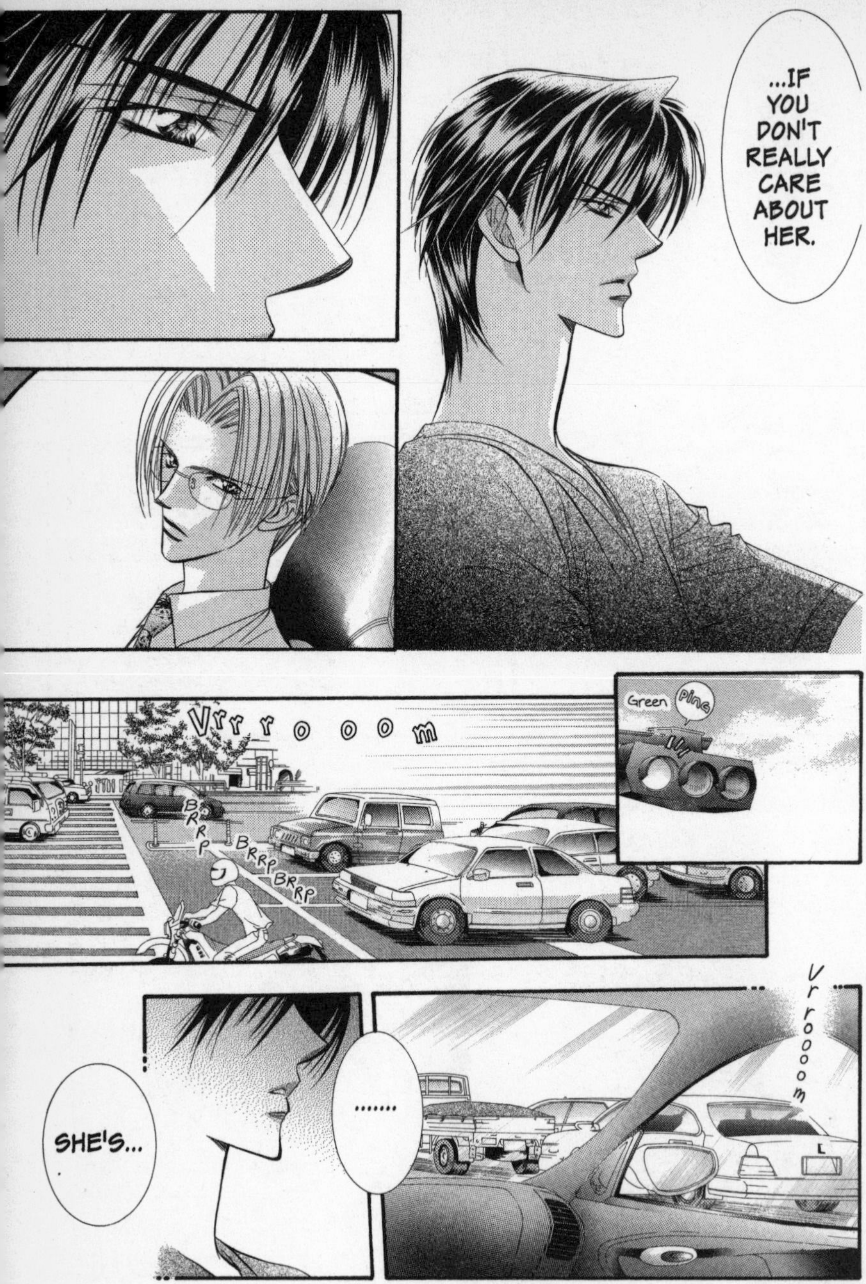
...IF YOU DON'T REALLY CARE ABOUT HER.
Green
Ping
Vrr r o o o m
BRRP
BRRP
BRRP
Vr r o o o o m
......
SHE'S...

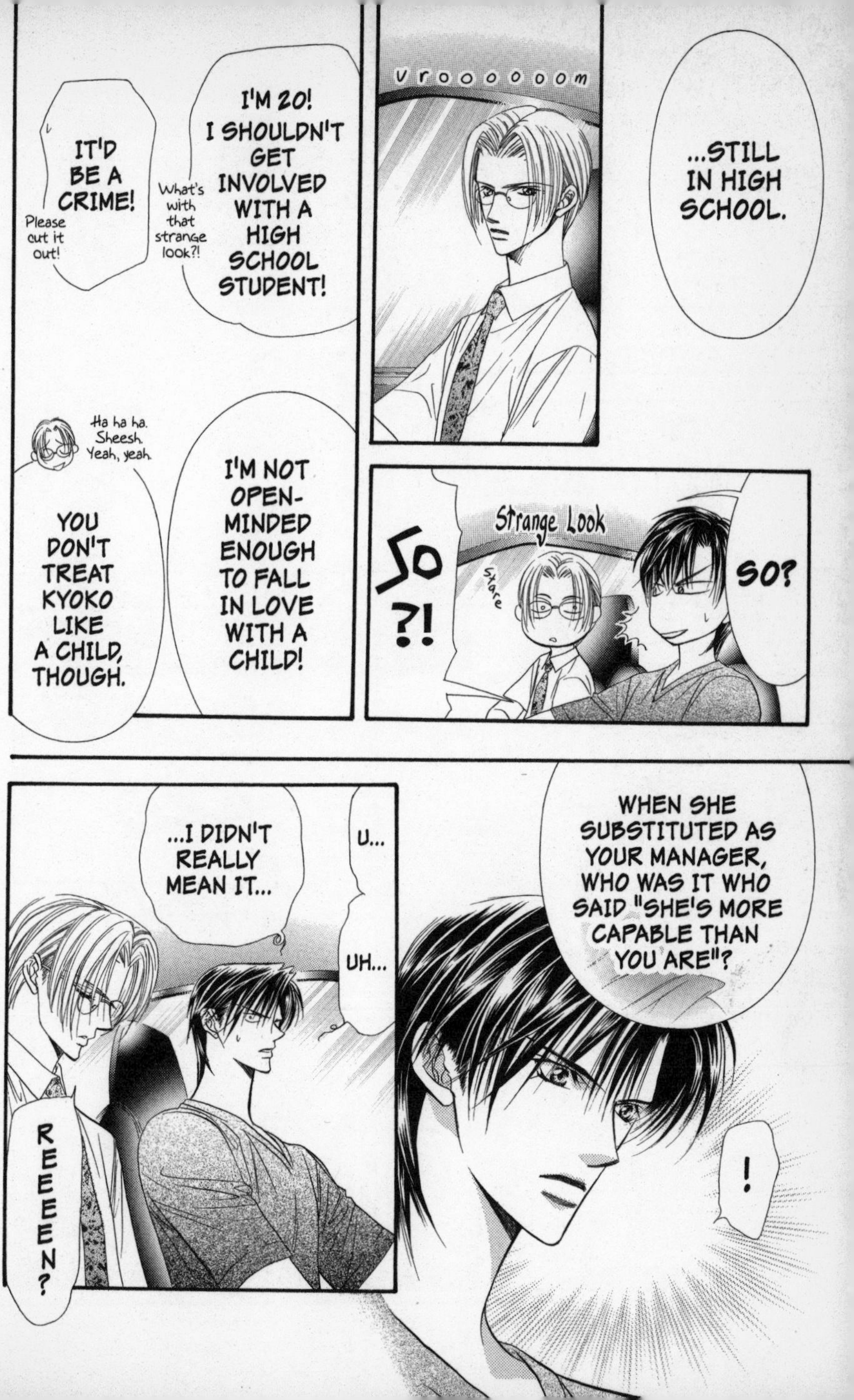
vroooooom
...STILL IN HIGH SCHOOL.
SO?
SO ?!
Strange Look
Stare
I'M 20! I SHOULDN'T GET INVOLVED WITH A HIGH SCHOOL STUDENT!
What's with that strange look?!
IT'D BE A CRIME!
Please cut it out!
I'M NOT OPEN-MINDED ENOUGH TO FALL IN LOVE WITH A CHILD!
Ha ha ha. Sheesh. Yeah, yeah.
YOU DON'T TREAT KYOKO LIKE A CHILD, THOUGH.
WHEN SHE SUBSTITUTED AS YOUR MANAGER, WHO WAS IT WHO SAID "SHE'S MORE CAPABLE THAN YOU ARE"?
!
U...
UH...
...I DIDN'T REALLY MEAN IT...
REEEEN?

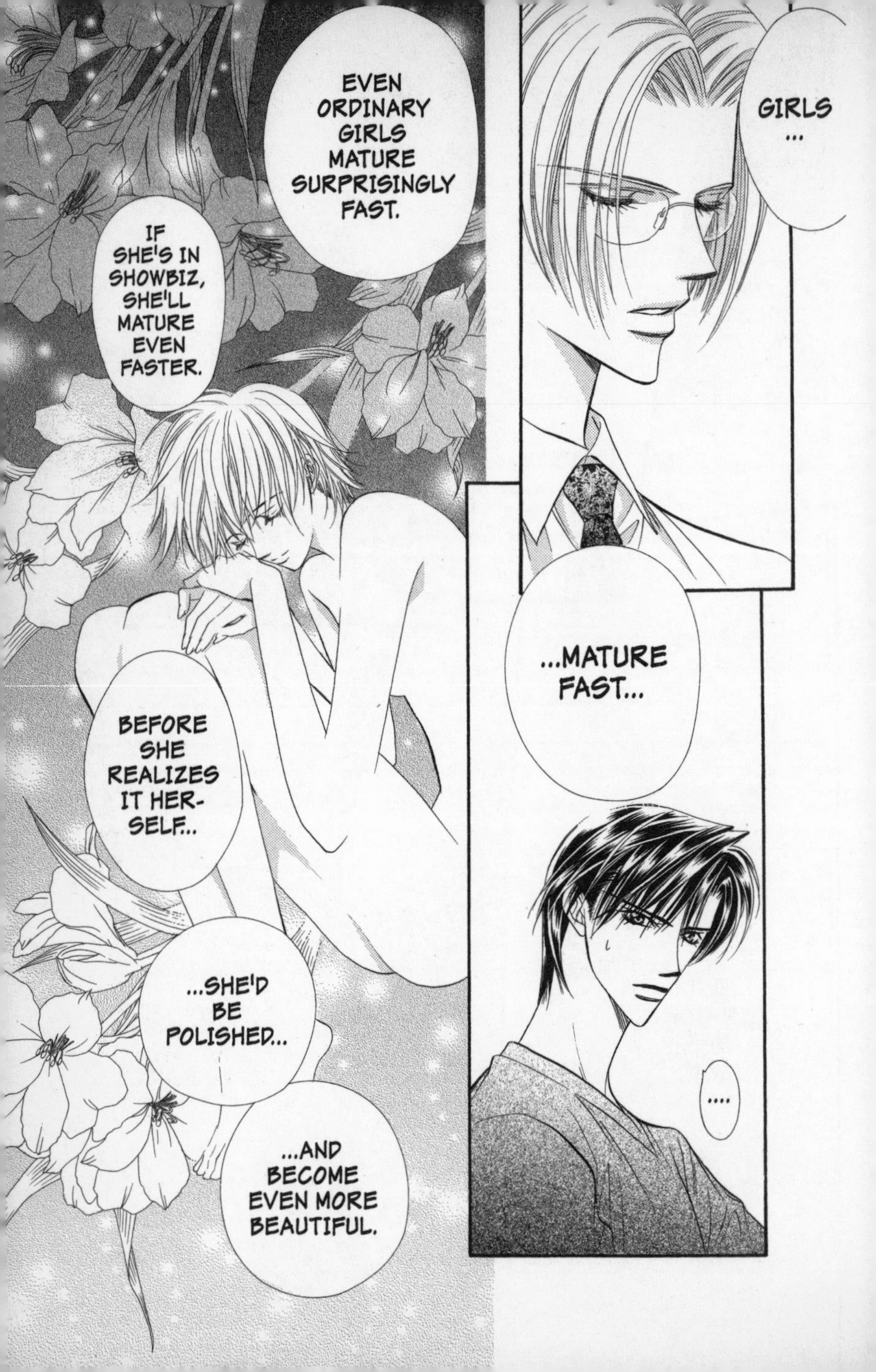
GIRLS ...
...MATURE FAST...
....
EVEN ORDINARY GIRLS MATURE SURPRISINGLY FAST.
IF SHE'S IN SHOWBIZ, SHE'LL MATURE EVEN FASTER.
BEFORE SHE REALIZES IT HER-SELF...
...SHE'D BE POLISHED...
...AND BECOME EVEN MORE BEAUTIFUL.

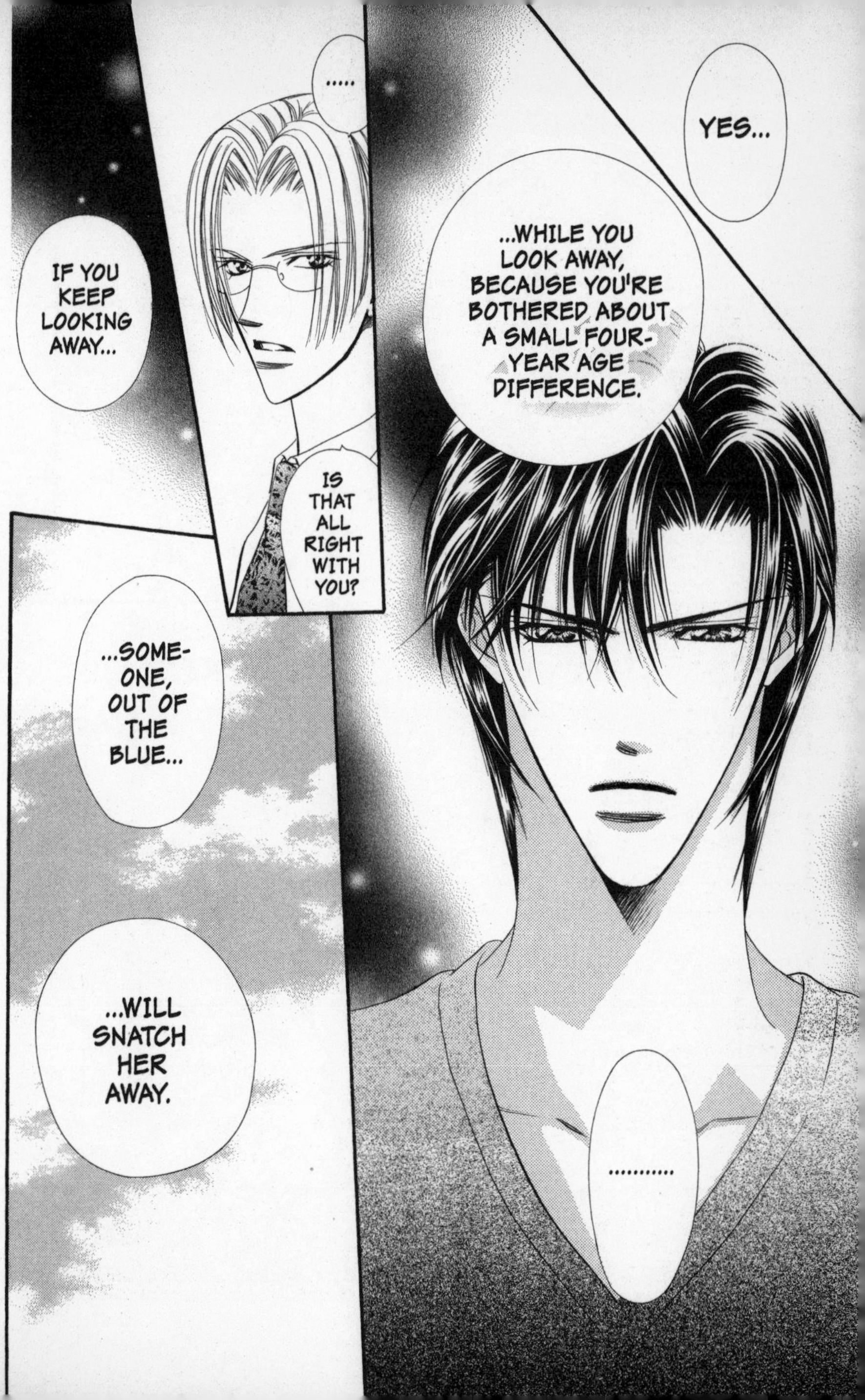
YES...
...WHILE YOU LOOK AWAY, BECAUSE YOU'RE BOTHERED ABOUT A SMALL FOUR-YEAR AGE DIFFERENCE.
....
.....
IF YOU KEEP LOOKING AWAY...
IS THAT ALL RIGHT WITH YOU?
...SOME-ONE, OUT OF THE BLUE...
...WILL SNATCH HER AWAY.

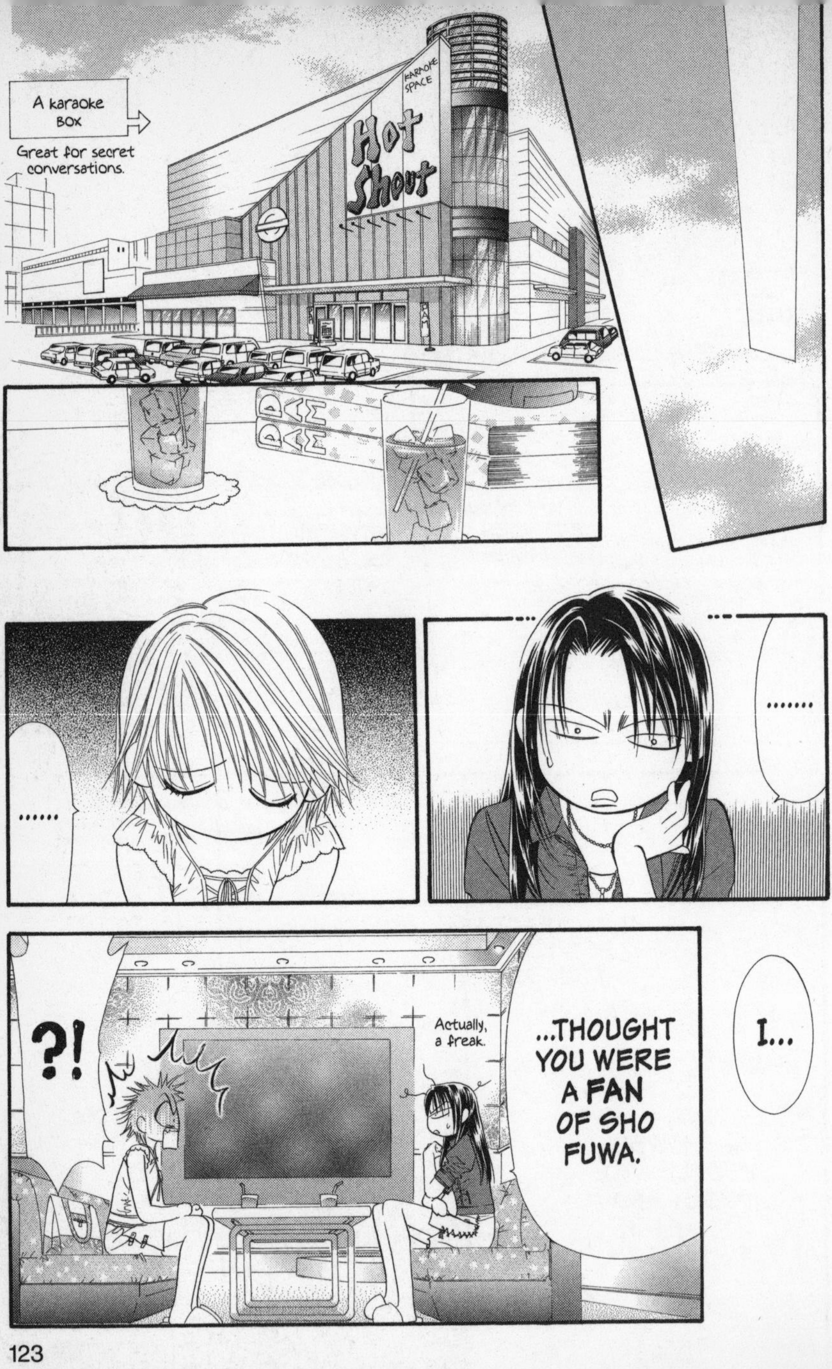
A karaoke BOX
Great for secret conversations.
KARAOKE SPACE
Hot Shout
......
......
I...
...THOUGHT YOU WERE A FAN OF SHO FUWA.
Actually, a freak.
?!

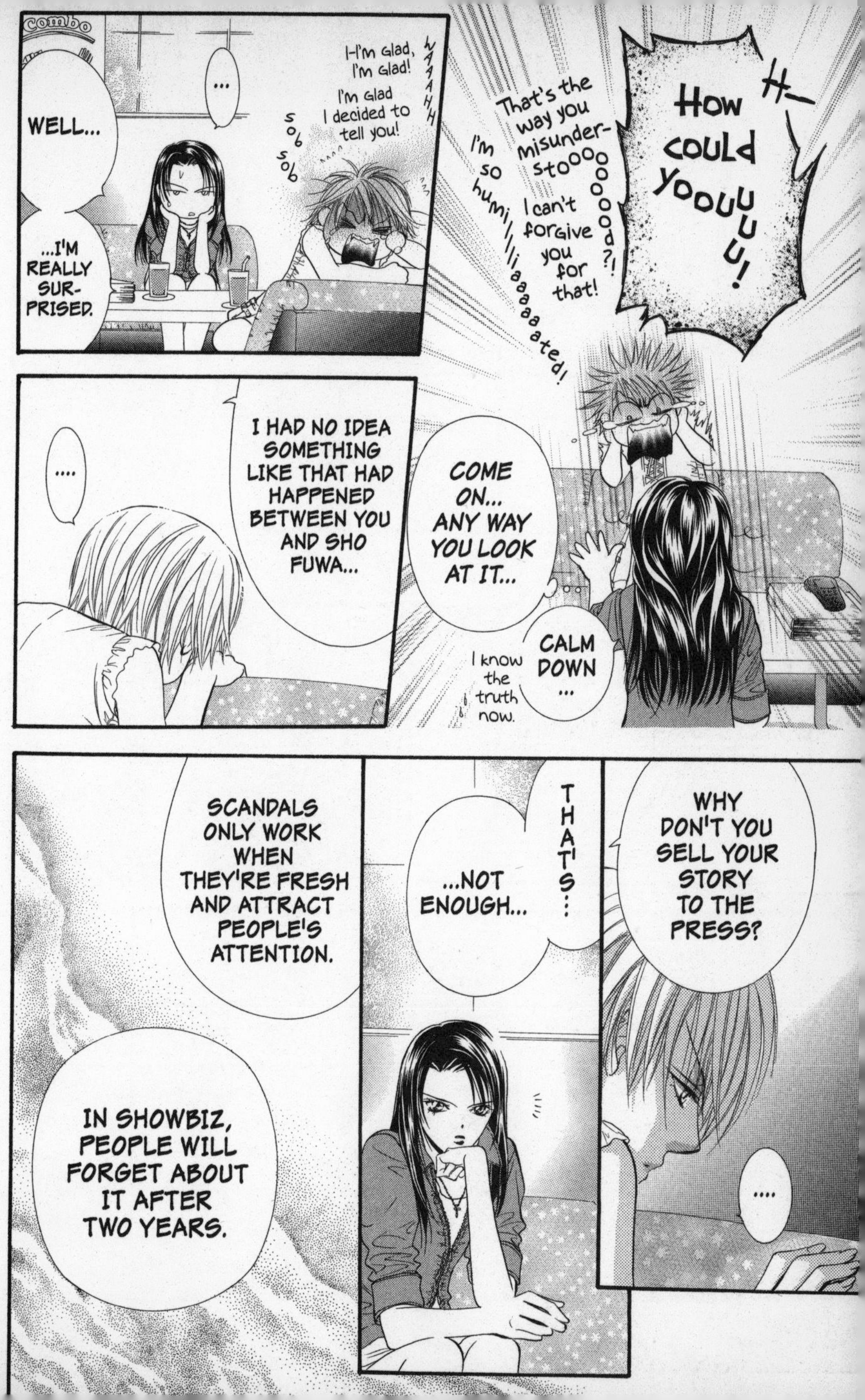
H—
How could yoouuuuu!
That's the way you misunder-stoooooooood?!
I can't forgive you for that!
I'm so humiliaaaaaated!
I-I'm glad, I'm glad!
I'm glad I decided to tell you!
WAAAAHH
sob sob
...
WELL...
...I'M REALLY SUR-PRISED.
COME ON... ANY WAY YOU LOOK AT IT...
CALM DOWN...
I know the truth now.
I HAD NO IDEA SOMETHING LIKE THAT HAD HAPPENED BETWEEN YOU AND SHO FUWA...
....
WHY DON'T YOU SELL YOUR STORY TO THE PRESS?
....
THAT'S...
...NOT ENOUGH...
SCANDALS ONLY WORK WHEN THEY'RE FRESH AND ATTRACT PEOPLE'S ATTENTION.
IN SHOWBIZ, PEOPLE WILL FORGET ABOUT IT AFTER TWO YEARS.

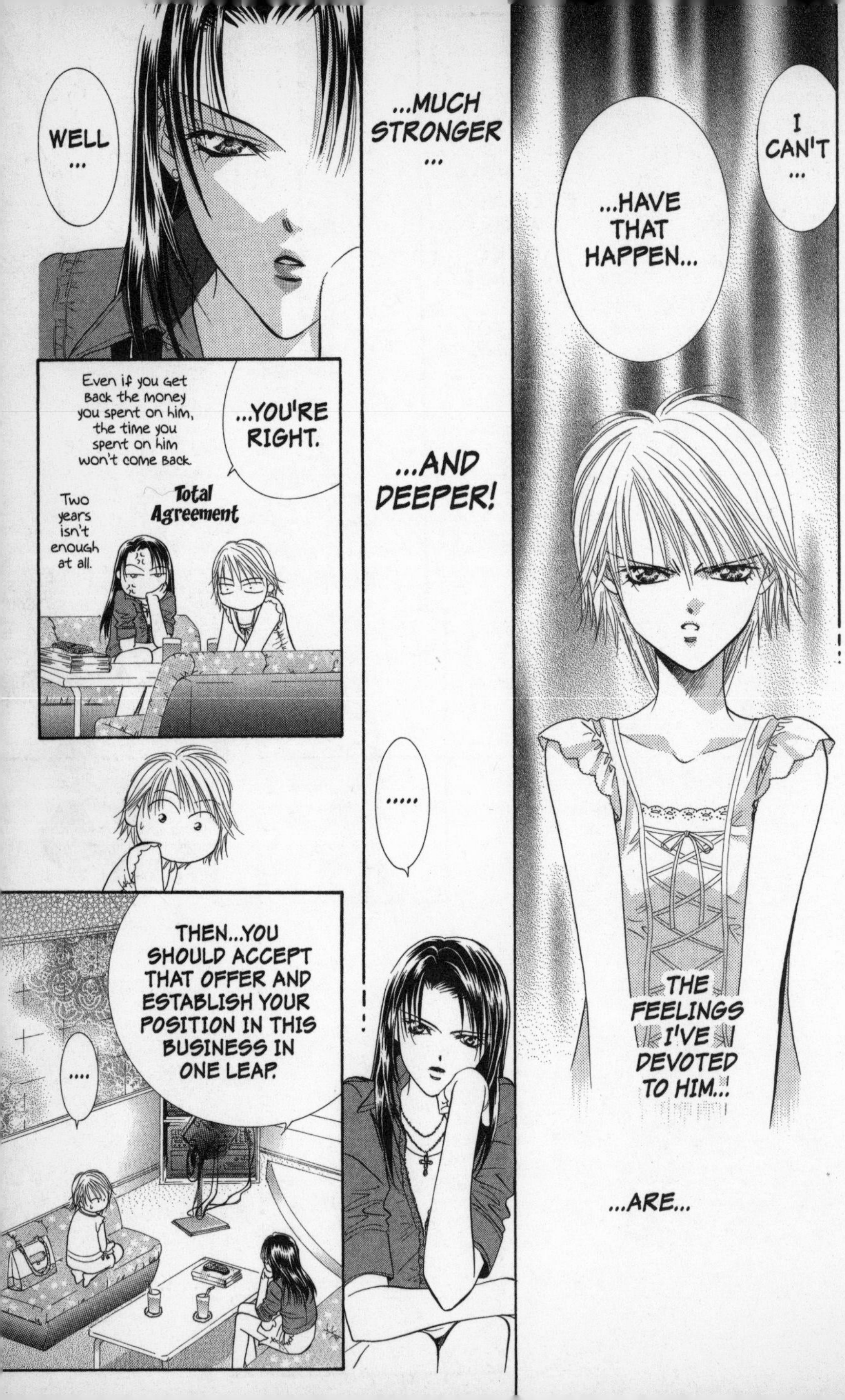
I CAN'T...
...HAVE THAT HAPPEN...
THE FEELINGS I'VE DEVOTED TO HIM...!
...ARE...
...MUCH STRONGER...
...AND DEEPER!
WELL...
...YOU'RE RIGHT.
Even if you get back the money you spent on him, the time you spent on him won't come back.
Total Agreement
Two years isn't enough at all.
.....
THEN...YOU SHOULD ACCEPT THAT OFFER AND ESTABLISH YOUR POSITION IN THIS BUSINESS IN ONE LEAP.
....

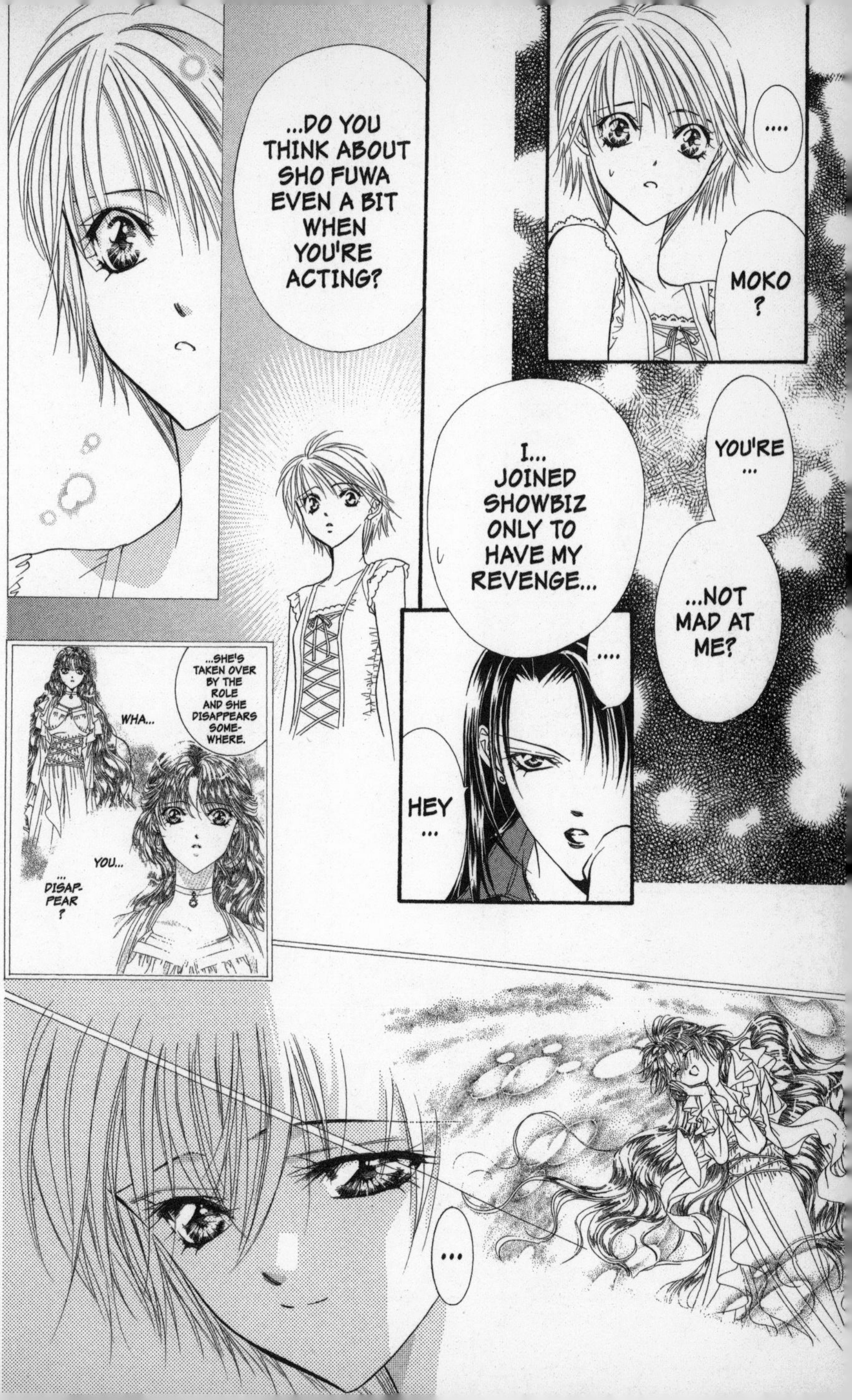
....
MOKO?
YOU'RE...
...NOT MAD AT ME?
....
HEY...
I... JOINED SHOWBIZ ONLY TO HAVE MY REVENGE...
...DO YOU THINK ABOUT SHO FUWA EVEN A BIT WHEN YOU'RE ACTING?
...SHE'S TAKEN OVER BY THE ROLE AND SHE DISAPPEARS SOME-WHERE.
WHA...
YOU...
...DISAP-PEAR?
...

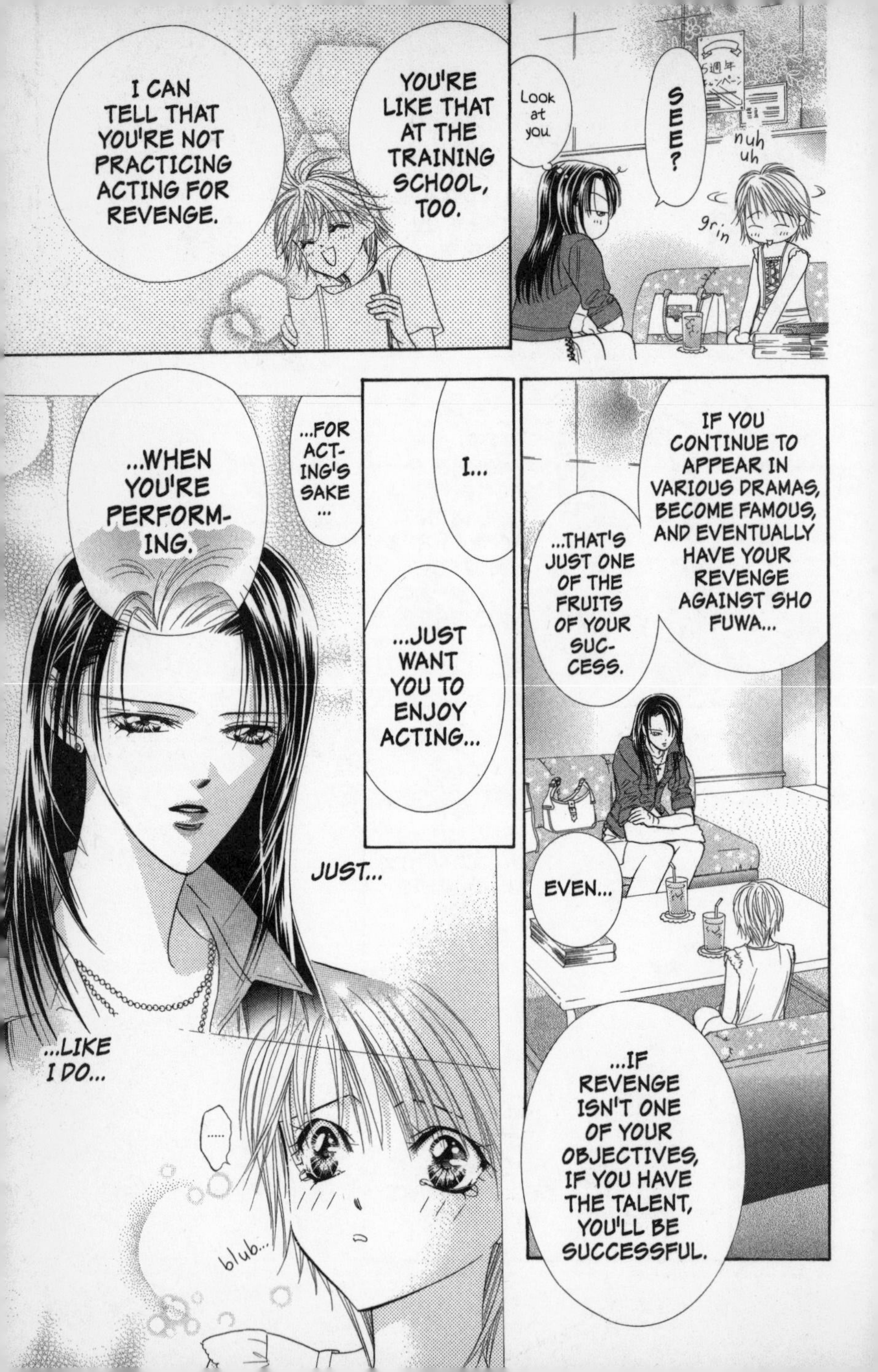
SEE?
Look at you.
nuh uh
grin
YOU'RE LIKE THAT AT THE TRAINING SCHOOL, TOO.
I CAN TELL THAT YOU'RE NOT PRACTICING ACTING FOR REVENGE.
IF YOU CONTINUE TO APPEAR IN VARIOUS DRAMAS, BECOME FAMOUS, AND EVENTUALLY HAVE YOUR REVENGE AGAINST SHO FUWA...
...THAT'S JUST ONE OF THE FRUITS OF YOUR SUC-CESS.
EVEN...
...IF REVENGE ISN'T ONE OF YOUR OBJECTIVES, IF YOU HAVE THE TALENT, YOU'LL BE SUCCESSFUL.
I...
...JUST WANT YOU TO ENJOY ACTING...
...FOR ACT-ING'S SAKE...
...WHEN YOU'RE PERFORM-ING.
JUST...
...LIKE I DO...
......
blub...

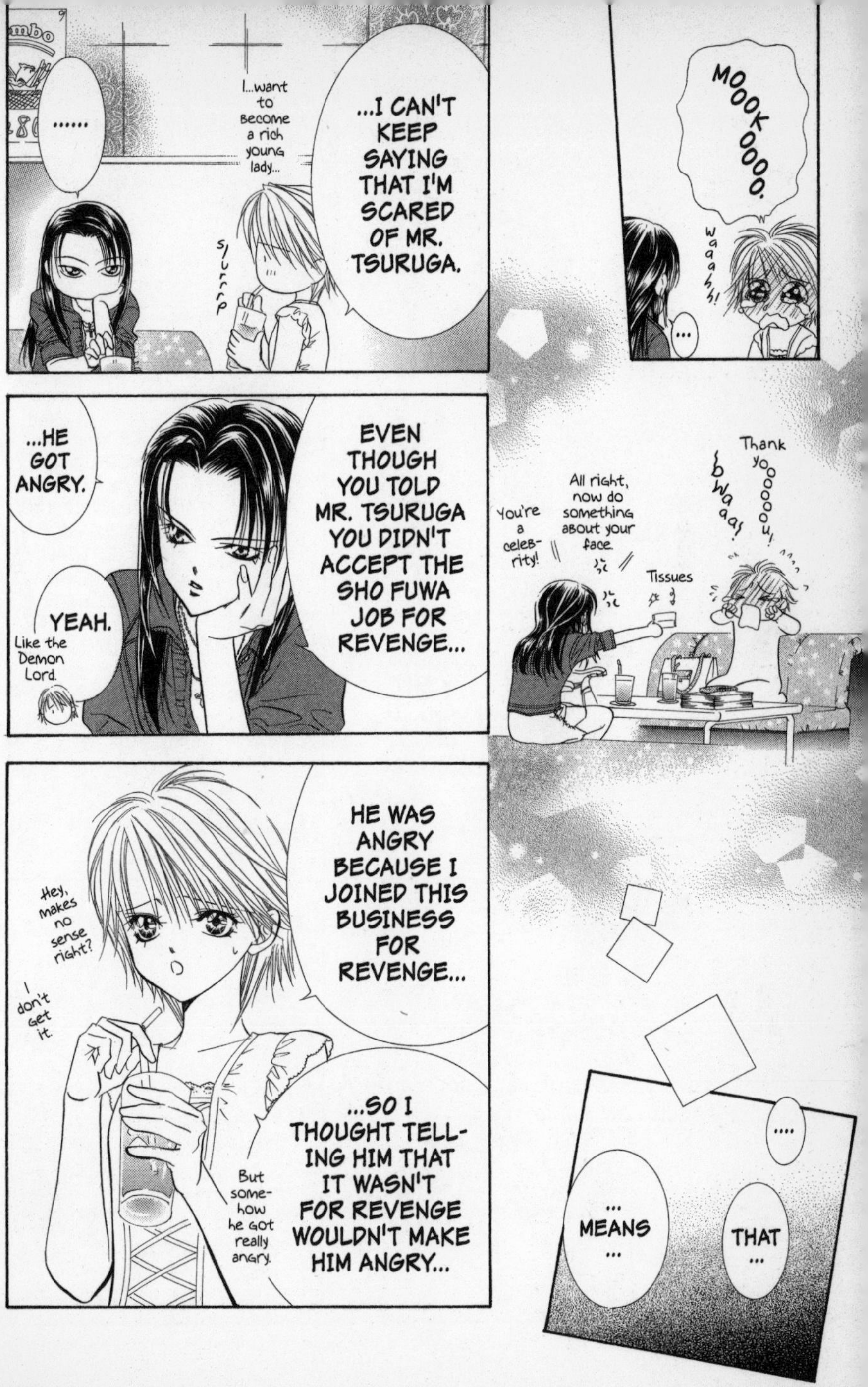
MOOOKOOOO.
Waaahh!
...
...I CAN'T KEEP SAYING THAT I'M SCARED OF MR. TSURUGA.
I...want to become a rich young lady...
slurrrp
......
Thank yooooooou!
bwaaa!
All right, now do something about your face.
You're a celebrity!
Tissues
EVEN THOUGH YOU TOLD MR. TSURUGA YOU DIDN'T ACCEPT THE SHO FUWA JOB FOR REVENGE...
...HE GOT ANGRY.
YEAH.
Like the Demon Lord.
HE WAS ANGRY BECAUSE I JOINED THIS BUSINESS FOR REVENGE...
Hey, makes no sense right?
I don't get it.
...SO I THOUGHT TELLING HIM THAT IT WASN'T FOR REVENGE WOULDN'T MAKE HIM ANGRY...
But somehow he got really angry.
....
THAT...
...MEANS...

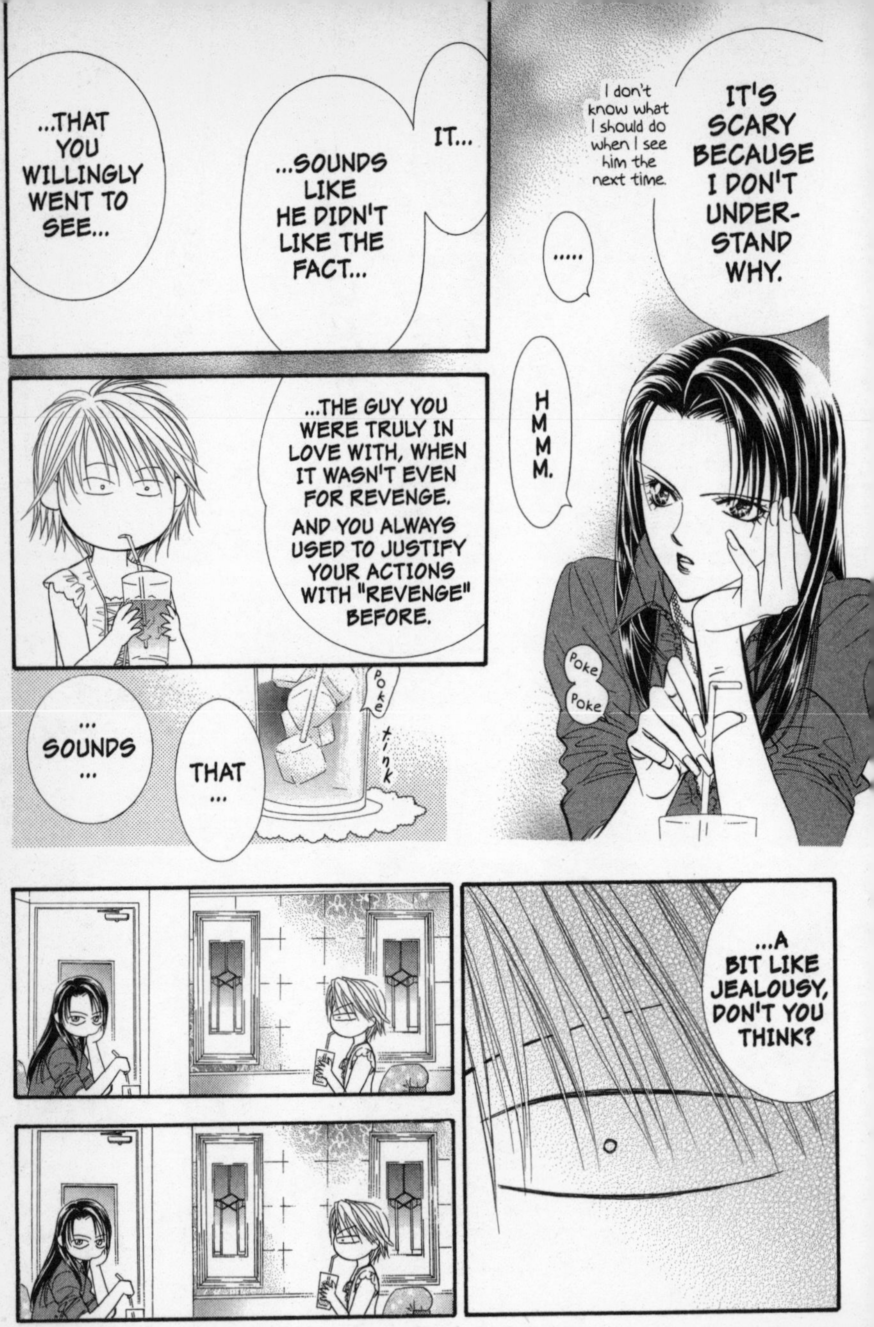
IT'S SCARY BECAUSE I DON'T UNDERSTAND WHY.
I don't know what I should do when I see him the next time.
.....
HMMM.
IT...
...SOUNDS LIKE HE DIDN'T LIKE THE FACT...
...THAT YOU WILLINGLY WENT TO SEE...
...THE GUY YOU WERE TRULY IN LOVE WITH, WHEN IT WASN'T EVEN FOR REVENGE.
AND YOU ALWAYS USED TO JUSTIFY YOUR ACTIONS WITH "REVENGE" BEFORE.
Poke
Poke
Poke
tink
THAT ...
... SOUNDS ...
...A BIT LIKE JEALOUSY, DON'T YOU THINK?

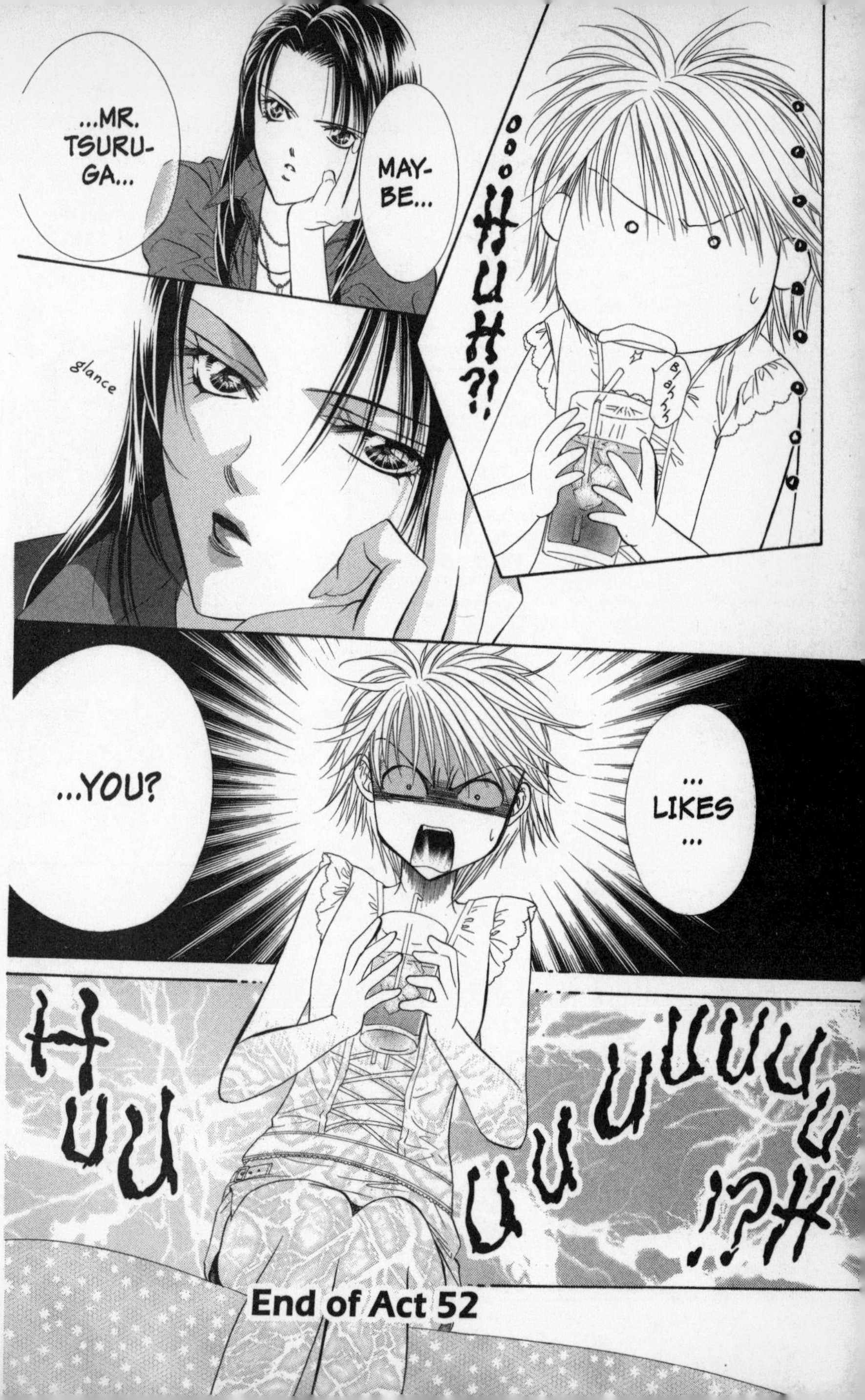
...HUUH?!
Blahhh
MAY-BE...
...MR. TSURUGA...
glance
...LIKES...
...YOU?
HUUUUUUUUH?!
End of Act 52

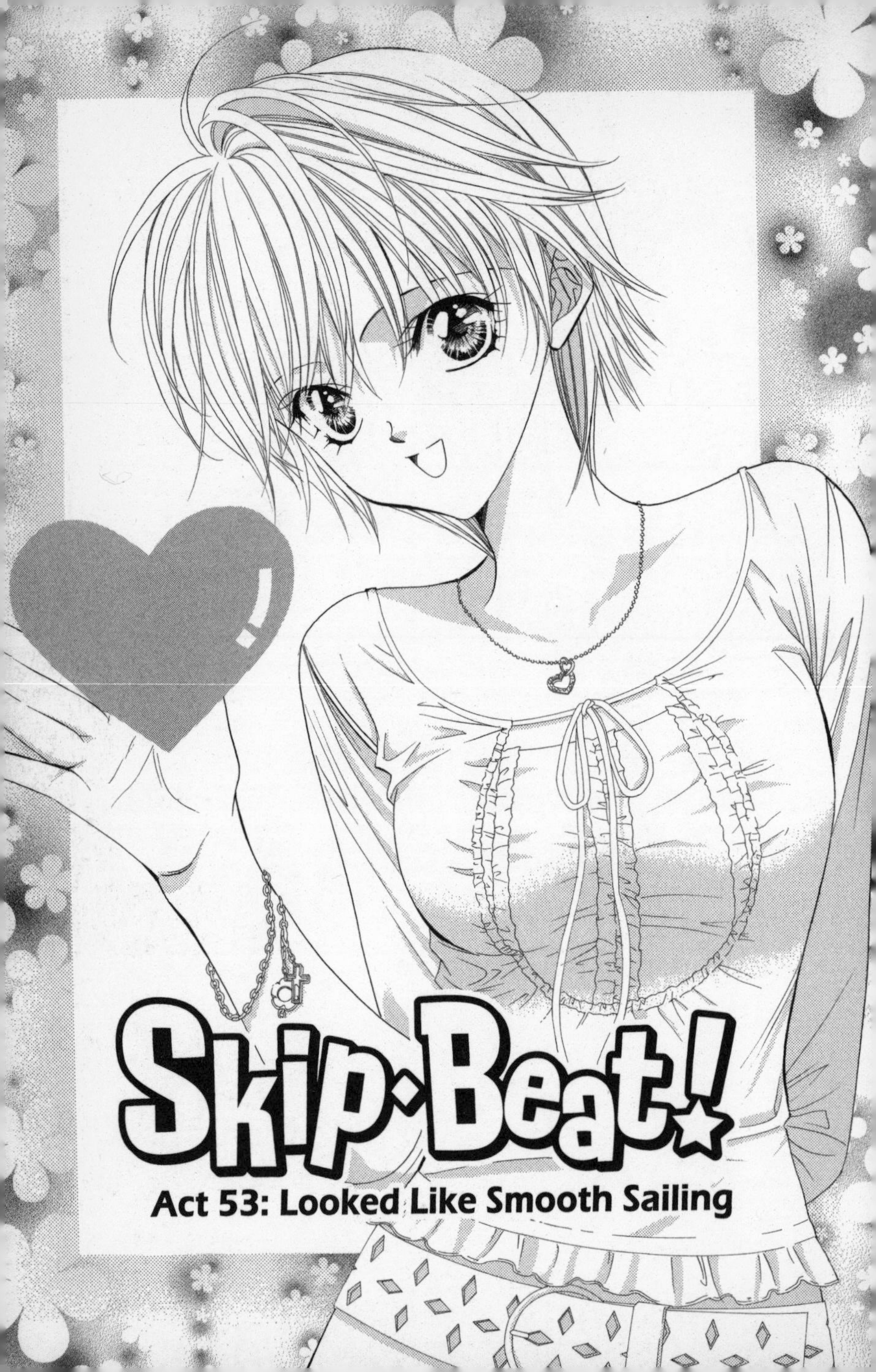
Skip·Beat!
Act 53: Looked Like Smooth Sailing

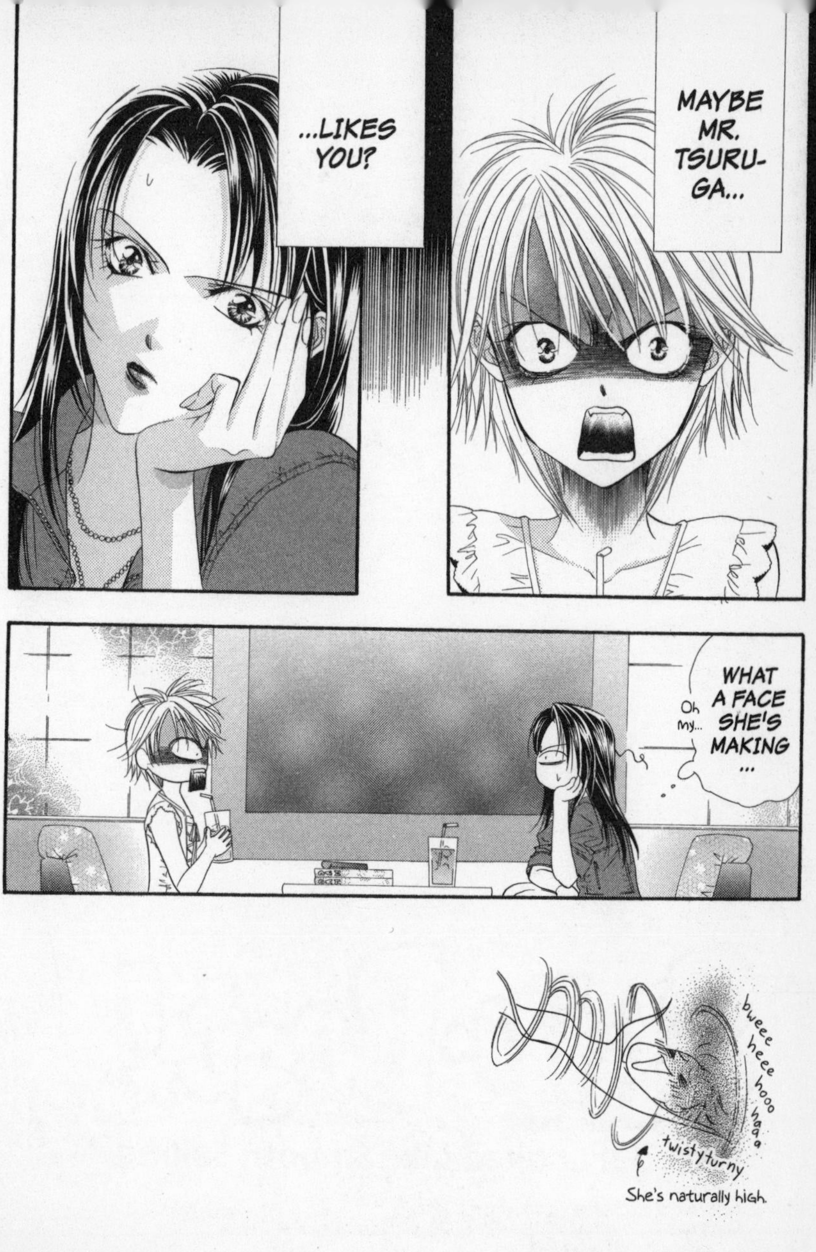
MAYBE MR. TSURU-GA...
...LIKES YOU?
WHAT A FACE SHE'S MAKING ...
Oh my...
bweee heee hooo haa
twistyturny
She's naturally high.

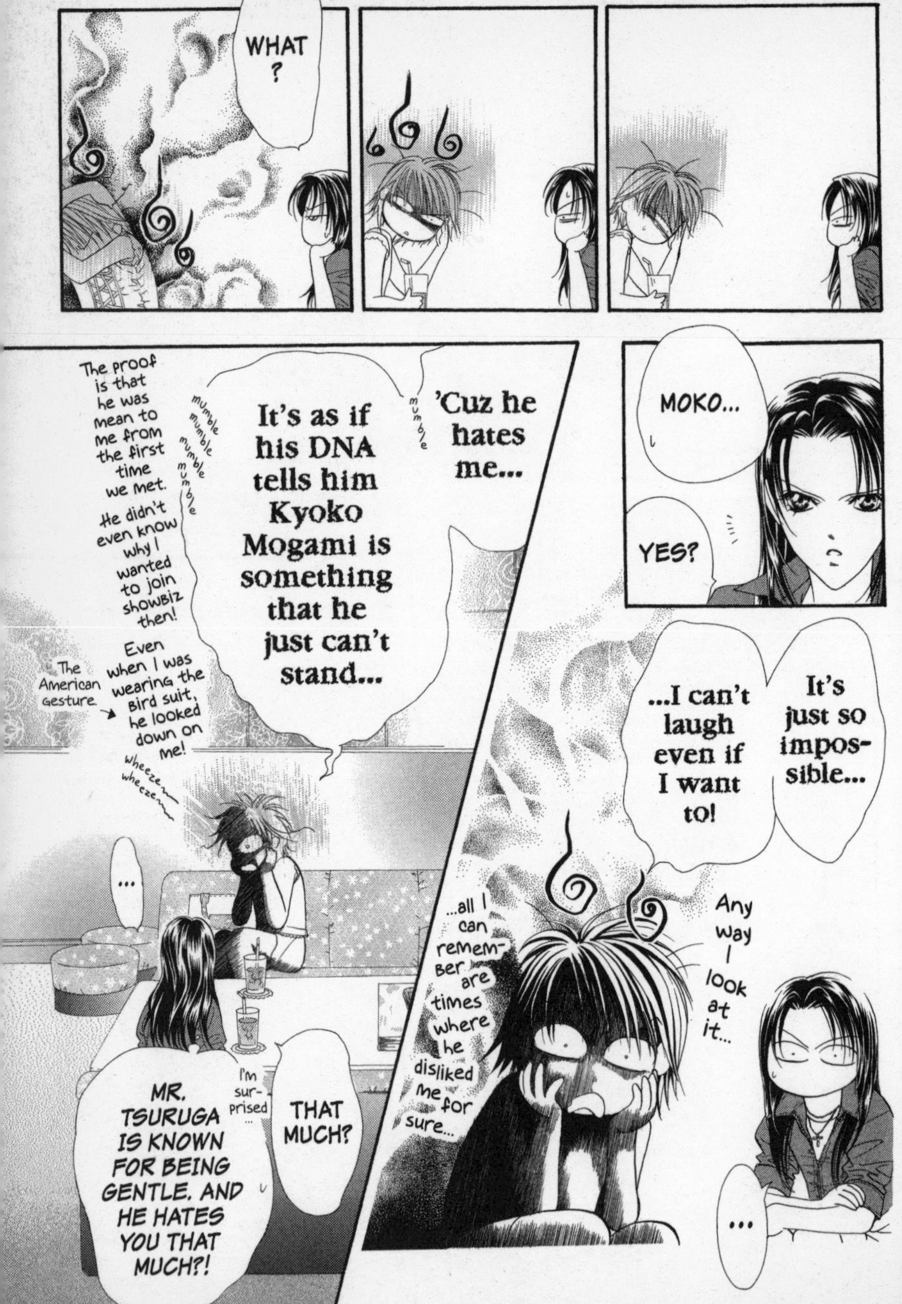
WHAT ?
MOKO...
YES?
It's just so impossible...
...I can't laugh even if I want to!
Any way I look at it...
...all I can remember are times where he disliked me for sure...
...
'Cuz he hates me...
mumble
It's as if his DNA tells him Kyoko Mogami is something that he just can't stand...
mumble mumble mumble mumble
The proof is that he was mean to me from the first time we met.
He didn't even know why I wanted to join showbiz then!
Even when I was wearing the Bird suit, he looked down on me!
The American Gesture.
wheeze wheeze
...
THAT MUCH?
I'm surprised ...
MR. TSURUGA IS KNOWN FOR BEING GENTLE. AND HE HATES YOU THAT MUCH?!

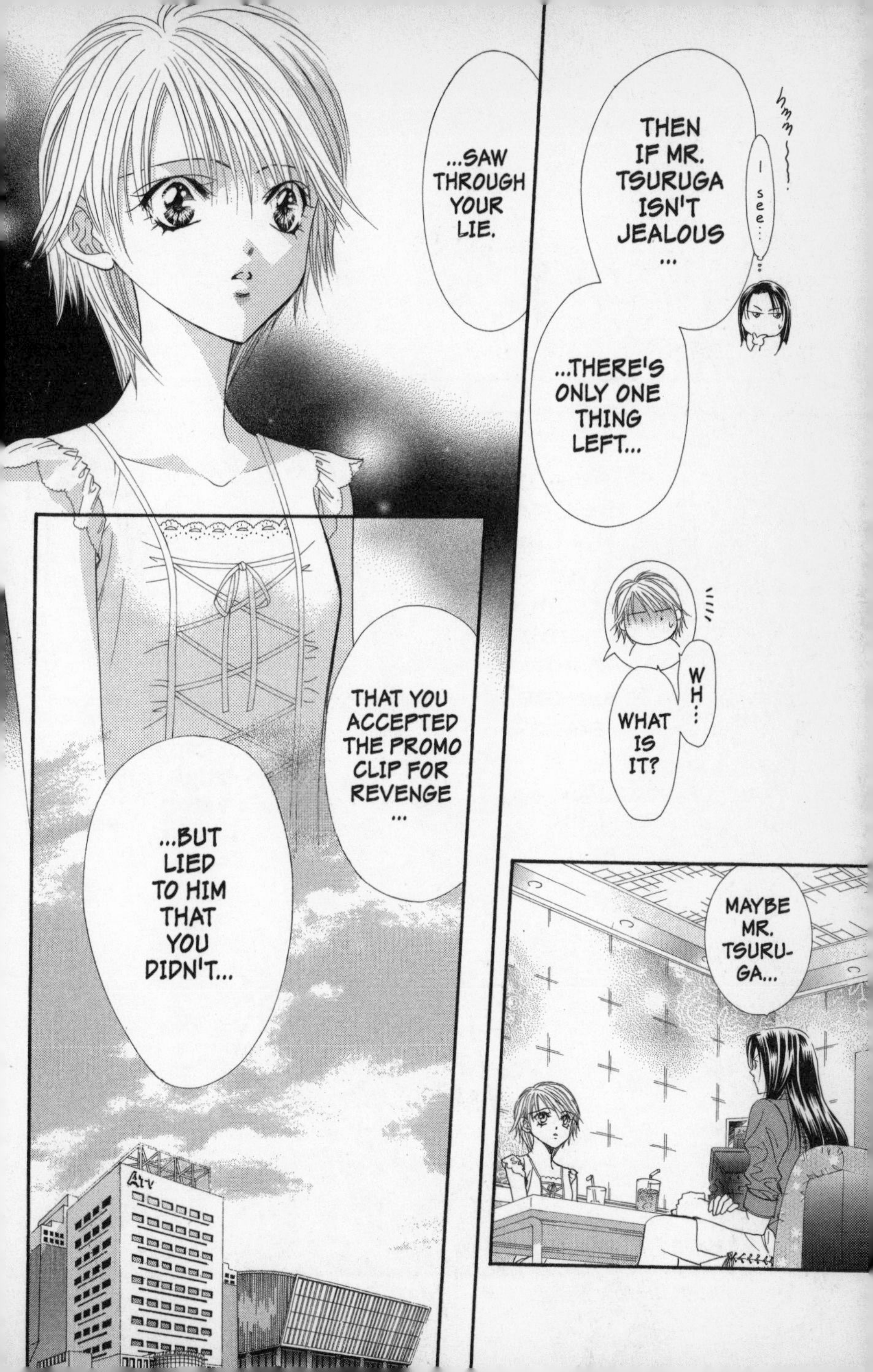
hmm~~~
I see...
THEN IF MR. TSURUGA ISN'T JEALOUS...
...THERE'S ONLY ONE THING LEFT...
WH...
WHAT IS IT?
MAYBE MR. TSURU-GA...
...SAW THROUGH YOUR LIE.
THAT YOU ACCEPTED THE PROMO CLIP FOR REVENGE...
...BUT LIED TO HIM THAT YOU DIDN'T...

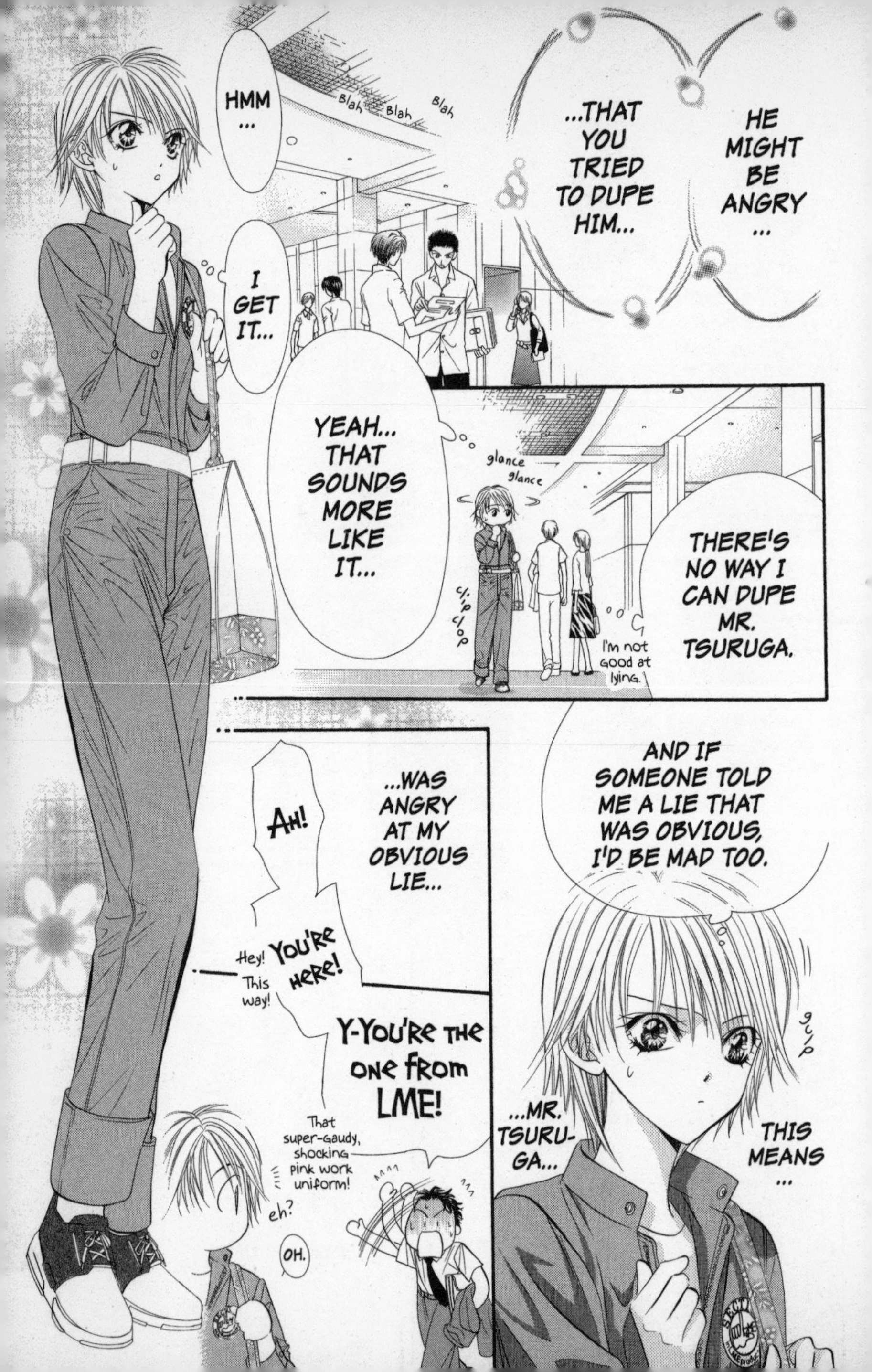
HE MIGHT BE ANGRY...
...THAT YOU TRIED TO DUPE HIM...
Blah Blah Blah
HMM...
I GET IT...
THERE'S NO WAY I CAN DUPE MR. TSURUGA.
I'm not good at lying.
glance glance
YEAH... THAT SOUNDS MORE LIKE IT...
clip clop
AND IF SOMEONE TOLD ME A LIE THAT WAS OBVIOUS, I'D BE MAD TOO.
THIS MEANS...
gulp
...MR. TSURUGA...
...WAS ANGRY AT MY OBVIOUS LIE...
AH!
YOU'RE HERE!
Hey! This way!
Y-YOU'RE THE ONE FROM LME!
That super-gaudy, shocking pink work uniform!
eh?
OH.

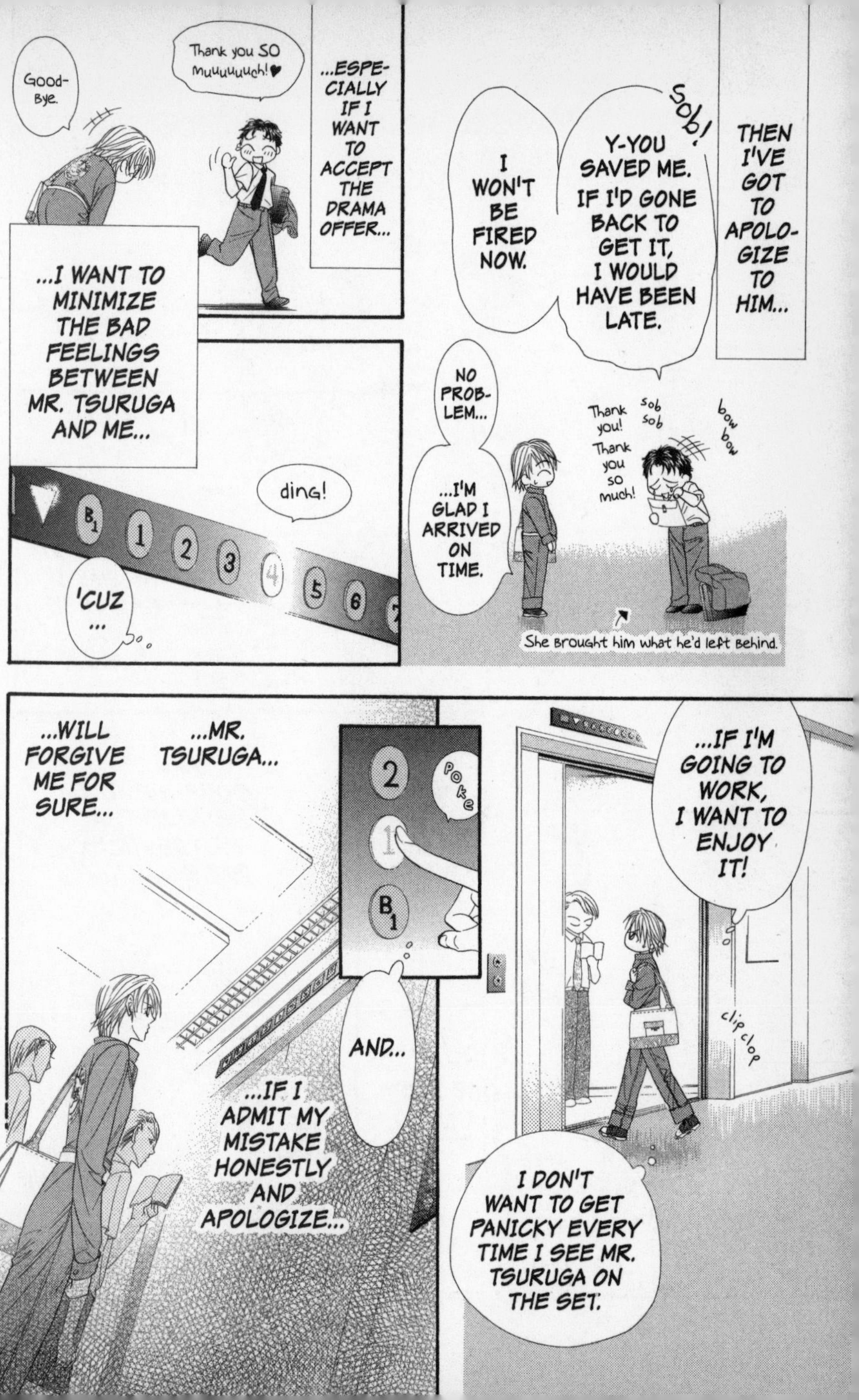
THEN I'VE GOT TO APOLOGIZE TO HIM...
Sob!
Y-YOU SAVED ME. IF I'D GONE BACK TO GET IT, I WOULD HAVE BEEN LATE.
I WON'T BE FIRED NOW.
bow bow
sob sob
Thank you! Thank you so much!
NO PROBLEM...
...I'M GLAD I ARRIVED ON TIME.
She brought him what he'd left behind.
...ESPECIALLY IF I WANT TO ACCEPT THE DRAMA OFFER...
Thank you SO muuuuuuch!♥
Good-Bye.
...I WANT TO MINIMIZE THE BAD FEELINGS BETWEEN MR. TSURUGA AND ME...
ding!
'CUZ...
...IF I'M GOING TO WORK, I WANT TO ENJOY IT!
clip clop
I DON'T WANT TO GET PANICKY EVERY TIME I SEE MR. TSURUGA ON THE SET.
Poke
AND...
...IF I ADMIT MY MISTAKE HONESTLY AND APOLOGIZE...
...MR. TSURUGA...
...WILL FORGIVE ME FOR SURE...

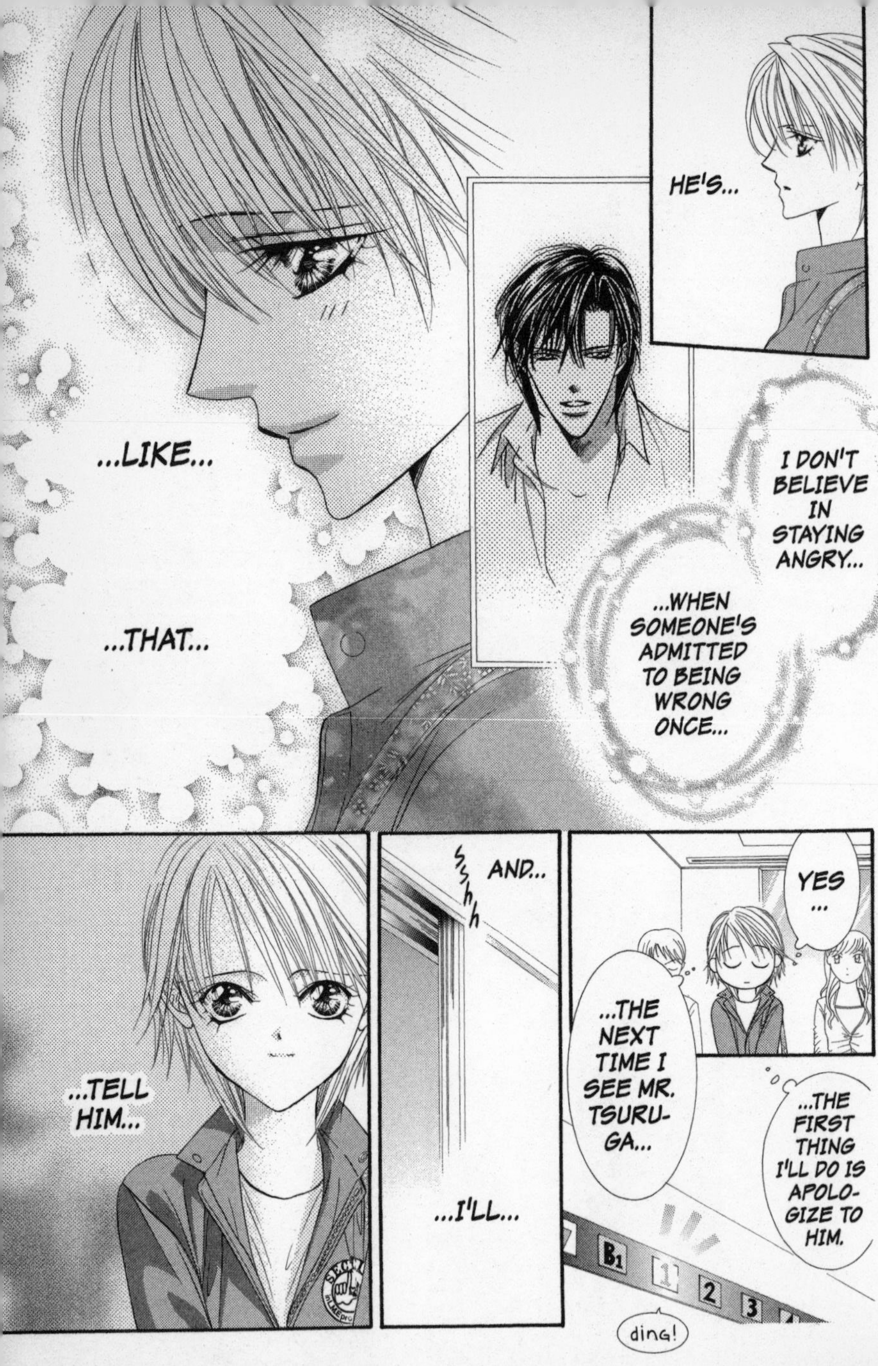
HE'S...
I DON'T BELIEVE IN STAYING ANGRY...
...WHEN SOMEONE'S ADMITTED TO BEING WRONG ONCE...
...LIKE...
...THAT...
YES ...
...THE NEXT TIME I SEE MR. TSURU-GA...
...THE FIRST THING I'LL DO IS APOLO-GIZE TO HIM.
B1 1 2 3
ding!
shhh
AND...
...I'LL...
...TELL HIM...

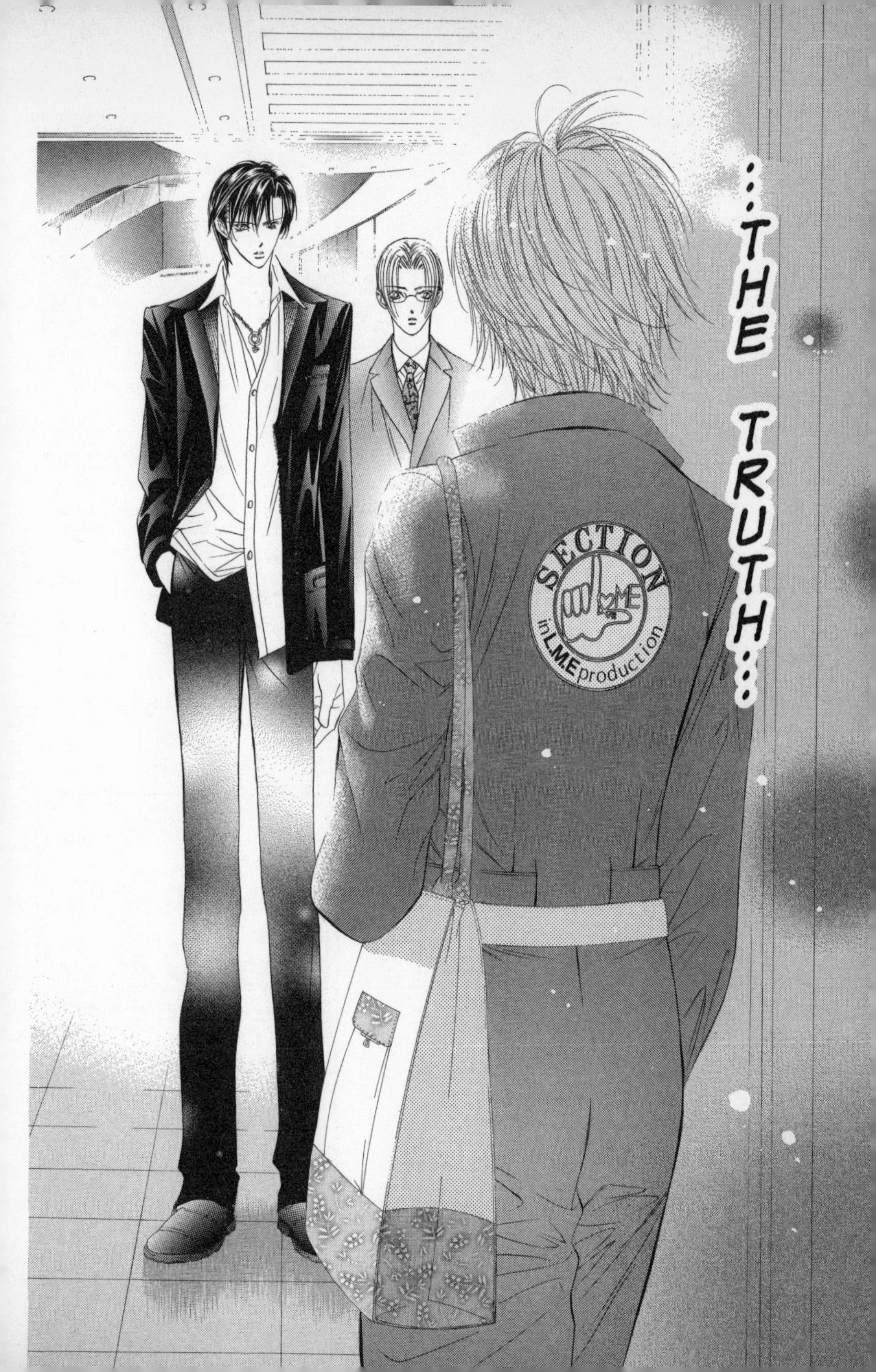
..THE TRUTH..
SECTION
LOVE ME
in L.M.E production

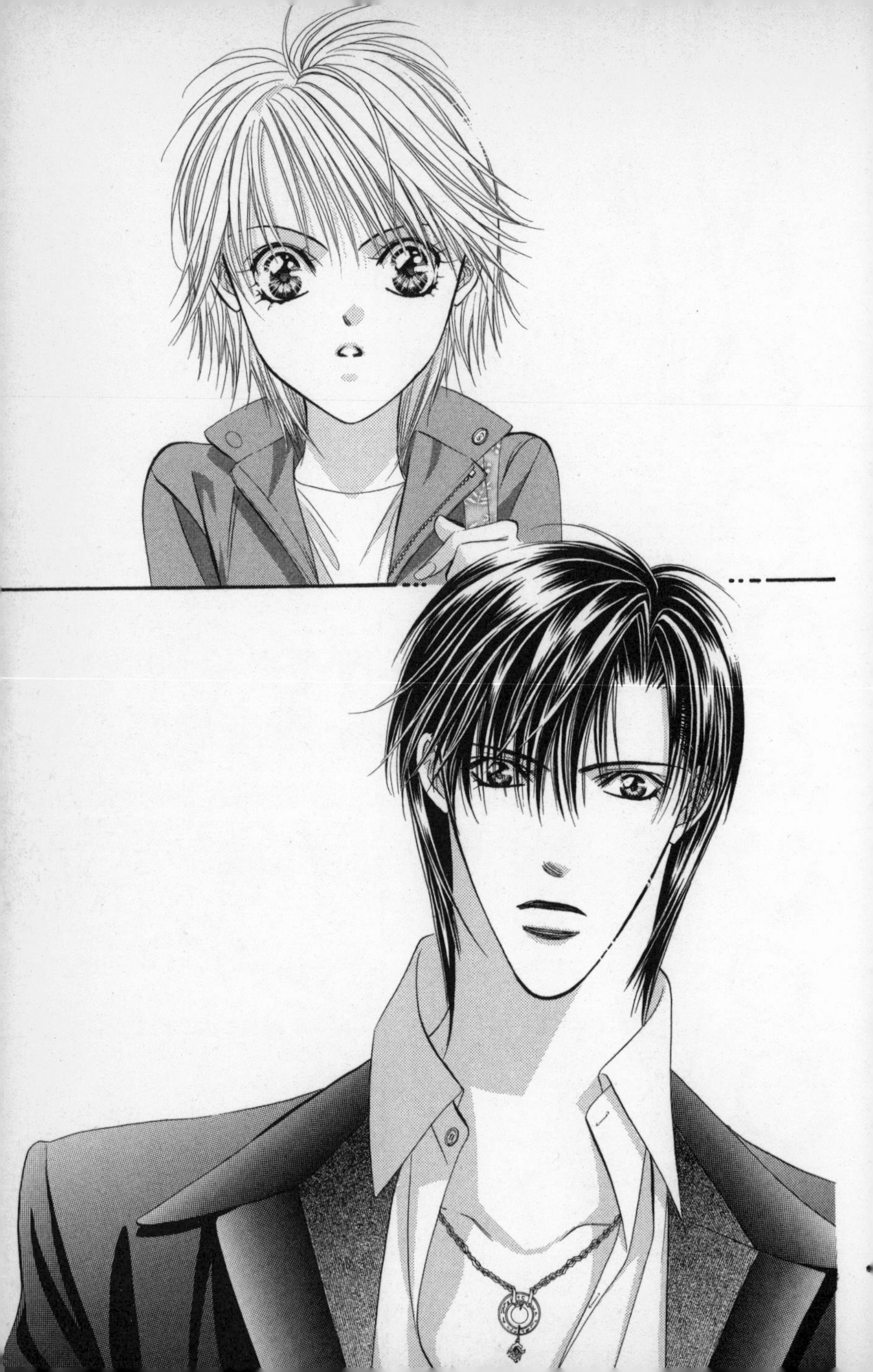

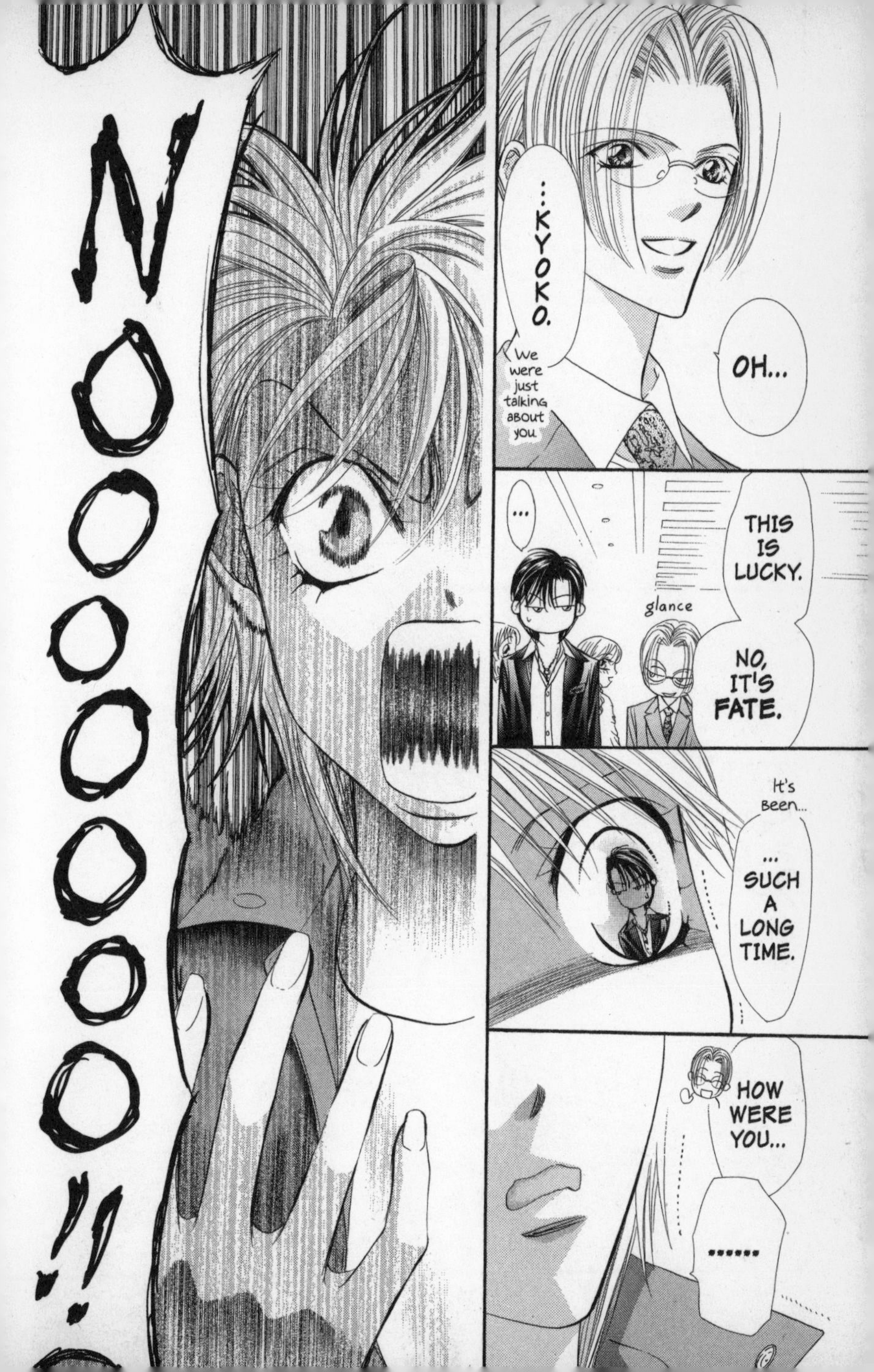
OH...
...KYOKO.
We were just talking about you.
THIS IS LUCKY.
NO, IT'S FATE.
glance
...
It's been...
...SUCH A LONG TIME.
HOW WERE YOU...
......
NOOOOOOOO!!

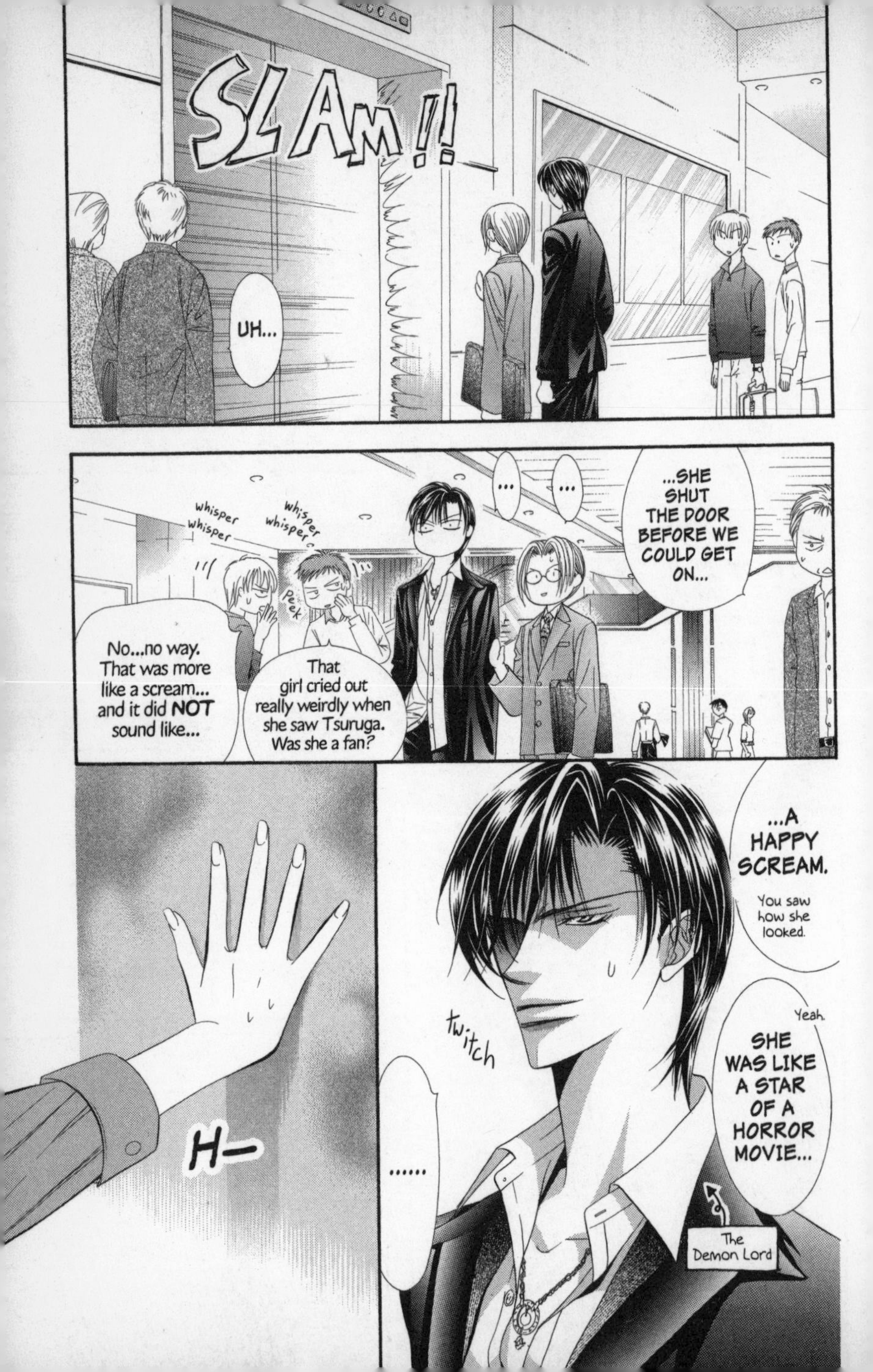
SLAM!!
UH...
...SHE SHUT THE DOOR BEFORE WE COULD GET ON...
...
...
whisper whisper
whisper whisper
Peek
That girl cried out really weirdly when she saw Tsuruga. Was she a fan?
No...no way. That was more like a scream... and it did **NOT** sound like...
...A HAPPY SCREAM.
You saw how she looked.
Yeah.
SHE WAS LIKE A STAR OF A HORROR MOVIE...
twitch
......
The Demon Lord
H—

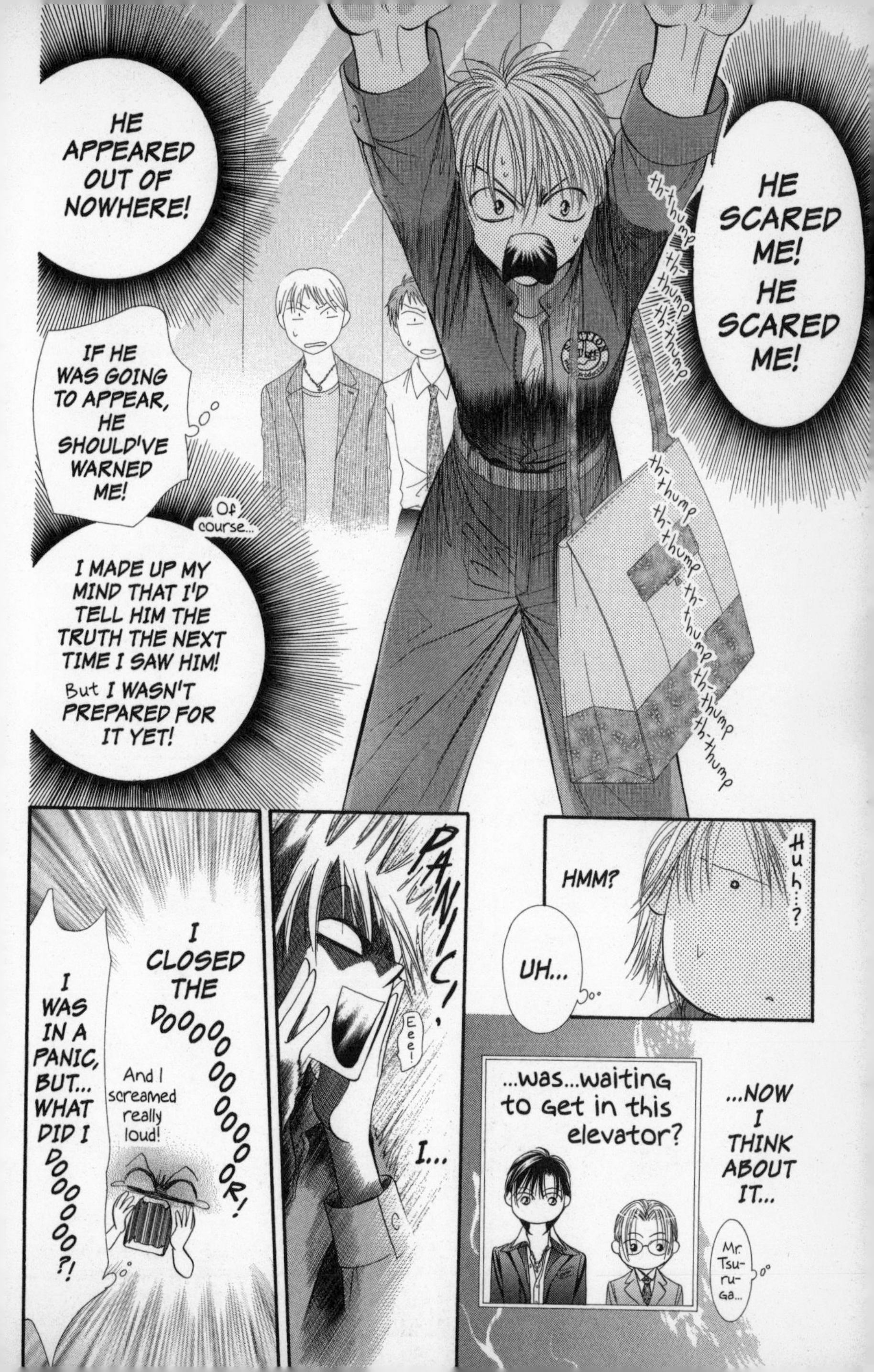
HE SCARED ME! HE SCARED ME!
th-thump th-thump th-thump
HE APPEARED OUT OF NOWHERE!
IF HE WAS GOING TO APPEAR, HE SHOULD'VE WARNED ME!
Of course...
th-thump th-thump th-thump th-thump th-thump
I MADE UP MY MIND THAT I'D TELL HIM THE TRUTH THE NEXT TIME I SAW HIM!
But I WASN'T PREPARED FOR IT YET!
Huh...?
HMM?
UH...
...NOW I THINK ABOUT IT...
Mr. Tsu-ru-ga...
...was...waiting to get in this elevator?
PANIC!
Eee!
I...
I CLOSED THE DOOOOOOOOOOOOOR!
I WAS IN A PANIC, BUT... WHAT DID I DOOOOOOO?!
And I screamed really loud!

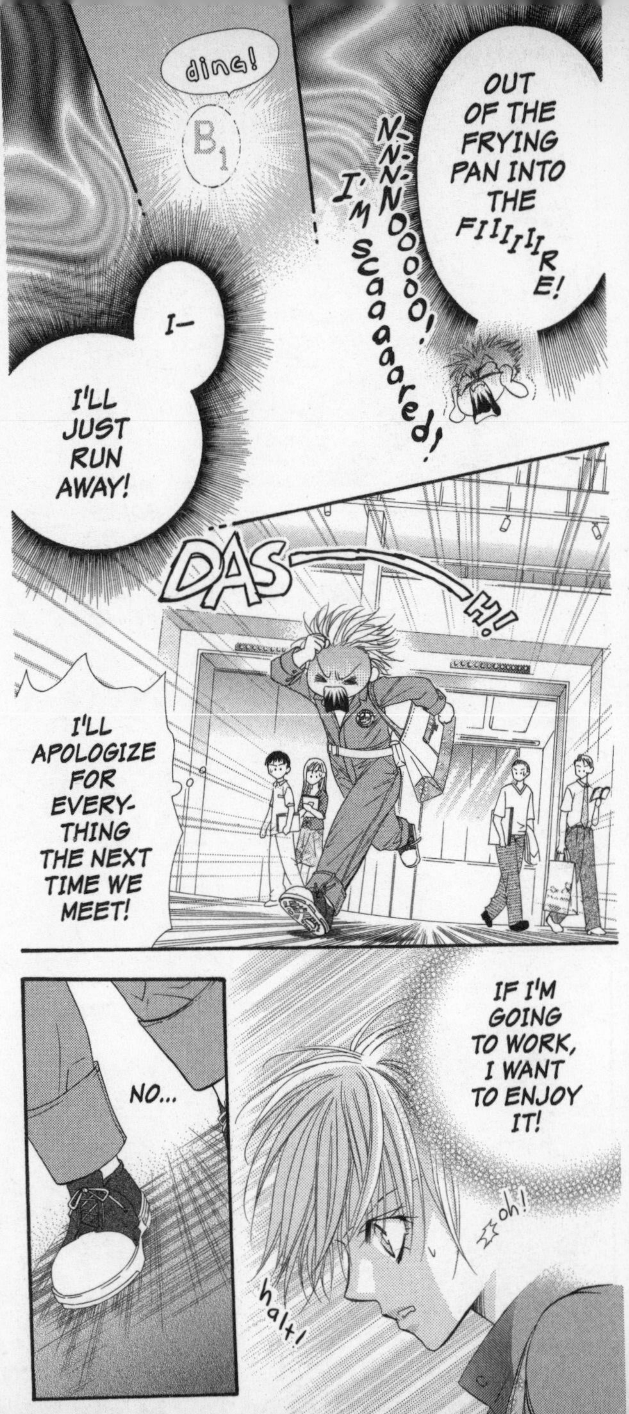
OUT OF THE FRYING PAN INTO THE FIIIIIIRE!
N-N-N-NOOOOO! I'M SCAAAARED!
ding!
B_1
I—
I'LL JUST RUN AWAY!
DASH!
I'LL APOLOGIZE FOR EVERYTHING THE NEXT TIME WE MEET!
IF I'M GOING TO WORK, I WANT TO ENJOY IT!
oh!
halt!
NO...

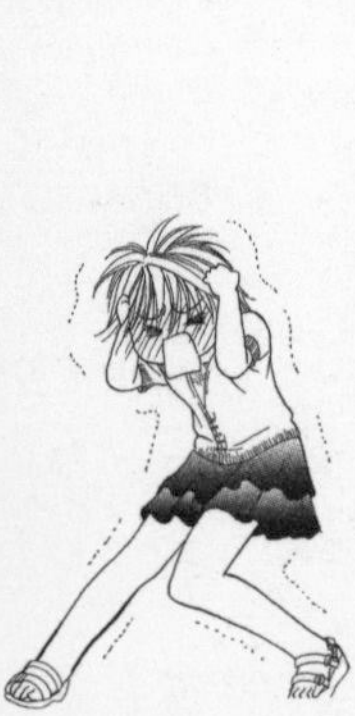

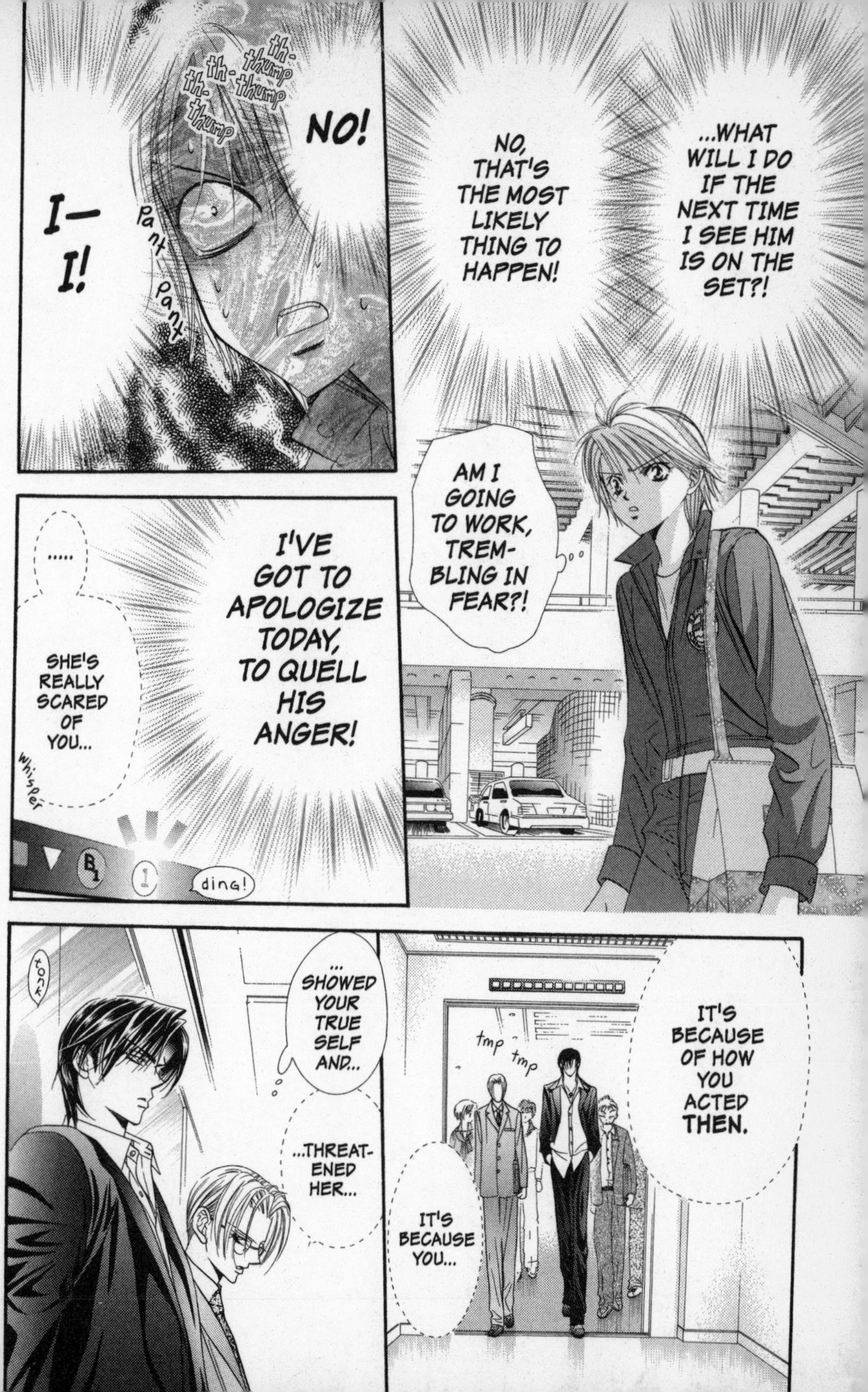
...WHAT WILL I DO IF THE NEXT TIME I SEE HIM IS ON THE SET?!
NO, THAT'S THE MOST LIKELY THING TO HAPPEN!
AM I GOING TO WORK, TREMBLING IN FEAR?!
th-thump th-thump th-thump
NO!
I— I!
Pant Pant
I'VE GOT TO APOLOGIZE TODAY, TO QUELL HIS ANGER!
.....
SHE'S REALLY SCARED OF YOU...
whisper
ding!
IT'S BECAUSE OF HOW YOU ACTED THEN.
tmp tmp
IT'S BECAUSE YOU...
...SHOWED YOUR TRUE SELF AND...
...THREATENED HER...
tonk

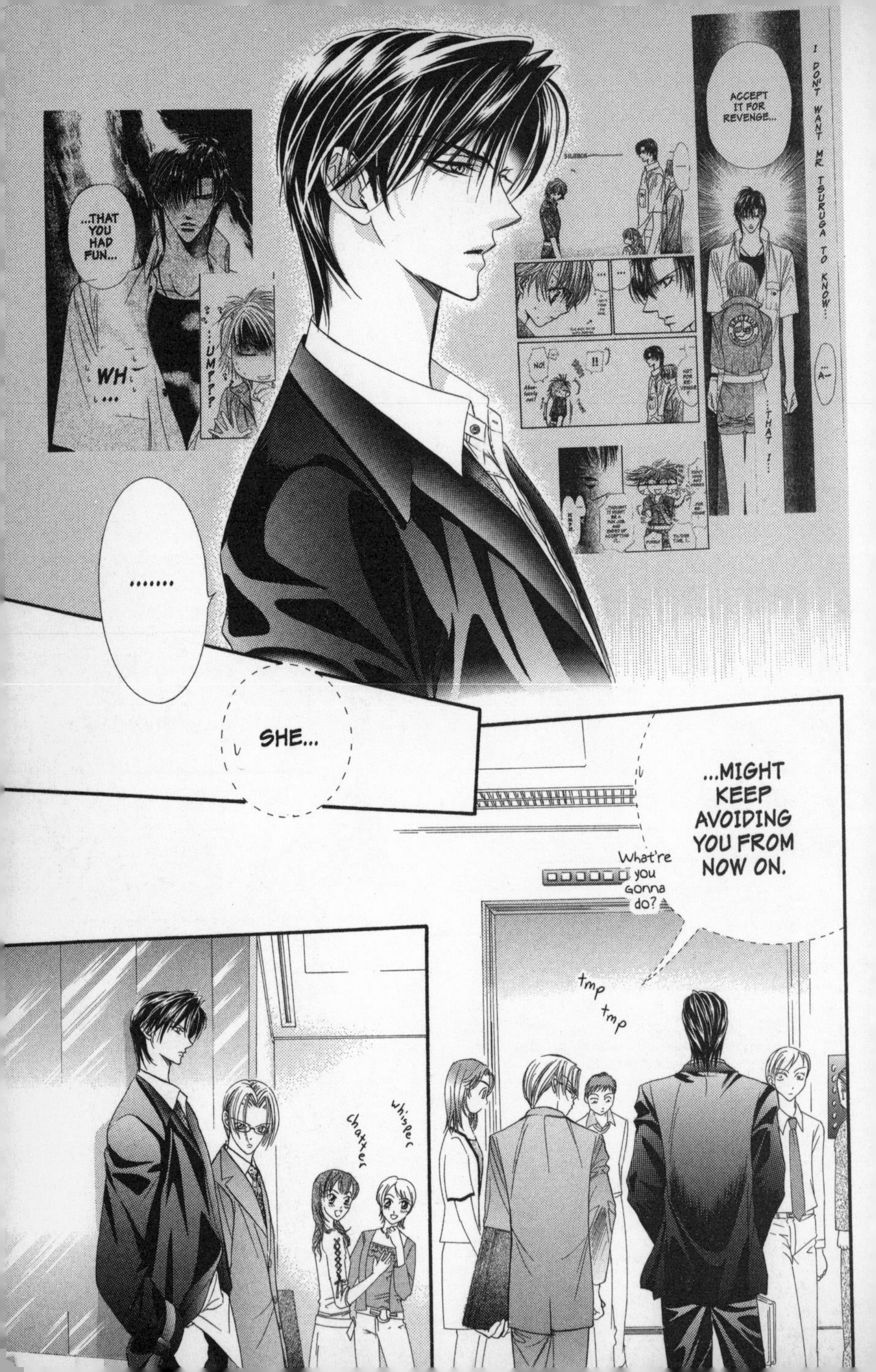
I DON'T WANT MR. TSURUGA TO KNOW...
...THAT I...
...A—
ACCEPT IT FOR REVENGE...
...THAT YOU HAD FUN...
...UMP??
WH...
....
SHE...
...MIGHT KEEP AVOIDING YOU FROM NOW ON.
What're you gonna do?
tmp tmp
whisper
chatter

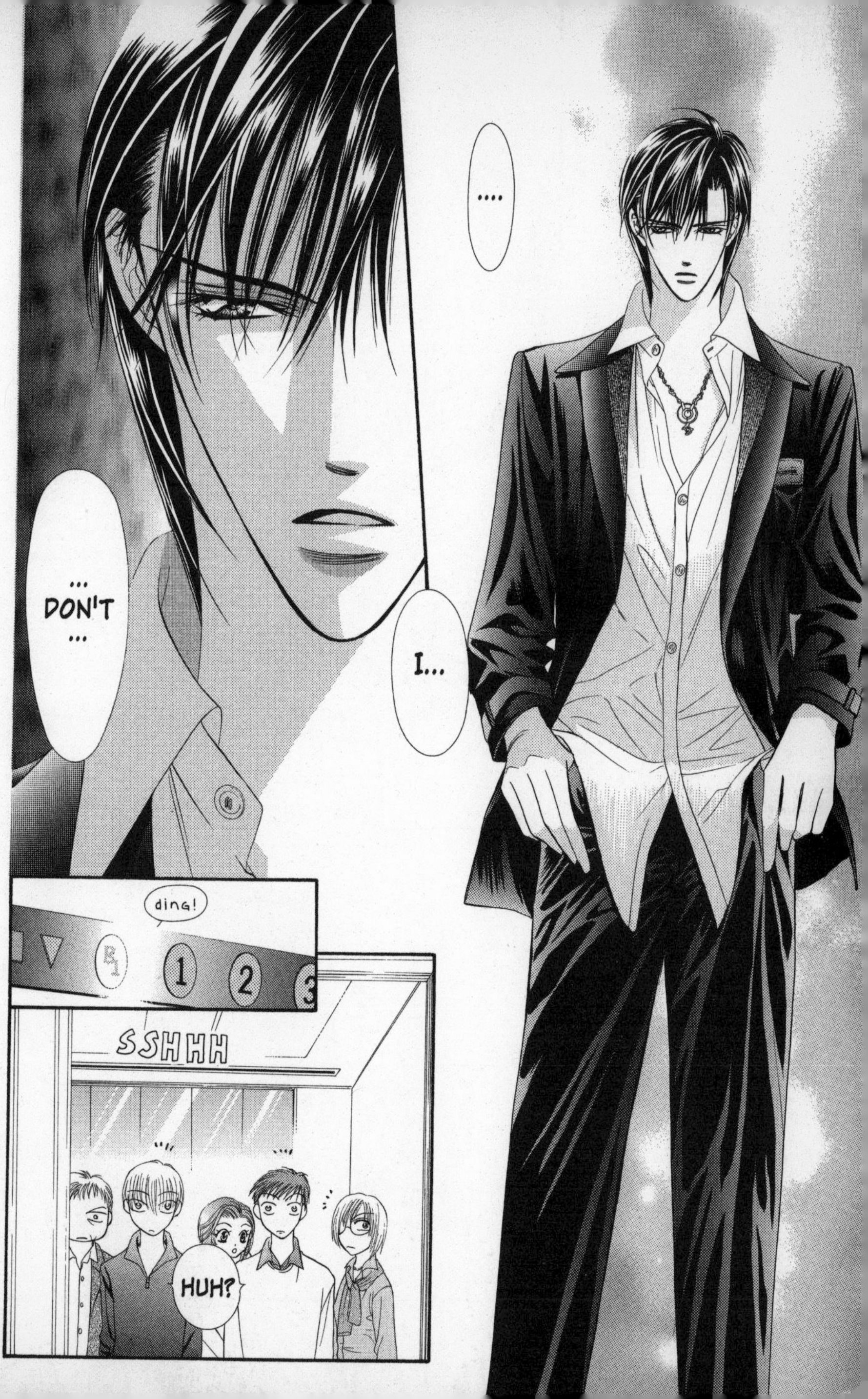
....
I...
... DON'T ...
ding!
SSHHH
HUH?

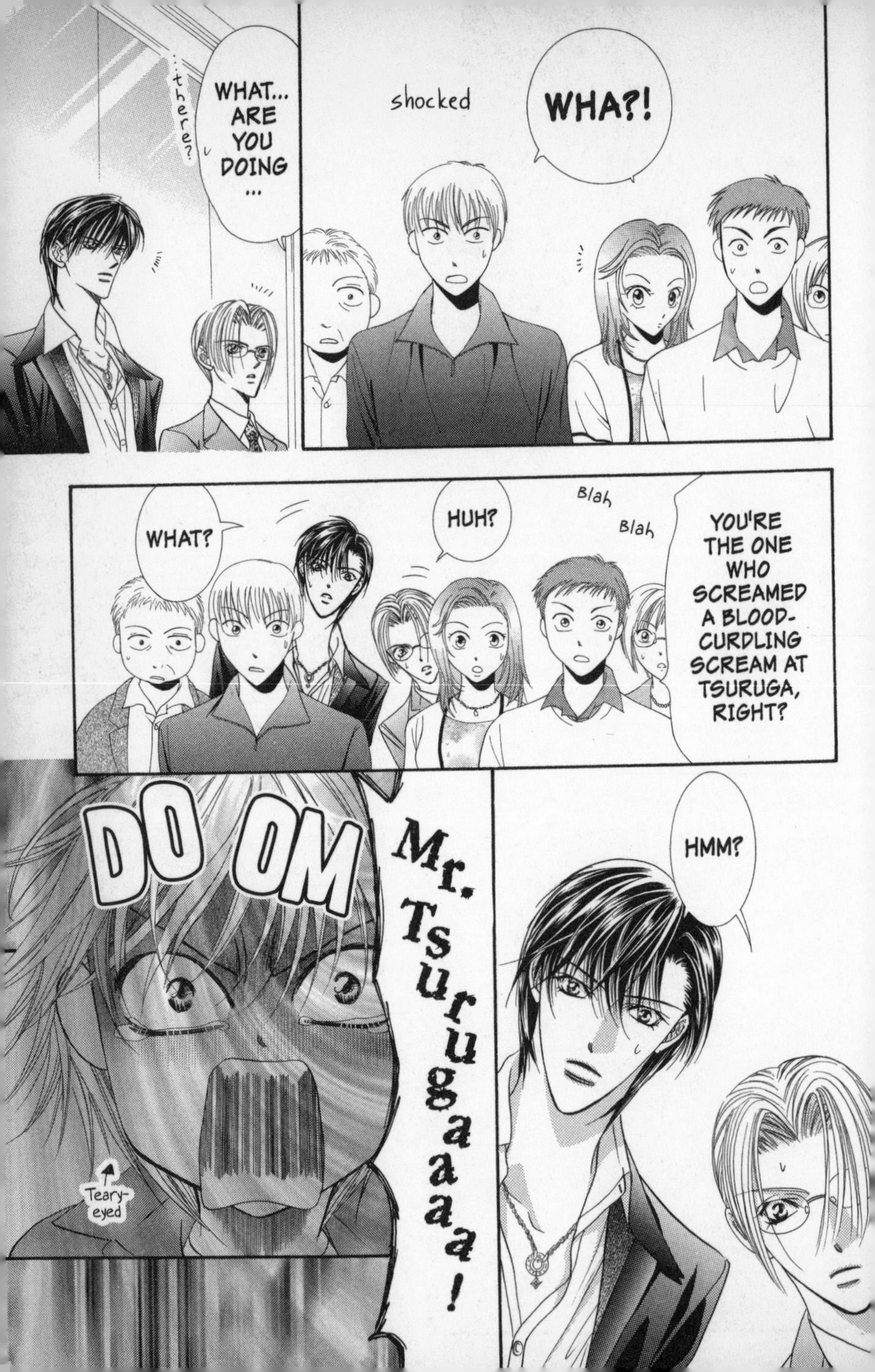

WHA?!
shocked
WHAT... ARE YOU DOING...
...there?
YOU'RE THE ONE WHO SCREAMED A BLOOD-CURDLING SCREAM AT TSURUGA, RIGHT?
Blah
Blah
HUH?
WHAT?
HMM?
DO OM
Mr. Tsurugaaaaa!
Teary-eyed

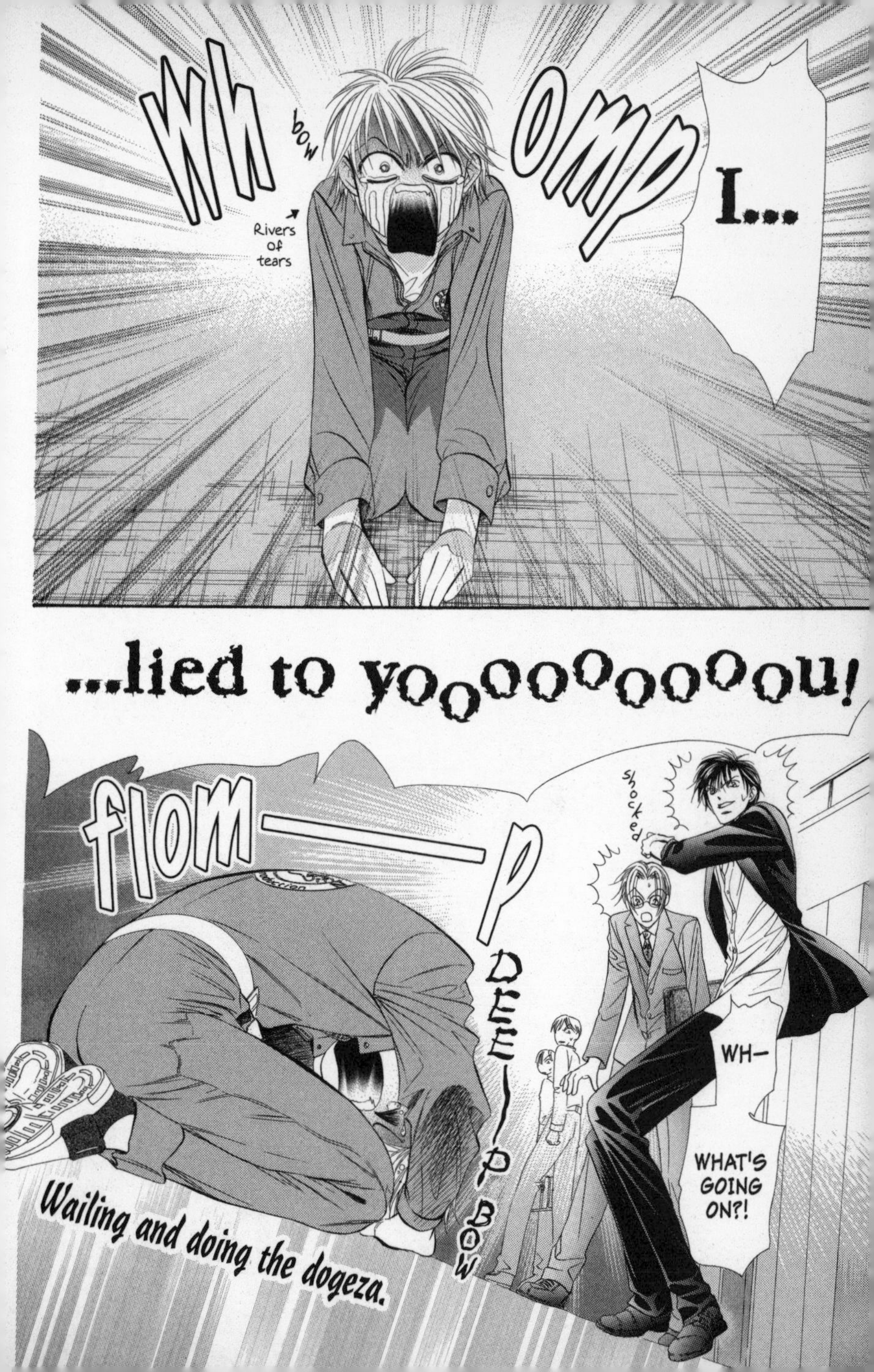
I...
Whomp
bow
Rivers of tears
...lied to yoooooooooou!
WH—
WHAT'S GOING ON?!
shocked
flom—p
DEE—P BOW
Wailing and doing the dogeza.

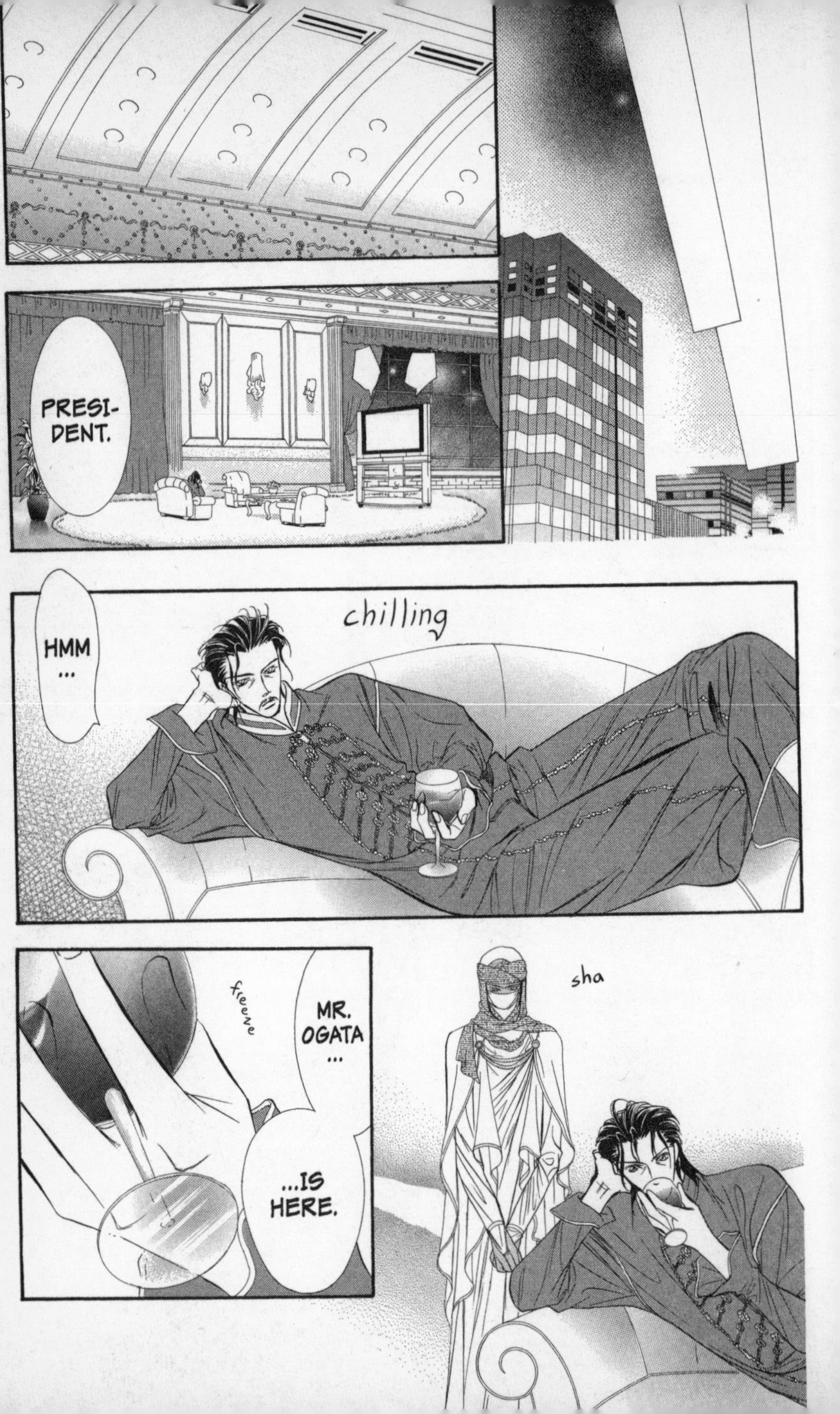
PRESI-
DENT.
chilling
HMM
...
sha
MR.
OGATA
...
freeze
...IS
HERE.

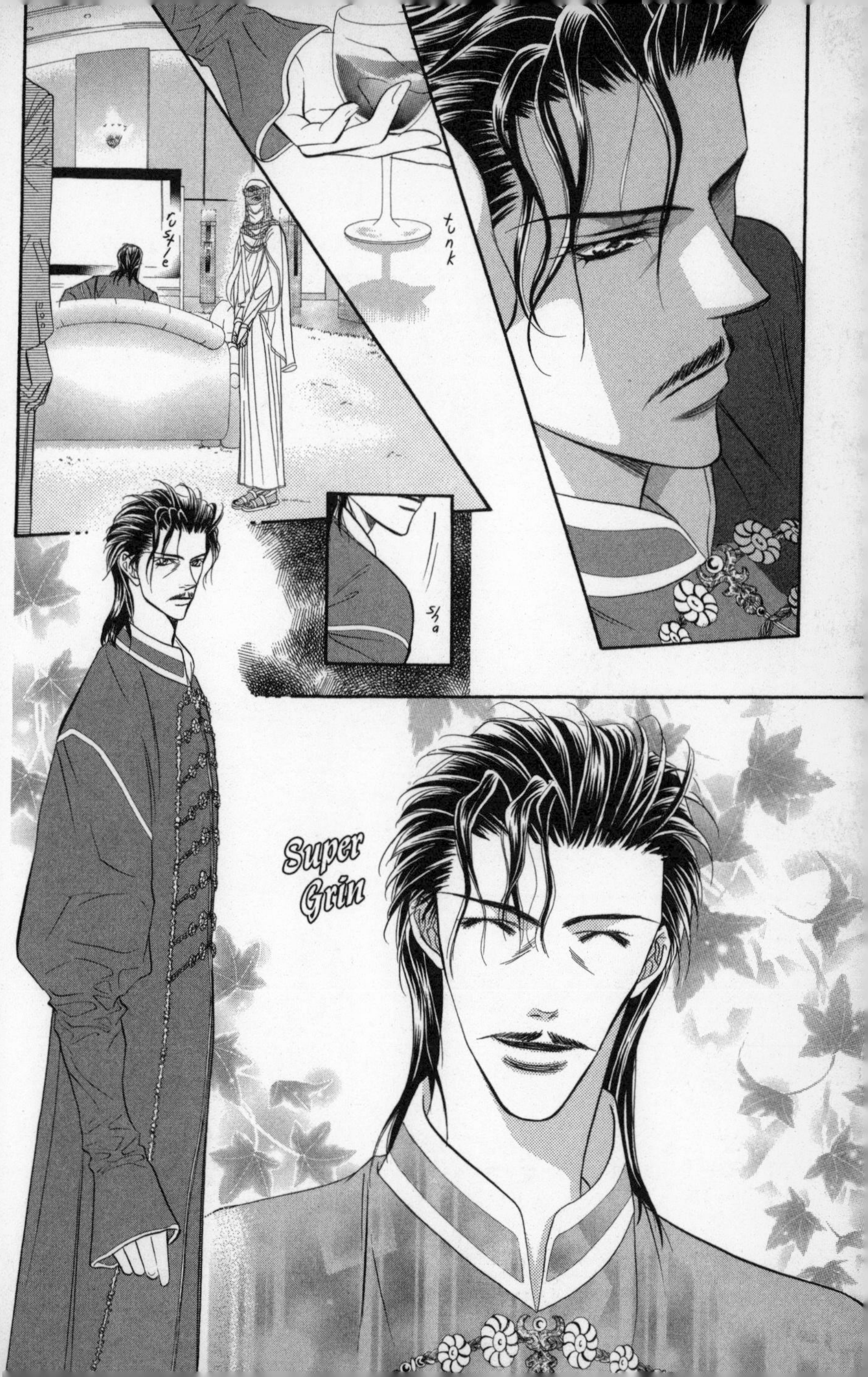
tunk
rustle
sha
Super Grin

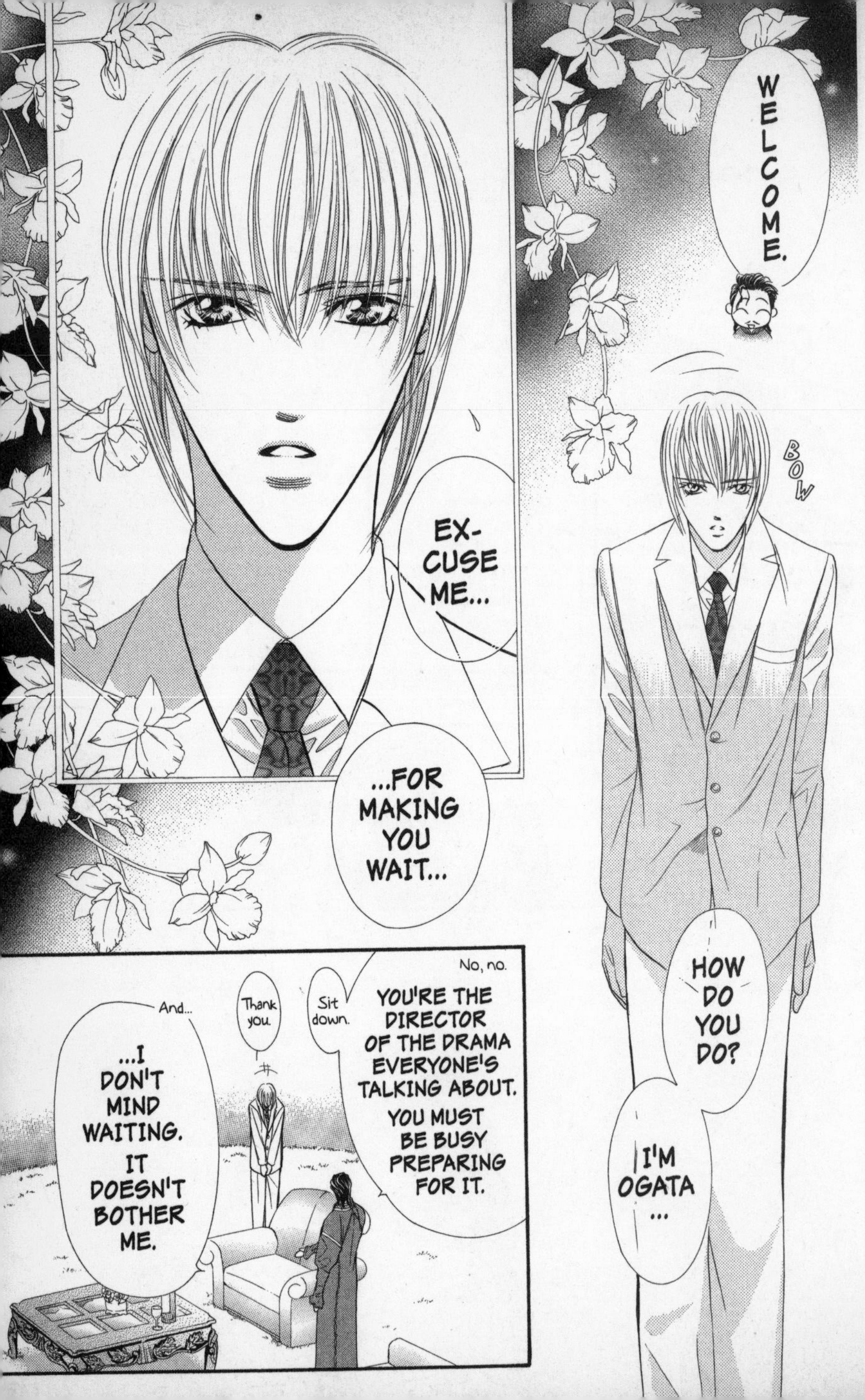
WELCOME.
BOW
HOW DO YOU DO?
I'M OGATA...
EX-CUSE ME...
...FOR MAKING YOU WAIT...
No, no.
YOU'RE THE DIRECTOR OF THE DRAMA EVERYONE'S TALKING ABOUT. YOU MUST BE BUSY PREPARING FOR IT.
Sit down.
Thank you.
And...
...I DON'T MIND WAITING. IT DOESN'T BOTHER ME.

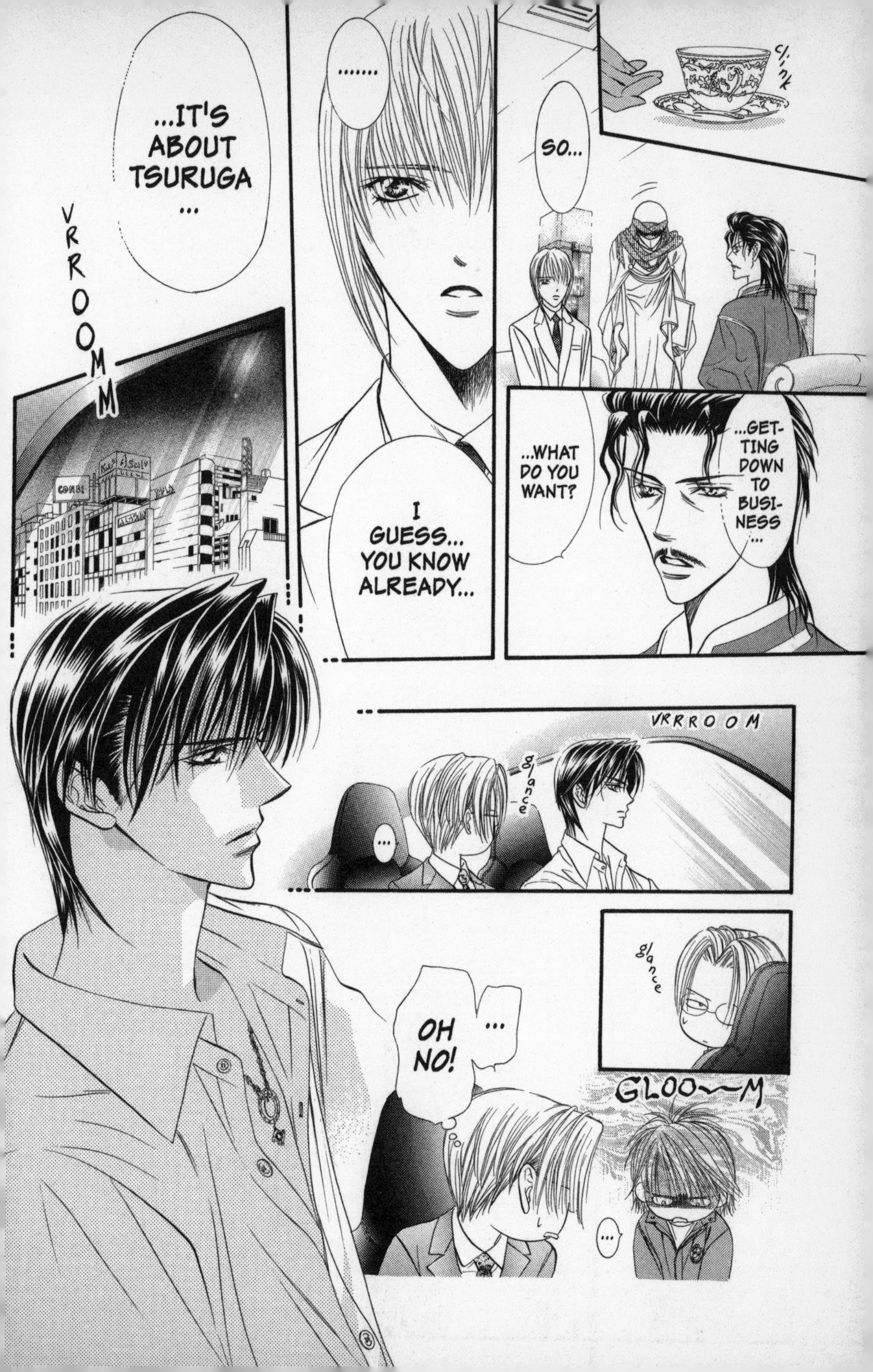
clink
So...
...Getting down to business...
...What do you want?
....
I guess... you know already...
...It's about Tsuruga...
VRROOMM
VRRROOM
glance
...
glance
GLOO~M
...
Oh no! ...

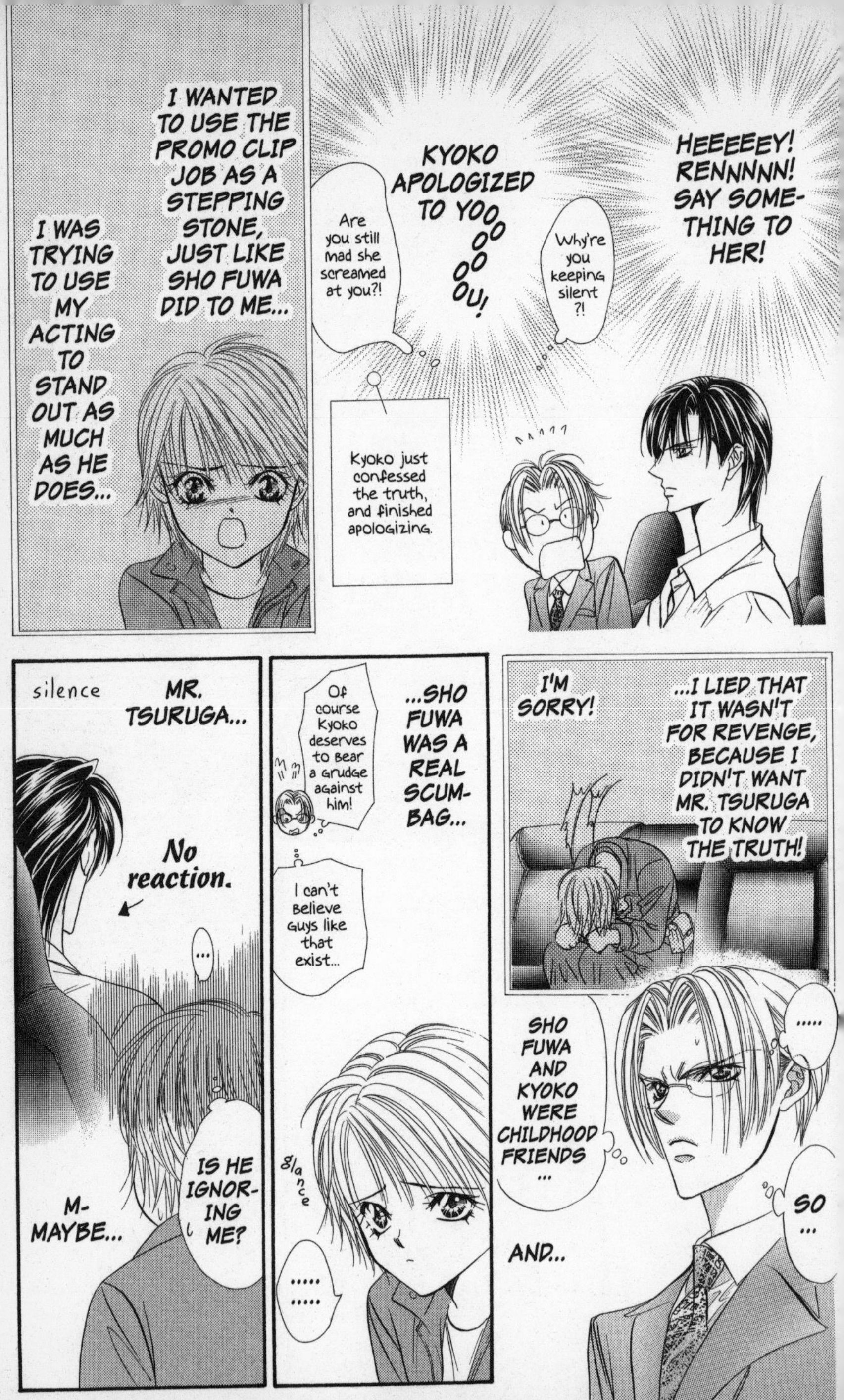
HEEEEEY! RENNNNN! SAY SOME-THING TO HER!
Why're you keeping silent?!
KYOKO APOLOGIZED TO YOOOOOOOU!
Are you still mad she screamed at you?!
Kyoko just confessed the truth, and finished apologizing.
I WANTED TO USE THE PROMO CLIP JOB AS A STEPPING STONE, JUST LIKE SHO FUWA DID TO ME...
I WAS TRYING TO USE MY ACTING TO STAND OUT AS MUCH AS HE DOES...
...I LIED THAT IT WASN'T FOR REVENGE, BECAUSE I DIDN'T WANT MR. TSURUGA TO KNOW THE TRUTH!
I'M SORRY!
.....
SO ...
SHO FUWA AND KYOKO WERE CHILDHOOD FRIENDS ...
AND...
...SHO FUWA WAS A REAL SCUM-BAG...
Of course Kyoko deserves to bear a grudge against him!
I can't believe guys like that exist...
glance
....
MR. TSURUGA...
silence
No reaction.
....
IS HE IGNOR-ING ME?
M-MAYBE...

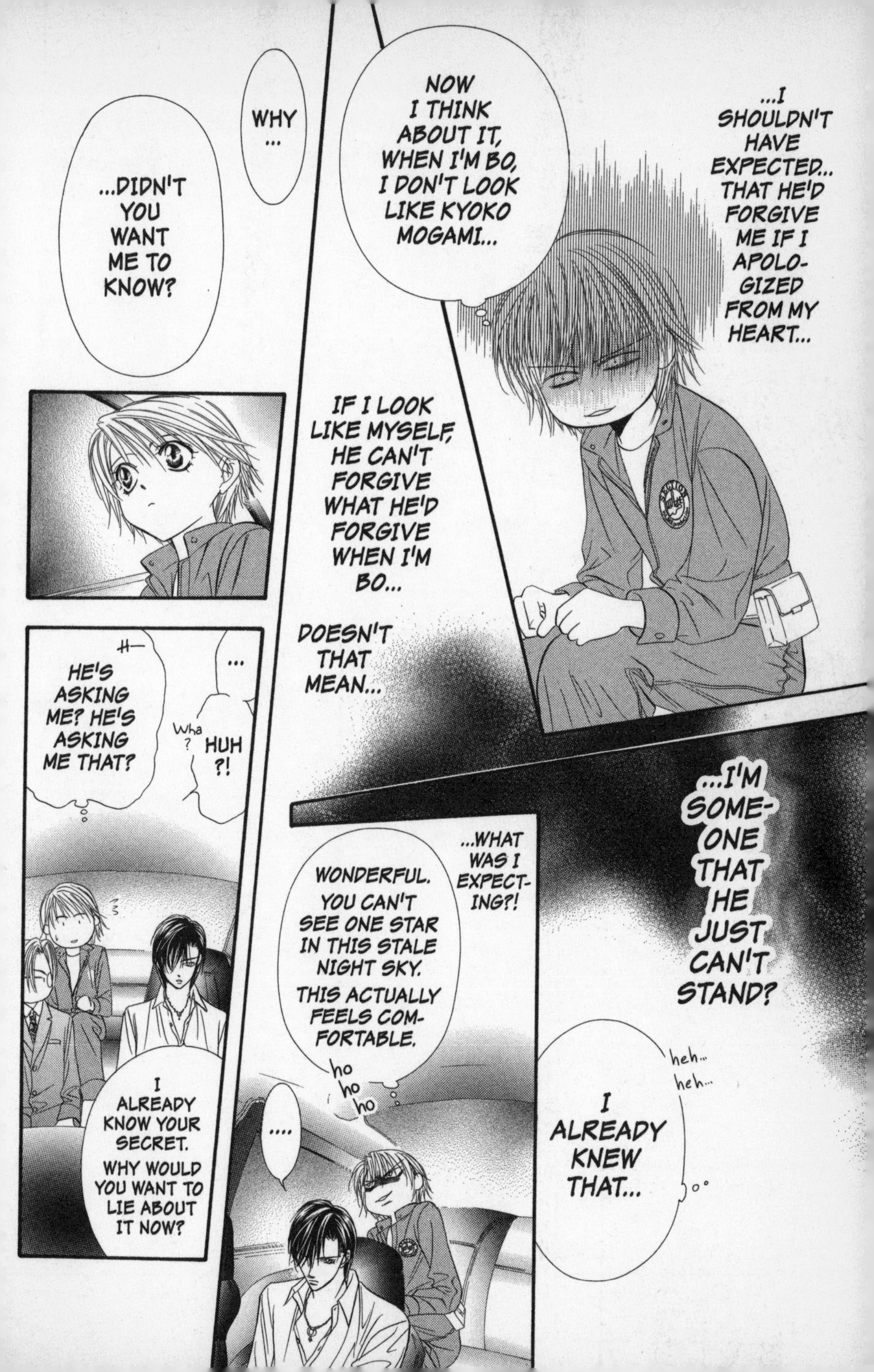
...I SHOULDN'T HAVE EXPECTED... THAT HE'D FORGIVE ME IF I APOLOGIZED FROM MY HEART...
NOW I THINK ABOUT IT, WHEN I'M BO, I DON'T LOOK LIKE KYOKO MOGAMI...
IF I LOOK LIKE MYSELF, HE CAN'T FORGIVE WHAT HE'D FORGIVE WHEN I'M BO...
DOESN'T THAT MEAN...
...I'M SOME-ONE THAT HE JUST CAN'T STAND?
I ALREADY KNEW THAT...
heh... heh...
...WHAT WAS I EXPECT-ING?!
WONDERFUL. YOU CAN'T SEE ONE STAR IN THIS STALE NIGHT SKY. THIS ACTUALLY FEELS COM-FORTABLE.
ho ho ho
....
WHY...
...DIDN'T YOU WANT ME TO KNOW?
...
HUH?!
Wha?
H— HE'S ASKING ME? HE'S ASKING ME THAT?
I ALREADY KNOW YOUR SECRET. WHY WOULD YOU WANT TO LIE ABOUT IT NOW?

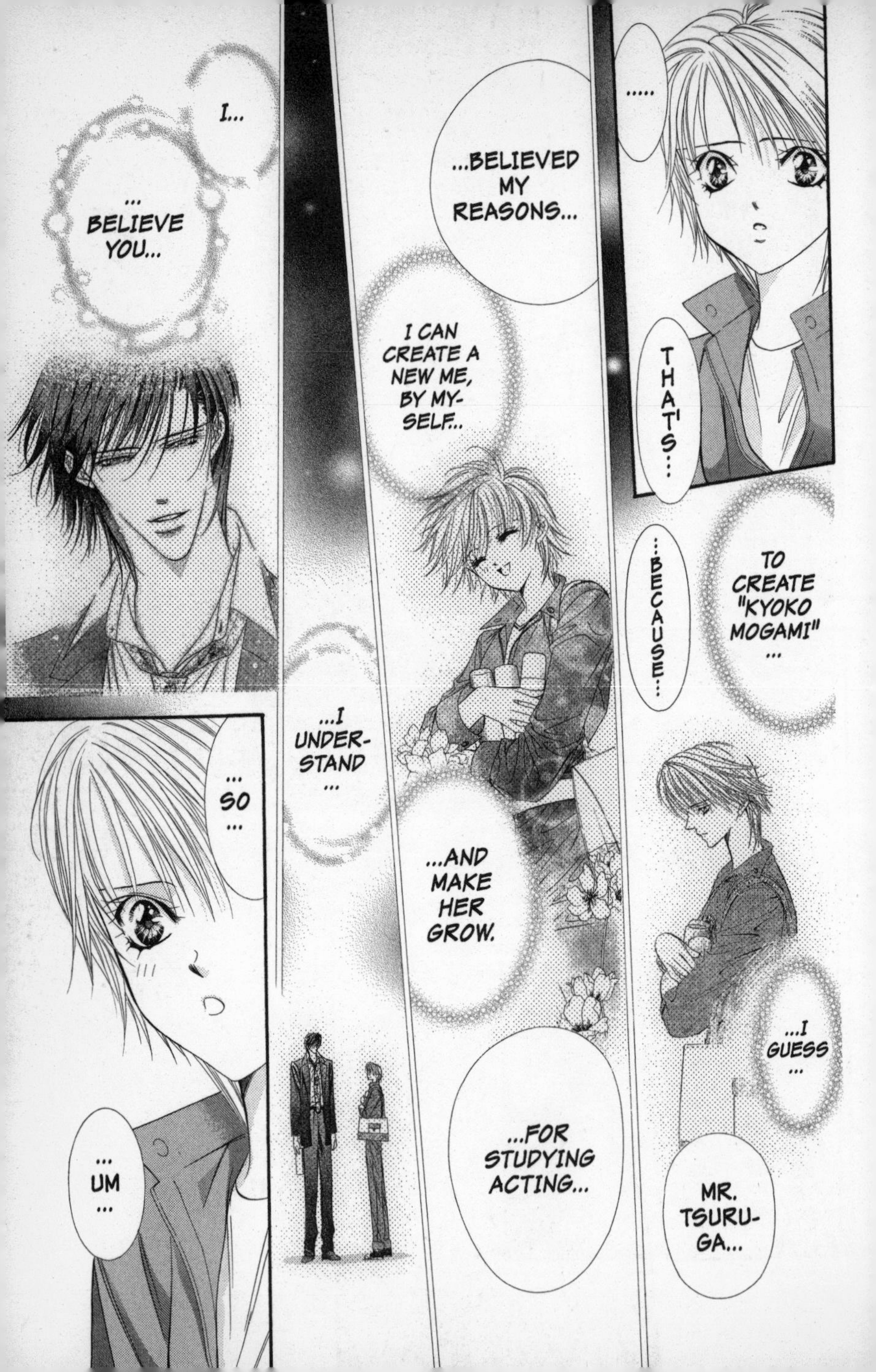
.....
THAT'S...
...BECAUSE...
TO CREATE "KYOKO MOGAMI"...
...I GUESS...
MR. TSURUGA...
...BELIEVED MY REASONS...
I CAN CREATE A NEW ME, BY MYSELF...
...I UNDERSTAND...
...AND MAKE HER GROW.
...FOR STUDYING ACTING...
I...
...BELIEVE YOU...
...SO...
...UM...

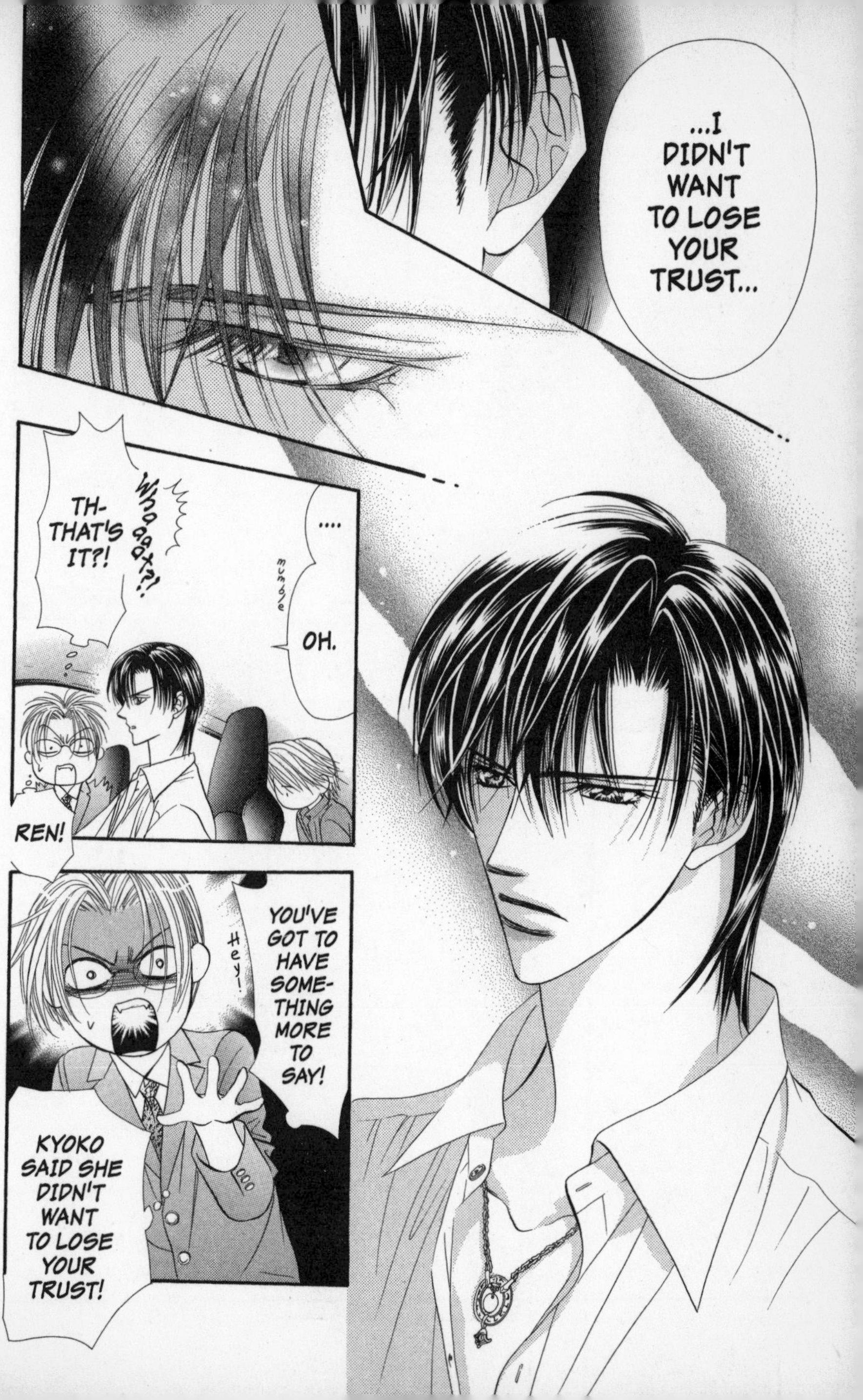
...I DIDN'T WANT TO LOSE YOUR TRUST...
....
mumble
OH.
TH-THAT'S IT?!
Whaaat?!
REN!
YOU'VE GOT TO HAVE SOMETHING MORE TO SAY!
Hey!
KYOKO SAID SHE DIDN'T WANT TO LOSE YOUR TRUST!

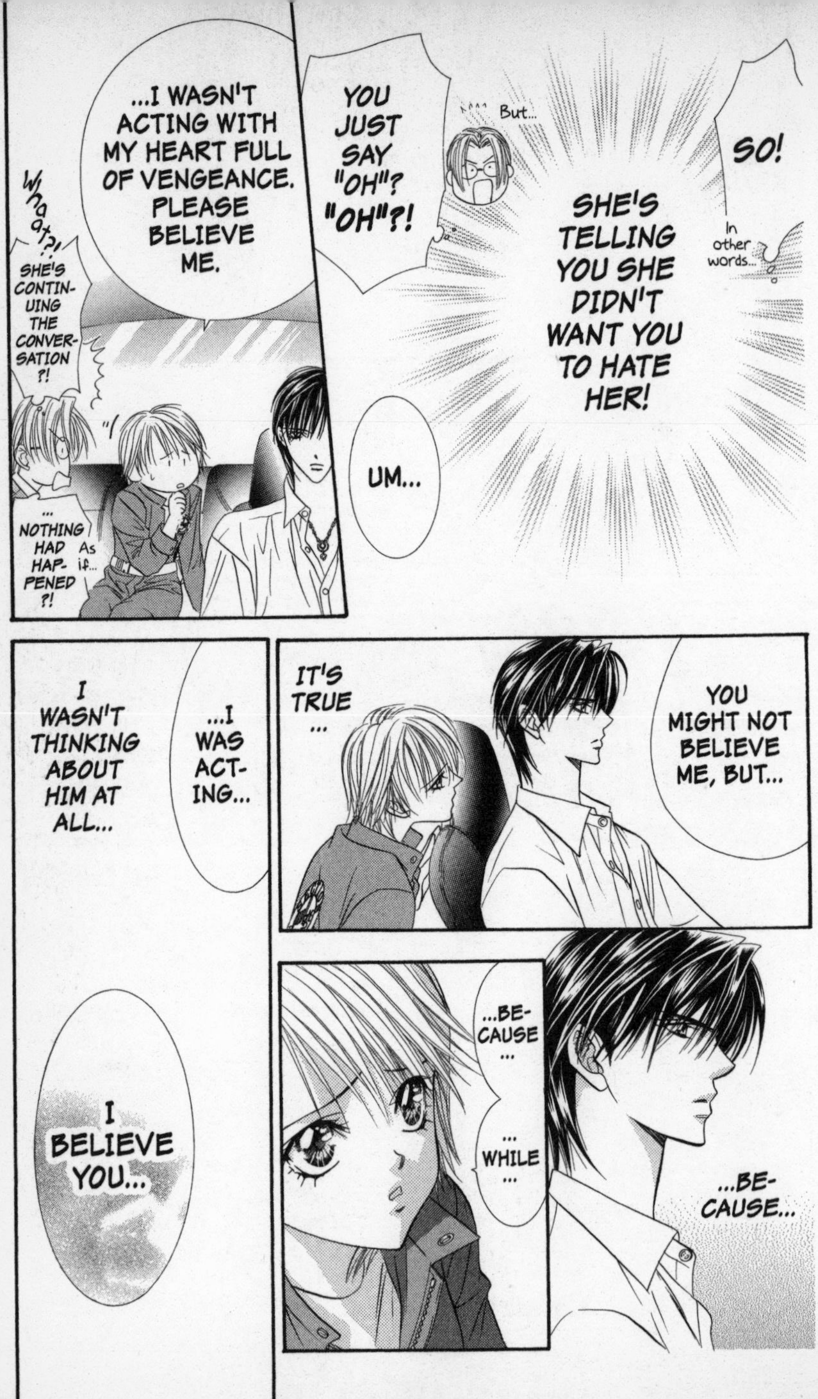
SO!
In other words...
SHE'S TELLING YOU SHE DIDN'T WANT YOU TO HATE HER!
But...
YOU JUST SAY "OH"? "OH"?!
UM...
...I WASN'T ACTING WITH MY HEART FULL OF VENGEANCE. PLEASE BELIEVE ME.
What?!
SHE'S CONTINUING THE CONVERSATION?!
...NOTHING HAD HAPPENED?!
As if...
YOU MIGHT NOT BELIEVE ME, BUT...
IT'S TRUE...
...BE-CAUSE...
...BECAUSE...
...WHILE...
...I WAS ACTING...
I WASN'T THINKING ABOUT HIM AT ALL...
I BELIEVE YOU...

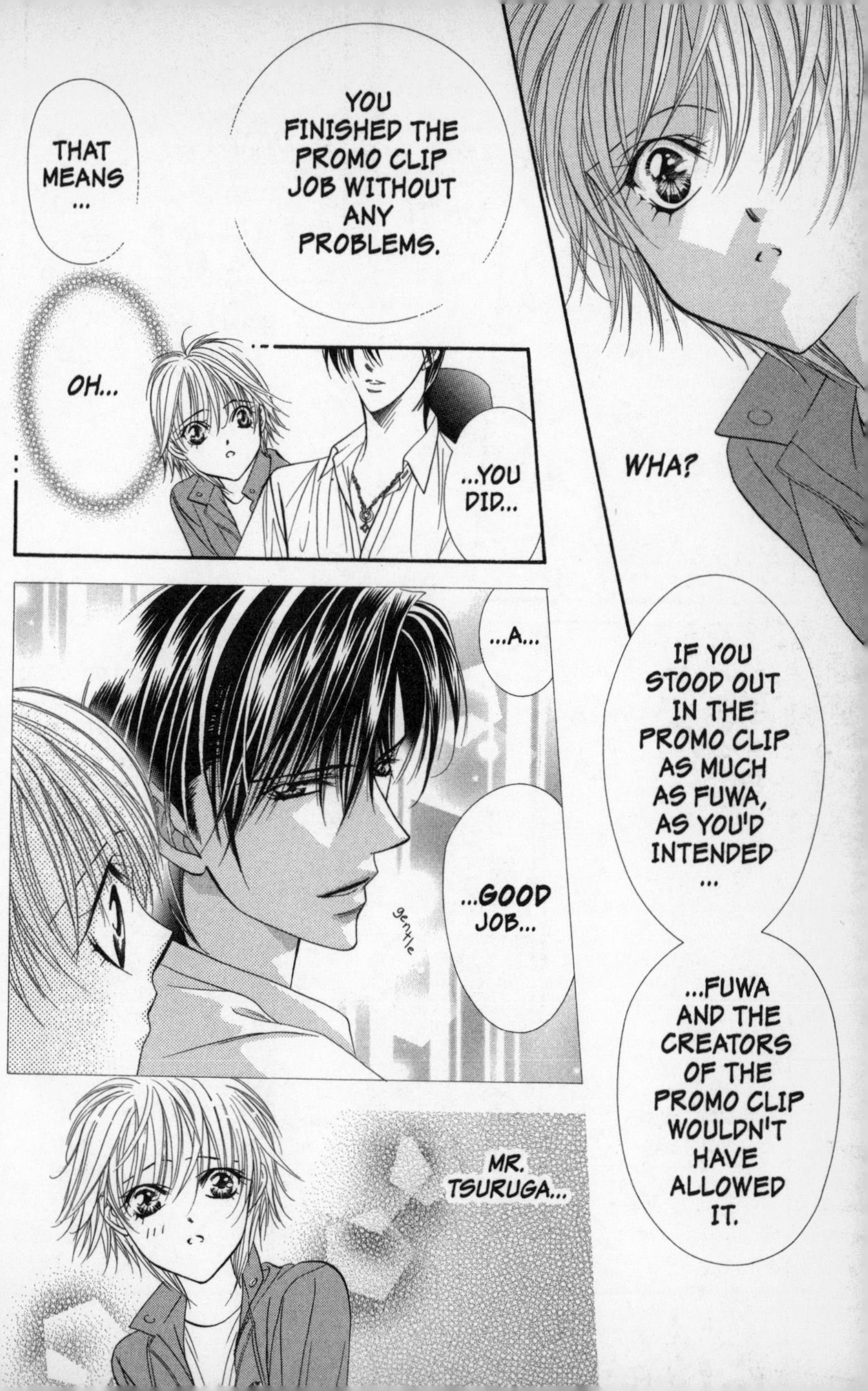
WHA?
IF YOU STOOD OUT IN THE PROMO CLIP AS MUCH AS FUWA, AS YOU'D INTENDED ...
...FUWA AND THE CREATORS OF THE PROMO CLIP WOULDN'T HAVE ALLOWED IT.
YOU FINISHED THE PROMO CLIP JOB WITHOUT ANY PROBLEMS.
THAT MEANS ...
...YOU DID...
OH...
...A...
...GOOD JOB...
gentle
MR. TSURUGA...

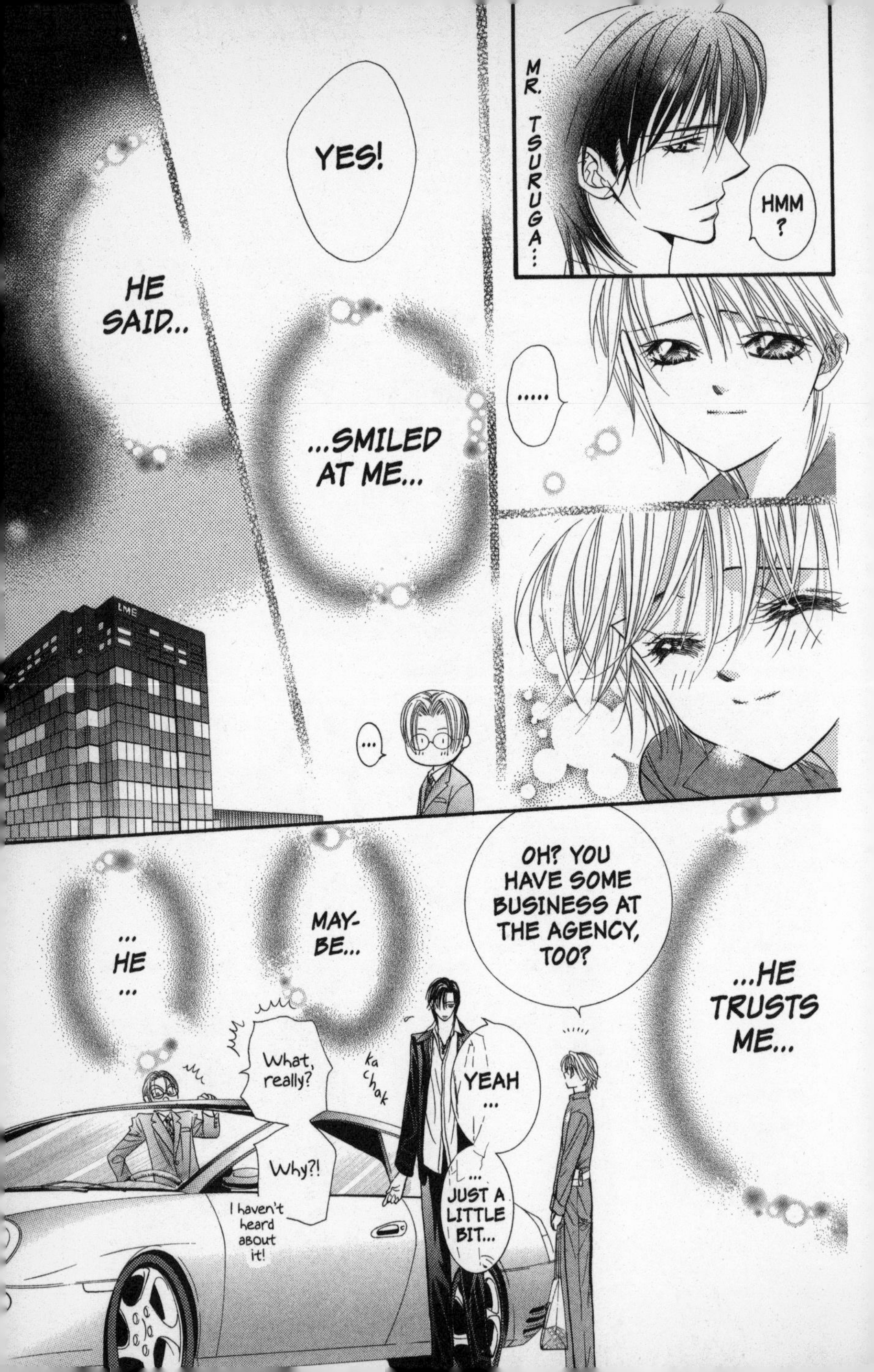
MR. TSURUGA...
HMM?
.....
YES!
...SMILED AT ME...
...
HE SAID...
...HE TRUSTS ME...
OH? YOU HAVE SOME BUSINESS AT THE AGENCY, TOO?
YEAH ...
... JUST A LITTLE BIT...
MAY-BE...
... HE ...
What, really?
ka chak
Why?!
I haven't heard about it!

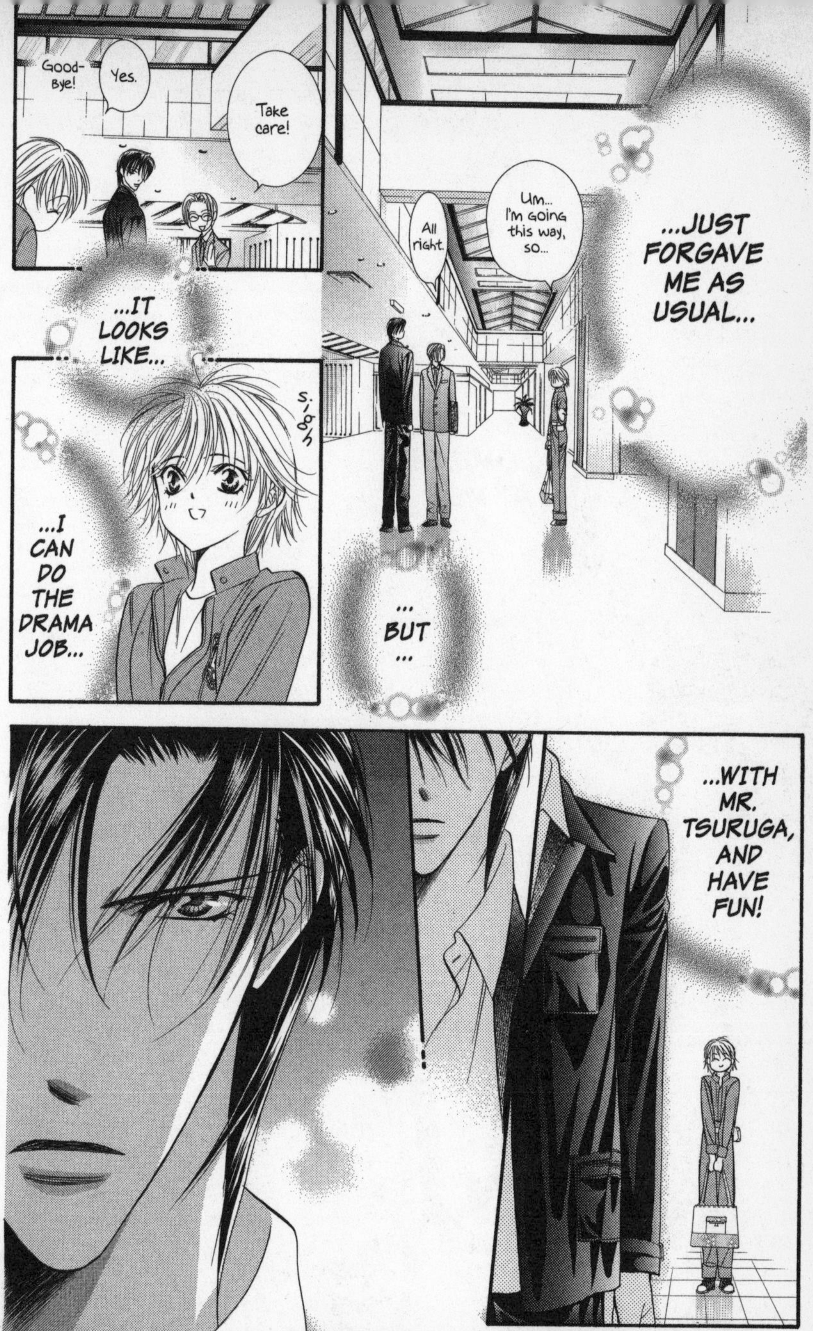
Um... I'm going this way, so...
All right.
...JUST FORGAVE ME AS USUAL...
Take care!
Yes.
Good-Bye!
...IT LOOKS LIKE...
sigh
...I CAN DO THE DRAMA JOB...
...BUT...
...WITH MR. TSURUGA, AND HAVE FUN!

End of Act 53

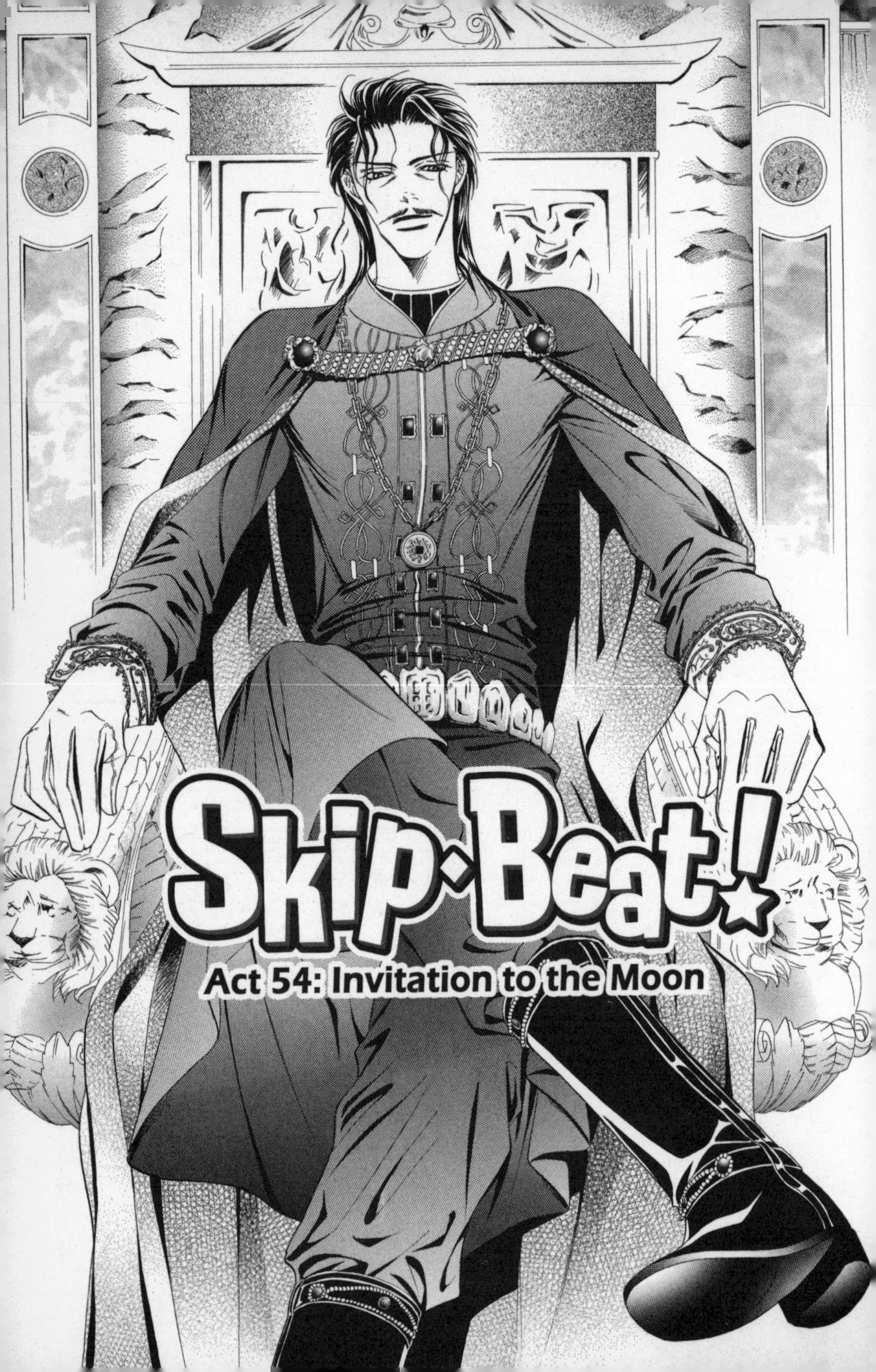
Skip·Beat!
Act 54: Invitation to the Moon

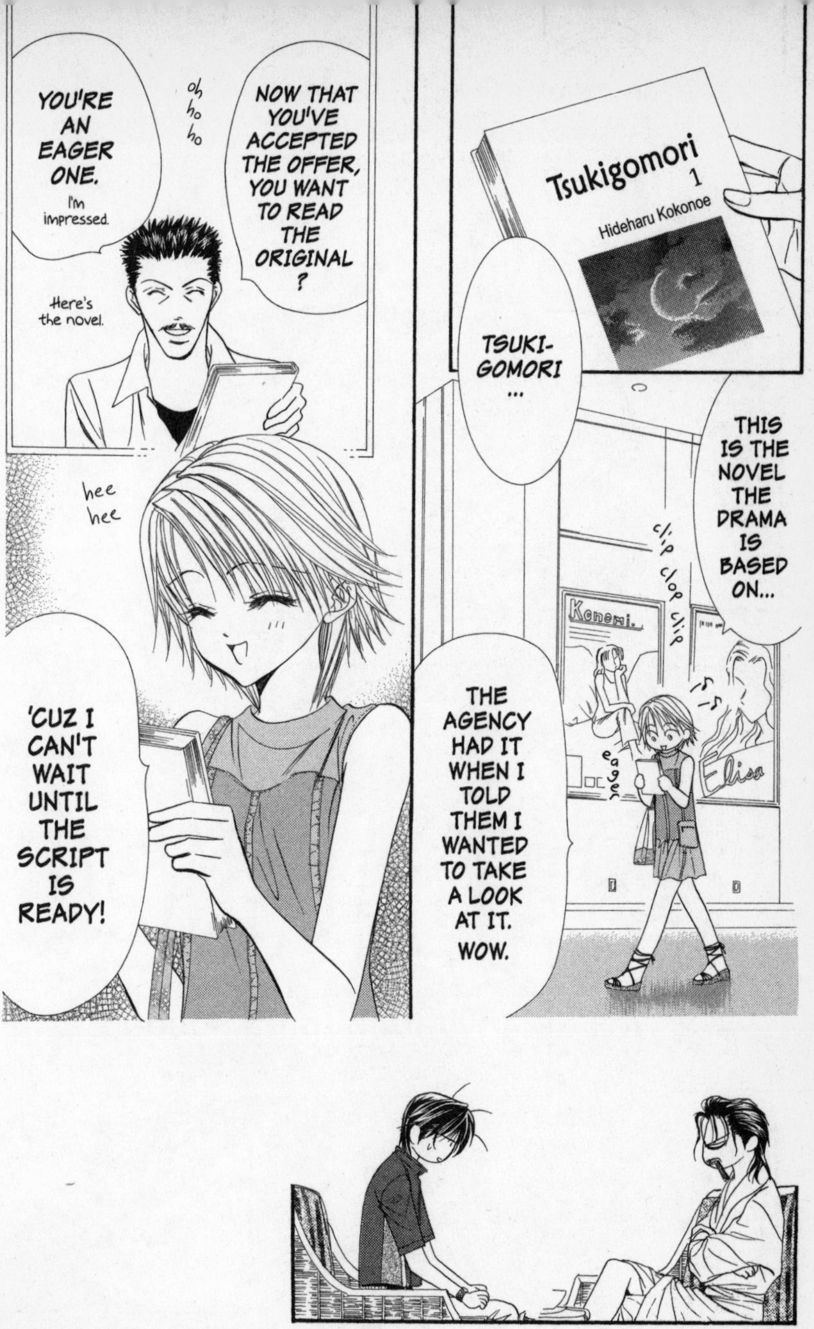
Tsukigomori
1
Hideharu Kokonoe
TSUKI-GOMORI ...
THIS IS THE NOVEL THE DRAMA IS BASED ON...
clip clop clip
eager
THE AGENCY HAD IT WHEN I TOLD THEM I WANTED TO TAKE A LOOK AT IT. WOW.
Konomi.
Elisa
NOW THAT YOU'VE ACCEPTED THE OFFER, YOU WANT TO READ THE ORIGINAL?
oh ho ho
YOU'RE AN EAGER ONE.
I'm impressed.
Here's the novel.
hee hee
'CUZ I CAN'T WAIT UNTIL THE SCRIPT IS READY!

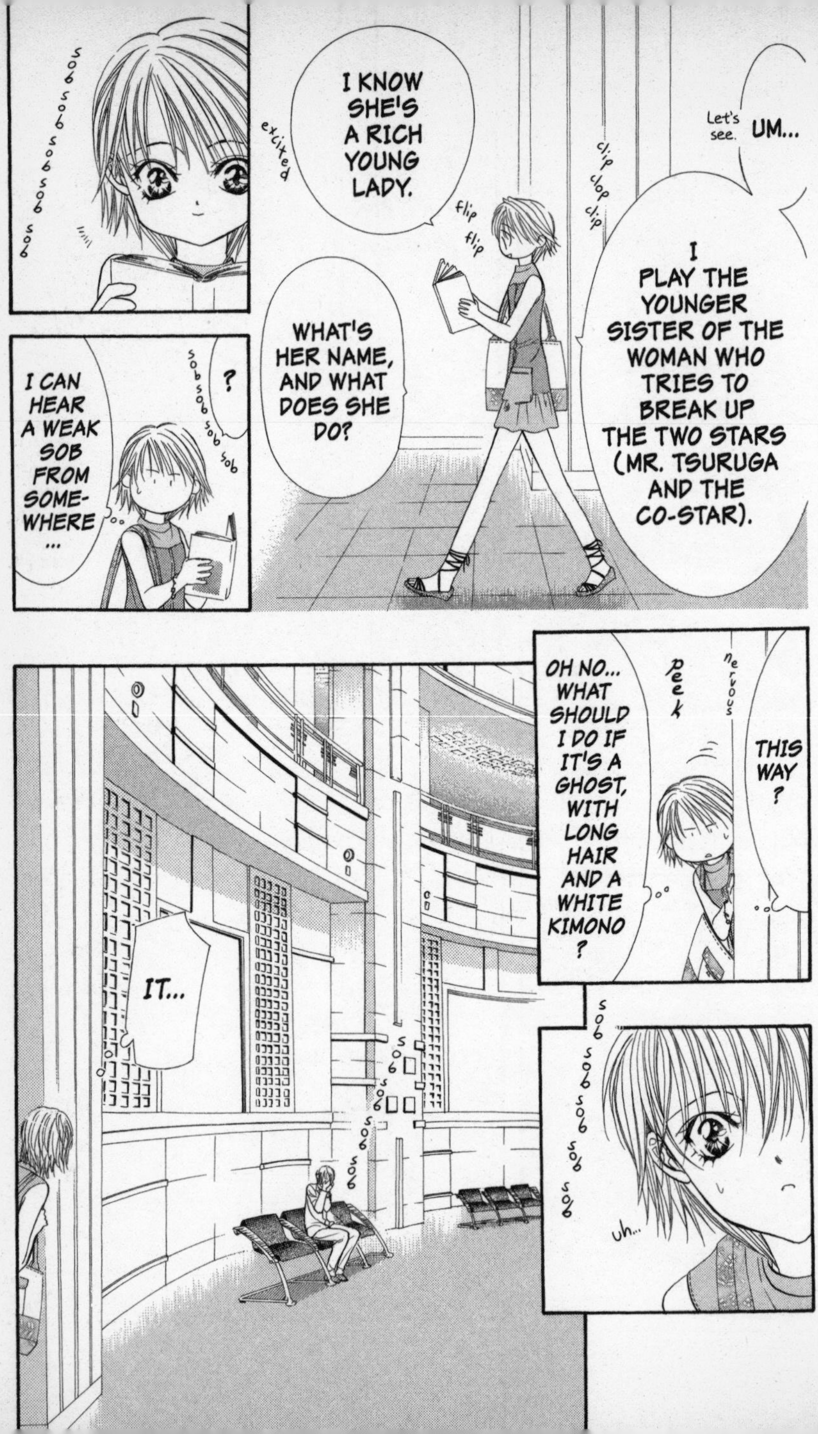
Let's see.
UM...
I PLAY THE YOUNGER SISTER OF THE WOMAN WHO TRIES TO BREAK UP THE TWO STARS (MR. TSURUGA AND THE CO-STAR).
clip clop clip
flip flip
WHAT'S HER NAME, AND WHAT DOES SHE DO?
I KNOW SHE'S A RICH YOUNG LADY.
excited
sob sob sob sob sob sob
?
sob sob sob sob
I CAN HEAR A WEAK SOB FROM SOMEWHERE...
THIS WAY?
nervous
peek
OH NO... WHAT SHOULD I DO IF IT'S A GHOST, WITH LONG HAIR AND A WHITE KIMONO?
sob sob sob sob sob
uh...
sob sob sob sob
IT...

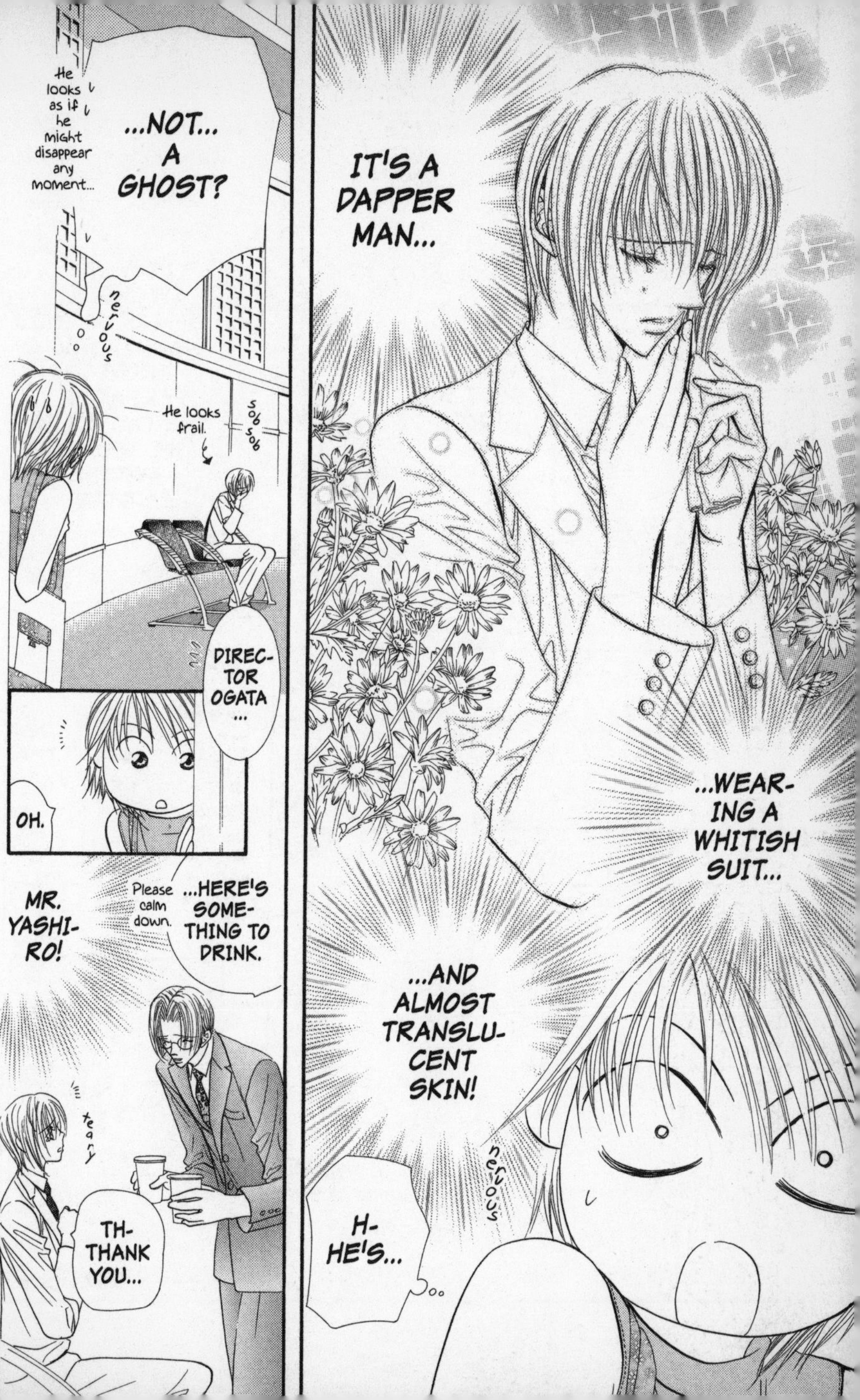
IT'S A DAPPER MAN...
...WEARING A WHITISH SUIT...
...AND ALMOST TRANSLUCENT SKIN!
nervous
H-HE'S...
...NOT... A GHOST?
He looks as if he might disappear any moment...
nervous
sob sob
He looks frail.
DIRECTOR OGATA...
OH.
...HERE'S SOMETHING TO DRINK.
Please calm down.
MR. YASHIRO!
teary
TH-THANK YOU...

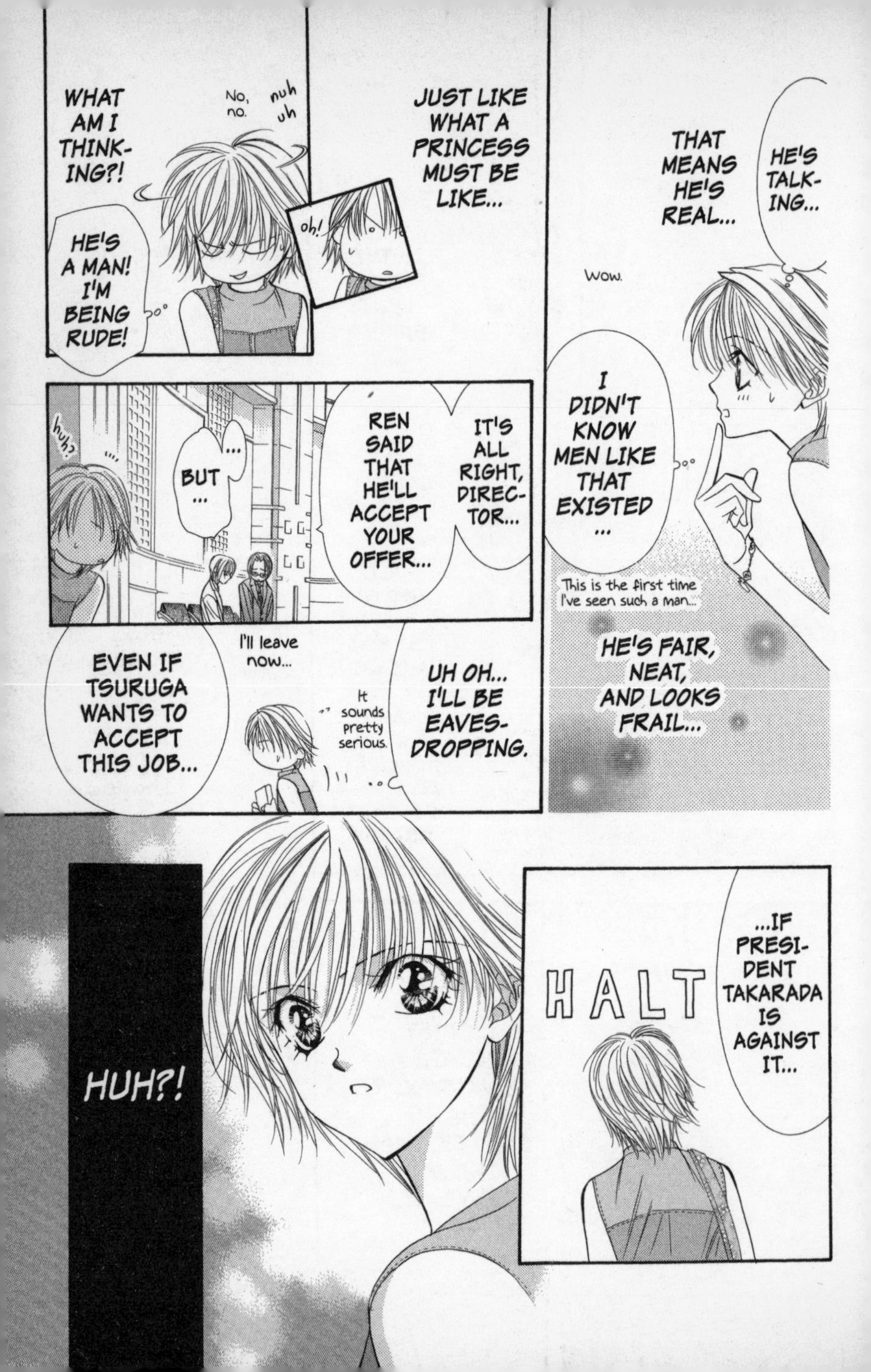
HE'S TALKING...
THAT MEANS HE'S REAL...
Wow.
I DIDN'T KNOW MEN LIKE THAT EXISTED...
This is the first time I've seen such a man...
HE'S FAIR, NEAT, AND LOOKS FRAIL...
JUST LIKE WHAT A PRINCESS MUST BE LIKE...
nuh uh
No, no.
WHAT AM I THINKING?!
oh!
HE'S A MAN! I'M BEING RUDE!
IT'S ALL RIGHT, DIRECTOR...
REN SAID THAT HE'LL ACCEPT YOUR OFFER...
... BUT ...
huh?
UH OH... I'LL BE EAVESDROPPING.
It sounds pretty serious.
I'll leave now...
EVEN IF TSURUGA WANTS TO ACCEPT THIS JOB...
...IF PRESIDENT TAKARADA IS AGAINST IT...
HALT
HUH?!

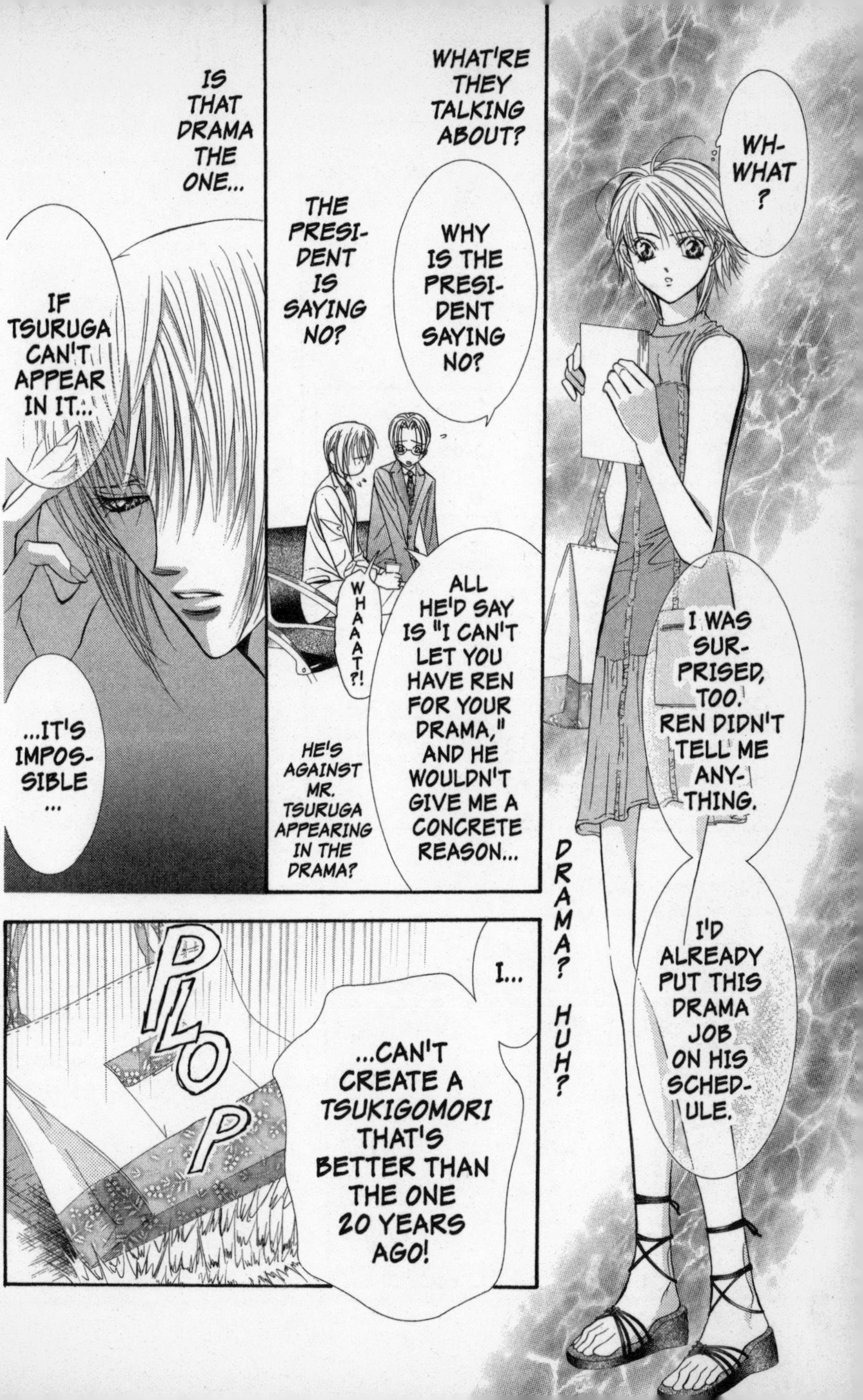
WH-WHAT?
I WAS SURPRISED, TOO. REN DIDN'T TELL ME ANYTHING.
I'D ALREADY PUT THIS DRAMA JOB ON HIS SCHEDULE.
DRAMA? HUH?
WHAT'RE THEY TALKING ABOUT?
WHY IS THE PRESIDENT SAYING NO?
THE PRESIDENT IS SAYING NO?
WHAAAT?!
ALL HE'D SAY IS "I CAN'T LET YOU HAVE REN FOR YOUR DRAMA," AND HE WOULDN'T GIVE ME A CONCRETE REASON...
HE'S AGAINST MR. TSURUGA APPEARING IN THE DRAMA?
IS THAT DRAMA THE ONE...
IF TSURUGA CAN'T APPEAR IN IT...
...IT'S IMPOSSIBLE...
I...
...CAN'T CREATE A TSUKIGOMORI THAT'S BETTER THAN THE ONE 20 YEARS AGO!
PLOP

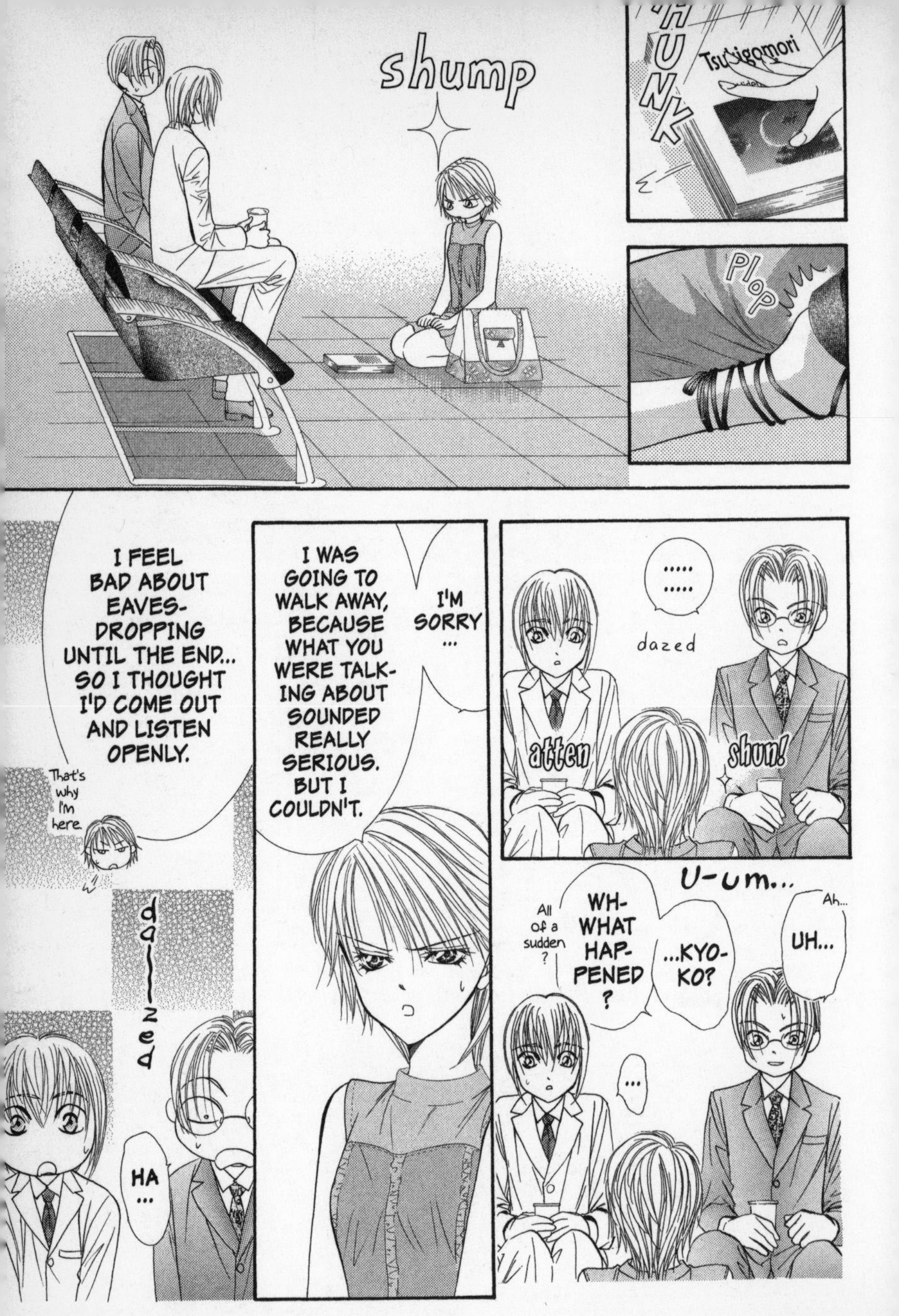

HUNK
Tsukigomori
Plop
shump
.....
.....
dazed
atten
shun!
U-um...
Ah...
UH...
...KYO-KO?
WH-WHAT HAP-PENED?
All of a sudden?
...
I'M SORRY...
I WAS GOING TO WALK AWAY, BECAUSE WHAT YOU WERE TALKING ABOUT SOUNDED REALLY SERIOUS. BUT I COULDN'T.
I FEEL BAD ABOUT EAVES-DROPPING UNTIL THE END... SO I THOUGHT I'D COME OUT AND LISTEN OPENLY.
That's why I'm here.
dazed
HA...

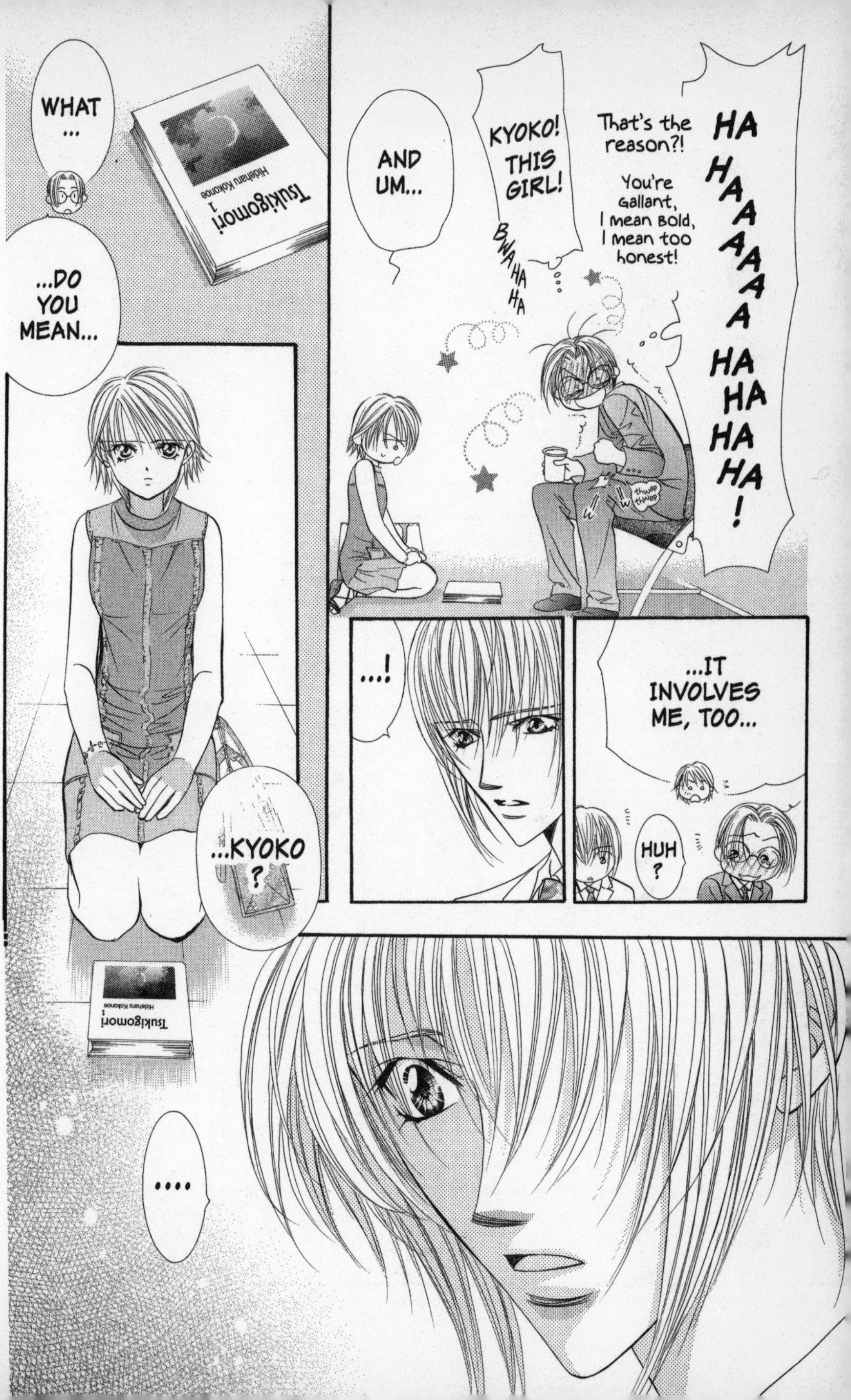
HA HAAAAAA HA HA HA HA!
That's the reason?!
You're Gallant, I mean Bold, I mean too honest!
KYOKO! THIS GIRL!
BWAHAHA HA
AND UM...
thwap thwap
...IT INVOLVES ME, TOO...
HUH?
...!
WHAT ...
...DO YOU MEAN...
Tsukigomori 1
Hideharu Kokonoe
...KYOKO?
Tsukigomori 1
Hideharu Kokonoe
....

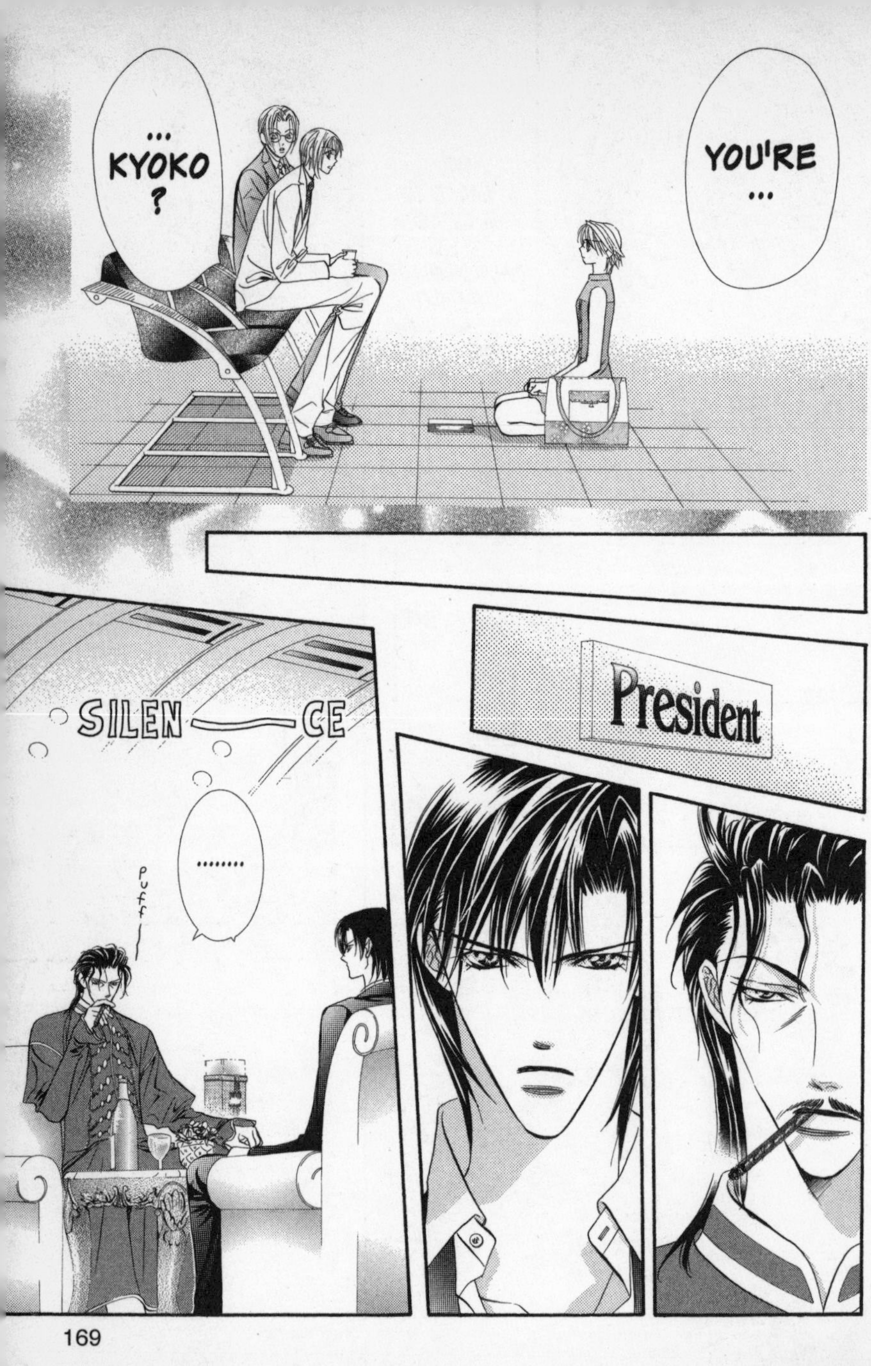
YOU'RE ...
... KYOKO ?
President
SILEN——CE
....
Puff

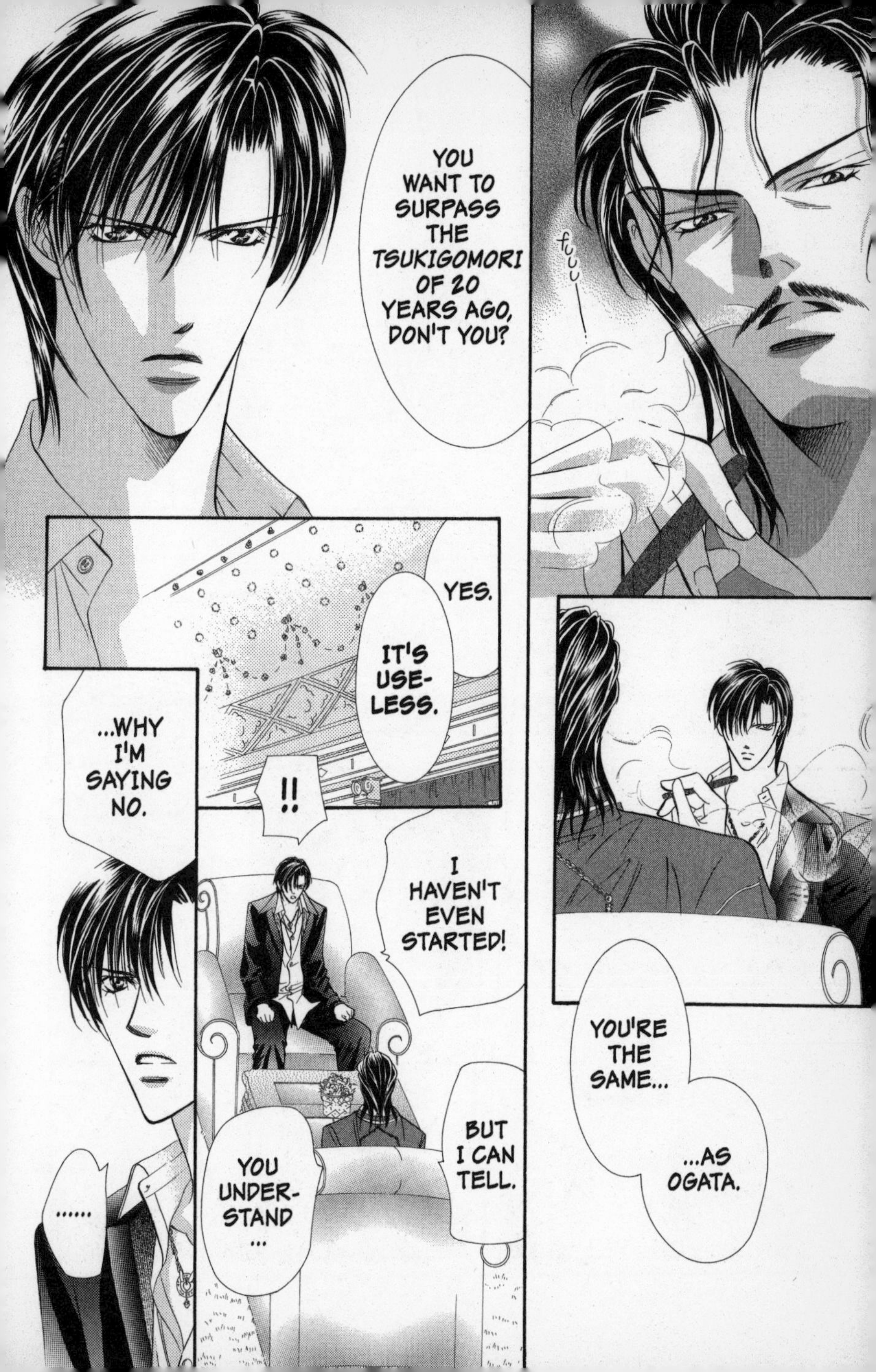
FUUU—
YOU WANT TO SURPASS THE TSUKIGOMORI OF 20 YEARS AGO, DON'T YOU?
YES.
IT'S USELESS.
!!
I HAVEN'T EVEN STARTED!
YOU'RE THE SAME...
...AS OGATA.
BUT I CAN TELL.
YOU UNDERSTAND...
...WHY I'M SAYING NO.
......

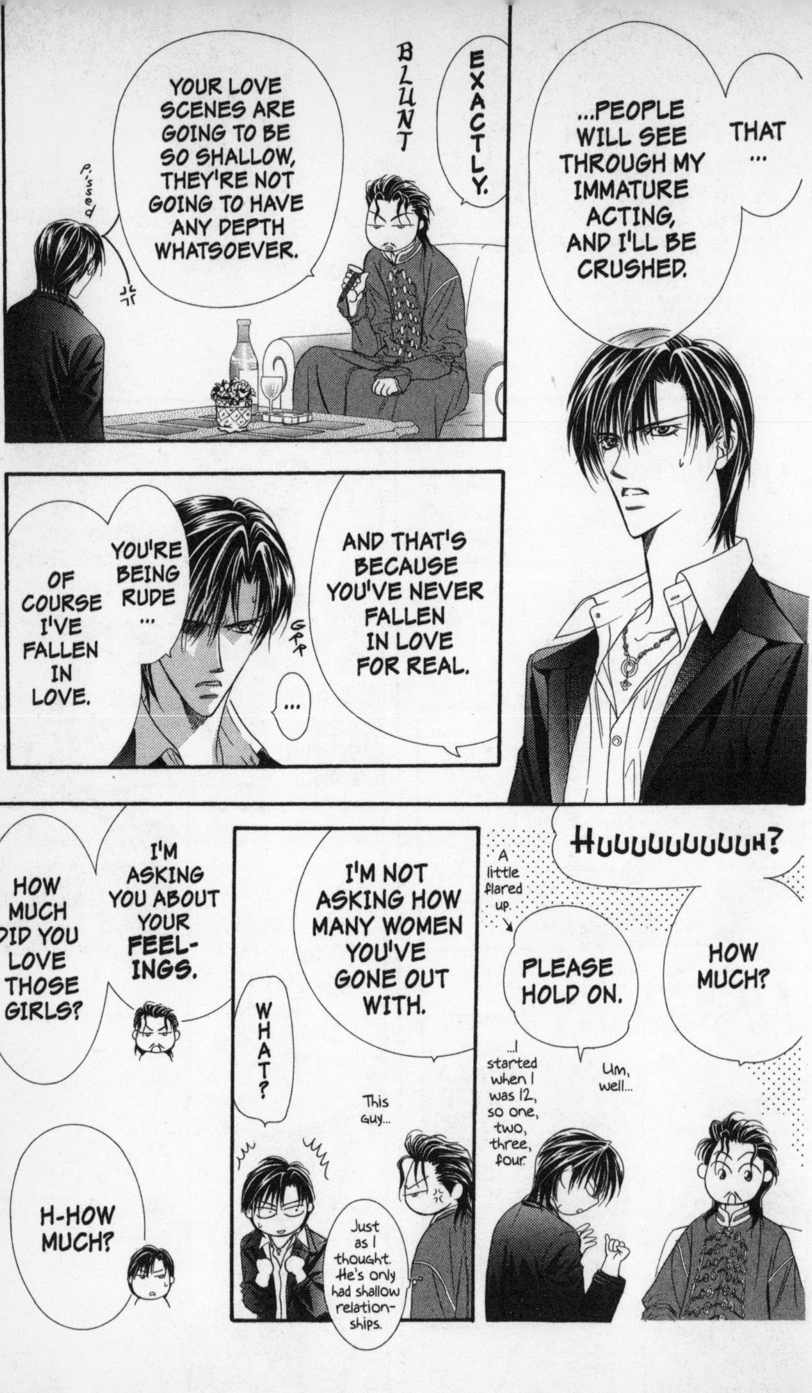
THAT ...
...PEOPLE WILL SEE THROUGH MY IMMATURE ACTING, AND I'LL BE CRUSHED.
EXACTLY.
BLUNT
YOUR LOVE SCENES ARE GOING TO BE SO SHALLOW, THEY'RE NOT GOING TO HAVE ANY DEPTH WHATSOEVER.
Pissed
AND THAT'S BECAUSE YOU'VE NEVER FALLEN IN LOVE FOR REAL.
GRR
...
YOU'RE BEING RUDE ...
OF COURSE I'VE FALLEN IN LOVE.
HUUUUUUUUUH?
HOW MUCH?
A little flared up.
PLEASE HOLD ON.
Um, well...
...I started when I was 12, so one, two, three, four.
I'M NOT ASKING HOW MANY WOMEN YOU'VE GONE OUT WITH.
WHAT?
This guy...
Just as I thought. He's only had shallow relationships.
I'M ASKING YOU ABOUT YOUR FEEL-INGS.
HOW MUCH DID YOU LOVE THOSE GIRLS?
H-HOW MUCH?

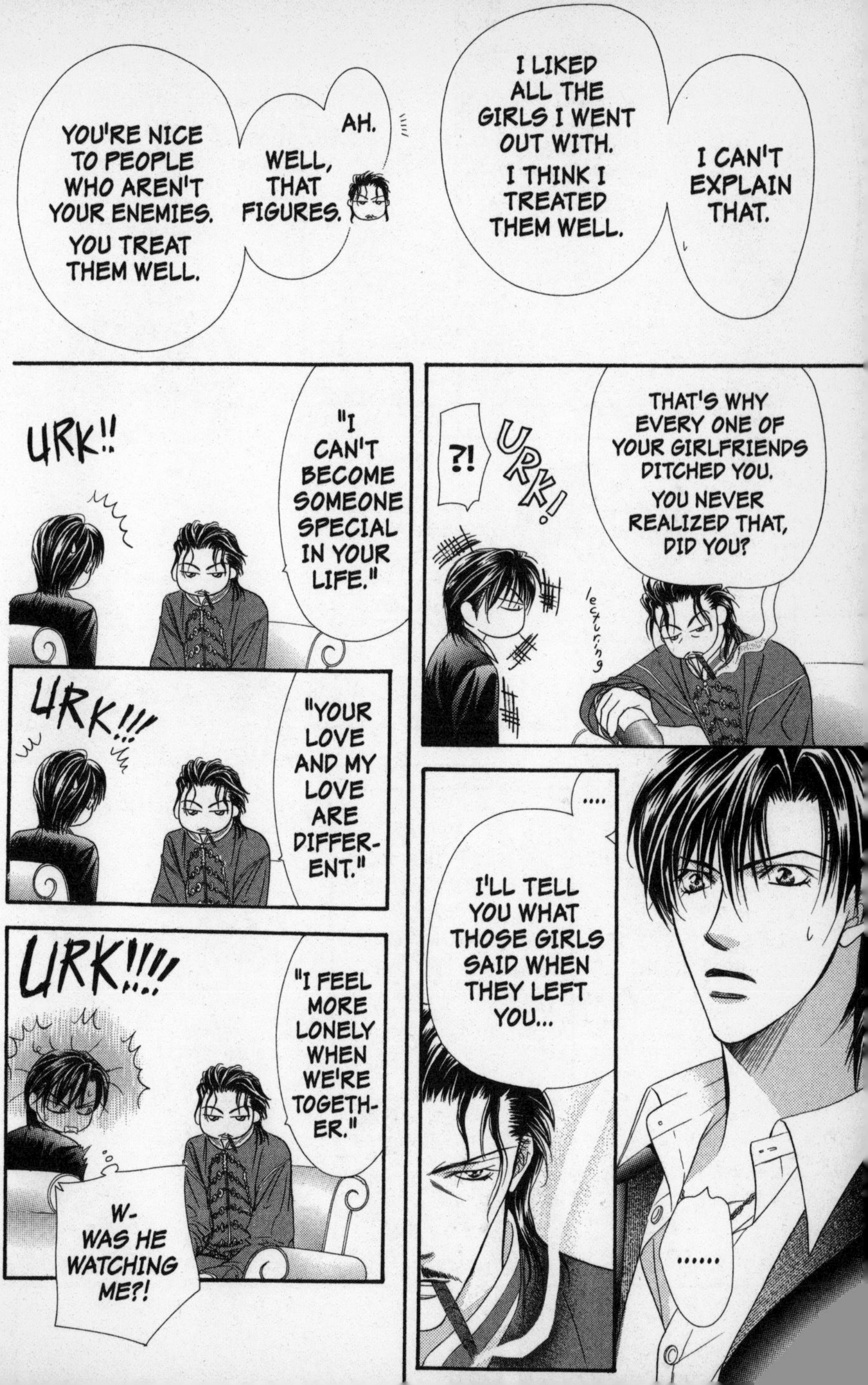
I LIKED ALL THE GIRLS I WENT OUT WITH. I THINK I TREATED THEM WELL.
I CAN'T EXPLAIN THAT.
AH. WELL, THAT FIGURES.
YOU'RE NICE TO PEOPLE WHO AREN'T YOUR ENEMIES. YOU TREAT THEM WELL.
THAT'S WHY EVERY ONE OF YOUR GIRLFRIENDS DITCHED YOU. YOU NEVER REALIZED THAT, DID YOU?
?!
URK!
lecturing
....
I'LL TELL YOU WHAT THOSE GIRLS SAID WHEN THEY LEFT YOU...
......
"I CAN'T BECOME SOMEONE SPECIAL IN YOUR LIFE."
URK!!
"YOUR LOVE AND MY LOVE ARE DIFFER-ENT."
URK!!!
"I FEEL MORE LONELY WHEN WE'RE TOGETH-ER."
URK!!!!
W- WAS HE WATCHING ME?!

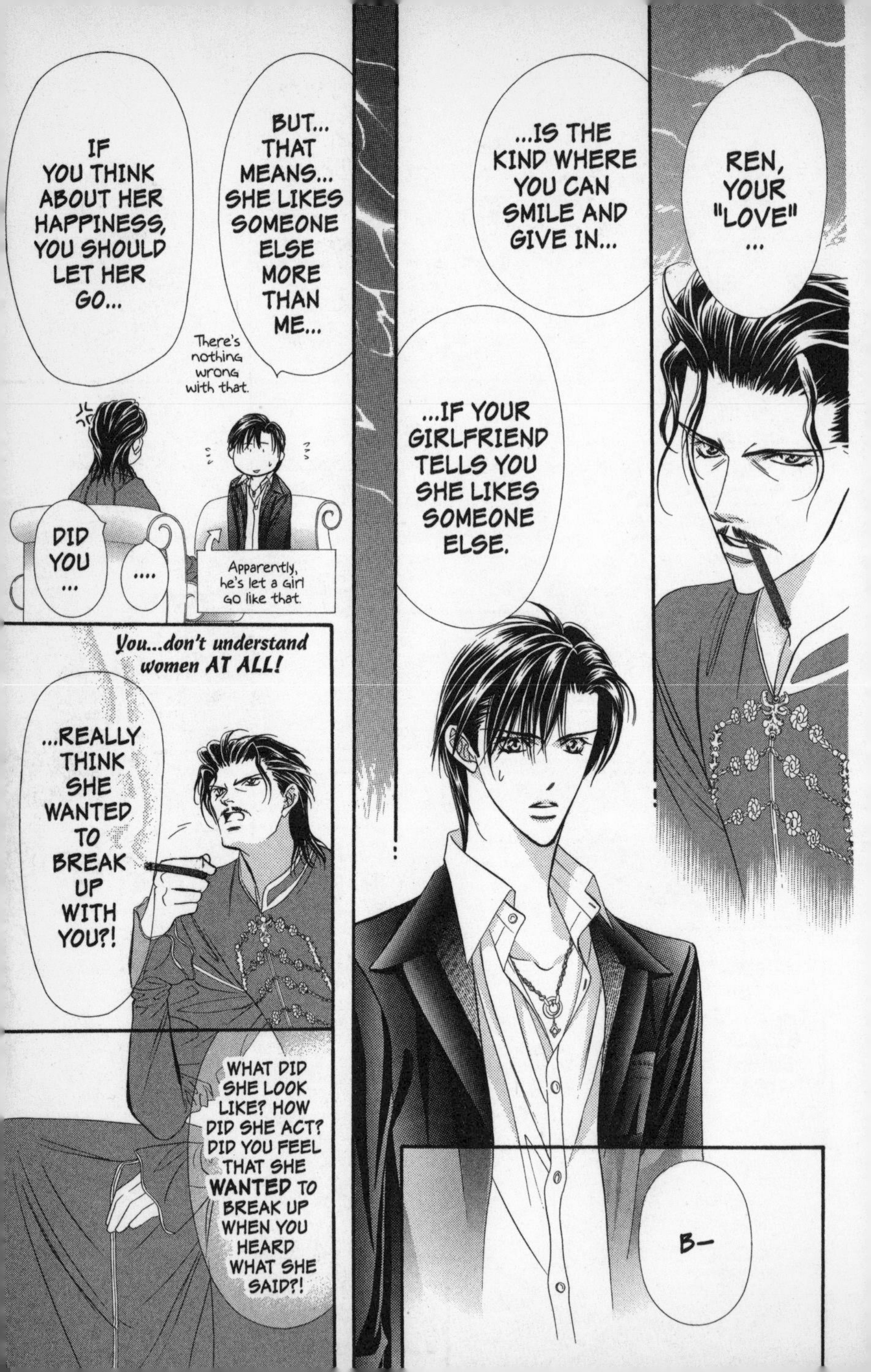
REN, YOUR "LOVE" ...
...IS THE KIND WHERE YOU CAN SMILE AND GIVE IN...
...IF YOUR GIRLFRIEND TELLS YOU SHE LIKES SOMEONE ELSE.
B—
BUT... THAT MEANS... SHE LIKES SOMEONE ELSE MORE THAN ME...
There's nothing wrong with that.
IF YOU THINK ABOUT HER HAPPINESS, YOU SHOULD LET HER GO...
Apparently, he's let a girl go like that.
....
DID YOU ...
You...don't understand women AT ALL!
...REALLY THINK SHE WANTED TO BREAK UP WITH YOU?!
WHAT DID SHE LOOK LIKE? HOW DID SHE ACT? DID YOU FEEL THAT SHE WANTED TO BREAK UP WHEN YOU HEARD WHAT SHE SAID?!

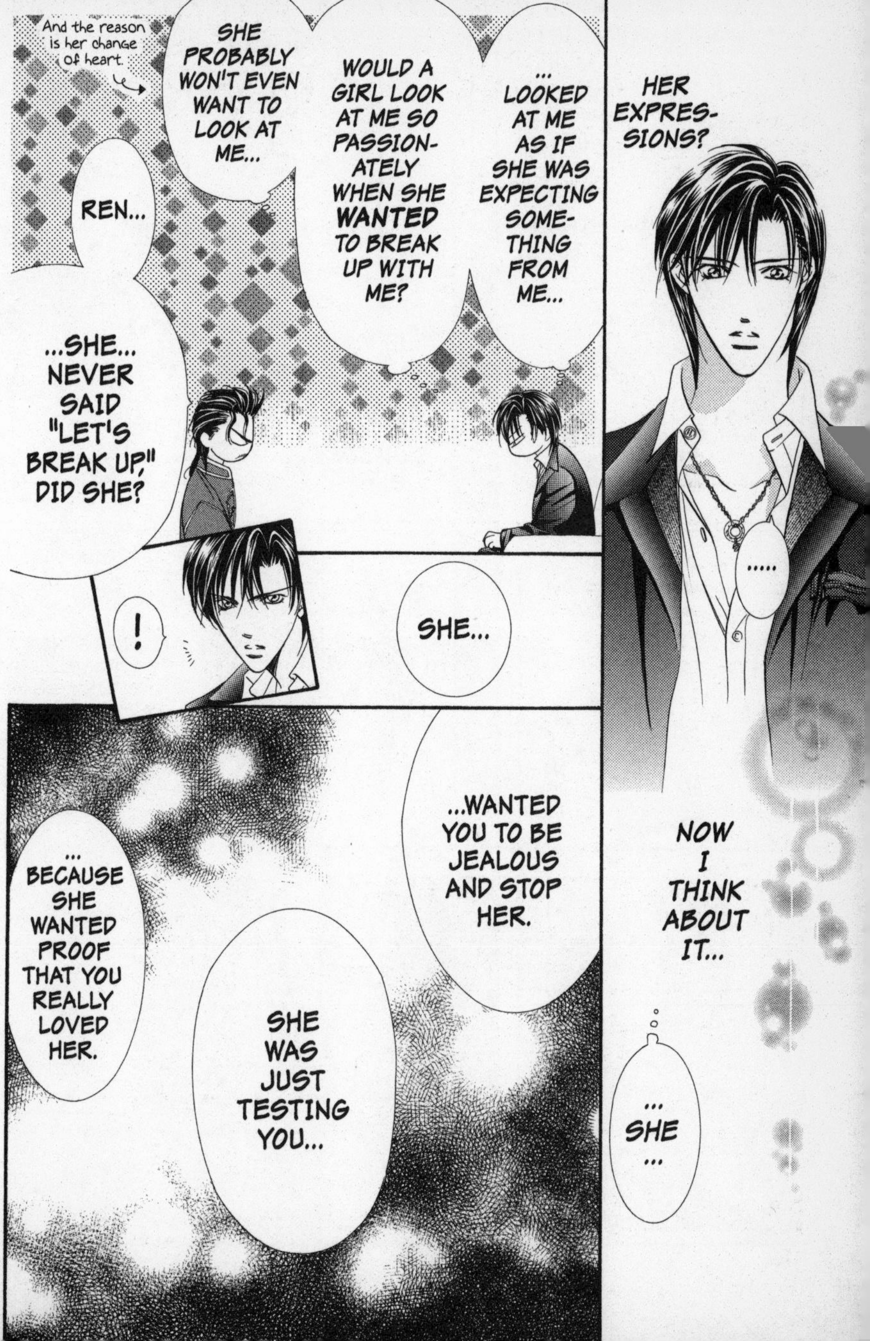
HER EXPRESSIONS?
.....
NOW I THINK ABOUT IT...
... SHE ...
...LOOKED AT ME AS IF SHE WAS EXPECTING SOMETHING FROM ME...
WOULD A GIRL LOOK AT ME SO PASSIONATELY WHEN SHE **WANTED** TO BREAK UP WITH ME?
SHE PROBABLY WON'T EVEN WANT TO LOOK AT ME...
And the reason is her change of heart.
REN...
...SHE... NEVER SAID "LET'S BREAK UP," DID SHE?
SHE...
!
...WANTED YOU TO BE JEALOUS AND STOP HER.
SHE WAS JUST TESTING YOU...
...BECAUSE SHE WANTED PROOF THAT YOU REALLY LOVED HER.

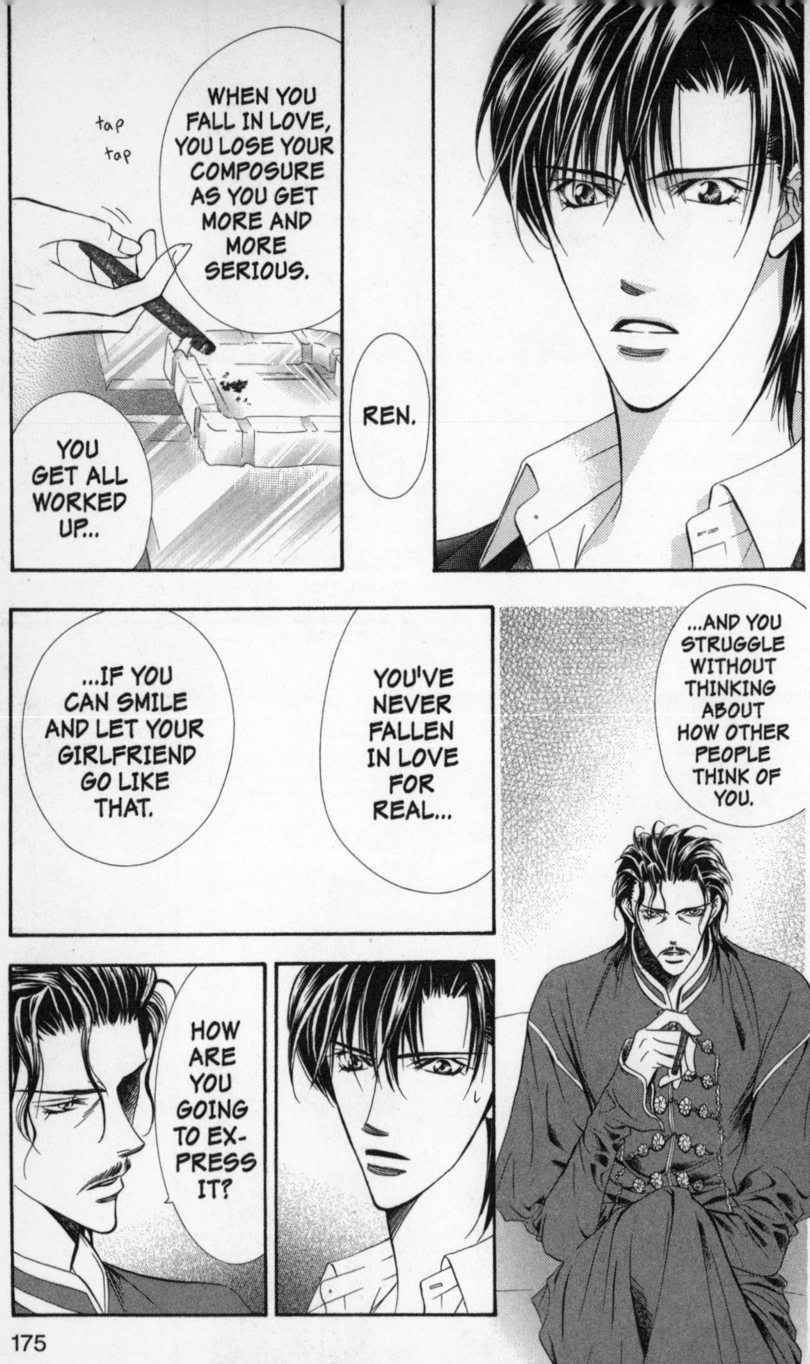
REN.
tap tap
WHEN YOU FALL IN LOVE, YOU LOSE YOUR COMPOSURE AS YOU GET MORE AND MORE SERIOUS.
YOU GET ALL WORKED UP...
...AND YOU STRUGGLE WITHOUT THINKING ABOUT HOW OTHER PEOPLE THINK OF YOU.
YOU'VE NEVER FALLEN IN LOVE FOR REAL...
...IF YOU CAN SMILE AND LET YOUR GIRLFRIEND GO LIKE THAT.
HOW ARE YOU GOING TO EXPRESS IT?

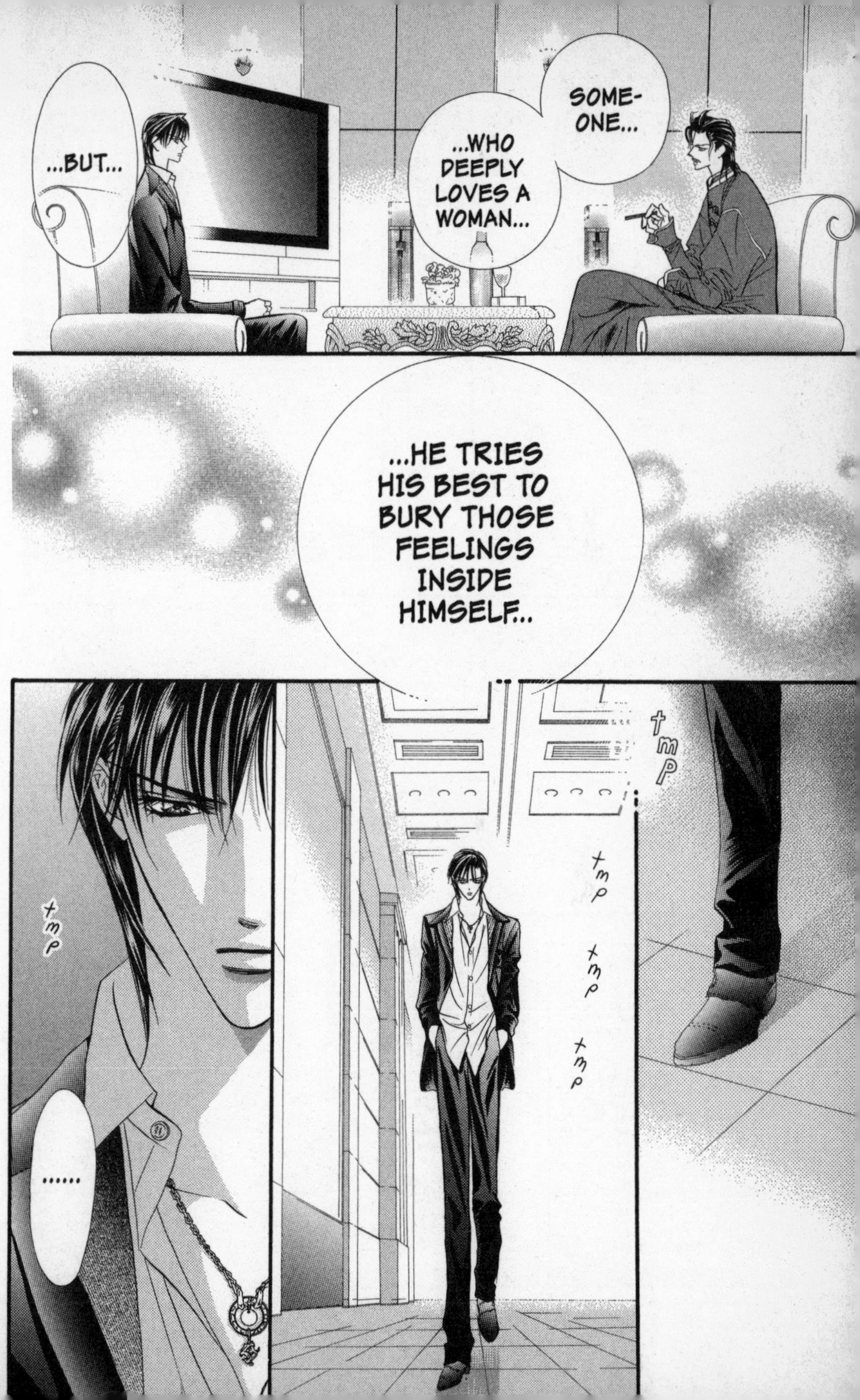
SOME-ONE...
...WHO DEEPLY LOVES A WOMAN...
...BUT...
...HE TRIES HIS BEST TO BURY THOSE FEELINGS INSIDE HIMSELF...
tmp
tmp
tmp
tmp
tmp
......

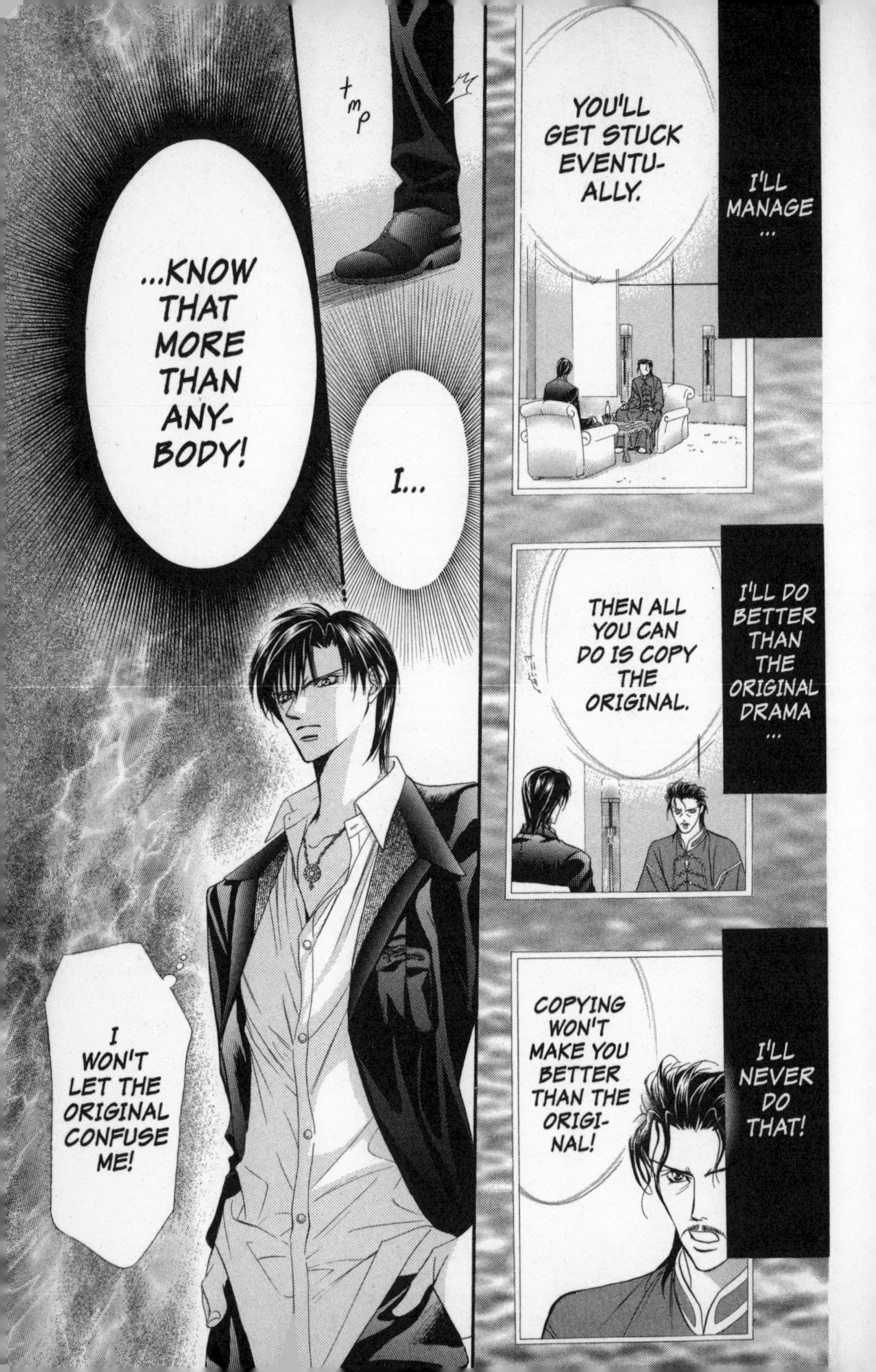
I'LL MANAGE ...
YOU'LL GET STUCK EVENTUALLY.
I'LL DO BETTER THAN THE ORIGINAL DRAMA ...
THEN ALL YOU CAN DO IS COPY THE ORIGINAL.
I'LL NEVER DO THAT!
COPYING WON'T MAKE YOU BETTER THAN THE ORIGINAL!
tmp
I...
...KNOW THAT MORE THAN ANYBODY!
I WON'T LET THE ORIGINAL CONFUSE ME!

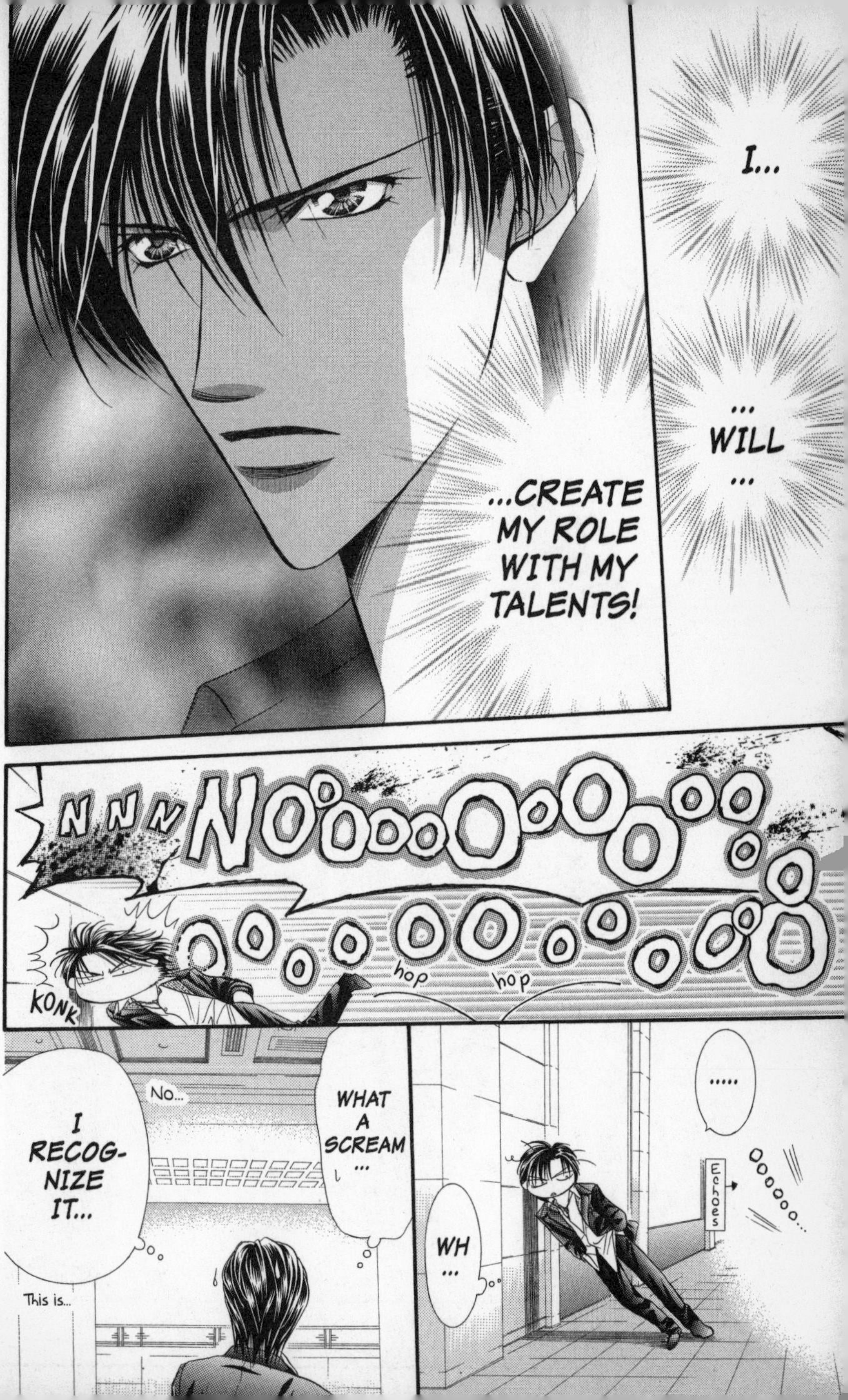
I...
...WILL...
...CREATE MY ROLE WITH MY TALENTS!
NNNNOOOOOOOOOOOOOOOOOOOOOOOOOO
hop hop
KONK
.....
Echoes
Oooooo...
WH...
WHAT A SCREAM...
No...
I RECOG-NIZE IT...
This is...

TH—

Tsukigomori
Hideharu Kokon 1

I KNEW IT...

THIS IS TERRRRRIBLE!

BWAAAAAH!

K-KYOKO?! WHAT'S WRONG?!

?!

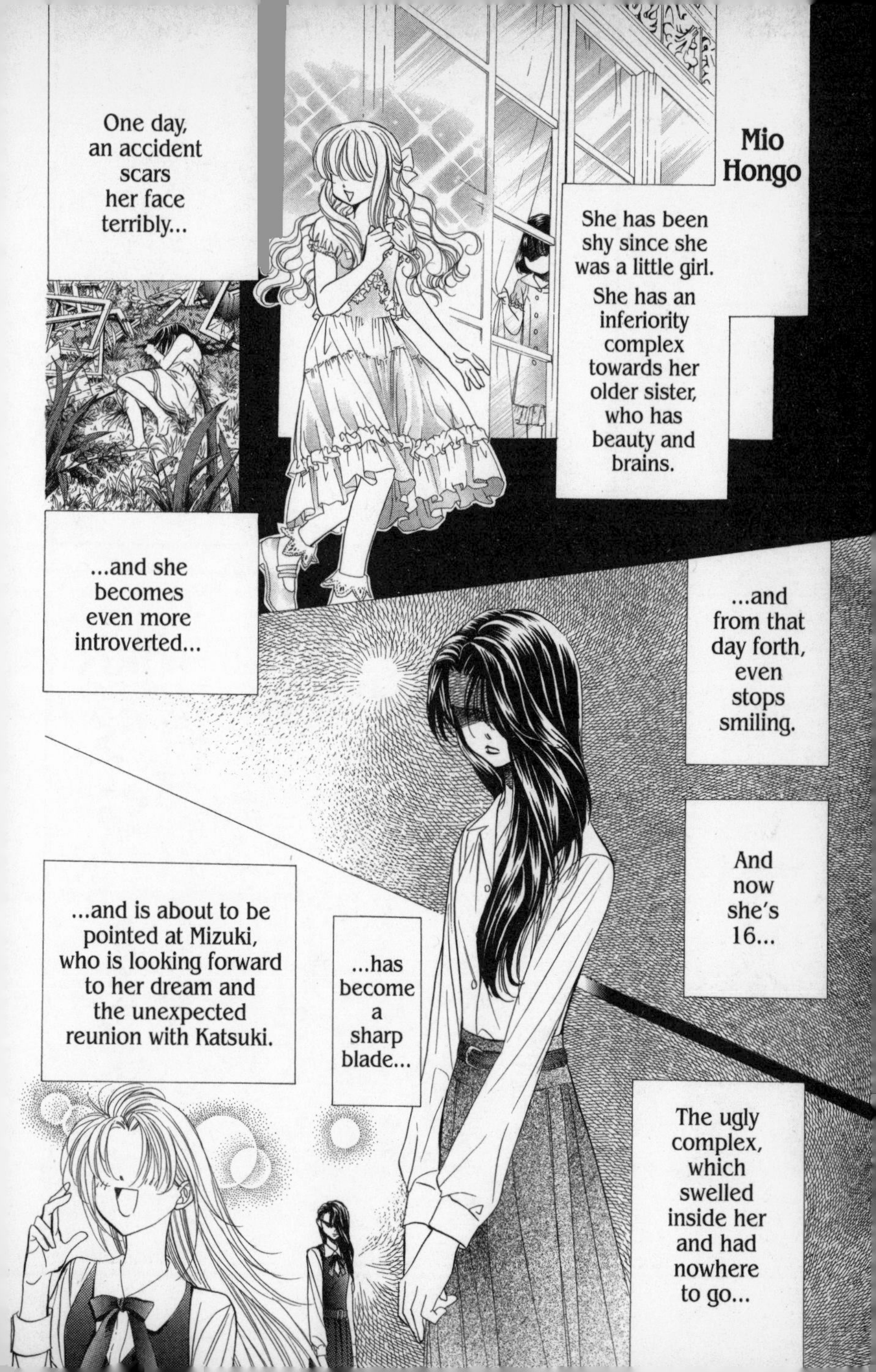
Mio Hongo
She has been shy since she was a little girl.
She has an inferiority complex towards her older sister, who has beauty and brains.
One day, an accident scars her face terribly...
...and she becomes even more introverted...
...and from that day forth, even stops smiling.
And now she's 16...
The ugly complex, which swelled inside her and had nowhere to go...
...has become a sharp blade...
...and is about to be pointed at Mizuki, who is looking forward to her dream and the unexpected reunion with Katsuki.

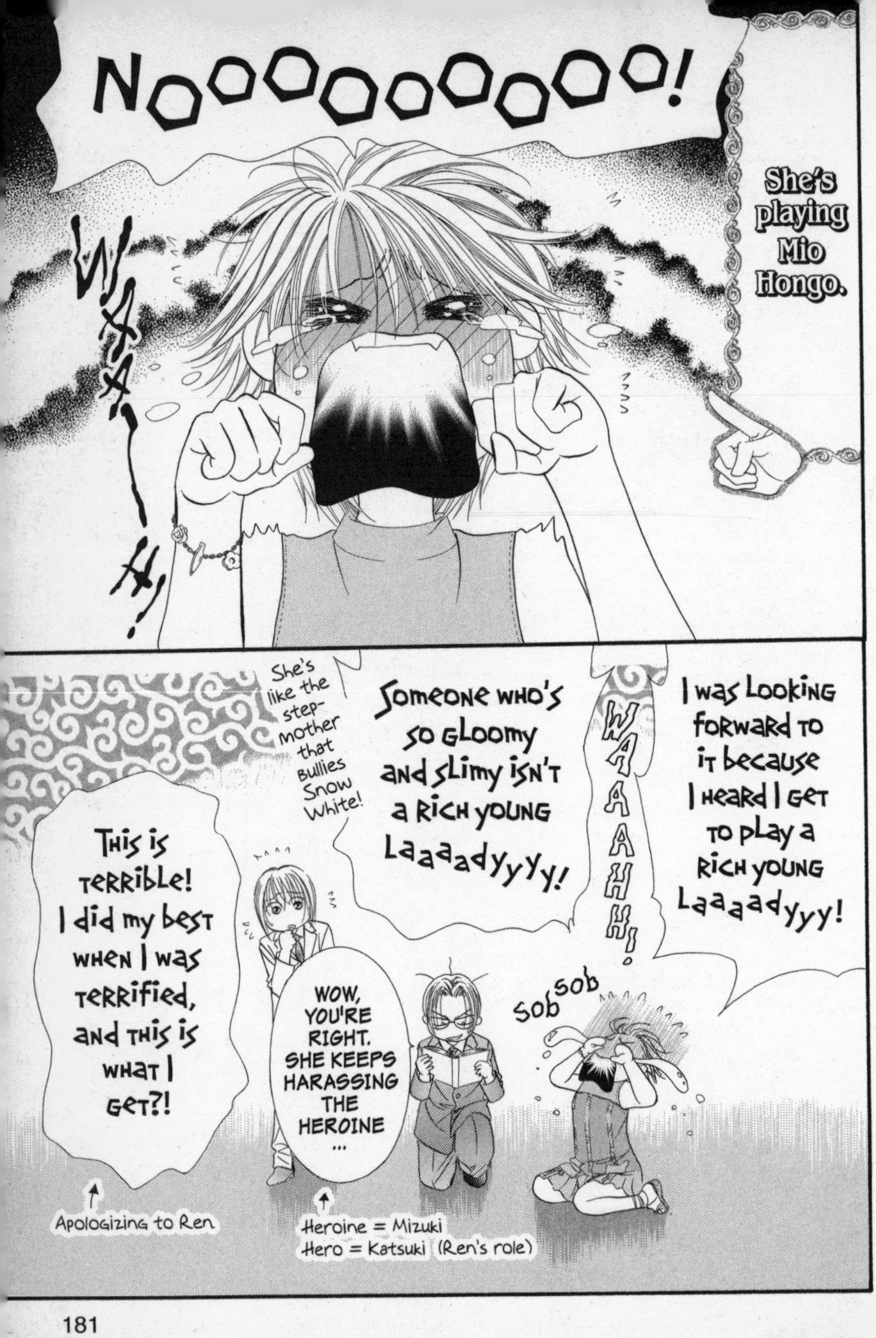
NOOOOOOOOOO!
She's playing Mio Hongo.
WAAA—H!
I was looking forward to it because I heard I get to play a rich young Laaaadyyy!
WAAAAHH!
Someone who's so gloomy and slimy isn't a rich young Laaaadyyyy!
She's like the step-mother that bullies Snow White!
sob sob
WOW, YOU'RE RIGHT. SHE KEEPS HARASSING THE HEROINE ...
This is terrible! I did my best when I was terrified, and this is what I get?!
Apologizing to Ren
Heroine = Mizuki
Hero = Katsuki (Ren's role)

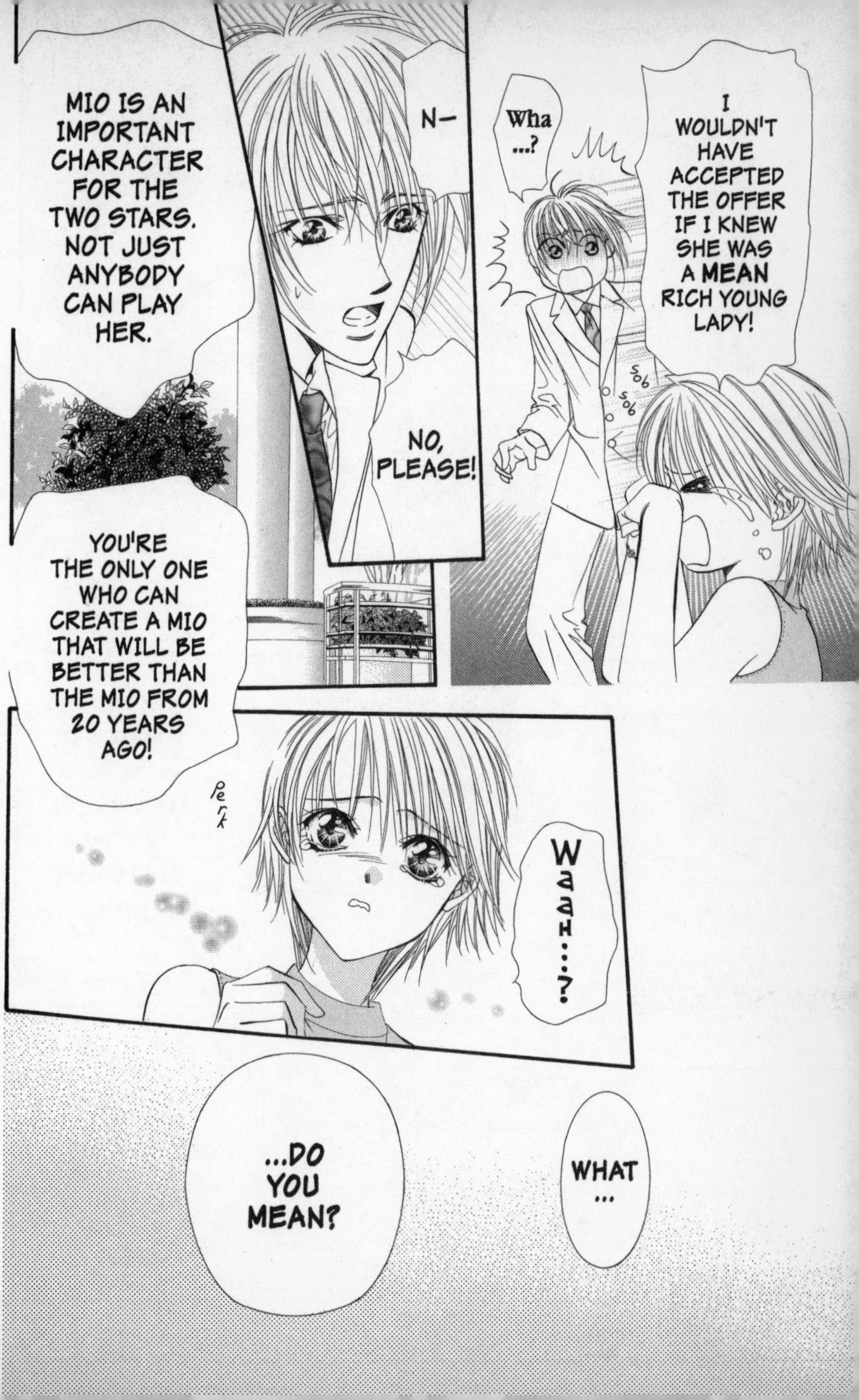
I WOULDN'T HAVE ACCEPTED THE OFFER IF I KNEW SHE WAS A MEAN RICH YOUNG LADY!
sob sob
Wha ...?
N—
NO, PLEASE!
MIO IS AN IMPORTANT CHARACTER FOR THE TWO STARS. NOT JUST ANYBODY CAN PLAY HER.
YOU'RE THE ONLY ONE WHO CAN CREATE A MIO THAT WILL BE BETTER THAN THE MIO FROM 20 YEARS AGO!
Waah...?
Perk
WHAT...
...DO YOU MEAN?

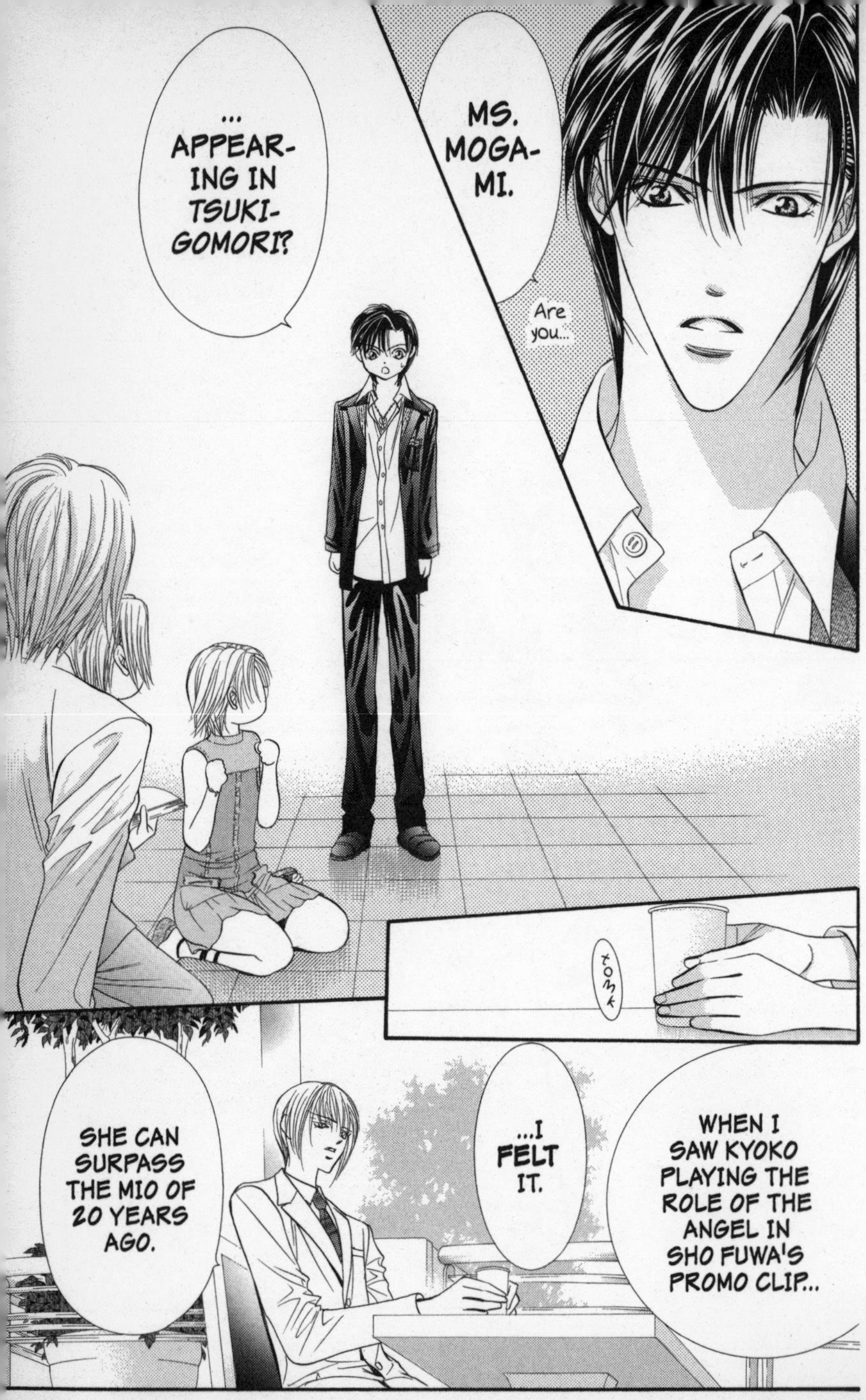
MS. MOGA-MI.
Are you...
... APPEAR-ING IN TSUKI-GOMORI?
tonk
WHEN I SAW KYOKO PLAYING THE ROLE OF THE ANGEL IN SHO FUWA'S PROMO CLIP...
...I **FELT** IT.
SHE CAN SURPASS THE MIO OF 20 YEARS AGO.

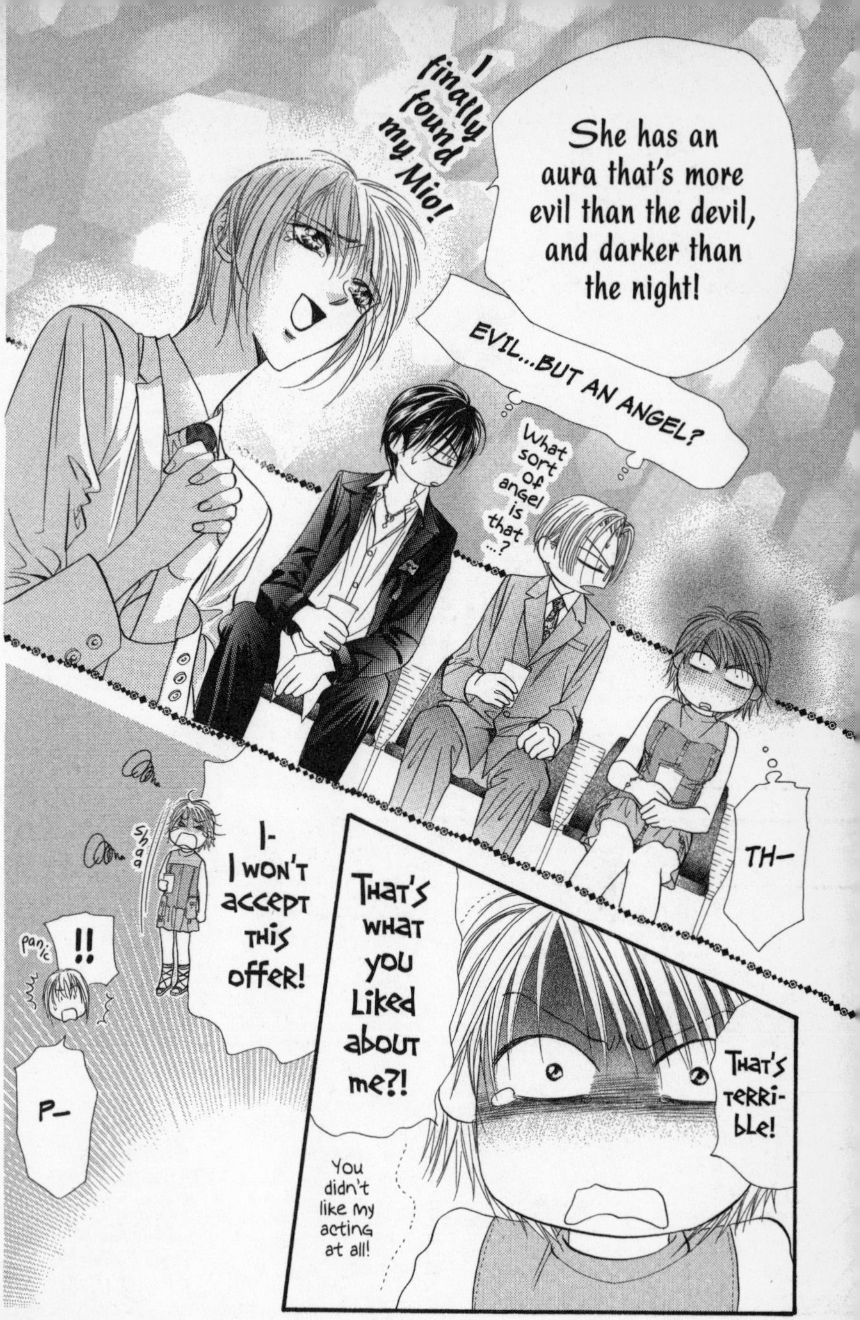

She has an aura that's more evil than the devil, and darker than the night!
I finally found my Mio!
EVIL...BUT AN ANGEL?
What sort of angel is that ...?
TH—
That's terrible!
That's what you liked about me?!
You didn't like my acting at all!
I- I won't accept this offer!
Shaa
!!
panic
P—

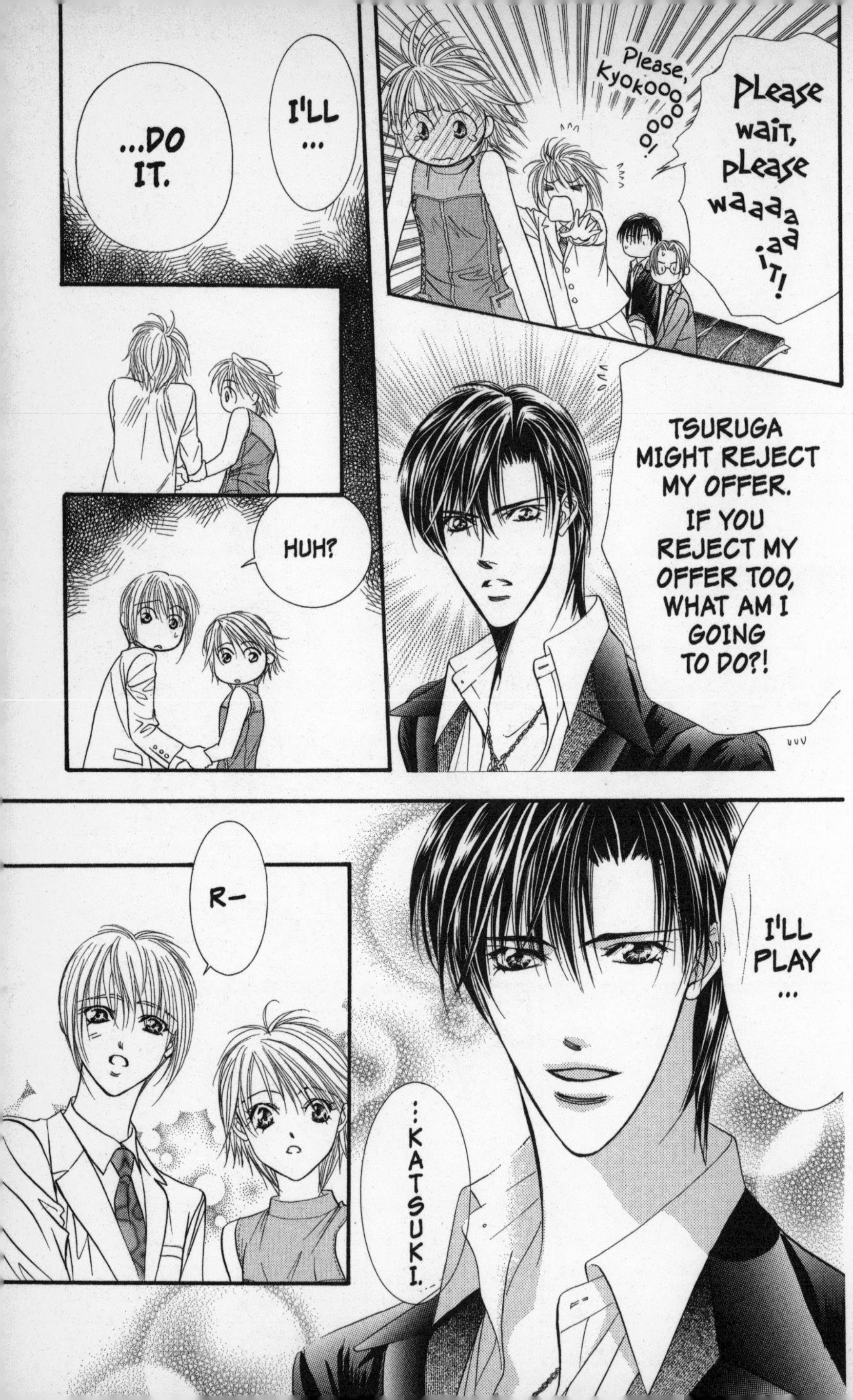
Please wait, please waaaaaaait!
Please, Kyokooooooo!
I'll...
...do it.
Tsuruga might reject my offer.
If you reject my offer too, what am I going to do?!
Huh?
I'll play...
...Katsuki.
R–

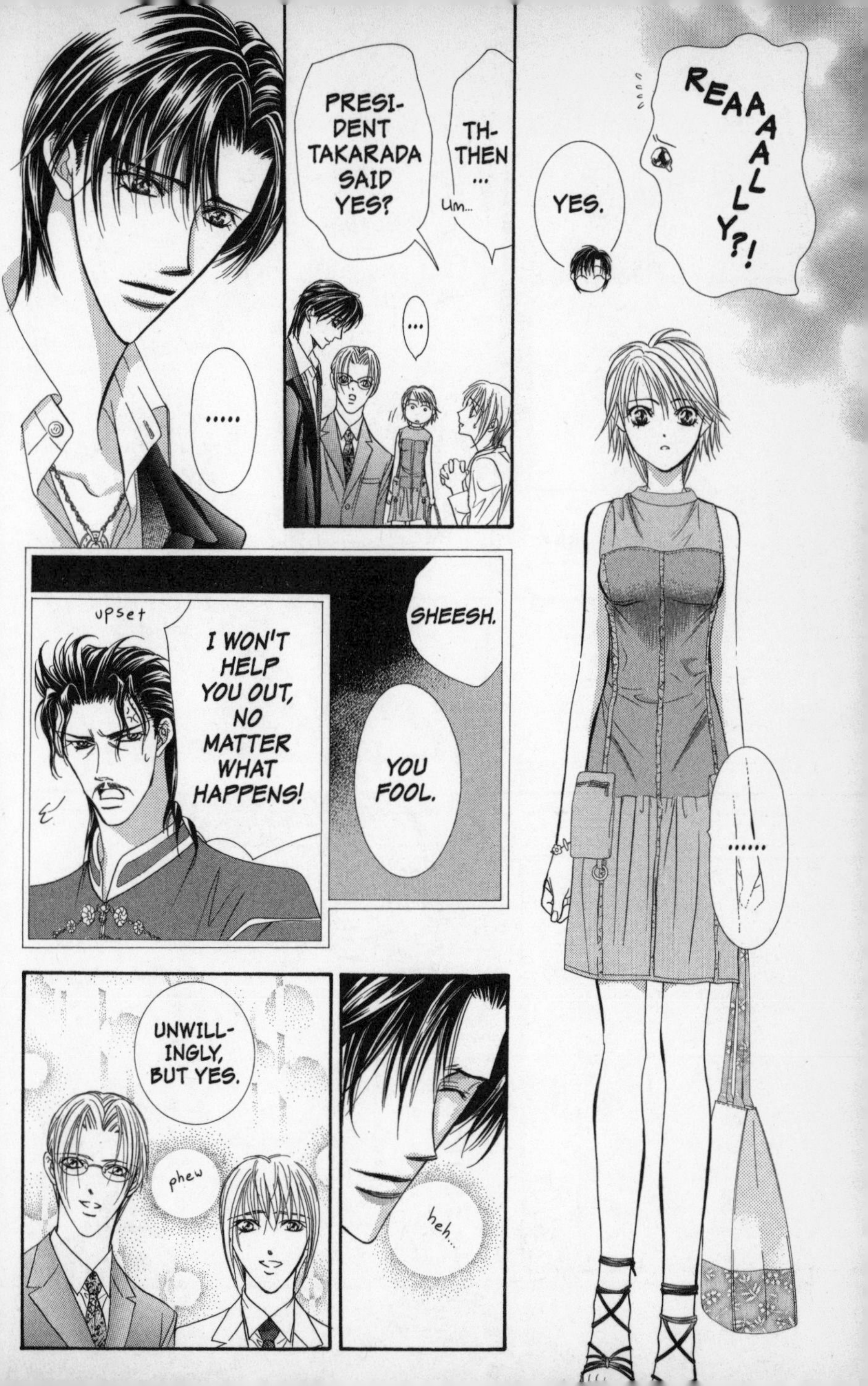
REAAAALLY?!
YES.
......
TH-THEN ...
um...
PRESIDENT TAKARADA SAID YES?
...
......
SHEESH.
YOU FOOL.
upset
I WON'T HELP YOU OUT, NO MATTER WHAT HAPPENS!
heh...
UNWILLINGLY, BUT YES.
phew

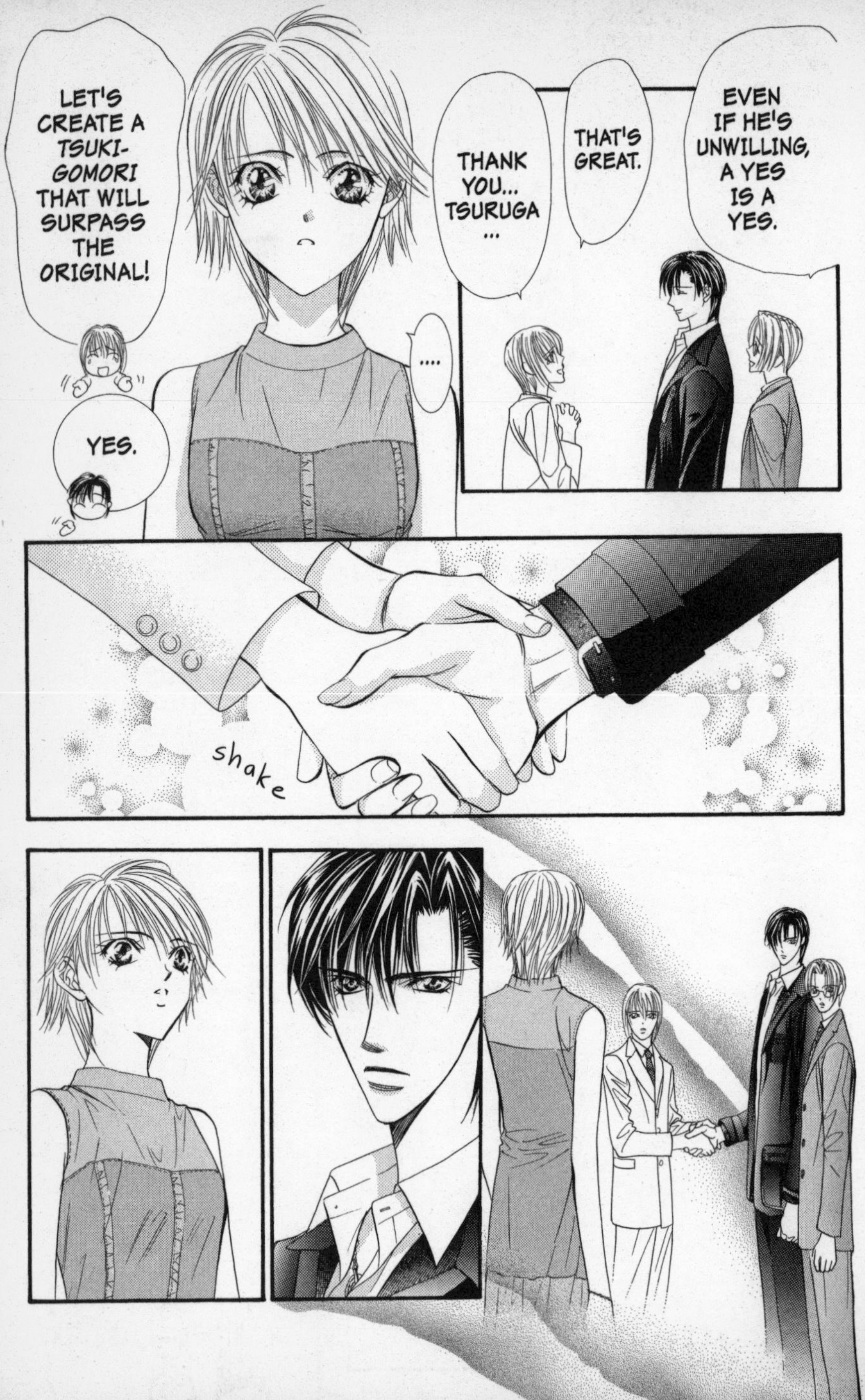
EVEN IF HE'S UNWILLING, A YES IS A YES.
THAT'S GREAT.
THANK YOU... TSURUGA ...
LET'S CREATE A TSUKI-GOMORI THAT WILL SURPASS THE ORIGINAL!
YES.
....
shake

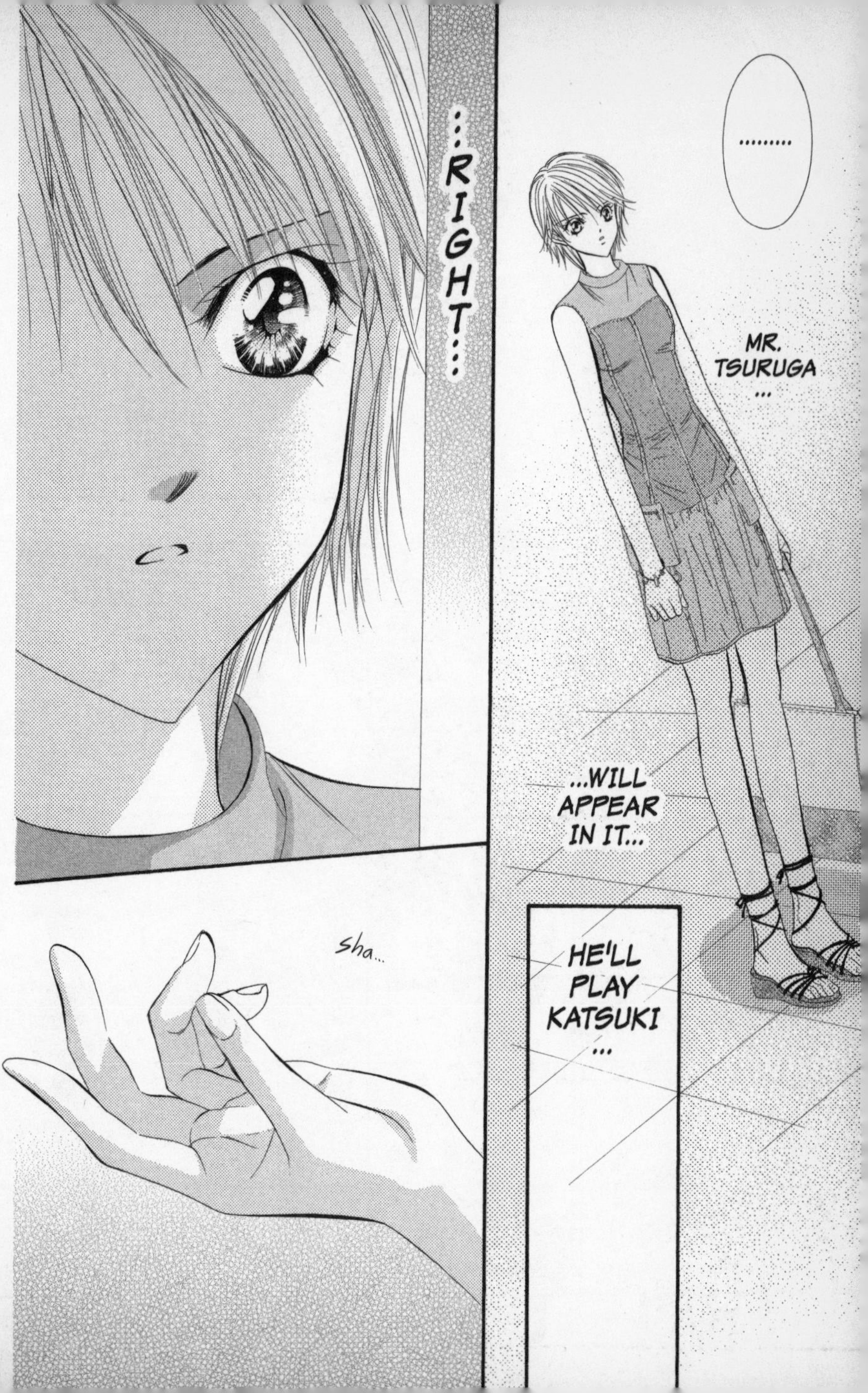
....
MR. TSURUGA ...
...WILL APPEAR IN IT...
HE'LL PLAY KATSUKI ...
...RIGHT...
sha...

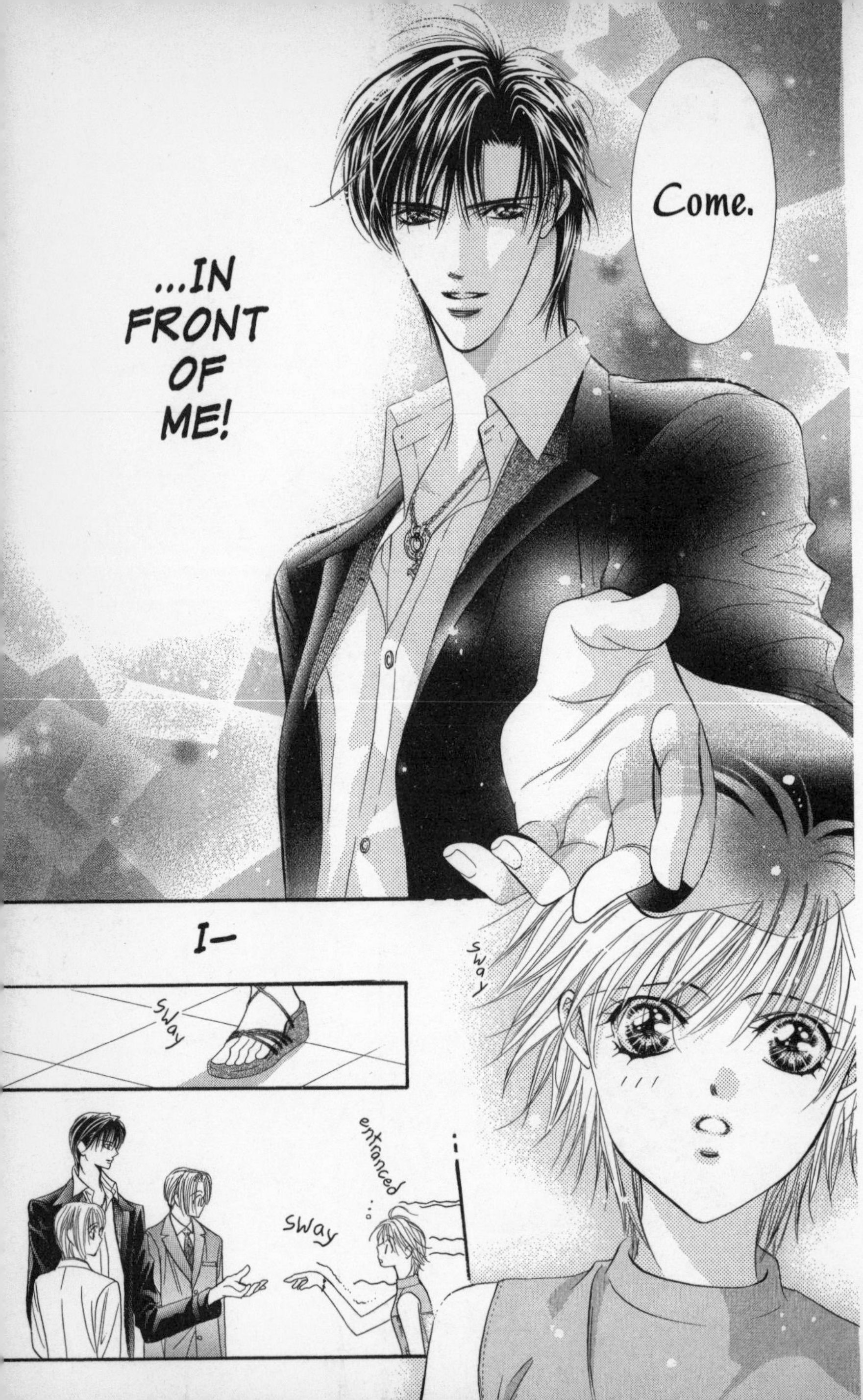
Come.
...IN FRONT OF ME!
sway
I—
sway
entranced
sway

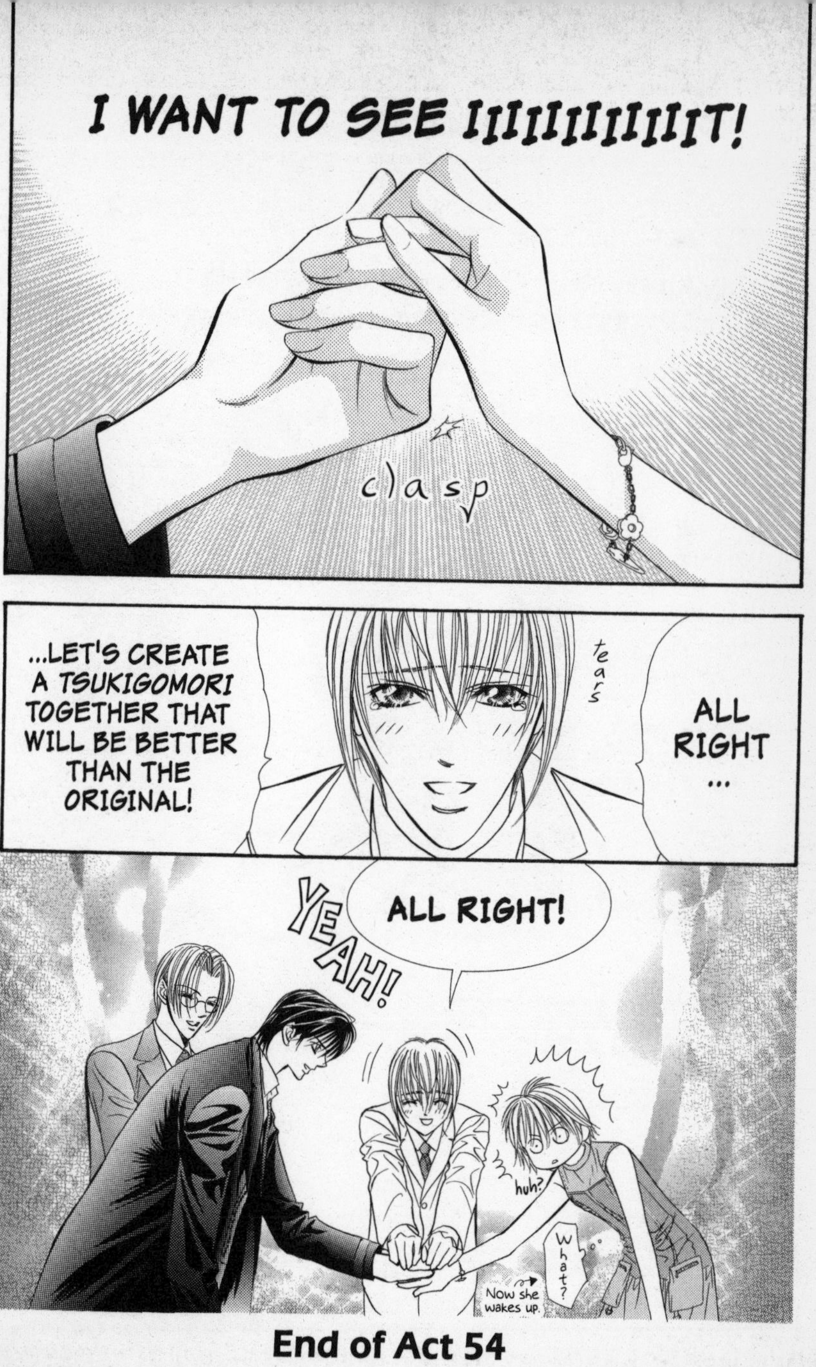
I WANT TO SEE IIIIIIIIIIIIT!
clasp
ALL RIGHT ...
tears
...LET'S CREATE A TSUKIGOMORI TOGETHER THAT WILL BE BETTER THAN THE ORIGINAL!
ALL RIGHT!
YEAH!
huh?
What?
Now she wakes up.

End of Act 54

Skip-Beat! End Notes
Everyone knows how to be a fan, but sometimes cool things
from other cultures need a little help crossing the language barrier.

Page 5, panel 1: Jidaigeki
Japanese period dramas such as the movies *Rashomon*, the *Zatoichi* series,
Azumi, and *Ran*, and the TV dramas *Edo o Kiru*, *Tsukikage Ran*, and the
annual taiga drama on NHK.

Page 28, panel 3: Moko
Hio thinks of the kanji for "ferocious tiger."

Page 40, panel 6: Makie
Kyoko uses the kanji for rolled-up paintings,
but Moko is talking about "bait."

Page 78, panel 3: Tamagoyaki
Japanese rolled omelet. They come either sweet or salty, and can be filled with
colorful ingredients.

Page 85, side bar: The hawk cowers at the chicken...
The kanji for *o* in Hio means "hawk" or "falcon," and the *hi* means "fly."

Page 110, panel 5: Sweet potatoes
This image refers to the Japanese saying "to tell things in sweet potato-vine fashion," meaning you have to confess to one thing after another, the way sweet potatoes are pulled from the ground.

Page 113, panel 5: Kanashibari
The Japanese term for a form of paralysis that occurs due to the presence of a ghost or evil spirit. Kyoko's evil spirits can cause it in sensitive people.

Page 123, panel 1: Karaoke Box
A private room with a TV and karaoke set up. These rooms are more private than the open karaoke bar, and are good for small parties and shy singers. Karaoke box establishments often sell food and drinks.

Page 148, panel 2: Dogeza
Bowing from a sitting position and pressing your head against the floor. The most contrite bow possible.

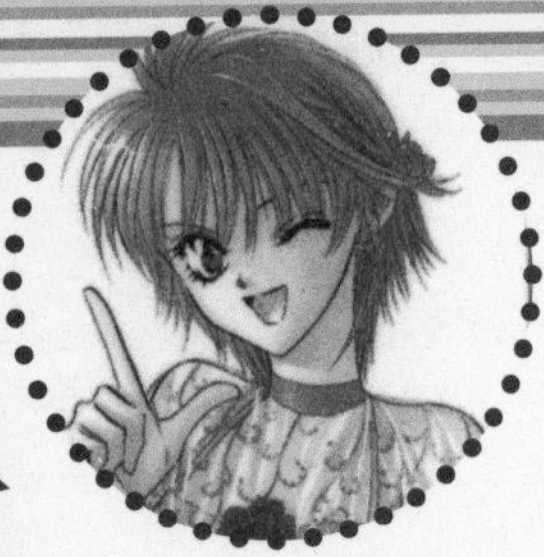

Yoshiki Nakamura is originally from Tokushima prefecture. She started drawing manga in elementary school, which eventually led to her 1993 debut of *Yume de Au yori Suteki* (Better than Seeing in a Dream) in *Hana to Yume* magazine. Her other works include the basketball series *Saint Love*, *MVP wa Yuzurenai* (Can't Give Up MVP), *Blue Wars*, and *Tokyo Crazy Paradise*, a series about a female bodyguard in 2020 Tokyo.

SKIP·BEAT!
Vol. 9
The Shojo Beat Manga Edition

STORY AND ART BY YOSHIKI NAKAMURA

English Translation & Adaptation/Tomo Kimura
Touch-up Art & Lettering/Sabrina Heep
Design/Yukiko Whitley
Editor/Pancha Diaz

Editor in Chief, Books/Alvin Lu
Editor in Chief, Magazines/Marc Weidenbaum
VP of Publishing Licensing/Rika Inouye
VP of Sales/Gonzalo Ferreyra
Sr. VP of Marketing/Liza Coppola
Publisher/Hyoe Narita

Printed in Canada

Published by VIZ Media, LLC
P.O. Box 77010
San Francisco, CA 94107

store.viz.com

Shojo Beat Manga Edition
10 9 8 7 6 5 4 3 2
First printing, November 2007
Second printing, December 2007

RATED T FOR TEEN

PARENTAL ADVISORY
SKIP·BEAT! is rated T for Teen and is recommended for ages 13 and up. This volume contains suggestive themes.
ratings.viz.com

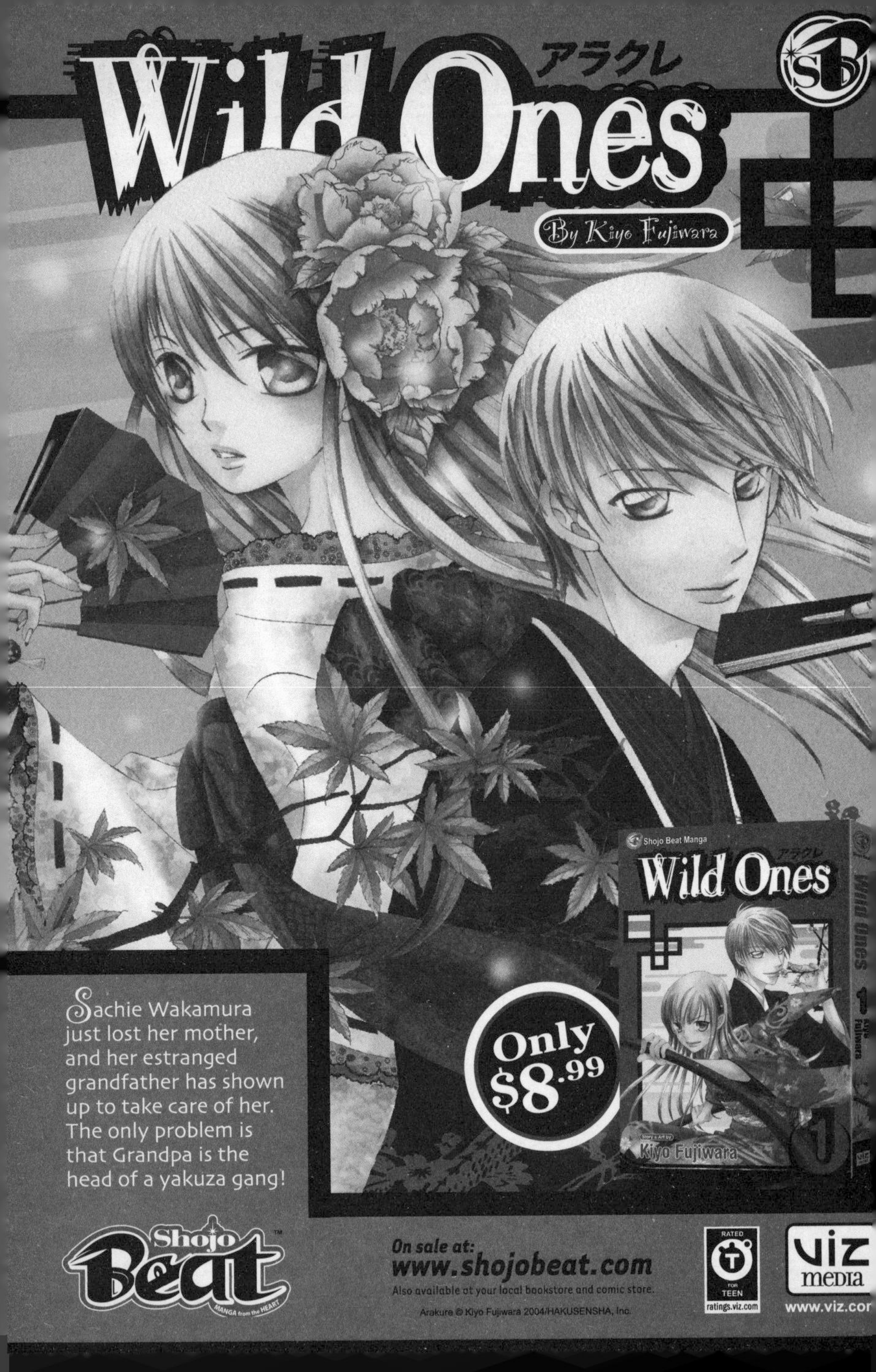

Wild Ones
アラクレ
By Kiyo Fujiwara
Shojo Beat Manga
Wild Ones
アラクレ
Story & Art by
Kiyo Fujiwara
Only $8.99
Sachie Wakamura just lost her mother, and her estranged grandfather has shown up to take care of her. The only problem is that Grandpa is the head of a yakuza gang!
Shojo Beat
MANGA from the HEART
On sale at:
www.shojobeat.com
Also available at your local bookstore and comic store.
RATED T FOR TEEN
ratings.viz.com
viz media
www.viz.com
Arakure © Kiyo Fujiwara 2004/HAKUSENSHA, Inc.

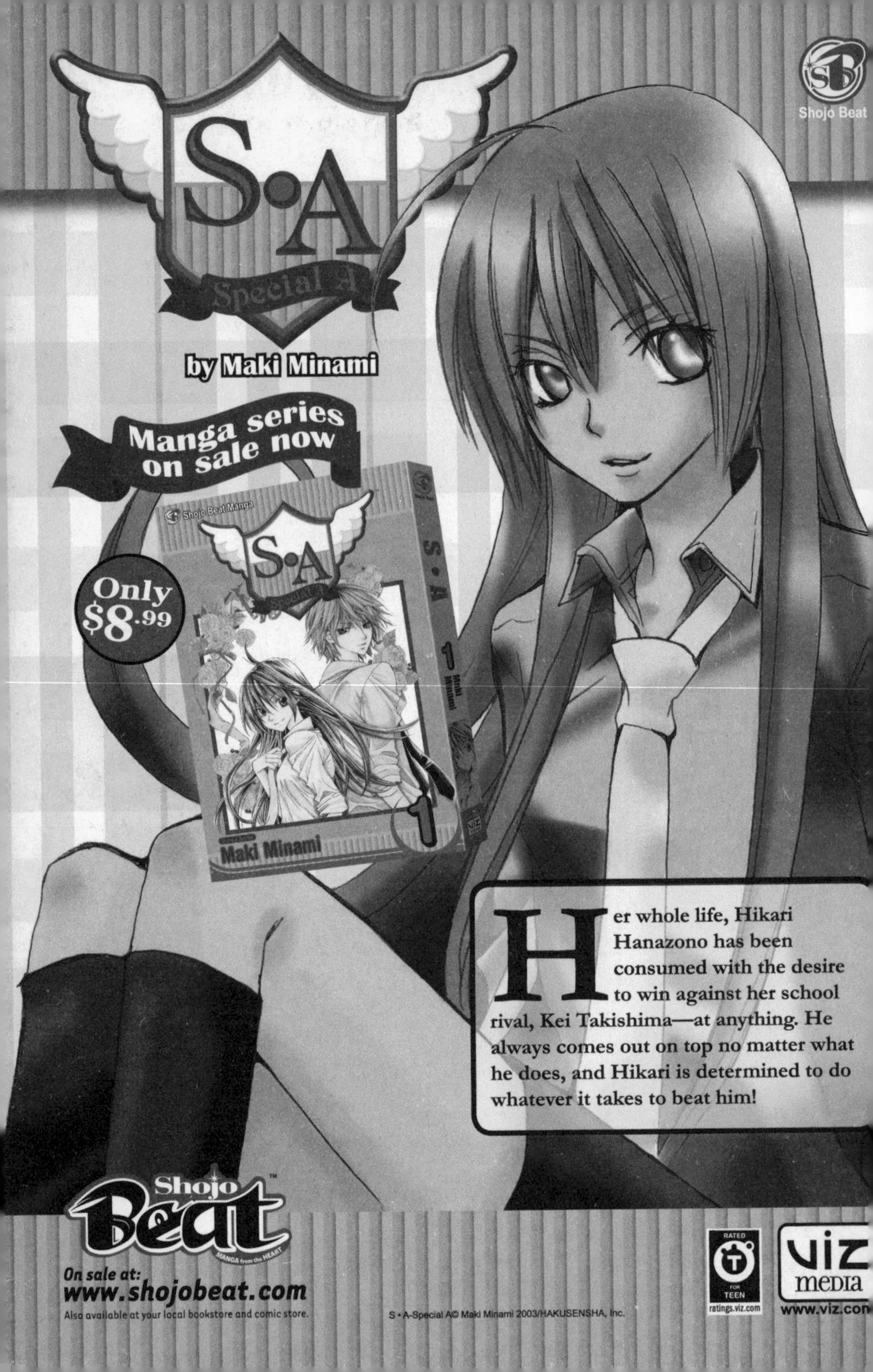

Shojo Beat
S•A
Special A
by Maki Minami
Manga series on sale now
Only $8.99
Shojo Beat Manga
Maki Minami
Her whole life, Hikari Hanazono has been consumed with the desire to win against her school rival, Kei Takishima—at anything. He always comes out on top no matter what he does, and Hikari is determined to do whatever it takes to beat him!
Shojo Beat
MANGA from the HEART
On sale at:
www.shojobeat.com
Also available at your local bookstore and comic store.
S • A-Special A© Maki Minami 2003/HAKUSENSHA, Inc.
RATED T FOR TEEN
ratings.viz.com
VIZ MEDIA
www.viz.com

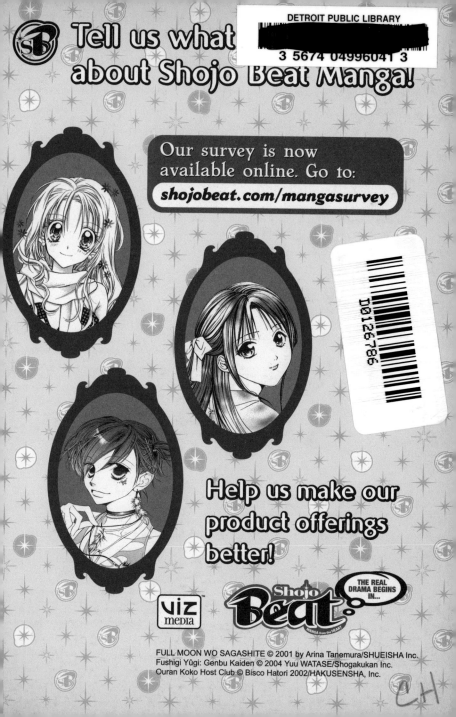

Tell us what about Shojo Beat Manga!

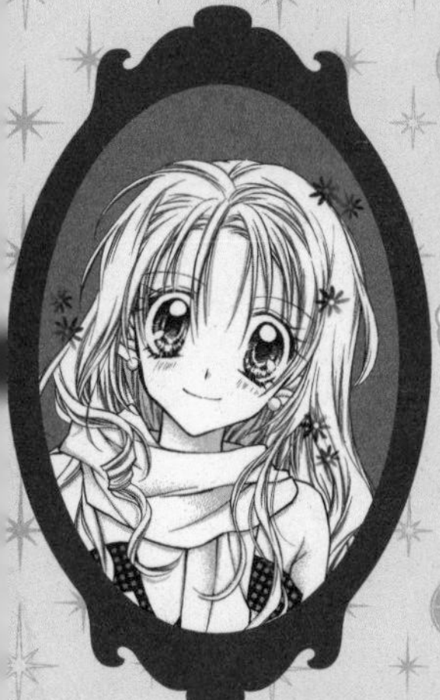

Our survey is now available online. Go to:

shojobeat.com/mangasurvey

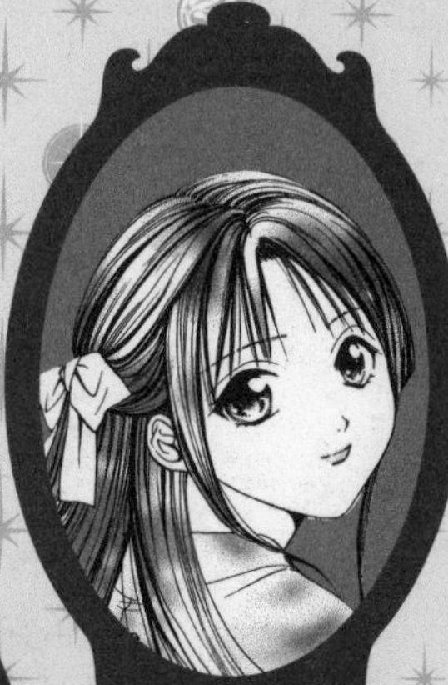

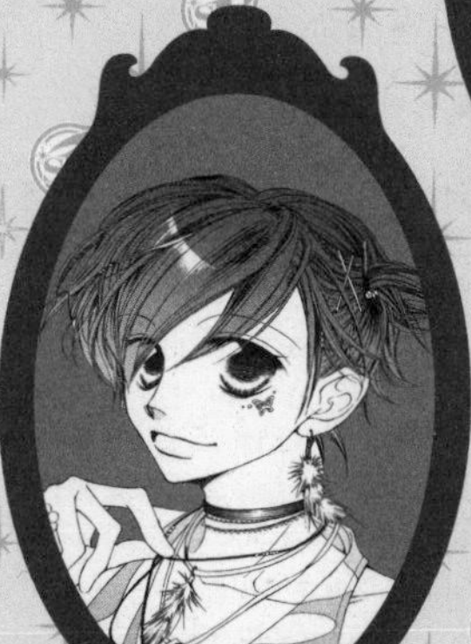

Help us make our product offerings better!

VIZ media

Shojo Beat — MANGA from the HEART

THE REAL DRAMA BEGINS IN...

CH